T0271192

Managing Creativity

What are the challenges and opportunities of managing people in creative industries? How are the tensions between creative and commercial pressures mediated?

The creative industries are an area of increasing economic importance. Yet creative industries and creative-based organizations are rife with problems such as whether and how control of the creative process should be exercised; the extent to which knowledge of creative production may be made explicit; and how the 'connection' between producer and consumer should be mediated. In *Managing Creativity*, a team of experts from a diverse range of fields – including management, fine art, music, the internet, design, theatre and publishing – discuss these and other problems concerning the relationship between management and creativity. Developing an appreciation of these problems is theoretically productive, not only because it throws new light onto our understanding of creative-based organizations, but also because it can be revelatory about organizations more generally.

BARBARA TOWNLEY is Professor of Management and Director of the Institute for Capitalising on Creativity at the University of St Andrews. Her research is in the area of creative industries, particularly the tensions that arise between artistic and commercial logics and how these are mediated. Her most recent book is *Reason's Neglect* (2008).

NIC BEECH is Professor of Management at the University of St Andrews and Lead Fellow in the Advanced Institute of Management. He is the founding chair of the British Academy of Management special interest group on identity and co-chair of the Scottish Network on Organizational Vitality. His research is focused mainly on the social dynamics of organizational life – the intertwining of people's identities, relationships and practices. He is co-author (with Eugene McKenna) of *Human Resource Management: A Concise Analysis* (Pearson, 2008).

Managing Creativity

Exploring the Paradox

Edited by

BARBARA TOWNLEY

NIC BEECH

CAMBRIDGE
UNIVERSITY PRESS

CAMBRIDGE
UNIVERSITY PRESS

University Printing House, Cambridge CB2 8BS, United Kingdom

Cambridge University Press is part of the University of Cambridge.

It furthers the University's mission by disseminating knowledge in the pursuit of
education, learning and research at the highest international levels of excellence.

www.cambridge.org
Information on this title: www.cambridge.org/9780521518536

© Cambridge University Press 2010

First published 2010

A catalogue record for this publication is available from the British Library

Library of Congress Cataloguing in Publication data
Managing creativity : exploring the paradox / [edited by] Barbara Townley, Nic Beech.
    p.   cm.
Includes bibliographical references and index.
ISBN 978-0-521-51853-6
1. Cultural industries.   2. Creative ability in business.   I. Townley,
Barbara, 1954–   II. Beech, Nic.   III. Title.
HD9999.C9472M36 2010
658.3´14–dc22   2009035022

ISBN 978-0-521-51853-6 Hardback
ISBN 978-1-107-40373-4 Paperback

For Dominique
For Linda and Rosie

Contents

Illustrations

Contributors

NIC BEECH is Professor of Management at the University of St Andrews and Lead Fellow in the Advanced Institute of Management. His research is focused mainly on the social dynamics of organizational life – the intertwining of people's identities, relationships and practices. He has particular interests in music and management and in organizational vitality. Nic is the founding chair of the British Academy of Management special interest group on identity and co-chair of the Scottish Network on Organizational Vitality.

MARTIN DIXON is currently a lecturer in music at the University of Glasgow. His doctoral thesis concerned Adorno's philosophy of musical composition and he retains an interest in the creative process, both as a theorist and as a composer.

JANE DONALD is Head of Sales and Marketing for Glasgow's Concert Halls. An important aspect of her remit is working with artists, media, audiences, finance and other managers in the promotion of the annual Celtic Connections festival. She has professional and academic interests in the theory and practice of performing arts management.

DORIS RUTH EIKHOF is Lecturer in Organization Studies at the Stirling Management School, University of Stirling, and Research Associate at the Wirtschaftsuniversität Wien, Austria. Her research interests include creative industries, changing forms of work and organization, women and work, work-life boundaries and social theories in organization studies. She has published in international academic journals and books and is co-editor of *Work Less, Live More? Critical Analysis of the Work-life Boundary* (Palgrave Macmillan, 2008).

LAURA GONZÁLEZ is an artist and writer. Her practice encompasses drawing, photography and sculpture, and her work has been exhibited in the UK, Spain and Portugal. She has participated in numerous conferences, including Research into Practice (2008), College Arts Association and the Association for the Psychoanalysis of Culture and Society (2007). When she is not following Freud, Lacan and Marx's footsteps with her camera, she lectures postgraduate students at the Glasgow School of Art.

ELIZABETH GULLEDGE is a graduate of Duke University and is studying for her doctorate at the Institute for Capitalising on Creativity at the University of St Andrews. She is researching into the nature, operation and maintenance of an institutional field with reference to book publishing.

PAUL JOHNSON is Senior Lecturer in Drama at the University of Wolverhampton, and Course Leader for the BA and MA programmes. His doctoral research was on the connections between science and live performance, and he has also published on experimental theatre and theatre in museums and heritage sites.

GUY JULIER is Professor of Design at Leeds Metropolitan University. His books include *The Culture of Design* (Sage, 2007 second revised edition) and *Design and Creativity: Policy, Management and Practice* (2009, co-edited with Liz Moor). He is Associate Editor of the new journal *Design and Culture* and an editorial board member of the *Journal of Visual Culture*. His current research is concerned with audit culture and political economies of design and design-led urban regeneration.

STEPHEN LINSTEAD is Professor of Critical Management at The York Management School, University of York. He was born in Barnsley into a working-class family, a direct descendant of a Royal Academician on his mother's side and a champion heavyweight boxer on his father's, at the beginning of the same summer that John Graham Mellor was born in Ankara. Some of his friends and colleagues think that it shows.

JULIAN M. LUXFORD is a senior lecturer in the School of Art History at the University of St Andrews. His research centres on late medieval art, architecture, texts and the historiography of art history. He has published extensively in these areas.

LOUISE MITCHELL is Director of Glasgow UNESCO City of Music and was previously Director of Glasgow's Concert Halls for twelve years. In that time she oversaw a wide-ranging concert programme, generated £13.5 million of funding and led the development of a regeneration strategy for two of Glasgow's most revered venues, the City Halls and Old Fruitmarket.

AMY PARKER is currently writing her PhD at the University of Glasgow. She has recently been appointed part-time lecturer in Music at Napier University, Edinburgh.

CHRISTOPHER RANDALL received his PhD in music composition from the University of Newcastle in 2009. He resides in north-eastern England where he works as a freelance composer.

AILEEN M. STACKHOUSE is a graduate of the School of Fine Art in Duncan of Jordanstone College of Art and Design, University of Dundee.

Aileen is an independent artist and thinker who constructs installations that use drawing, conversation, sculpture and photography to
reflect upon and describe the emergence and dissolution of imaginative thought and consciousness.

BARBARA TOWNLEY is Professor of Management at the University of St
Andrews and Director of the Institute for Capitalising on Creativity,
Scotland's centre for teaching and research in the Creative Industries
(www.capitalisingoncreativity.ac.uk). She has published extensively in
leading US and European academic management journals and her latest book is *Reason's Neglect: Rationality and Organizing* (Oxford
University Press, 2008).

CHRIS WARHURST is Professor of Labour Studies and Director of the
Scottish Centre for Employment Research in the Department of
Human Resource Management at the University of Strathclyde,
Glasgow. His research interests centre on labour process and labour
market issues and developments. He is currently co-editor of the jour-
nal *Work, Employment and Society.*

GREGOR WHITE is Division Leader for Computer Arts and Media at the
University of Abertay, Dundee. He has research interests in digital
media and online communities and works closely with the broadcast
sector in the development of interactive and social media products.

Acknowledgements

Work for this book was partially funded from an AHRC/ESRC/ DTI/ Arts Council England grant, number AH/E508456/1, *The Discipline of Creativity: Exploring the Paradox*. We should like to thank Paula Parish of Cambridge University Press for her support for the book and her help in bringing it to fruition. The editors would like to thank all the contributors for their contributions to the discussion and their willingness to respond to sometimes impossible deadlines. The editors are also extremely grateful to Mindy Grewar for her superb work in preparing the book for production. Anyone who has been through this process will realize how much work is involved in this. Her hard work and diligence on this while remaining so supportive is singularly recognized.

Introduction

1 | *The discipline of creativity*

BARBARA TOWNLEY AND NIC BEECH

The study of creative industries is important for theoretical and practical reasons. Theoretically, they offer a site of study that can help push forward the understanding of organization and management. The creative industries pose challenges because of the relative indeterminacy or unknowability of the process of creative production and the factors affecting its consumption (Caves 2002). This is in contrast to more traditional businesses where production and consumption are potentially much more knowable and controllable (Thompson *et al.* 2001). Creative industries and creative-based organizations are rife with dilemmas such as whether and how control of the creative process should be exercised; the extent to which knowledge of creative production may be made explicit; and how the 'connection' between producer and consumer should be mediated (Lampel *et al.* 2000). Developing an understanding of these dilemmas is theoretically productive, not only because it throws a new light onto the understanding of creative-based organizations, but also because it can be revelatory about organizations more generally. Organizational practice exemplified by the creative industries emphasizes coping with dilemmas and paradoxes, managing in states of uncertainty and unknowability, and thus challenges traditional thinking on managing people, production and marketing channels to the consumer. It highlights the practical reasons why we can learn much from a closer examination of creative industries and creative-based organizations. And as these organizations are recognized as making up an increasing, and increasingly important, section of Western economies (Bilton 2007, Work Foundation 2007), current organizational practice may benefit from an increased awareness of the traits of creative organizations (Glynn and Lounsbury 2005; Lash and Urry 1994). Hence an in-depth exploration of creative industries can help deliver a theoretical understanding that engages complexity, change and creativity along with a practical orientation that seeks to stimulate innovative practice in various aspects of organizing.

The creative industries?

An analysis of the 'creative industries' poses a number of challenges, however, not least the extent to which this group constitutes a discrete and distinct economic entity. The UK's Department for Culture, Media and Sport's (DCMS) definition covers a range for areas which includes advertising, architecture, art and antiques, crafts, design, designer fashion, film and video, interactive leisure software, music, performing arts, publishing, software and computer services, TV and radio (DCMS 2001).[1] For some, such a grouping neglects the diverse nature of the production processes and consumption patterns, with each having different production processes and markets, content distribution and experiences of growth and commercial value (Miège 1989). For this reason, some see the term 'creative industries' as the outcome of political manoeuvring, as government departments vie for ballast in arguments against the Treasury (Garnham 2005). The DCMS definition, however, identifies their commonality as lying in the generation and exploitation of intellectual property with the potential for wealth creation.

Just as their grouping is contested, so is their significance. The discourses that surround the creative industries are varied (Flew 2004; Hartley 2005; Hesmondhalgh 2007; Garnham 2005; Jeffcutt *et al.* 2000; Pratt 2005). For some, they typify the economic activity of post-Fordist, knowledge-based production (Florida 2002; Howkins 2001). They are seen as integral to the knowledge economy of high-value, knowledge-based industries, whose development relies on human not physical capital, and where value added comes from ideas and intangible assets (Leadbeater and Oakley 1999). It is a position that was given added emphasis with the UK's New Labour government identification of creative industries as part of its emphasis on the new knowledge economy (DCMS 1998, 2008). The 'culturalization' of economic life, typified by increasingly fragmented, volatile and competitive niche consumer markets and the growing importance of 'immaterial' needs and 'lifestyle', emphasizes 'aesthetic' design-intensive production for an increasingly differentiated customer base (du Gay and Pryke 2002). Within the contemporary business context, economic pressures of increased globalization and the heightened emphasis on consumption have emphasized the importance of creativity and of design and branding in competitive advantage (Cox

2005; Flew 2004). The 'experience' economy, characterized by the growing needs for cultural identity and social empowerment, and aided by technologies of knowledge generation, information processing and communication of symbols, further reinforce this. Although the differentiation of consumer groups, by virtue of the style of their consumption from music to fashion and art to living spaces, has long been acknowledged, the move to knowledge and cultural economies emphasizes the minutiae of distinctions (Bourdieu 1984), and the price and speed of the availability of products further stimulate the flux of creative consumptions and creative output.

Others identify a more limited economic role for the creative industries (Caust 2003; Garnham 2005). Seen as a panacea for regenerating old industrial areas, they are perceived as an extension of 'cultural industries', where art and culture are incorporated into broader social aims of regional regeneration and social inclusion. The focus is on a number of policy intents: creative regeneration, wealth creation, employment and social inclusion. Certainly there is a relationship between the upgrading of cityscapes and spaces and the rebranding of cities through public art, museums, architecture and an association with creative enterprises. Flagship cultural projects, such as the Guggenheim Bilbao, the Albert Dock, Liverpool, and Tate Modern, London, are allied to strategies of urban regeneration (bringing investment and consumers to raise the quality of life), and urban renewal (involving changes in structure and physical appearance). Increased leisure time and disposable income have also seen the burgeoning of cultural festivals and the growth of cultural tourism. However, the claims for cultural activity to enhance economic and social regeneration and improved prosperity are often guilty of exaggeration. Although land values may increase, creative clusters heavily dependent on life-style entrepreneurs and independents tend not to create ancillary employment or viable communities. Artists often have to rely on other jobs. Design consultancies, art and fashion outlets tend to have short lifespans. Flagship buildings do not necessarily regenerate a surrounding area. There remain problems of employment and social inclusion. Criticisms are voiced that creative industries reflect and rely on cultural ecologies, rather than being something to be created by policy engineering (Flew 2004; de Berranger and Meldrum 2000; Pratt 2004; Scott 1996, 1999; Tay 2005).

For yet others, the term 'creative industries' reflects the logical progression, identified in earlier writings, of symbolic creativity being organized around, and for, the market: the industrialization of culture and its commodification for the mass audience (Hesmondhalgh 2007). It is the consequence of the development of manufactured need, amusement and escape: 'mass deception' that ' ... no longer pretends to be art ... No object has an inherent value; it is valuable only to the extent that it can be exchanged' (Horkheimer and Adorno 1995: 158). Once culture had metamorphosed into the 'culture industry', from thence it easily transmutes into 'the creative industries' (Cunningham 2002; Garnham 2005). From this perspective, its emphasis parallels a growing disengagement of public support and patronage of cultural and artistic activity and the latter's gradual disciplining by the market through private gain.

Discourses such as these focus on the significance of the creative industries within broader socio-economic trends, rather than whether this group shares commonalities of experience that sets it apart from other organizations and industries. Work by Caves (2002) has perhaps been the most detailed on the ways in which the creative industries differ and the challenges they pose. For Caves the creative industries are different because they deal in 'experience goods'. The latter is where buyers lack information about a product prior to its consumption (a response to a book or film, for example, is not known until it is read or seen), and as a consequence, where satisfaction is subjective and largely intangible. What is being sold is that which cannot be captured. In this, Caves (2002) is similar to Hirsch (1972: 642) who describes the creative industries as dealing in 'non-material goods directed at a public of consumers for whom they generally serve an aesthetic or expressive rather than a clearly utilitarian purpose'. For Hirsch (1972: 642) the creative industries deal in 'the production, reproduction, distribution and consumption of symbolic forms'. As 'symbolic goods' (ideas, experiences, images), their 'value' is primarily dependent upon the play of symbolic meanings, in that they are 'dependent upon the end user (viewer, audience, reader, consumer) decoding and finding value within these meanings; the value of "symbolic goods" is therefore dependent upon the user's perception as much as on the creation of the original content, and that value may not translate into a financial return' (Hirsch 2000). Because the creative industries deal in experiential goods and commercial value only becomes known after the product is released to the market, there is considerable uncertainty about its likely demand.

Demand uncertainty, concerns about the unpredictable audiences and consumer responses, and the nature of the creative productive process itself, highlight the 'inherent unknowability' that characterizes the creative industries.

As an economist, Caves (2002) reminds us that the creative product is managed and organized to reach an audience. The creative industries involve the concretization of an image, or an insight, through whatever mode or medium for some form of economic return. Hence, we need to be aware of the materialization and commercialization of creativity and the importance of the institutional framework that underpins any artistic and cultural endeavour (Becker 1982). However, the nature of experience goods makes demand patterns highly unpredictable and production processes difficult to control, factors exacerbated by contestable notions of quality and 'originality' in their evaluation. The uncertainty of demand for the creative product, and the necessity of investing time, resources and the costs in production prior to its being evaluated, pose distinct managerial and organizational challenges. The structure and staffing of creative projects are often temporary, as are capital investments (DeFillippi and Arthur 1998). Success is highly dependent on the composition of project teams with individuals and groups working in a highly interactive and adaptive fashioning of the product. Why some products sell and others don't leads to considerable challenges for decision making, not only before, but after, production. Consumer data is susceptible to contradictory interpretations. Uncertainty pervades the creation of the product; the recognition of new talent; managing creative inputs; facilitation of the production process; the identification of the potential market and potential audiences; the prediction of the response of consumers; and predicting the potential longevity of the creative enterprise. Is it just a passing fashion or will it last? In all these areas there is an inherent tension between the freedom to be creative and keeping this creativity within manageable and productive bounds; the necessity of creating a 'creative space' for 'creative labour' to experiment, and maintaining the tension and balance between creativity and cost, autonomy and management control.

While forces of globalization, the centrality of knowledge as a force of production and post-Fordist production methods have implications for all types of production processes, including pressures to accelerate product development, rapid change and a greater degree of unpredictability and risk in the fluctuation of audience tastes and fashions, the creative industries deal with a higher degree of uncertainty in relation to all elements of the productive endeavour. High fixed costs of production influence production to reproduction ratios. Low to zero marginal costs of reproduction and distribution emphasize economies of scale and audience maximization. But the inherent public good or semi-public good nature of creative output (i.e. consumption by one person does not diminish its consumption by another) means there are difficulties of securing exclusivity or scarcity. There are also difficulties of capturing realizable demand through the price structure. Intricate value chains, where profit is extracted at key nodes in the chain, make control of production, investment and distribution complex. The difficulties of decision making that these areas present is further exacerbated by underlying tensions between creative/artistic and commercial logics.

A supposed antithesis

Whatever the political interpretation of the significance of the creative industries, Adorno's (2001) thesis of the importance of preserving the autonomy of the field of cultural production continues to inform approaches to understanding the 'creative industries', establishing an apparent antitheses between art and commerce, a cultural versus a commercial logic.

There are perhaps three claims for the role of 'creative art' and the 'creative artist'.[2] First, art is held to reflect 'true', authentic self-expression, and thus to be transcendent of mundane economics. The artist produces the 'auratic' work of art which loses its 'aura' in mechanical or electronic production (Benjamin 1973). The second is an argument about the distinctiveness of cultural goods. They are held to have a transformative rather than just a demand value, that is, they allow for the exploration of aspects of human experience and well-being. 'Art' reflects on human nature. Appreciation of 'art' is taken as an indicator of civilized activity. Art and culture are thus 'special' and distinct from other market goods and it is this that forms the opposition to the commodification of culture and the marketization of this important aspect of social life. Thirdly, and again relatedly, is the argument that art has a role to play in social endeavour. The artist's primary virtue is disloyalty, being on 'the dangerous edge of things', offering the challenging, 'political' role of critique. Although such positions may mistake or underestimate the relative, and the historical, interpenetration of the 'world of art' and the 'world of money', their presence underlies many disputes in the creative industries.

Given the apparent inherent tensions that arise between an artistic (A) and commercial (not A) logic, a number of strategies suggest themselves and feature in the organization of creative endeavour: either 'A' or 'not A' dominate; 'A' and 'not A' are separate over time through sequential phasing; or 'A' and 'not A' are spatially separate. But a number of questions suggest themselves. Is it possible to have a synthesis of the two? Or would this obliterate or silence the strengths of each? Is it possible to secure a form of 'rule bending' betwixt and between? Is it possible for them to co-exist contiguously? Are they in fact antithetical? It certainly indicates the need for more direct research as to whether there is in fact a problem: how pervasive and how frequently these tensions arise; how significant they are; and whether they are necessarily negative or might be seen as having a positive role to play.

This fundamental antithesis between art and commerce has been transposed into the antipathy between creativity and management.[3] Understood through a Romantic legacy, artistic creativity often appears antithetical to management. Traditionally, creativity has been associated with cultural and creative production: the opera, the work of art, drama, etc.; while management has been associated with control, planning and organizing, the antithesis of anything associated with creativity. The latter stifles or inhibits creativity; creativity needs to 'escape' the strictures of discipline. The association of creativity with play further reinforces this characterization. We should remind ourselves, however, that etymologically, 'creativity' comes from the Latin, *creare*, at once to generate or to give birth or to make or to produce (Gotz 1981). The animal and mechanical, the natural and the social, are integral to its meaning; the tensions are immanent. So let us look at the creativity and management that the creative industries encapsulate, the generation and giving birth of the artistic or creative image and the making and production of creative goods. Are creativity and management an etymological division of labour incarnate?

An entrenched antithesis between management and business and creative/artistic activity is in danger of blinkering us to some of their potential similarities. Both creativity and industry have at their root the process of transformation, although under different guises. Creativity takes that which is familiar and presents it in a different light. Industry takes the input of labour and raw materials and equally transforms them. (The problem arises with the image of 'industry' and its associations with industrial processes and mechanization.) The creative act is an act of managing self, managing others and managing objects. It is the activity of organizing, co-ordinating and directing. Success in both areas often involves collaborative practice, especially as the basis for innovation. Although emanating from different sources, there are perhaps in both management and art forceful pressures to innovate. The artist is obliged to innovate from that which went before in order to claim an individual voice. Within business, innovation of product or process is equally a form of 'market' imperative. Because there is the enactment of roles, both may be seen as delivering a type of performance. A performance is delivered upon some form of stage.

Both may also be seen as a form of practice. While this is largely recognized for the artist, the manager does not often see him- or herself as so engaged. A process of reflection on 'what it is that they do' and 'how they do what they do' is not traditionally part of a recognized discourse of management activity. The introspective nature of the artistic process as the individual 'struggles' in order to express a creative intent might on first glance place it well outside the norms of management activity. (Perhaps the only equivalent figure in management is that of the entrepreneur, often portrayed as the individual with a 'vision' that he or she struggles to materialize.) Because there is a greater awareness of practice in the artistic sphere and a greater degree of reflexivity, there is perhaps the greater possibility for critique, again something which is perhaps more absent from management activity. A greater awareness of management as practice, however, opens up discussion as to the importance of skill and craft in the exercise and execution of practice, a vocabulary that has been, unfortunately, sadly missing from discussion of management until recently (Gabriel 2002). Breaking from the traditional view of management as a role, or the disciplinary arm of industry, management as practice and the need for reflexivity and self-critique in achieving good performance have recently been emphasized (Gabriel 2002; Cunliffe 2002).

Given some of these apparent similarities, it is important to focus discussion on the nature of the relationship between creativity and management. However, it is also important to frame this discussion in a language that does not privilege one particular discipline over another, i.e., does not take as its starting point an 'artistic' or 'managerial' perspective. The disciplinary divide between creative programmes and management and the tension that arises between creative or artistic endeavour and commercial constraint (the stereotyped tension between 'art for art's sake' and 'grubby commercialism'), points to the need to bridge the disciplinary areas of management and creativity. There is also the recognition that while creative areas have much to learn from management in being able to realize creative endeavour, there is a lot that management can learn from the creative arts in terms of the way they manage their activities and the lessons that this might have for business (Morley and Silver 1977; Lampel *et al.* 2000; De Fillippi and Arthur 1998; Sutton 2001). It is thus important to frame an approach that does not favour one discipline over the other, but develops a common vocabulary privileging neither management nor creative endeavour. How to proceed?

Marks on paper

Let us start with the seeming contradiction between 'management' and 'creativity', this antithetical conjunction. What do we see in Figure 1.1? A musical composition, a written text, a published page, budgets, diagrams and balance sheets. What is the relationship between a compositional score for a music concerto, the trace outlines of an etching or design, the manuscript of a novel, a code for a software programme, an organization chart, a balance sheet or budget, a futures strategy diagram? What marks these out as fundamentally oppositional and opposed? What, if anything, do the images in Figure 1.1 have in common?

Let us take Caves' (2002) identification of the unknowability of the creative process as the intrinsic element or quality of the creative industries as our starting point and pose the question: how are management and artistic/creative endeavours known? One means is through their representations. The first step in making something manageable or able to be acted upon is to make it known, i.e. it is

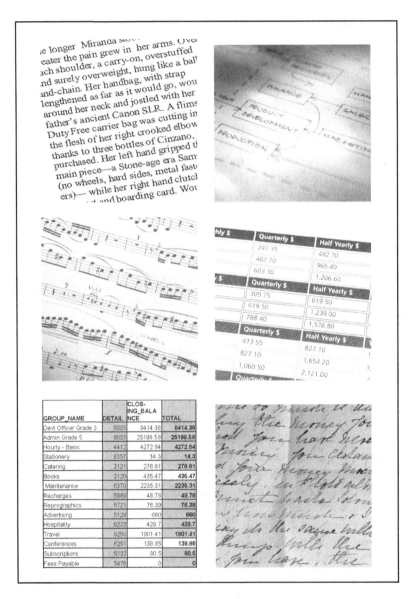

Figure 1.1 Disciplinary representations: marks on paper

to construct a framework that renders the 'unknowability' partially accessible. What 'marks' the above is precisely that. They are representations: a necessary stage in rendering knowable. These representations appear in the world ready labelled, signified, the carriers of meaning and interpretation. But, if we return to foundations, what is presented here are marks on paper.

All constitute 'compositional processes'. All constitute forms of how to (re)present that which is understood or grasped in some way. All rely on 'text'. These marks on paper use models from different disciplines in order to communicate. Musical composition uses the language of musical notation to present new ideas. A musical score is a form of conversation: 'notes are words'. Creative or artistic processes involve decisions as to how to edit, arrange or present material. Marks on paper also indicate patterns. They intimate the prospect or possibility of undetected patterns or new connections.

This is equally true of management. The 'marks on paper' that constitute management are no less creative and productive. An organization chart delineating authority lines and reporting structures, which may or may not bear a resemblance to organizational 'reality', renders organizations and organizational decision making potentially 'mapable'. A marketing survey is a tool that enables an 'unknown' audience reaction or response to be known in a particular way, with this knowledge then feeding into production and design. Strategic planning and the technologies that accompany this, SWOT analysis, etc., may be seen as processes of making the organizational world more tangible. Double-entry bookkeeping, originally devised by an occupation more often associated with the illumination of religious and learned manuscripts than the harbingers of commerce, introduced a method of accounting that was to provide the foundation of economic development. Although not often associated with such, the marks on paper that constitute accounting, as Hines (1988) notes, present a 'picture' of the organization. They create internal departmental divisions, internal and external boundaries (liabilities and externalities), and ultimately a 'picture' of economic health (profit and loss). Budgets act as a form of conversation (Hopwood 1973). These marks on paper (balance sheets, return on investment, cost benefit analyses, ERP, etc.) are significant for the opportunities they present of seeing management technologies as forms of composition.

Each representational technology symbolizes a discipline. These 'marks on paper' are representations that, upon being read by those who have the discipline and the skill to interpret them, present a way of interpreting or seeing the world, and a way of being in the world. Technologies are associated with discourses, familiarity with which

constitutes the 'art world' and the 'business world'. They bring forth
pictures. They deploy art, artifice and craft. Both art and management
use 'marks on paper' or models from different disciplines in order
to present and represent the world in certain ways. In essence, text
is an imperative, the foundation of sharing. It is that which may be
passed on to others. Management and artistic creativity may be presented or understood as forms of compositional processes. Discipline
informs this practice. As a form of power/knowledge, discipline is
simultaneously both restrictive and productive (Foucault 1977, 1980).
Disciplinary technologies present and represent the world in a certain
way, informing identity, discourse and practice and producing real
effects. A focus on 'marks on paper', on representation, allows us
to consider the conventions of representation and the discipline that
informs this practice. The questions raised by 'marks on paper' is
what is invested in them such that they become 'real', and being realized, what effect does this realization have (Latour 1999)?

It would appear that the problem of an assumed antithesis lies in
the boundaries that divide and separate disciplines from one another,
the conceptual frameworks and the specialized language that constitute the prisms or silos through which the world is made sense of and
ultimately judged. This suggests that the concepts of creativity (the
unknowable) and discipline (the act of rendering known) may provide
a means whereby common discussion between different areas may be
advanced, without privileging either a 'managerial' or an 'artistic' perspective. 'Reframing', taking creative approaches to other fields, and
placing the familiar in unfamiliar terrain, is integral to opening up a
dialogue between the two spheres. A focus on 'discipline' addresses
how communication across and between disciplines can take place
and how knowledge may be shared with others. But again the question arises, what are the processes whereby models of representation
may be communicated to and understood by others? What, if any, are
the bases of translation? Is it possible to translate between different
models and different fields? Is integration possible? Or desirable?

We can thus begin a discussion of creativity (and management) from
a perspective of discipline. A less dichotomized reading of creativity
and discipline would appreciate that there is creativity and discipline within any activity. It is to recognise discipline's dual-sided role
(Foucault 1977, 1980): its operation to restrain or constrain; and its
function in a creative or productive capacity. Creativity is intimately

related to discipline. Through constructing categories and boundaries, identities and the promotion of self-discipline, discipline may be understood as the necessary counterpart of creativity, inviting the paradox that the best way to examine aspects of creativity may be by focusing on the operation of discipline. The discipline of learning the area and its craft and the understanding of its rules is the necessary quid pro quo of being able to transgress them. While presenting a seeming straightjacket, the rigour of a discipline allows an element of play, experimentation with and within the canons in order to test boundaries. Discipline is the foundation of play and innovation, providing knowledge and an awareness of boundaries, with an awareness that boundaries are always pliable or fungible. Creative innovation necessarily involves the combination of newness and familiarity. That which is created has to be recognized as being linked or connected in some form to that which went before, a tradition or a discipline. Without an element of familiarity, newness remains 'strange', unrelated to a context for, and of, interpretation. Discipline provides the link between precedents which are known and that which is different, is new or is innovative. Discipline is thus essential for creativity and innovation. It is the foundation of any creative enterprise. Creativity comes at the interface of these twin dimensions of discipline: its prohibitive and its productive side. The requisite balance between the two lies at the heart of creative endeavour in any field.

Disciplines present different traditions and draw upon different canons in order to make judgements as to what is rigorous or what is valid. An emphasis on discipline and a body of knowledge points to the crucial role played by the institutional support for the exercise of practice. The institutional foundations of practice grant legitimacy to that which is undertaken, no matter how seemingly individualized the practice is. It is an emphasis that indicates an awareness of an ecology, with all that this metaphor allows us to bring to the debate, in terms of widening our appreciation of activity from the 'gifted individual' or 'leader', to the systems, interactions and 'infrastructure' that support such endeavours.

The discipline of practice involves processes of self-discipline. The requirements of discipline present specific processes that must be engaged in, in order to train and acquire a body of knowledge. It is a training that disciplines an identity, the body, engagement with self and engagement with others. When disciplinary knowledge becomes internal to being, there is then the opportunity to embody it, to feel it, to play. Creativity is a physical activity; it has physical or observable results.

Understanding, using, applying, interpreting and manipulating compositional processes inform identity and practice and is equally informed by these. Excelling in compositional processes identifies those engaged with them as a craftsperson, one who has dedicated time, effort, energy to learning and developing a skill (Sennett 2008). It is the practice of craft that distinguishes the virtuoso from the parvenu, in terms of their recognition of, and genuflection towards, that which has gone before and the extent to which this informs their practice. Composition, however, lays the basis for, but is not itself, the actualization of creative action. Both in music and the leadership aspect of management, for example, the ideas and marks on paper can be brought to life in better or worse ways. Excellence in composition does not guarantee excellence in performance, and precision of composition does not eliminate the need for interpretation and expression in practice. And in reality, many compositions in various forms of music and management require considerable improvizational skill on the part of the performer. In much early keyboard music the melody is composed along with indications of counterpoint harmony and bass, but the performer is expected to improvize much of the music as part of the performance. Similarly, no amount of organizational charts and management plans and techniques eliminate the need for interpersonal skills in management practice. In neither case can the performer simply 'read the script'. Hence in both fields, practitioners need to be skilled in 'composing as you go'. Making the score come to life is a matter of skill built up through hours of practice. Skilled practitioners, therefore, need to employ creative capacity as they operate within their disciplinary foundations.

Bequeathed by a Romantic legacy, creativity and discipline are often depicted as antithetical. Like the antagonistic twins that inhabit our cultural hinterland, creativity and discipline are forever in conflict. What we propose, however, is a both/and combination that refuses to materialize into an either/or division. It is not until things are seen in these terms that there is a chance for dialogue. It is a perspective that allays some of the dangers of seeing management and art as divided practices. They are not necessarily oppositional. As the etymology of *creare* reminds us the creative and the disciplined are offsprings of the same womb.

And thus are we suggesting reconciliation, the abandonment of paradox, through recourse to 'the linguistic turn'? No. We are suggesting that paradox is apparent because of the failure to delve sufficiently, remaining at the surface manifestation of that which is presented. In essence what is being contrasted is not 'management' versus 'creative'. Our focus is the operation of the disciplines that enables each to be manifest as artistic licence and organizational possibility. How each unfolds, the degree of disciplinary constraint that is involved in an activity and the possibilities of creative licence are worked out in situ, in practice. There is not necessarily a predictable outcome. Or, rather, there is necessarily not a predictable outcome. It is also to suggest the possibility that this reconceptualization might offer a new way of thinking of, and acting within, these tensions. The focus on 'ways of seeing', taking creative approaches to other fields, placing the familiar in unfamiliar terrain (and vice versa), is integral to opening up a dialogue between the two spheres. Might there be the possibility of dialogue?

The framework for the book

We explore the symmetries and interactions between the creative arts and management by examining the relationship between discipline and creativity as it is understood and practiced in the creative industries. Caves' (2002) characteristics of the creative industries are chosen as an organizing framework for our discussion. Caves identifies five distinguishing characteristics or properties of creative industries that make its organization and management complex and unpredictable: (a) the inherent unknowability of the outcome and success of creative endeavour prior to its practice (the *nobody knows* property); (b) the intrinsic motivation beyond economic concerns (*art for art's sake* property); (c) the range of factors that sustains appreciation of creative work (*infinite variety* property); (d) the reliance on the skills of a number of talented individuals for creative production (*motley crew* property); and (e) attempts at securing the durability of creative products (*time flies* and *ars longa* properties).[4]

In considering these areas, the book seeks to foster dialogue by drawing authors from various creative and management disciplines. The aim is not to reduce dialogue to monologue. That is, we have not sought to impose 'resolution' or a singular order upon the work presented here. There are points of agreement and coincidence between disparate chapters, some complementary themes and motifs that resonate throughout. Equally there are tensions and possibly paradoxical situations when different ideas collide. We regard this as a basis for dialogical engagement, maintaining and appreciating some differences, whilst also facilitating agreements, debates and disagreements. In exploring creativity's links with discipline, the chapters question disciplinary boundaries by exploring areas of synergy and overlap between the diverse areas of creative practice and management. In making the links between the different disciplinary backgrounds with which we engage, we have been guided by artists (a fine artist, a performance artist and a musician/composer) who engaged with us in debate. Thus the reader will find in the introductory piece to Part I some of their spoken words that help highlight or reinforce the particular point that we are making.

The question remains, however, what are the implications for performance and research that this dialogue engenders in management and creative practice? To this we have no singular answer. We and all the contributors to this book have made our marks on paper. We have painted the picture, provided the score. We hope that it might help others open up their performance possibilities.

Notes

1 Different countries have different groupings of creative industries, and place different emphases on their import. In the USA, for example, the creative industries are primarily seen as copyright industries: 'engaged primarily in the generation, production and dissemination of new copyrighted material'.

2 'Art' is used here in a very general sense to encompass each form of creative activity identified in the term 'creative industries'.

3 Creativity and art are not synonymous: creativity is not by itself art. Rather, creativity refers to a spark or innovation, a cognitive or experiential process that moves something from place A to place B. And in this sense creativity is a process that occurs across a whole range of activities and disciplines.

4 Caves (2002) also stresses the importance both of complex temporal co-ordination and the timeliness of creative production (the 'time flies' property) and the division in the labour market in terms of talent and skills and differing abilities to command high rewards (A and B list properties). We do not discuss these properties here, not seeing them as being sufficiently distinguishing features of the creative industries. Timely co-ordination, for

example, is a feature of the construction industry, while 'A' and 'B' lists identify the operation of a lot of labour markets.

References

Adorno, T. W. and Bernstein, J. M. (ed.) (2001) *The Culture Industry: Selected Essays on Mass Culture*. London: Routledge.

Becker, H. (1982) *Art Worlds*. Berkeley and Los Angeles: University of California Press.

Benjamin, W. (1973) *Illuminations*. Glasgow: Fontana/Collins.

Bilton, C. (2007) *Management and Creativity. From Creative Industries to Creative Management*. Malden, MA: Blackwell Publishing.

Bourdieu, P. (1984) *Distinction: A Social Critique of the Judgement of Taste*. London: Routledge and Kegan Paul.

Caust, J. (2003) 'Putting the "arts" back into arts policy making: how arts policy has been captured by the economists and marketers'. *The International Journal of Cultural Policy*, 9(1): 51–64.

Caves, R. (2002) *Creative Industries: Contracts Between Art and Commerce*. Cambridge, MA: Harvard University Press.

Cox, G. (2005) *Cox Review of Creativity in Business*. Norwich: HMSO.

Cunliffe, A. (2002) 'Social poetics as management inquiry: a dialogical approach'. *Journal of Management Inquiry*, 11(2): 128–46.

Cunningham, S. (2002) 'From cultural to creative industries: theory, industry and policy implications'. *Media International Australia*, 102: 54–65.

de Berranger, P. and Meldrum, M. (2000) 'The development of intelligent local clusters to increase global competitiveness and local cohesion: the case of small businesses in the creative industries'. *Urban Studies*, 37(10): 1827–35.

DeFillippi, R. and Arthur, M. (1998) 'Paradox in project-based enterprise: the case of film making'. *California Management Review*, 40(2): 125–39.

Department for Culture, Media and Sport (DCMS) (1998) *Creative Industries Mapping Document*. London: DCMS.

(2001) *Creative Industries Mapping Document*. London: DCMS.

(2008) *Creative Britain – New Talents for the New Economy*. London: DCMS.

du Gay, P. and Pryke, M. (2002). *Cultural Economy*. London: Sage.

Flew, T. (2004) 'Creativity, cultural studies and service industries'. *Communication and Critical/Cultural Studies*, 1(2): 176–93.

Florida, R. (2002) *The Rise of the Creative Class: and How it's Transforming Work, Leisure, Community and Everyday*. New York: Basic Books.

Foucault, M. (1977) *Discipline and Punish: The Birth of the Prison*. London: Allen Lane.

Foucault, M. and Gordon, C. (ed.) (1980) *Power/Knowledge: Selected Interviews and Other Writings, 1972–1977*. New York: Pantheon Books.

Gabriel, Y. (2002) 'On the paragrammatic uses of organizational theory'. *Organization Studies*, 23(1): 133–51.

Garnham, N. (2005) 'From cultural to creative industries'. *International Journal of Cultural Policy*, 11(1): 15–29.

Glynn, M.A. and Lounsbury, M. (2005) 'From the critics' corner: logic blending, discursive change and authenticity in a cultural production system'. *Journal of Management Studies*, 42(5): 1031–55.

Gotz, I. (1981) 'On defining creativity'. *Journal of Aesthetics and Art Criticism*, 39(3): 297–301.

Hartley, J. (ed.) (2005) *Creative Industries*. Malden: Blackwell.

Hesmondhalgh, D. (2007) *The Cultural Industries*. London: Sage.

Hines, R. (1988) 'Financial accounting: in communicating reality, we construct reality.' *Accounting, Organizations and Society*, 13(3): 251–61.

Hirsch, P. (1972) 'Processing fads and fashions: an organization-set analysis of cultural industry systems'. *American Journal of Sociology*, 77(4): 639–59.

(2000) 'Cultural industries revisited'. *Organization Science*, 11(3): 356–62.

Hopwood, A.G. (1973) *An Accounting System and Managerial Behaviour*. Farnborough, Hants: Saxon House.

Horkheimer, M. and Adorno, T.W. (1995) *Dialectic of Enlightenment*. New York: Continuum.

Howkins, J. (2001) *The Creative Economy*. London: Penguin.

Jeffcutt, P., Pick, J. and Protherough, R. (2000) 'Culture and industry: exploring the debate'. *Studies in Cultures, Organizations and Society*, 6: 129–43.

Lampel, J., Lant, T. and Shamsie, J. (2000) 'Balancing act: learning from organizing practices in cultural industries'. *Organization Science*, 11(3): 263–9.

Lash, S. and Urry, J. (1994) *Economies of Signs and Space*. Thousand Oaks, CA: Sage.

Latour, B. (1999) *Pandora's Hope*. Cambridge, MA: Harvard University Press.

Leadbeater, C. and Oakley, K. (1999) *The Independents: Britain's New Cultural Entrepreneurs*. London: Demos.

Miège, B. (1989) *The Capitalization of Cultural Production.* New York: International General.

Morley, E. and Silver, A. (1977) 'A film director's approach to managing creativity'. *Harvard Business Review,* 55(2): 59–69.

Pratt, A. (2004) 'Creative clusters'. *Media International Australia,* 112: 50–66.

—— (2005) 'Cultural industries and public policy: an oxymoron?' *International Journal of Cultural Policy,* 11(1): 31–44.

Scott, A.J. (1996) 'The craft, fashion, and cultural-products industries of Los Angeles: competitive dynamics and policy dilemmas in a multisectoral image-producing complex'. *Annals of the Association of American Geographers,* 86(2): 306–23.

—— (1999) 'The cultural economy: geography and the creative field'. *Media, Culture & Society,* 21: 807–17.

Sennett, R. (2008). *The Craftsman.* New Haven, CT: Yale University Press.

Sutton, R.I. (2001) 'The weird rules of creativity'. *Harvard Business Review,* 79(8): 96–103.

Tay, J. (2005) 'Creative cities', in J. Hartley (ed.) *Creative Industries.* Oxford: Blackwell Publishing.

Thompson, P., Warhurst, C. and Callaghan, G. (2001) 'Ignorant theory and knowledgeable workers: interrogating the connections between knowledge, skills and services'. *Journal of Management Studies,* 38(7): 923–42.

Work Foundation (2007) *Staying Ahead: The Economic Performance of the UK's Creative Industries.* Available: www.theworkfoundation.com (accessed 28 January 2009).

Inherent unknowability

Introduction to Part I

Caves' (2002) identification of 'inherent unknowability' refers to the 'nobody knows' principle that characterizes the creative industries, in that nobody knows the outcome and success of a creative endeavour prior to its practice. 'The artist does not know and cannot pre-test whether her creative vision will prove equally compelling to others. Still worse, she cannot tell whether her conception has been successfully extracted from her inner vision and turned into an external creative product' (Caves 2002: 5). As we deal with audience response in Part III ('infinite variety'), here we focus on the 'inherent unknowability' that stems from the creative process itself, i.e., the uncertainty that accompanies the creative act. Harbouring a plethora of 'synonyms' such as innovation, novelty and originality, 'creativity' raises several issues. Is it possible for creativity to claim an institutional locus? Is creativity the defining element of artistic endeavour to the exclusion of all else? Or is it on a par with scientific creativity, or any act that is an act of illumination?

Much has been written on the nature of creativity, how it is identified and understood and the contexts that might enhance or dissipate its focus (Amabile 1998; Amabile *et al.* 1996, 2005; Cummings 1965; Ford and Gioia 1995; Jalan and Kleiner 1995; Scott 1965; Sternberg 1999; Woodman *et al.* 1993). Debate veers between creativity as mysterious, inspirational, the gift of the gods or the 'eureka' moment reflecting the exercise or gift of genius, versus creativity as the everyday experience of bringing into being something different from that which went before (Meyers and Gerstman 2007). From the work of McKinnon and colleagues onwards there has been interest in the extent to which creativity in different areas or domains overlaps, whether it is art-specific or resides in all human endeavour (McKinnon 1956; Ford 1996). Other strands of the debate focus around whether creativity is a unitary concept, and whether there are different types of creativity according to whether a problem is well defined and the nature and extent of the pressures to realize new solutions (Bleakley 2004; Unsworth 2001). Allied to this are questions as to whether creativity appears 'as if from nothing' and is therefore seen as quite transformative or is something more generic. As the latter, creativity is sometimes used interchangeably with innovation (often thought of as the implementation of ideas), and tends to concentrate more on focused solutions to problems and stresses the importance of diligence, persistence and commitment (Drucker 1998), as opposed to revolutionary ideas for radical change. Becker (1982), also, has identified problem-solving processes as underlying forms of creativity in the arts.

Also debated is whether creativity is individualistic or more collaborative (Drazin *et al.* 1999; Taggar 2002). Its depiction can be quite individualized, thought of as being an intrinsic motivation (Amabile 1998). Others argue that the 'lone genius' personification of creativity is something of a romantic myth and question the degree of individuality involved in a creative process (Hargadon and Sutton 2000; Marotto *et al.* 2007; Tschang and Szczypula 2006). Favouring an analysis that sees creativity as a collective endeavour, this supports a more ecological account of its emergence (Jeffcutt 2004; Perry-Smith and Shalley 2003; Ford 2000). Creativity has been variously described as the ability to think flexibly and imaginatively, the outcome of play and imagination, and being reflective of a relative balance between analysis and interpretation or sensing (Hargadon and Sutton 1997, 2000; Lester *et al.* 1998; Montouri 2003; Sutton and Hargadon 1996). This prompts debates as to whether creativity is spontaneous or may be learnt and taught; is unusual or ubiquitous; universal or culture-specific; imaginative and intuitive or knowledge- and skills-based. A more 'exclusivist' interpretation sees creativity associated with human capacity for originality and innovation. Its association with autonomy and self-expression stresses its independence from the control of others. A less idealized interpretation emphasizes the social 'codes', conventions and expectations through which creativity is understood and recognized. Basically, the debate focuses on whether creativity is the ineffable and instinctive or more tangible and testable (or, more crassly, emotional or rational), the extent to

which it is the product of determinable factors or unexpected occurrences and incongruities: essentially, the extent to which the creative
process may be rendered 'knowable' and to a degree determinable.

Our chapters in the first section (Stackhouse, Dixon and Linstead),
where we focus on the creative act and on producing the creative
product, reflect some of these themes. In essence they converge on
the 'unknown' of the creative process and the means through which
individuals make sense of creative activity and the production of artistic product. Stackhouse gives a detailed description of the creative
processes entailed in creating fine art. Of interest here, is how what
is to be depicted is initially hidden or 'unknown' to the artist. In this
she echoes others. Listen to the following descriptions of the artistic
process:

> The artist is good at orientation to that which is under-determined. The
> artist is good at going into an empty space and making something happen.
> The artist deals with, and constructs, choice within constraints and choice
> in the unknown. (Musician/Composer)

> There needs to be an openness as to what might happen, a capacity to
> hear and to notice, by being receptive. (Performance Artist)

These descriptions point to the indeterminacy, the lack of speci-
ficity and the 'unknown' that the artist addresses when faced with
starting a new work. They also point to an ability, or comfort – one
might almost say training – in being in such a position, of being able
to exist in, or hold onto, this indeterminacy for a greater period of
time than others might feel comfortable with:

> Ideas come from talking to people, accidents, things that happen. They
> eventually submerge into the 'final' work. It is a process of looking, see-
> ing, watching and observing. It's behaving towards chance as though
> chance does not exist. It is embracing randomness. This is tied in with the
> creative process. There is no such thing as 'inaction'. Some [actions] are
> more active and reflexive than others. (Fine Artist)

It is also the ability while being in this space to be able to experiment, reinvent and reimagine:

> Creativity is how to get out of your box and see things as a different
> world ... Creative thinking is not being put off by 'no' ... Artists make
> unusual connections and challenge assumptions ... It's flexible, thinking
> on your feet, making things happen from nothing or very little ... It's a

combination of the huge, vastness and universal and the intimate. And putting them together. (Performance Artist)

Only by engaging in the process of creation does the artist become aware of the creative object that 'demands' to become known. Stackhouse describes the processes involved in making a creation 'known'. In this, there is a strong awareness of the discipline that makes this possible. Creativity is recognized as being linked to the discipline of a long apprenticeship and full immersion in the field for successful innovation and creativity. Discussions of how artists understand the creative process are replete with the motif of discipline, again echoing other artists' descriptions of their work:

I keep describing the world that I see. I believe that any discipline does this. Any person engages in the same process, but they just use different methods. We absorb what we perceive about the world and bring it back again in a slightly altered form. (Fine Artist)

Listen to a musician and composer describe his work:

Discipline is the means through which noise is turned into music. It is the means by which the incalculable is rendered into choice. (Musician/ Composer)

The creative act is described as a process whereby that which is unknown, or known in another way, becomes translated into an image to be re-presented to itself. It is the concretization of the image. Discipline is the means through which noise is turned into music or the means by which the incalculable is rendered into choice. This process is achieved through a keen awareness of the craft of work:

The drawing is already there even though I don't know what it is yet. The good bits are when I make a mark and I think that's working, where it didn't before. [Pointing to the painting] These marks are not as tedious and boring as these marks are. But they aren't as pure. Drawings move from chaos into clarity. (Fine Artist)

Part of discipline is self-discipline:

There are strategies that artists used over the years, to use the personal, to develop the personal into performance. There is personal and interesting, and there is personal and self-indulgence. The line is crucial. You look at ideas and then you look at the medium. (Performance Artist)

An allied theme that emerges from Stackhouse's detailed description is the importance of 'labour', of how the artist is aware of the posture and activity of the body during the making of the artistic creation and of the physicality of work and the physicality of the materials that are engaged within the making of the work. The labour involved in the productive process is often missing from discussions of artistic production. 'Labour', the activity of the body is that which is repressed, giving way to the higher-minded activity of 'art', thus denying, or obfuscating the physical. But as this Fine Artist reminds us: 'When I produce a drawing, it's hard labour. There are parts of the work that can be repetitive and tedious. Repetition and tediousness is part of it. It gets boring and extremely painful.'

The interplay between work, labour and the produced work is a theme that is taken up by Dixon in his discussion of the narratives, or generic stories, available in discourse to describe the creative process. Dixon identifies the narratives of the 'quiet poetic process of creativity' and its contrasting theme of 'intemperateness'. What is missing in these narratives, for Dixon, is the 'moment' of decision. Like Stackhouse, he identifies the importance of action in creation, the 'leap into the unknown' when the decision is made to take one course of action or another, the bringing into being of the marks on paper that completes, if only temporarily, the 'inherent unknowability' of creating. An awareness of the discipline of the creative process presents decisions as a form of 'constrained choice'. The creative process is seen as the attempt to 'codify' elements of that which is known, and an attempt to deal with or make more 'manageable' that which is not. In this, his depiction of the artistic process suggests that there are similarities between the artistic process and the managerial process of decision making under uncertainty, or decision making under risk, evoking the distinction between action rationality and decision rationality (Brunsson 1985). Dixon's essay suggests that there are parallels between the processes of good decision making and effective creativity. Both are good at overcoming indecision. It is this role for discipline that informs a less idealized interpretation of creativity.

The final chapter in this section, by Linstead, picks up Dixon's theme of the narratives of creativity, placing them in a broader sociohistorical context than that of the individual in the creative process. Linstead considers some of the themes of 'intemperateness' in his discussion of creativity, its political implications and the historical linkages between 'creativity' and the carnival. In his discussion of The Clash, creativity is seen as the testing of (disciplinary) boundaries, of being a process of challenge and transgression. In this, Linstead further reinforces Dixon's argument about the importance and significance of creativity's links with action.

References

Amabile, T. (1998) 'How to kill creativity'. *Harvard Business Review*, 76(5): 77–87.
Amabile, T., Conti, R., Coon, H., Lazenby, J. and Herron, M. (1996) 'Assessing the work environment for creativity'. *Academy of Management Journal*, 39(5): 1154–84.
Amabile, T., Barsade, S. G., Mueller, J. S. and Staw, B. M. (2005) 'Affect and creativity at work'. *Administrative Science Quarterly*, 50: 367–403.
Becker, H. (1982) *Art Worlds*. Berkeley and Los Angeles: University of California Press.
Bleakley, A. (2004) 'Your creativity or mine? A typology of creativities in higher education and the value of a pluralistic approach'. *Teaching in Higher Education*, 9: 463–75.
Brunsson, N. (1985) *The Irrational Organization: Irrationality as a Basis for Organizational Action and Change*. Chichester, NY: John Wiley.
Caves, R. (2002) *Creative Industries: Contracts Between Art and Commerce*. Cambridge, MA: Harvard University Press.
Cummings, L. (1965) 'Organizational climates for creativity'. *Journal of Academy of Management*, 8(3): 220–7.
Drazin, R., Glynn, M. and Kazanjian, R. (1999) 'Multilevel theorizing about creativity in organizations: a sensemaking perspective'. *Academy of Management Review*, 24(2): 286–307.
Drucker, P. (1998) 'The discipline of innovation'. *Harvard Business Review*, 63(3): 149–57.
Ford, C. (1996) 'Theory of individual creative action in multiple social domains'. *Academy of Management Review*, 21(4): 1112–42.
    (2000) 'Creative developments in creative theory'. *Academy of Management Review*, 25(3): 284–6.
Ford, C. and Gioia, D. (1995) *Creative Action in Organizations*. London: Sage.
Hargadon, A. and Sutton, R. I. (1997). 'Technology brokering and innovation in a product development firm'. *Administrative Science Quarterly*, 42: 16.
    (2000) 'Building an innovation factory'. *Harvard Business Review*, 78(3): 157–66.
Jalan, A. and Kleiner, B. (1995) 'New developments in developing creativity'. *Journal of Managerial Psychology*, 10(8): 20–3.

Jeffcutt, P. (2004) 'Knowledge relationships and transactions in a cultural economy: analysing the creative industries ecosystem'. *Media International Australia incorporating Culture and Policy*, 112: 67–82.

Lester, R., Piore, M. and Malek, K. (1998) 'Interpretive management: what general managers can learn from design'. *Harvard Business Review*, 76(2): 86–96.

Marotto, M., Roos, J. and Bart, V. (2007) 'Collective virtuosity in organizations: a study of peak performance in an orchestra'. *Journal of Management Studies*, 44(3): 388–413.

McKinnon, D. (1956) 'Personality and the realization of creative potential'. *American Psychologist*, 20: 273–81.

Meyers, H.M. and Gerstman, R. (2007) *Creativity: Unconventional Wisdom from 20 Accomplished Minds*. Basingstoke: Palgrave Macmillan.

Montouri, A. (2003) 'The complexity of improvisation and the improvisation of complexity: social science, art and creativity'. *Human Relations*, 56(2): 237–55.

Perry-Smith, J. and Shalley, C.E. (2003) 'The social side of creativity: a static and dynamic social network perspective'. *Academy of Management Review*, 28: 89–106.

Scott, W. (1965) 'The creative individual'. *Academy of Management Journal*, 8(3): 369–401.

Sternberg, R. (ed.). (1999) *Handbook of Creativity*. New York: Cambridge University Press.

Sutton, R.I. and Hargadon, A. (1996) 'Brainstorming groups in context: effectiveness in a product design firm'. *Administrative Science Quarterly*, 41: 685–718.

Taggar, S. (2002) 'Individual creativity and group ability to utilize individual creative resources: a multilevel model'. *Academy of Management Journal*, 45(2): 315–30.

Tschang, F.T. and Szczypula, J. (2006) 'Idea creation, constructivism and evolution as key characteristics in the videogame artefact design process'. *European Management Journal*, 24(4): 270–87.

Unsworth, K. (2001) 'Unpacking creativity'. *Academy of Management Review*, 26(2): 286–97.

Woodman, R., Sawyer, J. and Griffin, R. (1993) 'Toward a theory of organizational creativity'. *Academy of Management Review*, 18(2): 293–321.

2 | To *draw thought* – how *can* this be done differently?

AILEEN M. STACKHOUSE

I suggest that the seeker forget what he has learned, neglect what he has heard and read, and listen to his own experience.

(Reik 1948: 330)

This chapter describes the manner of thinking involved in the creation of an ongoing sequence of art works which began in 2004 with *A twenty-eight day drawing for conversation* and continued in 2006 with *How* can *this be done differently?* The most recent work, *Drawing undone,* a collaborative drawing installation with Cordelia Underhill, took place in 2007 at Dundee Contemporary Arts Centre. Each of these works uses drawing as a research tool to reflect on aspects of creative processes and thought. I emphasise that the works function in relation to each other and should not be treated as separate entities, also that the sequence is unfinished and so far inadequately addresses all that I want it to address. I do not envisage a conclusion at this time, or at any time – these works continually evolve – these works are way stations (Dallow 2003).

Drawing enables those who use it as a thinking tool to respond flexibly and imaginatively to any given problem. It enables and maintains enduring connections between non-verbal thought processes and those of spoken or written language. This chapter will touch on my own practice-led doctoral research (Stackhouse 2006) throughout which I developed the use of drawing and introspection as a systematic and disciplined approach to access and study subjective states of thinking apparent throughout the various stages of creative action (Vermersch 1999).

I believe that physical and tactile engagement with materials and the world acts as a catalyst for intuitive, and consequently innovative, conceptual manipulation of perceptions of the world and the nature of reality. Fresh points of view and original actions are produced by rigorous questioning and curiosity concerning this perceived nature.

The visual documentation of drawings provides *points of attention* regarding individual awareness of the intertwining sensations of the spoken, read and written word, the visual image, the hand, the eye and the ear.

When reading the following text I would ask the reader to do so as slowly as they can bear, to read each sentence more than once, to speak each sentence aloud (Goulish 2000). To vocalise brings a different understanding; brings the writing of drawing closer to the drawing. The sometimes fractured, repetitive and hesitant structure of the text is deliberate and is intended to mirror the painstaking processes of creativity. The purpose of the work is to raise questions in the mind of the reader rather than answer them.

> We enter into thought ... only by questioning. We go from question to question to the point where the question, pushed towards a limit, becomes response ... (Blanchot 1993: 108 in Peters 2003)

The image is not what it seems. The artist asks us to look more closely at what we see before us – there *is* more here than meets the eye.

We can *speculate* about what the artist wishes us to see and what he wishes us to think about. We can *speculate* about the reactions of others who look at/see the image and we can *know* about our own reaction (which *will* change over time). When I first saw this image my reaction was one of delight. My heart leapt in response and my breath caught within me – and then bubbled to the surface as laughter – even now while writing these words my breath catches and bubbles again. I looked and I knew that this image was not what it seemed, a man leaping from a window. I knew (or I think I know) that no one was harmed in its making. I do not want to know how Klein made the image, what sleight of hand or trickery was involved. What I, as the observer, take from the image is akin to the feeling I sense when I read the following words by Maurice Merleau-Ponty:

> ... the artist launches his work just as a man once launched the first word not knowing whether it will be anything more than a shout ... The meaning of what the artist is going to say *does not exist* anywhere – not in things, which as yet have no meaning, nor in the artist himself, in his unformulated life. (Merleau-Ponty 1945)

In Yves Klein's image I recognise the decision to leap into the void, in Merleau-Ponty's words I recognise the struggle of wanting to

Figure 2.1 Yves Klein (1960) *Leap into the Void*. Shunk-Kender
(©) Roy Lichtenstein Foundation, © ADAGP, Paris and DACS, London 2009

express … what? –express not knowing? – wanting to express what I
see and understand – and express what I see and *do not* understand? –
Wanting to express the clamour and chaos of everyday life – the wonder and the ennui bound up in its living – to speak about this struggle
and be understood?

For *this* artist the impulse to make art resembles a decision to
jump – to jump from, to jump to, to jump into, to jump up and to
jump down. It begins with hesitation and hovering at the edge of *not
knowing* how to do this … this unknown *thing – then* the urge to
make becomes irresistible, unbearable, and the decision is taken to

Figure 2.2 Aileen Stackhouse (June 2004) *A twenty-eight day drawing for conversation*. Installation, Dundee Contemporary Arts Centre. 'I do not draw how I want to draw.'

leap. There is no knowing *where* the movement will take us when the feet first rock forward, flex and push down, when the body lifts, out and up, rises into the air and when – for a fraction of a second – we experience flight (Breugel c.1555–8). The ensuing tumble through the rushing air and the thudding impact of the ground beneath us resonates up through the body (a reverse echo of the fall) and we either lie broken or stand up and begin again. For the person who falls it is momentous – for the rest of the world it goes unnoticed.

The image *is* not what it seems. There *is* more here than meets the eye.

An invisible background history exists of considering the processes of thought involved in the making of art. An invisible and continuing/ous arrival exists at the realisation that I did/do not completely understand what I was/am investigating. Explanations using words were/are not comprehensive or adequate. The meaning did not – *does not exist* anywhere (see Merleau-Ponty above). I knew that these words I used were not saying what I wanted them to say. I knew that if I continued to use these words the work would become something other … *these* words would take the meaning of the work somewhere

different – somewhere that was not *here* where *this* creating mind
existed now. All the drawings that I had made up to this point in the
research only scratched at the surface of what I wanted to communicate. I spent hours gazing at them as if *they* knew how to tell me
what to do, as if *they* would speak – and yet it was *I* who had made
them, not the other way round. I knew how to draw, I could draw, I
did draw and I do draw but I did not draw how I *sensed* I wanted to
draw. I would grasp and lift the pencil and hold it poised – ready. I
would stare at the paper before me, I would move the pencil towards
the surface and I would approach *and* I would know as soon as the
connection was made that I had missed ... missed what? Missed the
time, the place – had the paper moved? Had I moved? Had the pencil moved? Had time moved? What slippage had occurred between
my sensing of coming to what it was that I wanted to draw and my
action of drawing? All of these questions are too literal to describe
what it was that was taking place between my mind, my eye, my hand
and the paper's surface. I *could not* draw my gap in understanding. I
could only gesture towards the space it occupied. These works began
to emerge at a time when I was trying to pin down a creative methodology in response to the demands of the academic institution. Were
these demands unrealistic? Are there some kinds of knowledge and
understanding where, ultimately, observation intrinsically interferes
with their operation?

According to modern physics (especially the quantum theory), when one
comes down to the atomic and subatomic level of size, the observing instrument is even *in principle* inseparable from what is to be observed, so that
this instrument cannot do other than 'disturb' the observed system in an
irreducible way: and indeed it even helps to create and give form to what is
observed. One may compare this situation to a psychological observation,
which can likewise 'disturb' the people being studied, and thus take part
in the process that one wants to learn about, as well as 'create' and shape
some of the very phenomena that can be observed. (Bohm 1998: 38)

I argue that some creative practices do not bear literal explanation.
Detailed academic explanation and rationalisation can and *do*
undermine the complex processes of thought involved. The repetitive
manipulation of materials and objects by the creative practitioner,
which to the onlooker can seem meaningless, is inextricably intertwined with an attentive state that cannot be objectively measured

but is highly attuned and holds the potential for creative leaps in understanding of ideas and motivation. Much of *this* artist's practice takes place within the imagined space of the mind. Using the imagination is of primary importance in rehearsing alternative outcomes to express the sensed – yet unseen – sequence of actions and impressions that concern the mind throughout its observation and experience of the world. Such rehearsal of processes enables internalisation and sets in motion transformations of awareness that result in externalisation of ideas. The ensuing transformations develop at their own momentum, any imposition of another pace will not be maintained and cannot be forced.

There are inherent difficulties involved in the systematic observation of self whilst creating work. A balance has to be weighed between an awareness which watches with attention but does not *appear* to affect the actions of making, and an awareness which exerts an influence that subtly moves the action of making towards a performance to self. The intention is to highlight oblique transitions in thinking and practice that necessitate a more intense and reflective focus. The most obvious drawback to using introspection as the primary approach for monitoring the fluctuating presence of recurrent elements during the creative process is establishing its veracity as a body of experiential knowledge for the wider research community. Nevertheless I believe these descriptions of engagement with the thinking inherent in creativity are *fundamental* to reaching a genuinely informed and serious understanding of process (Petitmengin-Peugeot 1999; Varela 1999; Vermersch 1999).

The image is *not* what it seems. There is *more* here than meets the eye.

Imagination is an intelligence which is highly underrated in our approaches to research. It is the basic tool that all people use to approach and understand new areas of experience and to revision [*sic*] what they already know. (McNiff 1998: 184)

Some observers of the work wanted more than I could give them. They wanted to know why I was doing what I was doing, *what* it was that I was drawing, what I was doing it *for*. When I did not have answers or reasons that satisfied them (and I did not – for I had no answers or reasons for myself – except that the work and the way of working was a way of thinking about thought) they supplied their own, they made the drawing into something meaningful for them, they described the drawing to themselves and they began to know it in *their own* way – making it *be like* something they recognised – making the drawing *represent* something – unwilling to come to the thought that the drawing was unknowable and that I, as the artist, accepted that it was unknowable. This being the case ... why was conversation with thinkers from disciplines other than Fine Art so important for me? The following passage is an extract from notes of one of a series of conversations with the philosopher Professor Nicholas Davey. These notes were not made during the conversation but immediately after he had left the drawing installation. Their fragmentary nature gestures toward the recognition, delineation and negotiation of shared conceptual concerns:

... in two conversations before this drawing began we briefly discuss what it is I am striving to achieve with this **descrying** ... Nicholas has spoken of sites of difficulty ... which it seems to him are the basis of what my drawing is ... spaces of attention that I link with my breakdown of varying volumes of attention ... we speak of the nature of the pointing finger ... the open hand ... how the site of difficulty I negotiate is an anti space ... it seems to ... **not** exist ... except in our imagination ... my recognition of my attempt to draw what **seems** to not exist and cannot be described using words implies that it does exist ... refers to space which is not ... the drawing of what is ... not there ... and cannot be seen or described ... drawing this as ... sensation ... rather than picturing ... (Davey and Stackhouse 2004)

The artist puts things together – elements, ideas, features, *stuff* – that did not exist together before (Boden 2004). For the artist this action points to an idea, a relationship or an abstraction that they wish to call attention to – a way of seeing. This action can be considered and deliberate, planned, thought-through, foreseen, imagined and predictable. This action can also result in juxtapositions that are accidental, fortuitous, ugly or beautiful. These mistakes and errors of judgement often produce creative actions that are more challenging than those which are predictable *precisely* because they are unplanned and possess the element of surprise. The paradox of their existence cannot be denied and holds a stronger attraction because that existence triggers questions which build on the circularity of previous experience – why did *this* happen? Why does it *look* like this? What happens if I do this now? The action of putting elements together is not intended to focus attention on individual elements or their appearance. It is the relationship between the elements which sets out the space for the imagination to function/operate more freely – unbound by considerations of what the artwork should *be* – unbound by what it should *look* like, and allow the return to what the artwork *is* and what it *does*. The relationship is not meant to reach or propose a conclusion – it is a way of understanding an area of disquiet in the mind of the artist. The relationship of elements may appear nonsensical to the observer, they may never have considered such interactions – they may not have noticed that there existed a potential gap in understanding – and thus for them there is no gap. It can be argued that simply placing the incongruent elements together will create an answering question in their thinking (Crook 2005).

The image is not *what* it seems. There is more *here* than meets the eye.

The drawing was dismantled, cut into sections and placed outside prior to storage. While it lay outside on the ground the rain began. I watched raindrops fall on its surface – each impact dislodged a fine spray of charcoal and graphite powder – and left a clear circle behind framed by a spattering of darkness. I decided to hang the soaking paper on the outside walls to dry and see what these accumulated marks would become. The heavy summer rain did not stop for a further four weeks. The drawing became so sodden that it began to fragment – to tear and fall down under its own weight. As it unpeeled from the walls my daily inspection of puddles of rain water and dirt collecting within its new folds and gullies revealed sculptural shapes and landscapes marked and traced by the weather and not by my hand. The physical appearance of these tracks came closer to what I was trying to draw than the drawing had itself when *I* had been the mark maker. The marks more accurately described the *sensed* cognitive action of drawing, its ephemeral nature, its reference to the *now*. I began to systematically photograph, to select and frame and fix what was there before my eyes. If I drew these marks (in fact I would not be able to – it was impossible) it would not be the same – my drawing would be too considered – it was the *initially* accidental nature of their emergence which was important, which *was the thing itself*.

This pull towards other (to something which made no sense, which was real but was also not real) was/is a recurring rhythm in the making of art.

The image is not what *it* seems. There is more here *than* meets the eye.

While drying the drawing fragmented still further, huge crumpled forms and small distorted shapes were created by the action of the rain as size. (Size /siz/n: a weak glue or gluey material used for stiffening paper or rendering it sufficiently water-resistant ... for stiffening fabric ... [origin obscure] Chambers 2003.)

The constituent parts of the work were hung again in the original experimental space according to the order in which they had been drawn (as closely as my memory permitted). Once reconstructed the work's new and alien form raised fresh questions in my imagination, questions triggered primarily by the tactile sensations experienced in manipulating the paper and its recalcitrant behaviour while in my grasp. Its new characteristics meant that it had become more rigid and resistant to pressure. It made a different noise – it sighed, creaked, crackled and groaned. Once suspended it arched over and around the observer – moved constantly, turned and swayed, unfolded and presented different semblances of itself. I had intended to draw back into the drawing with charcoal and graphite, to re-emphasise and retrace my own marks and those of the rain. I decided not to – I sensed that such actions would interfere with the work's (my?) trajectory of meaning. Instead I decided to use light and air to call attention to the perceived forms and marks created by the rain. I added electric fans to maintain and accelerate the drawing's own motion, and lighting to accentuate its hidden landscapes. The drawing now became an actor on its own stage, the play was unknown – its hidden narrative to be guessed/imagined by the observer.

The images are not what *they* seem. There is more here than *meets* the eye.

What I am describing is experience of being, I am not investigating in the objective world, I am investigating sensitivity. (Hess 2001)

In 2006 I was asked by Generator Projects, an artist-led organisation in Dundee, Scotland, to make a new work for exhibition along with performance and installation artist Andy Wake. I had never worked in the same space as another artist before and I knew that this experience would shed new light on my practice. During two weeks in October I made a new drawing utilising the ways of working developed from *A twenty-eight day drawing for conversation.*

The project gave me the opportunity to systematically apply creative behaviours revealed by my research to an actual drawing situation within a set time limit.

Once more I started from a blank sheet. The immense expanse of creamy white paper buckled and bent as it was unrolled and held many possibilities for ... what? The potential for the fall? (*Do not fly too close to the sun.*) The sound of its unrolling cracked the air and resounded around the walls and the ceiling, its whiteness fractured the darkness of the room. The contemplation of the perceived long moments of its unrolling and the sound as it was manhandled up onto the wall and into place produced an answering resonant tremor in my chest and my hands. I stood before the paper astonished *again* at its emptiness – willing this moment to last forever – unwilling to ever mark. The paper was complete, it was always so – the paper needed nothing else – *it would never need anything else.* The paper was perfect in and of itself. I became conscious of my hands, my fingers flexing and nervously moving through the air as if in rehearsal (I am conscious of their movement *now* as I remember). I halted their flight and brought them down by my sides.

At these times of beginning a work I recognised that the risk always existed that I would be unable to draw anything at all, that I would become paralysed by fear or that I would simply be unable to think of any mark to make. This risk is continuously present and is part of any work, and such risk is bound together with choice. I knew that, as the artist, I could choose *not* to mark – to keep this work permanently in this moment – to suspend its possibilities, its potential. Or I could choose to begin to mark and then choose to stop, leaving the work seemingly unfinished and yet *I* would have finished with it – for me there would be no purpose in its continuation. *Every* and *any* mark was a choice, a decision which responded to a set of givens – (*here* is the paper in this room, *here* is this time *now*, *here* am I and *here* is the mark-making implement and *here* is my hand and *here* is my mind) – I choose to mark *now* ... I choose not to mark *now* ... I choose to mark *here* ... *now* ... I choose to *not* mark *here* ... *now* ... *this* space will remain unoccupied ... *this* space will be filled ... *this* mark will begin here ... this mark will end *here*.

All drawings/art works inhabit this curious and liminal conceptual space which is not subject to the 'usual' passage of time – each constituent line, tone, shade, mark, denotes a constant *coming to*, a continual *apprehending* of the elusive present. This ambivalent and ambiguous state of awareness was/*is* a recurring phase in the imaginative process. The power of emptiness as a precursory catalyst to creative action was/*is* a seeming contradiction in terms. The extension of the moment – though wished for – of emptiness, of blankness was/*is* impossible. As soon as the paper was/*is* there (in fact *before* the paper is there) the mind's eye began/*begins* to fill this expanse with: images, lines, shapes, patterns; calls back previous experiences of drawing, proposes and combines new structures, forms and relationships. The emptiness is *never* empty while the artist's eye reflects upon the presence of this void – even *before* the hand lifts the intention is there to interact, to stir the surface, to probe beneath and beyond. The mark is already *there* though unseen, tangible and detectable as a magnetic force when the hand approaches and inserts *what was not there before.* For the mark *inserted* does not float on the surface of the paper but becomes enmeshed within its fibres – enters the interstices of its being.

I unrolled a second expanse of paper on the floor beneath the first on the wall. The two expanses generated an invisible field of latent energy. I unfolded a wooden ladder so that I could reach the top part of the drawing. I placed materials for drawing at intervals over the paper: charcoal, beeswax, turpentine and graphite powder (plus a cheese grater to grate the wax and mix all three ingredients, making a drawing substance which slips and slides across *any* surface and emits a penetrating aroma). I used a plasterer's float for drawing broad strokes and sweeps of iridescent granular darkness. I placed four shallow black containers filled with water to soak parts of the drawing that I cut from the larger whole in an attempt to recreate the infusive power of the rain. The four pools formed dark mirrors of sections of the drawing on the wall. From a distance the drawing on the floor was punctured by four black holes.

At the same time Andy Wake (2006) set out his work for the exhibition. At the end of the room he placed the pipe organ he had made. On the wall adjacent to my work a video projection played showing people drifting, seemingly without direction, through a dense and green wood. The timeless nature of their travel and lack of overt narrative was accompanied by the sound work he had composed using the organ. The film and the music were looped and played constantly within the enclosed space of the room. My consciousness of this peculiar combination of flickering coloured light from behind my back, the intensity of the surrounding sound, and the sensation of my own actions (actual and imagined) being conducted by this unfamiliar environment created an atmospheric soup whose elements nurtured the emergence of *How* can *this be done differently?*

... I move, and I move the mark/line, backwards and forwards – left to right – right to left and up down and round in a circle ... and again ... and again ... each noise I make assumes significance in relation to the sound projection. I find that I am timing my actions to those sounds, the arc of the drawn line lasts as long as the recurring held note – throughout the gradual amplification of the note's volume the marks I make increase in their density – the pressure used in their making shown by their blackness – the intense tone penetrates the folding and unfolding of my arm and hand and fingers – with clicks, shudders and cracks the noise appears to enter my skin, flesh and bones as well as my ears ... (Stackhouse 2006)

The drawing's evolution was bound by and responded to this new sound that I heard. I did not shut it off or attempt to ignore it, for it was too overwhelming and besides – *I wanted to listen*. The music filled the whole space with its unearthly tones – sounds of prayer bowls, vibrations and the *archaic* notes of the pipe organ all worked their way into my own awareness. They provided a stimulus that I would not have been able to create for myself, *another* mind was *here* – *another* imagining consciousness – *other* informed and structured the work ... *other* entered from the outside in addition to my structuring the work from the inside. I let the sound lead and I followed by marking *its* time – for in this work I did *not* want to lead ... *I wanted to watch what would unfold.*

The sound had other functions; it acted as a barrier – used to shut *all* extraneous stimuli out; as a filter – used to allow some stimuli through; and as a tool – used for focus on a particular stimulus, for example – what was my reaction to, or interaction with, *that* stimulus?

The time spent *away* from the drawing was as important as the time spent *with* the drawing. The physical presence of the work can obscure thought, attention is caught up in the detail of its appearance – can become fixated on one part rather than the whole. The drawing that exists in the imagination is as *real* as the actual drawing – the actual drawing cannot exist without the imagined one – yet the imagined drawing can, and frequently does exist, without the actual. The imagined drawing multiplies infinitely – the actual does not, constrained in its being by space and time. The imagined and the actual resonate constantly with each other. Thought bounds backwards and forwards between the two – considering what *had* happened ... what *is* happening ... and what *could* happen – considering what the drawing *had become*, what it *was becoming* and what it *could/would become*. The cognitive distance between the actualisation of what occurred on the surface of the paper and what unfolded in my mind while I was *apart* from the drawing – as well as being *a part* of the drawing *while* drawing – began to reveal an increasingly complex network of relationships – which drawing was/*is* more real, more genuine? This sensation was intertwined with my beginning to read about Deleuze's Difference and Repetition – my understanding of which was tempered by the experience of this new drawing (Williams 2003). I began to realise why I could not draw how I wanted to draw.

The detailed documentation of a work's progress is fundamentally important. Not only does it provide a record of the work's development – documentation also annotates spaces in thinking where a change in understanding of the creative process has taken place – or where that understanding has deepened. Documentation creates a discussion which refers to the original work, to the observer's memory of the work (or imagination of that work if they have not directly encountered it) and gestures towards the conceptual space in between. If the documentation is exhibited separately from the work, or after the work has taken place, then there exists a dislocation between the memory of the original and what is perceived by the eyes now.

At regular intervals throughout the drawing of *How* can *this be done differently?* I photographed or videoed moments of time and relationships which described what I saw and that signposted sites of activity where changes in understanding had been engendered. For example, the cut space which lifted the drawing away from the wall and the charcoal dust coating the floor; the visual appearance of lines on the surface of the paper when viewed from the side instead of from the front; the reflection of a section of drawing in water as well as gatherings of dust on the water's surface.

The composition of the photographs and the video images was critical in the attempt to capture and communicate what I was seeing.

Lack of light meant that exposure time for still photographs would extend over minutes but also meant that the image would show translucent shapes that were the traces of observers who had moved through the space. A new layer of the work was created that shadowed and enhanced my own perception of emerging patterns and provided a new platform for critical engagement and thought. The still images obviously did not include the sound – a vital component of the original work – the sound only existed as an echo in the minds of people who had seen the drawing. Looking at these images conjures a gap, a vacancy, but only for those who have experience of the whole. The images attend to single facets of the work and represent whole sequences of sensations/thoughts while making – these sequences form an imaginary edifice which trembles and threatens to dissolve the more closely it is approached – like a mirage the closer I get to finding out what it comprises – the further it moves away until it has vanished all together – and I am left with standing with sand in my eyes and mouth.

Conclusion – unknowability

How do I want to draw then? I want to draw *not* knowing – I want to draw *non* understanding – I want to draw emptiness – and so how do I draw? Inaccurately and with much stumbling. I want to draw the space before the drawing – to paraphrase Cixous (1998). Repetition of this impulse does not bind me, repetition enables the mind to enter a state of awareness where the mark made is so simple and clear that in the end there is only one mark at a time, each one and all unobscured by the presence of many others – where the eye skims over and tries to make sense when there is none, when there is *only* what *is*.

My own understanding remains incomplete and yet there is a gradual deepening of an already sensitised consciousness regarding the complex and mutable structures of creative process. The identification of significant elements is painstaking. It necessitates a subtle play between concentration and withdrawal of attention, a continual adjustment that accepts a wide range of sensory inputs whether or not they are overtly relevant. Such adjustments take time and require internal actions that shift in a predictably repetitive and yet erratic style amongst intuitive responses and detailed contemplation of all possible meanings (Goulish 2001). Any comprehension of meaning at any time is not fixed, it takes into account what has just occurred (the precipitating instance), what has taken place further away in time (the scenery, the backdrop) and an internal rehearsal of what may transpire (possible projections into the future). This approach provides a series of points of departure that do not begin and end in the studio or the gallery.

The nature of this approach ensures that it continues all the time, itself becoming a way of *being in the world*.

The image is not what it seems. There is more here than meets the eye.

References

Boden, M.A. (2004) *The Creative Mind: Myths and Mechanisms.* London: Routledge.

Bohm, D. (1998) *On Creativity.* London: Routledge.

Bruegel the Elder, Pieter (c.1555–58) *Landscape with the Fall of Icarus.* Museum of Fine Arts, Brussels.

The Chambers Dictionary (2003), Ninth edition.

Cixous, H. (1998) 'Without end, no, state of drawingness, no, rather, the executioner's taking off'. in *Stigmata: Escaping Texts*, new edn., 26–33. London: Routledge.

Crook, T. (2005) 'The anthropology of connections', in *Practice as Research workshop series, 2005*, Dundee.

Dallow, P. (2003) 'Representing creativeness: practice-based approaches to research in creative arts'. *Art, Design and Communication in Higher Education*, 2(1): 49.

Davey, N. and Stackhouse, A. (2004) (personal conversation).

Goulish, M. (2000) *39 Microlectures: In Proximity of Performance.* London and New York: Routledge.

(2001) 'Memory is this'. *Performance Research*, 5(3): 6–17.

Hess, F. (2001) *Felix Hess: Light as Air.* Heidelberg: Kehrer.

McNiff, S. (1998) *Art-based Research.* London: Jessica Kingsley.

Merleau-Ponty, M. (1945) 'Cezanne's doubt', in H. Dreyfus and P.A. Dreyfus (transl.) (1964) *Sense and Non-sense*, 9–24. Evanston, IL: Northwestern University Press.

Peters, G. (2003) 'The aestheticization of research in the thought of Maurice Blanchot'. *International Journal of Education and the Arts*, 4(2).

Petitmengin-Peugeot, C. (1999) 'The intuitive experience'. *Journal of Consciousness Studies*, 6(2–3): 43–77.

Reik, T. (1948) *Listening with the Third Ear: The Inner Experience of a Psychoanalyst.* New York: Grove Press.

Stackhouse, A.M. (2006) *Trahere: The sense of unease in making a mark; the practice of drawing and the practice of thinking.* PhD thesis: University of Dundee.

Varela, F.J. (1999) 'Present-time consciousness'. *Journal of Consciousness Studies*, 6(2–3): 111–40.

Vermersch, P. (1999) 'Introspection as practice'. *Journal of Consciousness Studies*, 6(2–3): 17–42.

Wake, A. (2006) *Organ Magnificent.* Mixed media installation/performance in 'The visitor and the other' exhibition, October 2006, Royal Scottish Academy, Edinburgh.

Williams, J. (2003) *Gilles Deleuze's Difference and Repetition: A Critical Introduction and Guide.* Edinburgh University Press.

3 | *Labour, work and action in the creative process*

MARTIN DIXON

In this chapter I argue that our coming to terms with the organisation of and any subsequent capitalising on 'creative'[1] activity today, will need to reckon with – but not decide between – differing and conflicting accounts of what brings about these so-called 'created' objects. The narrative accounts that are given pertaining to the origin of a created object, and the claims that are wrapped inside those accounts, I will refer to as 'genetic stories'. In summary, such accounts can be analysed into one of three categories: the story of *labour, work* or *action. Laborious* production will emphasise effort, toil, 'perspiration'; *workly* production will emphasise planning, craft, technique and execution; *actional* production will emphasise spontaneity, decisiveness and risk. Descriptions of formation and origination can be used to bestow upon an artefact a meaning and a value, the genetic story told of the work, be it laborious, workly or actional, inclines our opinion of it significantly. We suppose we *know* something essential of an artefact when we know (or think we know) from whence it came. Hence, we are liable to take an interest in what apparently took place 'behind the scenes' of a specific 'creative' act; we might have an interest in what we know, or imagine, to have precipitated or influenced the ultimate form and expressive contours of a composition. Letters, diaries, anecdotes, interviews and sketches hold the promise of relaying something of the forces that shape the complex circumstances and contingencies of production.

Indirectly, my arguments in this essay are designed to thwart the temptation to presume that artistic production as a whole cannot be intellectualised without in the same moment corrupting its essence. In no sense need one pass over the creative process in silence. I wish to show that the stubborn paradoxes and strategic silences that are seemingly borne of our attempts to think or describe creative processes, arise not from deep mysteries latent within the imagination, or from influences inaccessible within the souls of artists, but, more prosaically, from the proximity of irreconcilable hypotheses regarding the origins of objects. Like the paradoxes of Zeno, which are thought experiments turned merely to lure and entertain our guileless wits and are not, as they at first appear, windows onto an abyss of impossibility and irrationality, the paradoxes of creativity are relatively benign, arising more from our initial misapprehensions, hastily formed conclusions and culturally reinforced ideologies than from dark regimes of madness, inspiration and temperament. So, despite apparently bullet-proof arguments to the contrary, Achilles will catch the tortoise, and notwithstanding the blustering mood swings, the black silences, frustrations and uncertainties; notwithstanding bursts of creative excitement, the vertigo of endless possibility, that artists are often prone to, works of art can be made in an orderly, rational and manageable manner. And they are none the worse for that.

In taking this critical approach one rails against some powerful interests within the institution of art. By trafficking allure, mystery and perplexity surrounding the processes that produce artworks (carried over in the endless task of interpreting and revering the 'classics'), art stands to profit significantly: mystery produces the endurance of our fascination with its aesthetic objects; they endure through being remade in wonder. One might suppose that an unparadoxical art is not really art at all, but rather some routine, soulless, machine production. While this essay is clearly committed to the cause of aesthetic disenchantment, it does not thereby advocate the vulgarisation of art. Quite the contrary: there is indeed something incalculable, troubling and perplexing, in the midst of the creative process, but my conclusion will be that 'something' is perfectly rational. That something has a name: *the decision*.

The categories of labour, work and action I have adapted from Hannah Arendt's book, *The Human Condition* (1958). In outline, the concept of labour is characterised by circularity: the tasks faced by labour are (or seem) endless because they begin again as soon as they are over. Housework amounts to labour, as does gardening, correspondence, cooking, administration; it is always there, demanding our time and attention. Work, however, presents us with tasks which once complete, are complete forever. Completion closes the task and what we have done has a robustness and a permanence which is, or can be, a satisfaction to us. We can take up our finished work and feel proud of our achievement. If I execute a plan or build an object from a model, then I work. If I externalise a conception, and bring something into being, then I work. Work, rather than being circular, is directed towards some goal. Such objects as work produces are likely to have a use and, importantly, they are likely to possess the durability that they need to become property. As useful, identifiable, durable things, they can enter into the market place, they can be exchanged, as well as be added to the other forms of capital. No object is absolutely durable – use destroys durability – but the worked, artificial object endures to a great degree, and serves an important function in stabilising human life. The homes we return to, the objects that populate that home, all momentarily suspend the remorseless transitoriness of life. Objects protect us from the vagaries of nature, we construct a world within the world, a world that is ours, which meets our needs and desires, restores us and gives us a sense of who we are. Work, as fabrication, is just this act of world-building.

There is a strong conceptual distinction between work and labour; their etymology is quite separate. In European languages the words behave quite differently and the grounds for treating them as synonymous are weak. Very simply, while work is both verb and noun – the musical work (noun) is what is produced by the work (verb) of the composer – labour does furnish us with an equivalent noun form. I can say 'the work must be on my desk in the morning', but I cannot say 'the labour must be on my desk by morning'. Labour does not seem to materialise and become an object. While cultural history is precisely that of great works – monuments, books, palaces, bridges, temples – what has *labour* ever left behind? Labour does not endure; it leaves no permanent record of itself. The labour that was required of rural subsistence communities at harvest time leaves no trace, while the working of the land by the plough, scarifies and shapes. The labour that toiled to gather building stones is invisible; but the work of the craftsmen that fashioned and fabricated a wall from those materials, that marks terrain, that protects property, endures for centuries. But work, to a large extent, depends upon and is preceded by labour, an unskilled, repetitive accumulation of resources and materials, work that is only fit for animals, slaves or lower orders, or machines. Labour does not endure, but rather is only ever destined to be repeated. It is characterised by a remorseless and yet invisible circularity. And in cultures that value property and therefore durability and objecthood, labour and labouring is held only in contempt. Our work becomes laborious when we find it returning to the beginning (like the start of an academic year). We sweep the path clear of leaves only to have to repeat the task the next day, and the next year and every year afterwards.

In all European languages the words for labour connote trouble and pain. The English word 'travail', meaning laborious effort, comes from the old French word *trepalium*, meaning an instrument of torture. And we are ourselves caught inside these endless cycles: our body continually demands food, it must be washed and clothed and there is nothing that can be done about it. To be in the world, even one we made ourselves, requires us to labour.

If labour is circular, work directed towards goals, commodities and world-making, human action, however, has a quite different structure. Action has two parts: the deed and the ramifications. To act has a specific sense in Arendt, it means to begin, to initiate. In acting I set something in motion. And then what has begun must be carried through but with *no view of its end*. Perhaps the action is carried through by an instigator; perhaps it is carried through by others, but whatever the case, there is a context which must suffer (bear, sustain) the action. Every situation, every social body, trembles under the impact of an action. And every action ramifies in countless directions and permeates any number of further situations. An action is therefore also potentially boundless. If it is boundless then in acting, the agent cannot predict where the action will end or if, as it propagates, the action will yield the good or the bad. The crucial and devastating point is this: the results of action are unknown and unknowable by the agents. An action then is not calculable, it cannot be judged. The agent always confronts the unknown.

As becomes clear in the development of these ideas below, these three aspects of the active life matter hugely to art. What use has art for the laborious? In one sense, very little. Traditional art is orientated exclusively towards the production of durable objects of great status. The durability of the work of art is emblematic of their being. Rather ironically, Shakespeare's sonnets continually pit the endurance of the poem itself against the mortality of the poetic subject: while the beloved might grow old and die, the poem is ageless. Sonnet 18 is typical; it ends: *So long as men can breathe or eyes can see/So long lives this, and this gives life to thee*. The wager could not be more bold: Shakespeare's sonnet will last as long as humankind.

But labour need not be regarded as negative. If, as it did under modernity, artists became sensitive to the commodification of works, the works began to dematerialise. Artworks became sets of instructions which initiated laborious tasks (I am thinking here of Sol LeWitt's wall drawings), or landscape works which were both ephemeral and explicit in their reliance on repetitive labour (i.e. Richard Long and his line 'sculptures' made by the traces left by walking). While labour, from the standpoint of work, might seem unworthy or base, or a trouble or a torture, producing nothing of itself and invisible to history, this might very well be a distortion, the conclusion of a consciousness that has screened itself from the ordinary processes of life; that misrecognises them, that finds security – that is happiness – in the durability of objects rather than a permanence of change; that finds its happiness in things rather than in a sense of continuity with the past or with others. Property, endurance and exchangeability produce a false consciousness which cannot but value that which endures over that which perishes as it is consumed.

Clearly some aspects of aesthetic production require labour (instruments must be practiced, techniques must be learnt and sustained through diligent repetition, canvasses must be prepared, novels must be copied and bound), and aesthetic production requires work (plans must be executed, aesthetic works must be made to stand up and endure), but such work must somehow maintain itself within freedom, not within a more or less mundane logic of means and ends, toil and remuneration. There has to be 'something else', another ingredient, a quality that eludes both labour and work. Traditionally this element has been called 'inspiration', a divine spark that kick-starts the whole process. But, in the remainder of this chapter, I will try to argue that this element can be called *action* and it is here that the traditional discourses of affect and inspiration can be revisited and redescribed.

So, while it is easy to see that artists labour and work, do they act? Composition can seem laborious when we are moving in circles, when there is no end in sight, when we have toiled all day and produced nothing. Composition seems like work when the objective is clear (when we have a plan that we realistically expect to complete), it feels like work when we know what we are doing and why. Much of music can be taught and learnt, communicated and shared. Such knowledge would concern how certain aesthetic ends (forms, characters, effects), qualified by regulative criteria (such as unity, harmony, coherence, expressiveness, playability, balance, etc.) could actually be achieved through the proper deployment and manipulation of material means. Getting all this right, being reasonable and explicit in one's activity, allows it to become work and share in the genuine satisfaction that comes from 'world-making'. (And, speaking for myself, as someone who is becoming increasingly conservative in a compositional sense, it is a source of great frustration that the workly aspects of composition are so undervalued.)

However, action is incalculable: action takes place inside a sense of unknowing. But not all unknowns are alike. Hamlet's 'undiscovered country', that is, death, is of a quite different order to not knowing a phone number. There is a potential fallacy here. Action takes place inside a sense of unknowing, but does 'not knowing' produce action? It is a mistake – imprudent – to keep oneself in ignorance, to keep oneself in the dark when there is knowledge to be had, just so that what one does looks and feels like action. 'Go for it' and 'just do it' are the slogans for late capitalist assertiveness in the face of banal imponderables. In acting we appear brave, decisive, combative; we move forwards and change our lives. Deliberation is not given a chance. We are not allowed to be rational. Action now becomes foolhardiness.

It is arguable that creative processes involve large amounts of decision making. 'Where do I begin?' 'Is what I have good enough?' 'Is that character convincing?' 'Should I stop the composition now, or does it need more work?' All of these questions force the artist to make a decision. Yes or no? Let us consider the decision. The concept of decision pertains to a situation whereby the task of producing alternatives and prioritising them has come to an end and yet there remains more than one possible course of action, all of which are equally preferable or equally unattractive. If one course of action is obviously the best, there is no decision to be made, one knows what to do. But in a situation whereby our deliberations do not grant us this insight, something must be done, but what? What is for the best? What might be done next is, strictly speaking, incalculable because all my efforts to weigh the pros and cons of my options have produced only a stalemate. What must be done is action; I must take a step, a leap into the dark.

In musical composition, for example, insufficient technique leaves too much to be decided; or, what is worse, the decision making is

only apparent because, while there do exist criteria which could prop-
erly inform deliberation, they are either not known or not deployed.
Should I worry about which chord follows every other chord? Shall I
never know what instruments are capable of? Anxiety, which stems
from the pervasive sense of being ill-equipped, is generally the result.
Anecdotally, such anxiety, which drains exorbitant amounts of psy-
chic and intellectual energy, is often mistaken for 'creative temperament'. While we scream and shout and throw manuscript paper
around we feel active, we can believe ourselves heroes. While we don't
know what we are doing, we can maintain ourselves in the false belief
that we are acting. The composer, in a sense, is suspicious of reasoning about his or her work for the simple reason that it might thereby
be stripped of the quality of action.

An inspiration has absolutely that character of an inception, a beginning, a making possible. As was absolutely routine of artists and composers of the nineteenth and early twentieth centuries, Schoenberg's
own accounts of his compositional experience relied heavily on the
moment of inspiration, a moment that is typically accompanied by, or
is caused by, strong affective states of elation. Artists have an interest
in making themselves 'ready' for what is to be given to the artist –
the *inspiration*, whether it is thought to come spontaneously from
'beyond', as a Muse, a god, or Nature; or from 'within', memory,
inner nature, the subconscious.

Affective states seem to come in two flavours: reverie and intoxication, and either can be supposed to be felicitous to creative endeavour.
What is more, artists and creators have a particular proclivity for succumbing to, eloquently occupying, such states. Quietness, stillness,
contemplation and solitude are themes common of early Romantic
poetry, but such poems also reflect, sincerely, the mood of the poets
themselves. The poem, *given* in solitude, is dignified by the bearing
that conditions its coming into being, and the poem brings with it its
own originating context as theme, tone and subject matter. Similarly,
in nineteenth-century music, the *Träumerei*, the reverie, while being
a characteristic form in its own right, is also a theory – or a story –
of what brings art into being in the first place. It is also, of itself,
an object of reverie: listening and performance take place inside and
recapture a poetic reverie.[2] Poetry (now a general concept betoken-
ing all cogent aesthetic endeavour) permits poetic states of being –
characterised by high sensitivity and receptiveness – to circulate. And

poetry conditions souls, making them susceptible to the solicitations of the verities, of nature and of love. The Wordsworthian formula, recapitulated in his preface to the *Lyrical Ballads* of 1798, encapsulates this perfectly: 'I have said that poetry is the spontaneous overflow of powerful feelings; it takes its origin from emotion recollected in tranquility.' Aesthetic works stand before us as masterly, formally convincing and sincere, recollections of actual emotion, or actual lived experience.

Contemplative states reside on a continuum with their opposites: the dance, laughter, drunkenness and, at one extreme, reappear as pharmacological stupefaction. Where would the history of later nineteenth century art be without wine and opium? Where would post-1950 popular music be without LSD and Ecstasy? Because of the indulgent, excessive, hysterical and obsessive traits that art seems to tolerate, it can never quite rid itself of the daemonic. The formidable abilities of musical virtuosi – Paganini and Robert Johnson are the obvious examples – were attributed to super-human, *demonic* influence. It was Nietzsche, still entirely caught in the nineteenth-century ideology of creativity and physiology, who took this line of thinking to its most decadent extreme in the *Will to Power as Art*. For Nietzsche, aesthetic production was basically a pathological process, a great excrescence of those endowed with a powerful will.

By analogy, it is easy to see that both contemplative states and intoxication comport with the actional because both distance themselves from the laborious and the worked. Neither are any effort; neither can be sustained for long periods – one falls into such states – and both stand as a considerable remove from planning and calculation. But taking action could itself be thought of as a delirium, an intoxication of sorts, a flight beyond reason. The 'affective' stories attempt to account for aspects of creative experience that seem to fall outside the control of the artist and can lead to a picture of creativity as sudden, chaotic, impulsive and unmanageable. But action and the decision also share these characteristics. Intoxication enables us to act because the forces that would otherwise hold us back have been neutralised.

It is exactly this story that high modernism rejects out of hand. It declares its verdict on inspiration and the arrogant pronouncements of Genius rather abruptly, applying a ban to such ludicrous notions and turning its attention to the purely technical dimension of art. Now the story is one of brute calculation over whim and fancy. It deliberately impoverished sensibility, producing brash, brutal and unsentimental art. Mechanistic, systemic or process art replaced the effusive, indulgent masterpieces of the nineteenth century. The genetic story here might be one of mimetically adapting aesthetic production to the paradigm of rationalised, industrial production. Modernism valorises the ferocious productivity of the machine over delicate musings of the soul. But modernism still had its heroic, actional, aspects: the avant-garde after all were committed to aesthetic and social transformation, they flew in the face of public taste and mores.

The composer Arnold Schoenberg had long agonised about the apparent lack of connection between two of the themes of his *Kammersymphonie* op. 9. Many years after its composition he relates his disquiet and eventually triumph:

Directed only by my sense of form and the stream of ideas, I had not asked such questions while composing; but, as usual with me, doubts arose as soon as I had finished. They went so far that I had already raised the sword for the kill, taken the red pencil of the censor to cross out the theme b [the second theme]. Fortunately, I stood by my inspiration and ignored these mental tortures. About twenty years later I saw the true relationship. It is of such a complicated nature that I doubt whether any composer would have cared deliberately to construct a theme in this way; but our subconscious does it involuntarily. (Schoenberg 1975: 222–3)

In another essay, referring to the same epiphany, he writes:

This is also the place to speak of the miraculous contributions of the subconscious. I am convinced that in the works of the great masters many miracles can be discovered, the extreme profundity and prophetic foresight of which seem superhuman. In all modesty, I will quote here one example from the Kammersymphonie ... solely in order to illustrate the power behind the human mind, which produces miracles for which we do not deserve credit. In this example is unveiled the hidden relationship between two main themes. It is based on the appearance of steps of the melody, which, in the second theme, move miraculously in the opposite direction ... If there are composers capable of inventing themes on the basis of such a remote relationship, I am not one of them. (Schoenberg 1975: 85)

We might quibble over whether or not the themes are indeed connected, or over the means by which such an observation could be substantiated, or doubt that a connection so complicated could even be heard. But let us listen rather to the type of story that is being told here. For Schoenberg, there *is* a connection between the themes, it *matters* that there is a connection between the themes, and it matters how this connection came to be there at all. It is decisive that this connection was not planned or consciously intended by the composer. While Schoenberg, being a consummate craftsman, would not shrink from laying claim to the technical achievement were it his, he does not. Rather, his story draws on a difficult mix of psychology and theism; it is the miraculous contribution of the subconscious and yet also evidence of a gift from the 'Almighty', or the 'Supreme Commander', which is then left to the discipline of the artist and insight of the music analyst to make good. To the twenty-first-century ear such a story may strike one as quaint. But that is hardly the point. In trying to explain how this music came about, Schoenberg has entangled the 'fact' of these connected themes with miracles and the gift of inspiration. And what now? Can any evaluation of the *Kammersymphonie* or any evaluation of the composer ever really discount the compositional miracle that sits at its heart?

In the light of what has been presented so far, this story of Schoenberg's could be read in another way. Schoenberg's mental 'torture' signals the presence of a decision at the heart of this composition. That the second theme should be as it is, that it should be left in place, even in the absence of a rationale, was a decision. Was it the right decision? Decades elapsed before the agony was alleviated and a 'reason' was uncovered. The principle by which they could be connected was the reason. In retrospect, their connectedness justifies the decision, which can now change its status to that of an inspiration. Without demonstration of connectedness, Schoenberg's decision is simply an act of will that forced two things into a relationship. What one respects and understands here is that an artist had to make the initial decision in the absence of justification and without knowing whether or not his decision was the right one. This moment deserves the name of *action*.

Taking a sceptical stance, it is possible – even preferable – to say that the two themes connected only by chance. Could the genetic story here be that Schoenberg got *lucky*? Schoenberg, committed as he was to musical logic, would have no time for the arbitrary. But there is no shame in this, surely? No artist would ever renounce serendipity, but need one go so far as to say that a happy accident is a sanction from God? Let us pursue this question in a more extreme context. The picture of literary creation being roughly analogous to a room full of typewriter-wielding monkeys has entered the popular unconscious via the realm of probabilistic mathematics, where it is known as the 'infinite monkey theorem'. The conjecture is that if one left sufficient monkeys and typewriters alone for long enough, the complete works of Shakespeare (or some other significant body of work) might be produced 'accidentally'. In fact, the mathematics tells us the exact opposite. To all intents and purposes, the probability of *Hamlet* being 'written' entirely by accident is zero. When computer simulations began, rather ironically, to test the theorem (with the monkeys being replaced by hundreds of random number generators), small fragments of Shakespeare did actually materialise. An article in the *Times Literary Supplement* (2007: 36) reports that: 'The Monkey Shakespeare Simulator, in existence since 2003 with a hundred monkeys typing at a vastly accelerated speed, has produced just nineteen letters from *The Two Gentlemen of Verona* after 42,162,500,000 billion billion monkey years: "Valentine. Cease to". A separate simulation produced a fragment from the second part of *Henry VI*: "RUMOUR, open your ears."'

While the 'infinite monkey theorem' teaches us a great deal about the dangers inherent in sloppy reasoning with regard to probabilities, complex tasks, very large versus infinite numbers, our concern here is not with the mathematics. Nor is it with the demonstration that complex tasks, like the writing of masterpieces, are not best accomplished by blind, arbitrary mechanisms. But, rather, what is the nature of the story one can tell with regard to such strange fragments of text? In a sense, something truly remarkable was 'created' here. Discovered amidst trillions upon trillions of lines of random textual screed, such phrases are even more unlikely and more deserving of the status of the miraculous than anything Schoenberg could have produced. But who or what is responsible for these fragments of poetry? What is their origin? They seem oddly orphaned, bereft; almost ghostly. What they lack is a progenitor. The place of origin stands empty, with no higher cause at work. In effect, a new piece of poetry was made here. It is superficially the same as a piece of Shakespearean drama, but the genetic story behind the production matters hugely.

The infinite monkey theorem is only an extreme case of a very real and very productive tradition of aleatoric aesthetic processes, processes which are designed to break the link between the intentions of the artist and the resultant work. William Burroughs' 'cut-up' technique, John Cage's use of chance-based I Ching methods, the Surrealists and Dadaists, David Bowie and Thom Yorke of the English band Radiohead, have all deployed aleatoric techniques to produce material. In every case, there is a revaluing of the product by process. Popular culture might embrace cut-up technique so as to make rhetorical and stylistic liaisons with high modernist culture and shore-up avant-gardist pretensions. Dadaists use chance as a protest against meaning, the Surrealists use it to open up unconscious association, · de-repress desire and fantasy. The aleatorical does not foreclose genetic storytelling, it opens up a vast array of further possibilities and complications.

Aesthetic creation, if it contains a moment of action, cannot be rid of a certain darkness. Action begins but cannot control ramification. But there is an exhilaration to beginning because, in a sense, the action has no past; it is not entangled in chains of consequences and obligation. These come later. Even in writing, as one begins a sentence, there is a certain excitement at what might unfold. Aphoristic writing is shot through with that thrill of beginning, the freshness and impetus of starting out. But how soon we can feel caught by past decisions. How can we go back on an action? It is too late for that. And immediately the consequences of our actions burden us. The feeling can drive us to madness. But as Arendt (1998: 236) observes, there is a way out: 'The possible redemption from the predicament of irreversibility – of being unable to undo what one has done though one did not, and could not, have known what he was doing – is the faculty of forgiving.' If one is forgiven, one is released from the debt of the past and the deeds which haunt us. Forgiving is an act for the reasons already established: it is unconditional, it makes no bargain with the future, and it allows us to begin again.

Compositional action is concentrated at the beginning and forming sustains, suffers that beginning. Forming, like life, is irreversible. It must go on. The only actions that can adjust the remorselessness of forming are forgetting and forgiving (the return of the aria theme at the end of Beethoven's op. 111 sounds not like a forgetting of what went before, but a forgiving).

One last observation: contemporary technology has ruined aesthetic practice in one main respect. It allows us to be indecisive. What single thing would improve the quality of writing? Remove the delete key on a word processor. Deletion means that writing is not frightening enough. We can always retract what we say. We can act, delete, then pretend that it never happened and we stay in place. But when we write knowing that we cannot turn back, we write differently. We are gripped by a force of great moment.

Notes

1 The 'scare' quotes apply since the word 'creative' has become banalised into near ruin by both common parlance and informal theory.
2 There are countless stories relating the collaboration of dreams in composition: Coleridge's *Kubla Khan* came almost fully formed in an opium-induced slumber; Wagner dreamed of the resounding E flat chord that opens *Der Ring des Nibelungen*. Perhaps the most emblematic legend within the psychology of creativity is that relating to the chemist Friedrich August Kekulé's dream – he succumbed to sleep on a Clapham omnibus and upon waking the mysterious molecular structure of benzene was presented to him. See A. Rothenberg (1995), 'Creative cognitive processes in Kekulé's discovery of the structure of the benzene molecule', *American Journal of Psychology*, 108(3): 419–38.

References

Arendt, H. (1958) *The Human Condition*. Chicago: University of Chicago Press.
Schoenberg, A. (1975) *Style and Idea*. London: Faber and Faber.
Times Literary Supplement (2007) 1 June: 36.

4 | *Popular culture as* carnaval: *The Clash, play and transgression in the aesthetic economy*

STEPHEN LINSTEAD

... punk's spirit of negation lacks a utopian counterpart, and as a consequence its aggressive nihilism occasionally expresses itself as an attack upon the powerless rather than the powerful.

(Moore 2004: 308)

Punk's utopian heresies remain its gift to the world.

(Savage 2001: 541)

Introduction

In this chapter I explore the question of the appropriateness of the metaphor of carnival when applied to rock music generally, but in particular to the world of The Clash, with its strong visual identity and cartoonish sensibilities displaying eccentricity, *mésalliances*, ambiguity, profanation, transgression, ambivalent laughter and creative degradation – all classic features of carnival, identified by Mikhail Bakhtin. I highlight some of the post-Bakhtinian problems of dealing with a literary representation (carnival) of a lived social relation (which I term *carnaval*), and using that representation as a metaphor for a different lived social relation, without direct close engagement with the relevant (transgressive) features of that social relation itself. Whilst the work of The Clash provides useful material for the former analysis, an examination of their social milieu and interpersonal relations provides insight into processes of transgression and what Peter Stallybrass and Allon White (1986) call 'the dialectics of social classification'. That these social relations have a dark side that is not resisted without cost – a point that is often lost in the application of the carnival metaphor – is underscored by the conflictual and ultimately destructive dynamics of the band, their management and organization, despite producing perhaps the most musically complex, professionally influential, politically energized, commercially successful and artistically enduring body of work by any of the punk bands.

As Pat Gilbert (2004) points out, the subtitle of his biography of The Clash (*The Real Story of The Clash*) is not without irony. The story of the band is complicated: neither the people involved, nor the events that unfolded, were simple. Comparing Gilbert's accounts with those of Marcus Gray (2003) and Chris Salewicz's (2006) epic biography of Joe Strummer, the fluidity, ambiguity and contradictions confound any attempt at naïve clarity. 'The Clash' as narrative is an intertext, a weave of genres, a nexus of stories. Some are fragmented, incomplete, gentle, violent, obsessive, addictive, tragically vulnerable; some are of visions achieved, of visions unrealized, egotism, selflessness, friendship, betrayal, perhaps revenge, self-discovery; many are of lives changed forever, for better or worse. The story of the band is always, as Gilbert uniquely realizes, the stories of The Clash camp, and he argues that the wider social milieu that sustained them was one with which they finally lost touch in the last incarnation of the band. The bigger picture was integral to the unfolding identity of The Clash. But both the band and the people who made up the 'camp' and its environs were complex and 'invariably with an intelligence and insight that's rare in rock'n'roll' (Gilbert 2004: 2), although not everyone was so impressed with this 'customary entourage of lads, liggers and rock'n'roll poseurs' (Savage 2001: 488). The transparent motives that make for ease of storytelling are not always in evidence in this story – many of those Gilbert interviewed in fact seemed to be discovering their own thoughts and feelings in the telling. The Clash have been described as a world within a world, but perhaps a better description would be of several often contradictory worlds within a shifting and unstable universe.

The aesthetic economy and the carnival metaphor

In recent years the arena of popular culture, as a branch of what has come to be termed the 'aesthetic economy', has begun to be taken seriously by scholars of organization. Approaches here seem to take different directions. First, as long ago as 1972, Paul Hirsch was arguing that the structure of the industry (and its subindustries) was worthy of study in its own right – and the pace and nature of change in those industries has received continuing attention, summarized by Hirsch

in a later article (Hirsch 1972, 2000). Of particular interest here has
been the nature of new technology-mediated networks and organizational models, and the question of whether these have potential efficacy for other industries: cultural economy as *vanguard*. Another line
of inquiry, informed in part by media and cultural studies, argues that
popular media including literature, film, music and even cartoons offer
an alternative take on the realities of work, managing and organizing,
to those found in the mainstream texts of management. Issues such
as emotion, feeling, ambiguity, paradox, betrayal, sacrifice, senseless-
ness, waste, violence, politics or resistance are often suppressed or
rendered anodyne in texts that see themselves as part of a broader
field of management as a largely scientific endeavour. Work informed
by the arts in these areas usually seeks to restore complexity to these
issues, recognizing that conflict, outer and inner, personal, ethical
and political, is endemic to their experience and representation. Here
cultural economy is more *avant-garde* than vanguard (Henry 1984).
Critical approaches drawn from literary criticism, psychoanalysis and
cultural theory have contributed to this, and some have borrowed
from the work of Bakhtin to consider popular forms of writing, music
and cartooning as forms of carnival (Humphrey 2000).

As one example of such work, Chris Turner (2005) argues persua-
sively that since the 1980s, with the increasing incorporation of both
music and comedy into overtly commercialized rather than politicized
forms of entertainment, the cartoon series as genre, of which *The
Simpsons* is the contemporary paradigmatic exemplar, has replaced
rock'n'roll as the key arena of critique and the resisting voice of alternative culture. There are three significant differences, however, that
need to be borne in mind. First, the cartoon inherits the mantle of
Hogarth and his successors, in that the cartoonist is observer and
critic and is able to caricature from a position that does not necessarily identify him or her as spokesperson for a social group or generation. Rock'n'roll, on the other hand, is expected to be exactly
that – whilst voices are diverse, rock'n'roll is primarily a youth genre
and speaks for, or from within, a generation, even as those spokespersons and that generation themselves age (Bennett 2006; Frith 1988;
Grossberg 1992, 1997a, 1997b; Marcus 1989, 1994). It may also,
and most powerfully, articulate a perspective from within a class (or
the basis of a 'clash between rulers and ruled' as Marcus (1989: 12),
notes, citing Sebastian Conran's sleeve collage for The Clash's single
'White Riot'. That is to say, popular rock musical forms are more

sociological in their emergence than popular cartoon forms. Second, neither cartoonists nor their creations are faced with the problem of having to embody the personae they create, and live their lives on and off stage in the shadow of their mask, unlike artists working in the rock and pop music media – although both cartoonists and musicians have to make decisions about where they will locate themselves in relation to the core of the aesthetic economy, and often work together (see for example the work of Damon Albarn's Gorillaz project with cartoonist Jamie Hewlett[1]). Finally, and as a consequence of this difference, rock artists may experience great intensity and enormous tensions in their careers, literally facing and often succumbing to madness and death in the process of avoiding incorporation into that which they have invested their identity in resisting. It is this that represents the dark and dangerous side to carnival as a lived reality that is less obvious in its representational forms.

Joe Strummer, the lead singer and lyricist of The Clash, was said to have a 'cartoonist's view of the world' (visible in Julien Temple's 2007 film *The Future is Unwritten*) and a tour with the band was described by photographer Pennie Smith (1980) as being like 'a commando raid with the Bash Street Kids' (cartoon characters from multi-levelled UK children's comic *The Beano*). This view was also supported by Lester Bangs (2003) and Johnny Green (Green *et al.* 2003). The band even had a 'war artist' cartoonist (Ray Lowry) on their 1979 US tour who designed the album sleeve of *London Calling*, and also illustrated Green's book (Green *et al.* 2003; see also Lowry and Myers 2007). Simultaneously, carnival itself as a model for behaviour, and its proximity to rioting as a sort of joyous direct action, was an important element of The Clash's background and social experience, surfacing most inspirationally in their early classic, 'White Riot'. Yet at the same time, The Clash were signed to the biggest and perhaps most conservative record label of the day (CBS) and their struggle with the commercial demands of such a relationship ultimately took a toll on their creativity. Strummer was particularly torn between his ambition to make great music that would challenge people to question the way they thought and acted, and the need to be commercially successful in order to reach the widest possible audience – a tension that stretched him to the limit and arguably into hypocrisy. In this chapter, I will revisit the idea of carnival through the model of *carnaval*, the twentieth-century (Latin American) derivation of the European medieval tradition, which surfaces the dark side of the tradition, and

I will use it to interpret the multi-voiced story of The Clash, who were perhaps at times as much a lifestyle as a band.

The Clash carnival

Whilst Lawrence Grossberg argues that punk was a symptom of popular conservatism, in that it demanded a revaluation of affect and passion in music and social life, it was also a catalyst for it in signalling despair at the failure of those counter-cultural movements that had articulated youthful passion over the previous twenty years to affect any significant social changes. Ryan Moore (2004) develops an earlier observation by Jude Davies (1996: 17) that this emphasizes only part of the punk legacy, and that this stems from an approach to cultural studies that constructs music in terms of subcultural movements rather than historical moments, and sees them in terms of cycles of *authenticity* (origination) and *recuperation* (incorporation). Moore argues that punk generated two cultural forms: a *culture of deconstruction* that was associated with opposition, refusal, nihilism and the anarchic/chaotic position epitomized by the Sex Pistols; and a more positive *culture of authenticity* that was characterized by the do-it-yourself ethos, the proliferation of bands and labels. Whilst there are obvious problems with Moore's presentation of 'deconstruction' as negative, the idea of 'authenticity' is similarly problematic given the resonances of punk with postmodern thought and its problematizing of processes of signification, representation, communication, community and subject-formation (Davies 1996; Hebdige 1979; Marcus 1989). But there is a useful distinction to be made between the relatively short-lived first wave of punk and a form of punk as both music and subculture that did not develop dramatically into new musical directions nor subside into being little more than an aesthetic. This movement embodied some elements of punk purism and elitism in its 'hardcore' and 'straight-edge' versions with strict views of how the music should be played, on what instrumentation, how loud and for how long, but also mutated into forms of continuing contemporary relevance (the development of grunge, the continuing popularity of Rancid and the work of Green Day being examples). More significantly, perhaps, it came to sustain its own record labels, fanzines, websites and related venues and a continuing stream of creativity and emerging talent (Bennett 2006; Moore 2007).

The Clash, however, combined elements of 'deconstruction' and 'authenticity' without either extreme of nihilism or purism. Indeed, whilst they took a negative view of the present situation and its prognosis, they maintained a belief that something better, however uncertain, was possible and independent effort had a chance of generating this – and that both music and ideas developed alongside each other. They remained, in fact, enthusiastic *fans* of and *listeners* to a wide range of music (Fletcher 2005: 50), constantly experimenting and absorbing influences (often to their critical cost). The importance of performance in this cannot be underestimated, as noted earlier. The archetypal punk performance was one that addressed and engaged its audience, challenging them to be involved in it – and their involvement was frequently such that it brought the performance to an end. Such a performance was 'not a spectacle seen *by* the people: they live in it, and everyone participates because its very idea embraces all the people' (Bakhtin 1968: 7 cited in Gardiner 1992: 206 n.16, *emphasis added*). As Gardiner notes, the Situationist International took a similar position, arguing that the mass-popular media (modern spectacle) performed an anaesthetic function in turning spectators into passive consumers of images. This needed to be challenged by strategies of transgression and subversion (*détournement* to the Situationists, a concept close to Bakhtin's idea of the *carnivalesque* – which he opposed to the established and officially sanctioned *canonical* order). Both were 'a form of empowerment, which made possible an expansion of autonomy and creativity' (*ibid.*). Not only does this sound like The Clash's own declared objectives, but their mentor Bernie Rhodes (along with Malcolm McLaren) was influenced by Situationism (and its predecessor Lettrism) to the extent that the connections between the movement and punk are extensively documented by Marcus (1989). Langman (2008) closes the loop between punk and carnival, and it is to his discussion we will now turn.

For Langman (2008: 659), carnival is a means to explain 'the growing toleration, indeed desire, for transgressive expressions of embodiment, couture and sexuality' of which punk is one major form. The early transgressions of punk, as expressions of nihilism, involved grotesque imagery allied to transgressive violence, bodily adornment including piercings and often drug-mediated mutilation (Iggy Pop, for example, would cut himself with broken glass as part of his performance; The Clash's roadie Steve 'Roadent' Connolly would replicate this and burn himself with cigarettes). Designed to shock, but not simply to shock, they were a means not of critiquing dominant aesthetics (as Langman argues) but of rejecting them – creating a new aesthetic, new music, new dance, new audience behaviours by refusing the rules of mainstream music and aesthetics, creating something that appealed on its own terms. For Langman, just as mainstream escapist media were inadequate for the punks in the 1970s, the post-punk period of intensive globalization has seen the mainstream demand shift from escapism to incorporate sanctioned forms of 'lipstick' transgression (Langman 2008: 673; Marcus 1989). He argues that whereas for Marcuse (1964) the tolerance of oppositional subcultures was a 'steam-valve' strategy of repressive desublimation, to contain and neutralize discontent, the greater sophistication of late capitalism both incorporates and profits from the critique. The Clash's single 'Complete Control' offers an early example. For Langman, globalization has increased 'the alienation of work, the rationalization of everyday life and the inauthenticity of a commodified world' which has led to the 're-emergence of a culture of transgression, inversion and excess'. This, he argues, is the *essence of carnival culture* – but put in place by global capital (which created the demand and now sets itself to meet it), carnivalization 'has itself become a commodity that serves to alleviate the strains and tensions of the contemporary world and at the same time profits from providing amelioration' (Langman 2008: 660).

Langman draws on Bakhtin's (1968) depiction of carnival as a critique of social hierarchies and domination, and a space and time of resistance. The norms, practices, appearances, rituals and aesthetics (the canons) of the dominant in society were mocked and satirized as due deference and appropriate demeanour were jettisoned. Carnival constituted a 'second life', embodying a utopian urge to achieve a social configuration beyond existing social forms, emphasizing the common qualities of all humanity – especially those relating to the body, its products and its functions. Although it constituted only a momentary break from the constraints of normal everyday life, it brought down the pretentious, abstracted and idealized to a material level, to the ground of both death *and* rebirth: de-grading to emphasize the primary values of 'incompleteness, becoming, ambiguity, indefinability and non-canonicalism' (Clark and Holquist 1984: 312). Carnival combined the grotesque, the ludic, and the desublimated in

several features. The first, *eccentricity*, constitutes a refusal to accept
pre-existing social roles and enables free contact between people
of different social levels, allowing latent aspects of human nature
to express themselves, and anyone to be approached and addressed
by anyone else. This *familiarization* was also seen in '*mésalliances*'
where previously fixed (and incompatible) categories are combined.
It was also combined with a sense of 'gay time' or a heightened consciousness of the relativity of history – the inevitability of change and
transformation underscored by tying together contradictory events
and images. The downgrading process of *profanation* of official texts,
ceremonies and personages proceeded through parodies, debasement,
travesty, association with bodily functions, particularly excrement,
and the use of 'marketplace' or 'billingsgate' language – a particularly
strong, energetic, excessive and partly musical form of foul or abusive
language. Carnival *laughter* was a powerful collective form of folk
laughter that constituted an 'all-annihilating and all-renewing force'
expressing a distinctive ideological viewpoint diametrically opposed
to the logical and serious world of authority and officialdom – which
could be radical and ruthless. So powerful was the carnivalesque view
of the world expressed in folk laughter that from the end of the sixteenth century and the shift from feudalism to absolute monarchy,
followed by enlightened monarchies and republics, it was controlled,
repressed, trivialized and marginalized, as the medieval carnivals
became modern 'fairs'. The repression was perhaps most effective
in the nineteenth century, when the aesthetics of play were thought
inappropriate to bourgeois ideology.

However, though diluted in Europe, carnival was exported to
European colonies and to Brazil in particular. Here its history was
different. The frequent old world cultural assumption from the seventeenth century was that there was no sin possible south of the Equator,
such that there 'all wickedness was [but] amusement and play' (Von
Barlaeus cited in Parker 1997: 361). The 'two lives' of Bakhtin's folk
here become two worlds, one of which is daily life as a struggle (*luta*),
filled with work but also with considerable suffering, and often a
deadly serious affair full of exploitation and violence at the hands of
Northern oppressors and pirates.

Life, survival, is an eternal war. The struggle for our daily bread, the struggle for a miserable salary ... the struggle because of a lack of hope in itself,

everything in order to arrive at the end is simply a total struggle to the death. (João in Parker 1997: 364)

The other world of *carnaval* accordingly becomes a space in which struggles are playful but often violent, and where the acting body is lost into the mass of bodies, merging into the crowd in a flow of exchange and transformation, into the 'reality of the fantasy' and its consequent risk. Since the early colonial period there has been a further subdivision between the *carnaval da rua* (carnival of the streets), or *entrudo*, and the *carnaval do salão* (carnival of the ballroom or dance hall). The *entrudo* is a rough affair, reasonably represented as the sort of place where

To play (*brincar*) the carnaval is to dance, to drink, to fuck, to get high, to kill and to die. They are days to let out your emotions like a child. (João in Parker 1997: 365)

The *carnaval do salão* was a political development over many years, after repeated attempts to suppress the *entrudo*, beginning in the nineteenth century, had failed. It involved, briefly, building the *carnaval* around the samba schools, and after government support in the 1930s, this went on to produce the spectacular public festival (in Rio particularly) that is world famous. But the side of the *carnaval* that is lower-class, aggressive and potentially violent still exists in the background as a social reality. At the core of its popular mythology is the character of the *milandro,* a rogue or scoundrel, a 'dangerous good-for-nothing who is likely to be a criminal, a racketeer or a thief', but who becomes a cultural hero. His skill is his ability to live by his wits and continually circumvent the rules and regulations, to put something over on authority, a society that sees him as an assailant or a thief when he is simply seeking his own freedom, any way he can get it (Parker 1997: 370). So the *milandro* is no Robin Hood – he might rob from the rich but he won't give it to the poor, and he might on occasion rob from the poor as well if he thinks it necessary. He is a trickster, but he succeeds, sets an example to others and gives them hope that there might be a way to cheat the system after all.

Following Bakhtin, it is possible to argue that attempts to repress the carnivalesque impulse have effectively contained its main form of expression from medieval times, but that it has, since the nineteenth century at least, moved fluidly in all directions to find outlets where they present themselves. These have emerged especially in forms of popular culture that include films and TV, cartoons, car-boot sales and rock'n'roll. But Stallybrass and White (1986) caution that the high-low system of inversions is both more complex than Bakhtin is able to uncover, and that Bakhtin's folkloric approach deals with literary representations of carnival, of which his is only one. Two routes open up – one is that of Stallybrass and White to demonstrate how much the carnivalesque is part of a wider system of social understanding by plotting transgressions and inversions across literatures, and in so doing they open up the sublimation process to being understood as mapping the contours of bourgeois consciousness, the problematic and ambivalent space between 'high' and 'low'. Accordingly, 'repressive desublimation' may in fact be 'counter-sublimation' – expression, not by the lower classes under tolerance and licence of their desires so as to better contain them, but expression and acknowledgment by the bourgeoisie of their own hidden desires, so as to cope with them. The second complementary route is discussed by Chris Humphrey (2000) in terms of looking at different types of historical account and identifying specific cases of carnival activity happening, as a historically lived relation (and thus contradictory in specific ways) rather than being simply reported (abstracted and overly unified). He agrees with Stallybrass and White that in viewing it as political anthropology, its features can be seen to operate far beyond the boundaries of festivals and celebrations. The fact that Brazilian *carnaval* is a *contemporary* lived relation offers further significant insights into the sorts of dimension and contradiction that might have been neglected in earlier attempts to translate Bakhtin into cultural studies (the neglect of violence, for example). We can now turn back to The Clash and ask whether these carnivalesque resources help to make sense of the band and their pre-eminent but ambivalent position within the punk movement, and some of the contradictions implied.

'Like trousers, like brain'

The Clash's three founder members emerged from their backgrounds not as uneducated working-class kids but as art-school dropouts who had chosen a particular way of life because they did not want to do what society expected or allowed them to do. Mick Jones and Joe Strummer wanted to be musicians, Paul Simonon an artist or designer. Bernie Rhodes, a manager and successful designer, helped

them to think through what it was that had brought them to where
they were, and bring out its visual dimensions. In so doing, he created
links with Situationist practice and thought, and promoted the development of The Clash's own style of the grotesque that suggests affini-
ties with carnival. They shared the disaffections of punk, its refusal
of what was on offer, and indeed the impending shift to the right in
domestic and international politics – 'things will get tough. I mean
a fascist government. But people won't notice ... ' (Joe Strummer in
Miles 1980: 8) – but committed themselves to opposing the anaesthetic, distracting music of the time – 'we want to keep OUT that
safe soapy slush that comes out of the radio' (Miles 1980: 9) – and
argued that:

What we want to achieve is an atmosphere where an idea can grow and
be passed around. It's a question, I suppose, of spirit and how people feel.
(Miles 1980: 9)

In this The Clash are clearly aligning with a contemporary form of
carnivalesque space in which resistance can be expressed and worked
with, not solely as a safety valve; resonating with the historical view
of the carnivalesque spirit as being within and derived from the
people, mutating, being sublimated and evading or resisting that sublimation. Here they provide evidence in support of arguments within
the theorization of carnival that over-emphasize binaries, oppositions
and reversals, and those that carry this through into discussions of
popular culture and cycles of resistance and incorporation. The idea
of the *milandro*, drawn from Brazilian *carnaval* (but also found elsewhere in South American society), provides both a metaphor for the
trickster position that they often articulated, and goes some way to
explaining the serious implications of their apparent obsession with
guns and outlaws in their writing, their aesthetic and their own tastes.
The words of 'Cheat' from the first UK album indicate:

I have the will to survive
I cheat if I can't win
If someone locks me out
I kick my way back in

Or

Daddy was a bank robber
He never hurt nobody

> He just liked to live that way
> Loved to steal your money
>   ('Bankrobber')

The same voice is present in 'Hate and War', 'City of the Dead', 'Career Opportunities', 'Guns of Brixton' and 'Stay Free', in particular. Aesthetically too the band adopted images and dress designs reminiscent of outlaws and renegades – indeed by 1982 their version of the grotesque was a caricature of itself – and the respect for the individual living on his or her wits was also reflected in the people with whom they chose to surround themselves in the 'camp'. Working around the rules and boundaries, as the *milandro* does, also recognizes the inescapable element of violence involved if carnival is to be seen as a full breaking-down of boundaries, yet this does not necessarily degrade into nihilism. Violence, in fact, is dealt with at all levels in The Clash's oeuvre, extending from the street to terrorism, from police oppression and crime to state-sponsored domestic and global political violence, and the various processes and consequences of war. Their carnival is dangerous – the *milandro's carnaval*.

Somewhat unfairly given the pressures they faced and the microscope their behaviour was put under the band acquired a police record. The media scrutiny provoked the concern of local councils which resulted in close police attention wherever they played. They were searched after a gig in St Albans for no reason, but after the police found nothing they searched the band's bus to find pillow cases, keys and towels from a Holiday Inn in Newcastle where they had played the night before, and Joe and Topper were charged and bailed. The following week Joe was arrested for graffiti-spraying the band's name on a wall in Camden Town, London. As both cases came up on the same day, 300 miles apart, and neither court would reschedule, Joe and Topper were arrested for failing to turn up in Newcastle. In Glasgow after a violent gig, Joe was arrested for breaking a lemonade bottle and Paul, after being struck by a truncheon, was arrested for coming to his aid. In Hamburg Joe was arrested for striking a 'fan', who had invaded the stage to attack him, with his guitar. In London, as recorded in 'Guns on the Roof', Paul and Topper found themselves surrounded by armed police with helicopter support when shooting air rifles at what they thought were wild pigeons (which turned out to be homing racing pigeons). They were reported by commuters on a passing train as terrorists. Add this evidence to that presented in various accounts but most notably that of ex-roadie Johnny Green (Green *et al.* 2003) and the low-key outlaw profile – with the associated 'gang' identity they put forward in interviews and such songs as 'Last Gang in Town' and 'Four Horsemen' – sustains a *milandro* interpretation, although the band come across as pranksters rather than petty criminals (Gray 2003; Knowles 2003; Needs 2005; Parker 2003).

When deployed analogically, outside the festival context, there is always a problem of where and how to draw the boundaries of carnival, which provokes the temptation to solve the problem by the over-determination of binaries. With The Clash it would be possible to focus on the lyrics (the incorporation of foul language) and music (in effect, literary carnival) or on the aesthetics of the band (costumes, development of their own version of the grotesque); on the performances (which would interestingly motivate a crossover between street carnival and dance-hall carnival and the role of the body, and the performer-audience relationship); or on the lifestyle of the group qua group, the band members themselves, and the coterie of 'active supporters' or 'The Clash family'. Keeping in mind the idea of the carnivalesque spirit, then, the sort of problem noted by Stallybrass and White (1986) and Humphrey (2000) moves easily into a broader context of transgression and affirmation. Focusing on the lyrics, The Clash are less provocative than the Sex Pistols, but similarly less likely to use words simply for effect – 'Death or Glory' is a good example of the perfectly positioned and weighted use of the word 'fuck' as verb (see p. 126). *Eccentricity* and *profanation* are in plentiful supply (see 'Career Opportunities' for a rejection of the values of fitting in, whilst resigned to the fact that there may be 'no choice') and these are deployed with irony and subtlety at times as well as straight rejection, as with the critique of consumerism and suburban alienation in 'Lost in the Supermarket':

> I'm lost in the supermarket
> I can no longer shop happily
> I came in here for what I was missing
> A guaranteed personality

Furthermore, whilst punk is often regarded for its serious, melancholic and aggressive aspects, it is steeped in irony (Hebdige 1979) and some 'punk' bands were essentially comedic (e.g. Splodgenessabounds). But humour in Strummer's work is abundant and often economically deployed, revealing an ambivalence and, through his earlier 'folk' roots, displaying a carnivalesque ability to engage 'folk laughter' with serious critique.

The music is uneven in that at times it deploys unusual and unconventional structures, including extremely short and fast pieces with very simple melodic characteristics, but even from the early days it pioneers what might be seen as *mésalliances* – such as the incorporation of reggae with a very white lyric in '(White Man) in Hammersmith Palais'. This willingness to experiment is what takes The Clash out of the conventional punk frame but emphasizes the affirmative dimension of their carnival style. The band's version of the *grotesque* is similarly thoughtful and improvizational – set backdrops using collage, their own clothes (like the famous multi-zippered 'Clash trousers' designed by them with the collaboration of fashion designer friends) decorated with Lettrist stencils, spray-painted or drip-painted in the style of Jackson Pollock, the avoidance of conventional materials like denim and the improvizations with combat fatigues are attempts to be both grotesque and cool that succeed in the early days, even if they become grotesque and silly by the time of *Combat Rock*. This strong visual identity extended to album and single covers and to their daily surroundings (they themselves renovated their first rehearsal space). Strummer also cartooned his personal communications, lyric sheets and studio notes, and the band took cartoonist and artist Ray Lowry, who, like them, straddled cult and mainstream status, on their first US tour. (Lowry's work is included in Green *et al.* 2003; Ridgway 2006; Temple 2007 and limited editions of prints.) The grotesque excess in the representation of bodily images obvious in cartooning was also in evidence in their performances. Whilst punk bands demanded intensity in performance, and none more so than The Clash, all three guitarists also worked hard personally on 'throwing shapes', or using their body as a symbolic device, and improvising juxtapositions of bodily shapes between them as their performances unfolded.[2] Whilst The Clash never pushed the extremes of body decoration into the piercing, tattooing or self-mutilation typical of punk, they pushed their bodies in other ways reminiscent of Artaud's 'Theatre of Cruelty', fuelled by the ergogenic use of drugs (Joe Strummer developed the 'Strummerguard', a device of padding and insulating tape to protect his right forearm from being shredded by his guitar strings, so violent was his rhythmic attack on the instrument).

The prosthetic use of drugs was much in evidence and was a point of contention – all the band used alcohol and marijuana, even in the early days when they professed an anti-drugs position. They used speed in tablet form, but rejected the use of the cheaper amphetamine sulphate powder as it had anti-social side-effects. Generally speaking Strummer was perhaps naïvely in favour of drugs that he thought assisted creativity but did not create dependency, but Mick Jones was a heavy cocaine user and Topper Headon eventually succumbed to heroin dependency. Given the punishing work ethic of the band, who practised seven days a week (and played soccer to keep fit during their daily break – Joe even ran the Paris marathon under an assumed name in a very creditable time) their 'creative violence' was also part of the bodily excess that broke down the barriers between audience and performers typical of both punk and carnival. Where carnival 'celebrated the birth, decay and death of the body as well as its organic functions such as eating, drinking, farting, defecating and copulating' (Langman 2008: 660) and used this as an embodied critique of the normative and suppressive pressures of everyday life, punk refracted this through its philosophy of 'no future' into a critique of contemporary bourgeois capitalism. Spitting, violent collisions in dancing, ripping out seats, throwing objects at the band – all normally forbidden and dangerous audience behaviours – became part of the risk of punk display, the danger of its carnival, a danger taken out into the streets by simply wearing punk clothes. According to Vivienne Westwood (designer and partner of Malcolm McLaren):

> To wear them is to express an attitude and a commitment – and you have to be brave … you make a spectacle of yourself on the street, and a spectacle is a show of force inviting opposition … they can be as subversive a weapon as a book, poster or pamphlet. (adapted from original citation in Blair and Anscombe 1978: 62, cited in Henry 1984: 31–2)

The process of *familiarization* was also significant, both in the band's lyrics (one reason for talking about themselves was not to mythologize, but to demythologize, although the former predominates) and their practice of being accessible to their fans:

> This stuff about fans staying in our rooms and coming backstage is very important – the responsibility is to the fans, not only to keep in touch, but to show also that we do care … Our idea was not to live out their fantasies

for them but to show them that they could live out their own fantasies. (Mick Jones in *Melody Maker* July 1978, cited in Miles 1980: 26)

Voices on and voices off

In his analysis of the work of Dostoevsky and Rabelais, in which he developed his concept of carnival and its continuing modern relevance, Bakhtin developed the idea of *polyphony* (Greek *polyphonia* – many-voiced) adopted from nineteenth-century German writer Otto Ludwig. Polyphony, in Bakhtin's hands, indicates a text in which there are several characters' stories, told from the perspective of each, and the author does not adjudicate between them, does not subsume them under an authorial master narrative, nor displace them altogether by a monophonic text telling only the author's point of view. Truth becomes a matter of relativities, action one of perspectives. Polyphony has in recent years become a metaphor for a form of organizational communication in which the voices of others are heard equally, rather than being forced into denying their own diversity, and its potential creativity (Hazen 1993, 1994; Kornberger *et al.* 2006). However, Bakhtin was more circumspect than this in his own analysis and was aware that the move from literary to social to specifically organized forms was problematic. Whilst polyphony was not cacophony, it offered no reason to be optimistic about convergence, and in its most carnivalesque form was unmanageable – the quintessential opposite of the canonical tendencies of organization. This irony is commonly neglected in contemporary organizational discussions of polyphony. David Boje (1995) offers a metaphor for the polyphonic organization that goes a little further. He argues that organizations are complexes of stories, sometimes running in parallel, sometimes intersecting, sometimes clashing. The beginning of one story might be the middle of another story or the end of yet another one. He draws the analogy with John Krizanc's 1981 play, *Tamara*.

The play takes place in a house, in which scenes are played simultaneously in different rooms. When the scene ends the audience can choose to follow one of the characters, or stay where they are and see who comes in. There are literally thousands of combinations that an individual member of an audience could choose, and each would offer a different insight into what was happening. In such circumstances, it would be impossible ever to get the 'full picture'. But Boje (1995) argues that organizations are not just collections of stories and trajectories – they tend to be composed of departments, branches and sections, any of which is itself a collection or theatre of stories. A larger organization is a meta-theatre of dramas, a *Tamara* of *Tamaras* – or a *Tamara-land*. Boje (1995) develops this metaphor in specific contrast to the hyper-convergent metaphor of *Disneyland* in an analysis of the Disney organization, where management attempted to over-ride the competing stories with its own dominant perspective, and as Boje shows, failed to suppress the underlying conflict.

The problem with polyphony is that while equality can occur in novels and dramas, polyphony can only ever be metaphorical in practice, as there are always inescapable power differences between people in the everyday world. We all have stories, but we don't all have an equal chance of making our story stick. There is no reason to assume that simply hearing the voices of the powerless will promote change (Kornberger *et al.* 2006). As Boje (2008: 77) argues, polyphony can be manipulated by management, used as a means of getting input to decisions but without relinquishing power – in fact it extends management control over the process. For Boje polyphonic approaches have merely affirmed that stakeholder 'dialogues' remain hegemonic, and that polyphony is applied only metaphorically.

How does polyphony apply to The Clash? From one angle, given Bernie Rhodes' not entirely ironic insistence on 'complete control'; the avowedly 'Stalinist' way that former friends could be dropped if they didn't fit the emerging new image; the obvious power struggles within the band that led to Rhodes' dismissal and reinstatement; the sackings of Headon and Jones; the fact that three out of five members of the last line-up were 'hired hands'; and the often ungenerous way that the band dealt with those with whom they had professional relationships (that is, friends who became employees), we might think polyphony is either irrelevant or is part of the manipulative struggles that Boje identifies. Terry Chimes (the band's first drummer) was important internally as he was generally dissonant, and Rhodes found him useful as a foil (Gilbert 2004: 116), but Chimes was not publicly allowed a voice and was never included in interviews (Gilbert 2004: 113). But artistically polyphony was much more significant. Coming from a squat culture of ever open doors, shared or plundered resources, endless nights and constant conversation, The Clash were embedded in dialogue and, despite the well-documented breakdowns,

were stimulated by interaction with a coterie of friends and supporters, extending from roadies to journalists to fellow musical travellers
to fans and, on occasion, to people in general. When Joe Strummer
realized that having lots of people, some of whom may be drunk,
hanging around in the studio (especially the control room) was not
conducive to some aspects of the recording process, he created a 'spliff
bunker' of flight cases into which the merry-makers could withdraw
(which also doubled as a reflective space at times). Their company
stimulated the creativity of Joe in particular, and the band would
often emerge from the bunker with new material ready to record.
Whilst the band were by their own admission not intellectuals, they
were interested in ideas, in political issues, in what others thought, in
how they lived, and what they dreamed – and these voices are very
present in the output of the band (Salewicz 2006: 159). They always
tried to be aware of and sensitive to what their friends and public
thought and experienced, and although Joe in particular resisted the
label of 'spokesman for a generation', their discursive openness in
this way made it a natural ascription. At their most polyphonic, the
band declared themselves to be unmanageable, but the 'posse' kept
them in touch with a common vision (*The Tomorrow Show* 1981). As
Strummer's first wife Gaby observed, 'Strong personalities, who lose
the same vision, means trouble' (Salewicz 2006: 339). Eventually, the
polyphony faded, and the band folded.

Conclusion

Regarding the carnival metaphor, then, the term *carnaval* may well
be better applied in its reference to a lived rather than a folkloric reality. The Clash alert us to the extent to which 'repressive desublimation' and 'bourgeois counter-sublimation' may shape the tensions of
the field of production of popular music, and to the variety of ways
in which 'reversals' may be deployed and complicated. They illustrate
the creative potential but also the problematic character of polyphony within practical power relations. The band also, in themselves
deploying the apparent contradictions of 'year zero' rejection of the
automatic reproduction of stylistic features of genres and showing an
uncharacteristic (for punk) respect for and awareness of other rock
genres and their histories, note the ambivalent character of reversals.
For The Clash these reversals are not cyclical, and, in distinction from

traditional carnival and the customary adaptation of the Bakhtinian approach to popular culture, not themselves reversible, but something to be lived with. The Clash's carnival involves participation in a parade that is musically both broad (e.g. reggae, country) and longitudinal (e.g. Bo Diddley), global ('Washington Bullets', 'Rock the Casbah') and local ('White Riot', 'Complete Control', 'City of the Dead') and bridges these arenas by reinterpreting their relevance in terms of each other.

It is, at its best, an open aesthetic, and an inclusive ethic, recognizing both the utopian potential and the dangerous realities of the contemporary carnival of creativity.

Editor's Note: For a table showing the chart history of The Clash, please go to the end of Chapter 7.

Notes

1 Albarn collaborated in 2006 with former Clash bassist, Paul Simonon, Simon Tong of The Verve and Tony Allen of Fela Kuti as The Good, the Bad and the Queen, whose eponymous first album reached No. 2 in the UK and No. 49 in the USA in 2007.

2 The most comprehensive and accessible source for a visual understanding of the band from ephemera to performance is Strummer et al. (2008) which brings together both previously published and hitherto unpublished material.

References

Bakhtin, M. (1968) *Rabelais and His World*. Cambridge, MA: MIT Press.

Bangs, L. (2003) 'The Clash (1977)', in L. Bangs and G. Marcus (eds.) *Psychotic Reactions and Carburetor Dung*, 224–59. New York: Anchor Books.

Bennett, A. (2006) 'Punk's not dead: the continuing significance of punk rock for an older generation of fans'. *Sociology-London*, 40(2): 219–36.

Blair, D. and Anscombe, I. (1978) *Punk*. New York: Urizen Books.

Boje, D.M. (1995) 'Stories of the storytelling organization: a postmodern analysis of Disney as "*Tamara-Land*"'. *Academy of Management Journal*, 38(4): 997–1035.

(2008) 'Dialogics', in R. Thorpe and R. Holt, *The Sage Dictionary of Qualitative Management Research*, 77. London: Sage.

Clark, K. and Holquist, M. (1984) *Mikhail Bakhtin*. Cambridge, MA: Belknap Press.

Davies J. (1996) 'The future of "no future": punk rock and postmodern theory'. *Journal of Popular Culture* 29(4): 3–26.

Fletcher, T. (2005) *The Clash: The Complete Guide to their Music.* London: Omnibus Press.

Frith, S. (1988) *Music for Pleasure: Essays in the Sociology of Pop.* Cambridge: Polity Press.

Gardiner, M. (1992) *The Dialogics of Critique: M. M. Bakhtin and the Theory of Ideology.* London: Routledge.

Gilbert, P. (2004) *Passion is a Fashion: The Real Story of The Clash.* London: Aurum.

Gray, M. (2003) *The Clash: Return of the Last Gang in Town.* London: Helter Skelter.

Green, J., Barker, G. and Lowry, R. (2003) *A Riot of Our Own: Night and Day with The Clash – and After.* London: Orion.

Grossberg, L. (1992) *We Gotta Get Out of This Place: Popular Conservatism and Postmodern Culture.* New York: Routledge.

(1997a) *Bringing it All Back Home: Essays on Cultural Studies.* Durham, NC: Duke University Press.

(1997b). *Dancing in Spite of Myself: Essays on Popular Culture.* Durham, NC: Duke University Press.

Hazen, M.A. (1993) 'Toward polyphonic organization'. *Journal of Organizational Change Management,* 6(5): 15–22.

(1994) 'Multiplicity and change in persons and organizations'. *Journal of Organizational Change Management,* 7(6): 72–81.

Hebdige, D. (1979) *Subculture: The Meaning of Style.* London: Methuen.

Henry, T. (1984) 'Punk and avant-garde art'. *Journal of Popular Culture,* 17(4): 30–6.

Hirsch, P.M. (1972) 'Processing fads and fashions: an organization-set analysis of cultural industry systems'. *American Journal of Sociology,* 77(4): 639–59.

(2000) 'Cultural industries revisited'. *Organization Science,* 11(3): 356–61.

Humphrey, C. (2000) 'Bakhtin and the study of popular culture: re-thinking carnival as a historical and analytical concept', in C. Brandist and G. Tihanov (eds.) *Materializing Bakhtin: the Bakhtin Circle and Social Theory,* 164–72. Basingstoke: Houndmills; New York: Palgrave, in association with St. Antony's College, Oxford.

Kornberger, M., Clegg, S.R. and Carter, C. (2006) 'Rethinking the polyphonic organization: managing as discursive practice'. *Scandinavian Journal of Management,* 22: 3–30.

Knowles, C. (2003) *Clash City Showdown.* London: Pagefree Publishing.

Langman, L. (2008) 'Punk porn and resistance'. *Current Sociology,* 56(4): 657–77.

Lowry, R. and Myers, B. (2007) *The Clash*. Warwick: Angry Penguin.

Marcus, G. (1989) *Lipstick Traces: A Secret History of the Twentieth Century*. London: Penguin.

(1994) *In the Fascist Bathroom: Writings on Punk, 1977–1992*. London and New York: Penguin.

Marcuse, H. (1964) *One-Dimensional Man*. Boston, MA: Beacon Press.

Miles, B. (1980) *The Clash by Miles*. London: Omnibus.

Moore, R. (2004) 'Postmodernism and punk subculture: cultures of authenticity and deconstruction'. *The Communication Review*, 7(3): 305–27.

(2007) 'Friends don't let friends listen to corporate rock'. *Journal of Contemporary Ethnography*, 36(4): 438–74.

Needs, K. (2005) *Joe Strummer and the Legend of The Clash*. London: Plexus.

Parker, A. (2003) *The Clash: Rat Patrol from Fort Bragg*. London: Abstract Sounds.

Parker, R. (1997) 'The carnivalization of the world', in R. Lancaster and M. Di Leonardo, *The Gender/Sexuality Reader*, 361–77. New York: Routledge.

Ridgway, A. (dir.) (2006) *The Clash: Up Close and Personal* (film). Nassau: Stormbird.

Salewicz, C. (2006) *Redemption Song: The Definitive Biography of Joe Strummer*. London: Harper.

Savage, J. (2001) *England's Dreaming: Sex Pistols and Punk Rock*. London: Faber and Faber.

Smith, P. (1980) *The Clash: Before and After*. London: Eel Pie.

The Tomorrow Show (1981) NBC, 14 June. Available: http://uk.youtube.com/watch?v=JVygiX0KEEw (accessed 15 January 2009).

Stallybrass, P. and White, A. (1986) *The Politics and Poetics of Transgression*. London: Methuen.

Strummer, J., Jones, M., Simonon, P. and Headon, T. (2008) *The Clash*. London: Atlantic Books.

Temple, J. (dir.) (2007) *The Future is Unwritten* (film). London: Film4.

Turner, C. (2005) *Planet Simpson*. London: Ebury Press.

Art for art's sake

Introduction to Part II

Caves' (2002) identification of 'art for art's sake' highlights the importance of 'non-economic' satisfaction for creative producers, recognizing that their motivation, employment and participation in a creative process may be heavily informed by non-pecuniary factors.

> In creative activities ... the creator (artist, performer, author) cares vitally about the originality displayed, the technical prowess demonstrated, the resolution and harmony achieved in the creative act ... Asked to co-operate with humdrum partners in some production process, the artist is disposed to forswear compromise and to resist making commitments about future acts of artistic creation or accepting limitations on them. (Caves 2002: 4)

These rationales, however, may strongly impact the economic viability of a creative process, setting up inherent tensions between artistic integrity and financial performance, between artistic and commercial logics. If those involved in creative activities are deeply concerned with the technical perfection, originality, artistic merit, etc., to the extent that the consumers' reception of the product may not be considered, how are these tensions manifest and reconciled? To what extent, and how, do the pressures for commercialization of content impact on the creative process? How is the balance managed? 'Art for art's sake' thus encapsulates the conflict between the creative and the commercial, between an artistic and commercial imperative (Glynn 2000; Tschang 2007; Eikhof and Haunschild 2007). It raises the question of which disciplinary code is to dominate judgement and decisions. Is it possible to have 'art for art's sake'? What are the compromises that have to be, and are, made? How are these negotiated? What are the strategies for the mediation of an economic logic that has a monetary assessment of quality, with an artistic logic that uses an immanent aesthetics as a guidance of legitimacy? Is the characterization of the commercial/management discourse as 'humdrum'

appropriate? To what extent do these constitute structured antithetical antinomies?

Our chapters in this section (Luxford, Eikhof, Linstead) explore some
of the paradoxes and ambiguities that underpin 'art for art's sake'.
Luxford's essay traces its early nineteenth-century origins in the history of art and literature and illustrates the reversals of argument that
have accompanied its development from the nineteenth to the twentieth century. 'Art for art's sake' is an expression that came into use in
the nineteenth century in association with the Aesthetic Movement.
Its implication is of art as a self-contained domain concerned with
beauty and free from utilitarian purpose. The distinction is thus
drawn between artistic creativity and utilitarian commercial activity.
It augments the view of artistic production as progressing independently from, and independent of, other developments. From this legacy
comes the belief that only artists can create and judge art. 'Practice' in
a guild or group has given way to the conception of the individual artist; and from an undifferentiated group of producers and consumers,
production and consumption are rendered discrete and separate processes, embodying discrete and separate interests that necessarily conflict. Historically, 'art for art's sake' has underpinned debates about
art's links to beauty; the role and claims of the artist; the ability of
the artist to judge art; the role of art in politics; and art's moral role.
Note, however, that an emphasis on 'art for art's sake' does not preclude commercial interest. Only the independently wealthy or those
supported through public commission remain impervious to financial
necessity. The autonomy and the special intrinsic value that 'art for
art's sake' creates can also act to secure monetary value. In doing so
it highlights the interpenetration of the 'world of art' and the 'world
of money' and underlines the role of money, power, status, reputation
and fashion that entwines cultural production.

Part of the problem with the overly Romantic conception of 'art for
art's sake' is that it emphasizes the artistic process and downplays the
importance of the artistic product. From '*creare*', we see that creativity in both commerce and art is about production. It is the creation
of a product. Difficulties arise when a creative product becomes a
commodity for commercial exchange and the impact that this has
on the integrity of the artistic process. That it has an impact is not in
doubt; witness the distinction that is drawn between 'art' and 'commercial art'. Audiences have to be large enough to support creative

activity, but widening audience appeal is in danger of turning creative endeavour into mass entertainment and with this threatening artistic values. The need for replication is in danger of creating standardization. The balance between small-scale production and large-scale reproduction threatens the relative balance of cultural and economic capital. It threatens the conversion of the artistic or creative product into the 'ready made'.

However, if we genuinely embrace the ideas of paradox and dialogue, we must also accept that commercial exchange provides both a form of feedback on quality and value to the artist and provides artistic opportunity. The production of an artistic product that is not recognized by others as having any value carries a dialogic message to the artist. It could raise questions over the product quality, or raise doubts over the judgement of the (potential) audience, or questions of connection and distribution. Its potential interpretation is quite varied. In rock music, for example, there is a litany of famous bands that have either cancelled performances or played to tiny audiences. Those who play to a small audience may not derive commercial success, but they may achieve a performance outcome in an 'intimate' atmosphere leading to 'you should have been there' stories. Conversely, other artists have made a virtue of commercial sophistication and success (e.g. Tracy Emin), or produced commercially successful products commenting on the commerciality of others (e.g. the Sex Pistols, before their 'Filthy Lucre' reunion tour). Hence, the relationship between art for its own sake and the pull of commerciality is far from simple. It may not be as dichotomous as it appears, and it could even be the site of ironic artistically and commercially successful product. We cannot conclude that art and commerce are necessarily opposed, or that they simply combine in synergistic success. Rather, the tensions between successful integration and separate value provide a site for potentially fruitful dialogue.

Eikhof's discussion of contemporary German theatre addresses some of these paradoxes and ambiguities. Although the importance of non-economic forms of satisfaction derived from 'doing the work' raises a number of problems for managers and organizations, it might also work to management's advantage. Eikhof illustrates how 'art for art's sake' has become incorporated as the institutional logic or rationality of an institutional sphere, the theatre. Here the term has been so absorbed in modern sensibilities that it becomes an 'existential' claim around which identities and actions are narrated. It is unquestioned that there is 'art for art's sake' and that this contrasts with a 'business' or commercial logic. These two logics, however, are entangled in the theatrical labour market which incorporates both economic incentives and claims to cultural capital. As a form of capital, the claims of being motivated by 'art for art's sake' become amenable to calculation, and as such may be used to improve (economic) positions in the labour market. What is being played out here are the apparently different imperatives of different value spheres, the artistic and the economic, the 'world of art' and the 'world of commerce'; imperatives that may or may not be internalized into the specific value commitments of the individuals as they enact and live their roles. Eikhof's essay illustrates how the two imperatives of artistic endeavour and commercial pressures are inter-related and accommodated.

The role of art in politics reasserts itself in Linstead's discussion of The Clash, in which he traces their battle to promote the political message of their music while accommodating the commercial interests of their recording company. In tracing the interplay between creative imperative and the demands of commercial development, it is interesting to see how debates of the nineteenth and twentieth century are played out in the rampant commercialism of the late twentieth-century music industry.

As with any industry, there is an imperative to innovation within the creative industries. Innovation may be of a product (e.g. rock'n'roll's use of white performers for a white record-buying public in the segregated southern USA) or a process (e.g. desktop publishing). One factor influencing innovation is the standards of performance in the creative activity, i.e. the strength of its disciplinary constraints. The more tightly these are controlled, the more difficult is creative innovation. Very loose standards of performance, however, render variation less predictable and 'innovation' less readily discernible. The ease and degree of replication also influences the extent to which stylistic innovation freely diffuses to imitators, thus affecting the extent to which there is an incentive to invest in it. Although The Clash were heralded as truly innovative, Linstead sees 'industry' playing a major role in shaping how claims about creative innovation are asserted, maintained and controlled, thereby having a direct impact on what 'creativity' and innovation are. There is an interest in 'steering' innovation, so that it may be understood and recognized as such by the largest potential audience. It is this element that the music business seeks to exploit as a means of coping with the 'inherent unknowability' of the process. The ease with which this may be secured influences the extent to which the 'creative industries' can be rendered 'industry like', and its creative innovation influenced and predicted. Under the pressures of commercialization, i.e. standardization, where the production of creative material becomes the production of creative merchandise, there is the danger of an innovative voice, intent on 'pushing the envelope', becoming anodyne. The conflict between those engaged in artistic endeavour and how this is managed by those having a more commercial focus, and the extent and consequences of this form of conflict acting as a form of 'creative violence', are all raised in the history of The Clash. For Linstead, practicing 'art' in these circumstances requires an intimate knowledge of the 'rules of the game', so that artistic practice might at some level be shielded, and as a means of avoiding the objectification process whereby the productive self becomes the product. His conclusion that the links between commercialization and creative endeavour are much too complicated to be posed in binary divides continues the debates raised two centuries earlier.

References

Caves, R. (2002) *Creative Industries: Contracts Between Art and Commerce*. Cambridge, MA: Harvard University Press.

Eikhof, D. R. and Haunschild, A. (2007) 'For art's sake! Managing artistic and economic logics in creative production'. *Journal of Organizational Behavior*, **28**(5): 523–38.

Glynn, M. (2000) 'When cymbals become symbols: conflict over organizational identity within a symphony orchestra'. *Organization Science*, **11**(3): 285–98.

Tschang, F. (2007) 'Balancing the tensions between rationalization and creativity in the video games industry'. *Organization Science*, **18**(6): 989–1005.

5 | Art for art's sake: was it ever thus? A historical perspective[1]
JULIAN M. LUXFORD

Scholars and artists have attached the following labels, *inter alia*, to art for art's sake: phrase, term, expression, notion, claim, point of view, rubric, appeal, slogan, rallying cry, battle cry, principle, guiding principle, half-truth, formula, theory, ideology, creed, doctrine, dogma, movement, school, style, art, 'ism' (as in 'art for art's sake-ism'), philosophy, aesthetic philosophy, theology. While these are not necessarily mutually exclusive terms, their multiplicity and conceptual range immediately suggest that, regarded synoptically, the subject of this chapter involves not a distinct hypothesis or hypotheses but a contested and semantically complex conglomeration of ideas. It also hints at the range of academic disciplines which have a stake in art for art's sake: philosophy, history, art history, literary studies and sociology, to name the most obvious. Historically, proponents, opponents and neutral commentators on art for art's sake have advanced or (more usually) assumed particular definitions for it. But the common thread in these is simply that art is separate from other spheres of human experience and that this autonomy conveys privilege, with the corollary, not advanced by all writers on the subject, that such privilege extends to those who make art. These ideas have proven sufficiently useful and provocative to give art for art's sake a prominent place in over two centuries of aesthetic discourse, and to lodge the term, with a wisp of its underlying ideology, in the popular consciousness: a remarkable status for something grounded in early readings of Kantian metaphysics. This essay will do no more than map some of the most prominent ideas associated with art for art's sake, and briefly consider whether the commonly understood concepts it embodies can be applied to art of the period before its first recorded use in the early nineteenth century. The link with the concept of creativity fundamental to this book will be implicit throughout in the discussion of both art and aesthetics and the manipulation of ideology.[2]

The nineteenth century

So much attention has been devoted to the early history of art for art's sake that proof of the term's use prior to 1804 now seems unlikely to be discovered.[3] In that year, the Swiss writer Benjamin Constant wrote of *l'art pour l'art* with reference to contemporary studies of those sections of Immanuel Kant's *Critique of Judgement* (first published in 1790) dealing with aesthetics. Here Kant proposed that human consciousness perceives beauty in objects (not simply artistic ones) directly, unmediated by ideological concepts. Man's powers of aesthetic perception are thus disinterested: politics, ethics, religion, class, patriotism, emotion, etc., play no part in them. If such extraneous considerations enter in, then, according to Kant, the perception of beauty will be corrupted (Collinson 1992: 361–7). These ideas were extremely attractive to those with an interest in championing artistic talent and its products, because they seemed to demonstrate that, alone among humanity, artists possessed sufficiently exulted aesthetic judgement to create beauty as well as perceive it. (In fact, as John Wilcox (1953) has pointed out, only a mistaken or wilful reading of Kant could have produced such ideas.) The scholars with whose work Constant was acquainted belonged to a larger intelligentsia, chiefly Franco-German, caught up in the first flush of this and related enthusiasms. When the philosopher Victor Cousin used *l'art pour l'art* in an early treatise on aesthetics (1818), these notions of artistic autonomy had become more widespread, and the way he frames it – 'art is not a means; it is an end in itself' – reflects a general understanding which most nineteenth-century writers had of the term. There are no further recorded uses before the early 1830s, but thereafter it emerges with increasing frequency in the debates about freedom of artistic expression played out in the Parisian press. By 1838, when painting was first brought under the *l'art pour l'art* umbrella in the context of a major review (by the art critic Théophile Thoré-Bürger), the term was widely associated with the claims to freedom of expression on the grounds of aesthetic detachment made by (or for) novelists, poets and critics, Victor Hugo, Alexandre Dumas, Honoré de Balzac, Charles Augustin Sainte-Beuve and Frédéric Soulié among them (Wilcox 1953: 367–75).

During what can be called art for art's sake's 'early period', the writer and journalist Théophile Gautier stands out alongside Cousin for his interest in developing the theoretical possibilities of the term. The preface to his 1835 novel *Mademoiselle de Maupin* is widely considered a manifesto of art for art's sake (Harrison and Wood 1998: 97–100). The notion of a manifesto implies the existence of a distinct 'movement', but this would be overstating the case. Detailed sifting of the relevant literature shows that the term art for art's sake was applied with considerable breadth and looseness both in this period and throughout the nineteenth century. Gautier, who nevertheless understood that he championed widely held sentiments, wrote with a colour and partisanship sanctioned by context (a novel) and true to his own bohemian ideas about artistic licence. 'Nothing beautiful is indispensable to life … [t]he useless alone is truly beautiful,' he claimed. 'Everything useful is ugly, since it is the expression of a need, and man's needs are, like his pitiful, infirm nature, ignoble and disgusting.' Here, as in Kant, the beautiful embraces more than art; but the status of art, and literature in particular, is the narrative's *raison d'être*. Nothing else in Gautier's preface is remotely Kantian. It consists of a series of trenchant and often intemperate statements containing none of the cogency usually attempted in artists' manifestos. But Gautier's belief that artistic detachment is most potently expressed in what was perceived to be art's otiosity represents a sensible extrapolation from the ideas associated with Kant's theory of aesthetic disinterestedness. Its enduring attraction is attested by its restatement near the end of the century in another literary preface, that of Oscar Wilde's *Picture of Dorian Gray* (1891), which ends with the notorious (and clearly derivative) claim that 'All art is quite useless' (Harrison and Wood 1998: 862).

Between Gautier and Wilde the term art for art's sake was in more or less continuous use, with a brief lull during the middle years of the century. It came increasingly to be associated with fine art, and, from the late 1860s onwards, was linked explicitly (but not exclusively) to the Aesthetic Movement in English painting, literature and criticism. In poetry it is associated with such names as Stéphane Mallarmé, Charles Baudelaire, Algernon Charles Swinburne and Edgar Allen Poe. Swinburne was an important influence in the application of art for art's sake to English painting, identifying (with overt reference to Gautier) the dreamy, sensual nudes of the classicising Albert Moore as 'faultless and secure expression[s] of an exclusive worship of things formally beautiful'. He also praised the stylistically very different art of James NcNeill Whistler in similar terms: here, he declared, was painting which did not betray the mark of brush or maulstick, and thus distanced itself from the mundane processes of manufacture (Spencer 1972: 35–7). Two years earlier, in a now-famous essay on William Blake (1866), Swinburne had stated that 'art can never be the handmaid of religion, exponent of duty, servant of fact [or] pioneer of morality'. Such remarks were part of a calculated attack on a pervasive belief in the subservience of art to moral, political and ultimately divine ends, exemplified in the domain of the visual arts by John Ruskin's *ex cathedra* commentaries, and in poetry by Matthew Arnold and Alfred, Lord Tennyson. 'Art for Art's Sake! Hail, truest Lord of Hell!/ Hail Genius, Master of the Moral Will!/The filthiest of all paintings painted well/Is mightier than the purest painted ill!' Tennyson wrote, in a shot at both the ideas and perceived licentiousness of the Aesthetic Movement's proponents (Adams 1971: 164 n.4). For his part, Ruskin attacked Whistler's *Nocturne in Black and Gold: The Falling Rocket* (1875) as an 'ill-educated conceit' and a 'wilful imposture'.[4] Here, and in contemporary, essentially philistine, press coverage, there is plenty of evidence that the claims for art's autonomy articulated by Swinburne and espoused by the Aesthetic Movement were penetrating the collective artistic consciousness in England, despite the fact that the painters involved were often excluded from exhibiting their own works in such high-profile and prestigious contexts as the Royal Academy, which played the largest role of any institution in shaping the Victorian public's taste for art.

Numerous important artists of the Victorian period can be associated with the Aesthetic Movement and the term art for art's sake. Whistler, Moore, Frederic Leighton, Dante Gabriel Rossetti, Simeon Solomon and Edward Burne-Jones, for example, have all recently been studied in this context by Elizabeth Prettejohn (2007). In each case the conception and perceived purpose of artistic autonomy can be shown to have differed, but it is nevertheless possible to summarise the main beliefs attaching to art for art's sake by the close of the nineteenth century. First, art has no purposes other than aesthetic ones: this was the crux of Swinburne's argument, also outlined in the same year (1866) by Walter Pater, the Aesthetic Movement's influential but periodically curbed academic voice (Brake 2003: 230–1).[5] Second, artists are more liberally endowed with creativity, or, to return to Kant, aesthetic judgement, than others. Third, the creation of art is the most elevated activity possible for man. Fourth, artists create with no ulterior motives, and to the extent that they are influenced by morality, utility, politics, etc., they are not artists, and what they produce not art (it follows that philosophers, moralists, politicians and so forth cannot be artists) (Singer 1954: 344–52). Of course, it was not in the nature of the Aesthetic Movement's adherents, or that of their Romantic and bohemian precursors, to structure theories in this way, for to have done so would have smacked of the very philosophising they repudiated. But in fact the urgency with which art for art's sake is promoted in the writings of Gautier, Poe, Swinburne, Whistler and Wilde, sounds a distinctly ideological note (Singer 1954: 352). To the extent that these writers considered art and artists to have an entitlement to special status and recognition, their principle of aesthetic detachment is alloyed by ethics: art is no longer simply beautiful, but to some degree a servant of its maker's status. While this contradiction was not demonstrably a matter of contention, it suggests the difficulty (even artists being moral beings) of maintaining that any product of human endeavour could be completely free of the taint of ideology. This and related difficulties were largely overcome by subsequent developments in the conceptualisation of artistic autonomy, also associated with the term art for art's sake.

The twentieth century

During the early to mid twentieth century, the critical understanding of art for art's sake changed. The fundamental idea of aesthetic autonomy remained constant, but came to be supported through a more carefully constructed definition of the peculiar property which exulted art. This property was now identified as artistic form. Where nineteenth-century defence of artistic superiority would have rested – had its proponents been obliged to argue systematically for it – on imperfectly digested readings of Kant's ideas about aesthetic judgement, twentieth-century writers could appeal to a theoretical apparatus which identified form as the only intrinsic (and thus defining) property of art, sufficient not only as a basis for conclusions about quality, but also, as early academic art historians such as Alois Riegl and Heinrich Wölfflin showed, for an understanding of the development of style and composition. In fact, nineteenth-century ideas about artistic 'purity' adumbrated the isolation of form as art's

defining property.[6] A precocious instance occurs in the field of music,
an art with its own history of tension between the competing claims
of aesthetic autonomy, moral duty and public appeasement. Eduard
Hanslick's *The Beautiful in Music*, published in 1854, contained a
detailed if not consistently cogent explanation of the intrinsic separateness of music, not only from the world of non-artistic phenomena
but from the other arts as well (Dahlhaus 1989: 194–5; Goehr *et al.*
2001: 616). Claims for the extraordinary nature for the visual arts did
not receive commensurate formalist support for another half-century.
Ultimately, from a philosophical point of view, this support proved
no stronger than the pseudo-Kantian propositions it replaced. The
work of such critics as Clive Bell, Roger Fry and Henri Focillon did,
however, help to justify avant-garde detachment in a period when artists were frequently placed under moral and even physical pressure to
harness their talents to socio-political causes.

Let us step back from the threshold of formalism for a moment, and
examine some of the negative associations attached to art for art's
sake during the later nineteenth and twentieth centuries. These widen
our understanding of the way the term was understood, and also
point up the main political grounds of opposition to artistic autonomy which emerged in the wake of World War One and the Russian
Revolution. Ruskin and his moralist contemporaries were not alone in
expressing disapproval. In France, Pierre-Joseph Proudhon, champion
of the Realist school in painting exemplified by the work of Gustave
Courbet (who himself criticised 'the pointless objective of art for art's
sake'), characterised what art for art's sake stood for as naïve, disin-
genuous and irrational. Exercise of aesthetic judgement, he argued,
was inseparable from the application of moral judgement: when man
paints (or describes) himself, or his surroundings, the results are thus
bound to reflect his morality. If Proudhon's detailed arguments were
no more cogent than those they aimed to discredit, they do sketch a
basic objection to the assumption that artists could produce works
in a wholly disinterested state which was corroborated and echoed
in various ways over the following eighty years (Proudhon wrote in
1865). The author Max Nordau built on this criticism in his most
famous work, *Degeneration*, published in 1892, in which he pointed
out that in the emotional and psychological satisfaction they bring,
creative acts are of manifest utility to artists. With direct reference to
art for art's sake, both critics suggested the arrogance of those who

would hive art and artists off from morality and society. In doing so they reinforced a widespread condemnation, on grounds of unjustified elitism, of the disqualification of non-artists from aesthetic judgement (a disqualification usually implicit but which Swinburne and Whistler, among others, spelled out) (Harrison and Wood 1998: 373, 404–10, 804–5; Spencer 1972: 85; Swinburne 1912: 349–51).

These objections encapsulate the main negative assumptions on which early twentieth-century critics could draw. Some, like T. S. Eliot, who was particularly censorious of Walter Pater, had religious reasons for rejecting the idea of artistic autonomy. Art for them provided valuable support for social and religious causes (although nobody argued that this was its sole function). Eliot stated (1976: 442), with little apparent force, that the term art for art's sake had no more validity than 'an exhortation to the artist to stick to his job'. Predominantly, however, the disapproval was politically motivated; and it is above all in socialist criticism of the avant-garde, whose exponents were seen to ignore social and moral imperatives in pursuit of artistic aims at best useless and at worse pernicious, that the term art for art's sake was attacked. Across the arts, the avant-garde (insofar as it can be meaningfully reified) has generally resisted alignment with causes in favour of its practitioners' ideas about intrinsic artistic progress. Such ideas could be compellingly articulated, as Arnold Schoenberg's response to attacks on his twelve-note serialism suggests. In 'How One Becomes Lonely' (1937) (Schoenberg et al. 1984: 53), he wrote: 'I knew I had to fulfil a task. I had to express what was necessary to be expressed and I knew I had the duty of developing my ideas for the sake of progress in music, whether I liked it or not.' There is a strong presumption here of artistic (specifically musical) autonomy. However, to political theorists, such ideology appeared morally flawed. Avant-garde detachment, repeatedly and pejoratively labelled 'art for art's sake', was at best a bourgeois abrogation of social responsibilities and at worst, in its wilful refusal to mobilise art against repression, a servant of capital and, ultimately, fascism (Benjamin 1969: 242; Harrison and Wood 2003: 157, 422–9, 656–8). By and large, such political objections did not engage with the possible philosophical justifications for advocating artistic autonomy. A job of surpassing importance needed doing, and artists, whose particular skills would have made them valuable fellow-travellers, were not prepared to do it: such pragmatic considerations were sufficient to validate any censure.

But some Marxist critics did recognise a value in successful theoretical repudiation of the ideas attached to art for art's sake. Perhaps
the most detailed of their responses is contained in Arnold Hauser's
Sociology of Art (1974) (Hauser 1979). Hauser identified art for art's
sake with the claim of autonomy for artistic form. He understood that
he could not debunk this claim with reference to social duty, though
he asserted this duty at several points (e.g. 'The protest against the
doctrine of *l'art pour l'art* is a protest against … fleeing from the
responsibility of real life'). His most forceful argument centred on the
common-sense claims that art is produced not disinterestedly, but for
reasons possessed by artists (here he took up Nordau's cudgels); and
that even once time has obscured these reasons, the form of a piece –
his examples are musical, but the point is broadly applicable – will
always bear their mark (Hauser 1979: 426, 427, 438–9).

By the time Hauser wrote, few argued that artists as well as art
were beyond the moral and utilitarian compass of their social *milieux*.
As soon as claims for artistic autonomy were subjected to systematic
scrutiny, it must have become obvious that artists, whose special status was contingent on their involvement with art and not vice versa,
could not in fact be accorded any philosophically defensible privilege.
Artists retained a certain kudos, of course, but this related to their
ability to intuit and manipulate artistic form rather than any share
in its quiddity. The artist thus takes a step back in most formalist
discourse on artistic autonomy. This same discourse also relegated,
or at least refined, the concept of beauty in art. For Bell, Fry and
Focillon, beauty is not something which artistic form need possess.
From the early nineteenth century onwards, those who argued for
artistic autonomy had simply assumed all art to be beautiful. This
was, to say the least, a shaky presumption, and was singled out as
such as early as 1892 in Max Nordau's observation that '[Art for art's
sake's] inadequacy follows from the fact, among others, that it allows
absolutely no place for the ugly as an object of artistic representation'
(Harrison and Wood 1998: 804). To Nordau, as to the modern
observer, it must have been clear that many works of art, through
damage, poor execution, cultural abstraction, or otherwise, were,
if not actually ugly, certainly not beautiful either. Given this fact,
and also the often-deliberate absence of beauty in avant-garde works,
supporters of art's autonomy had to relinquish the notion that art
was synonymous with beauty. Bell and Fry both considered form an

aesthetic phenomenon, but with the qualification that this aesthetic was of a different type from that which constitutes beauty in nature.

Bell, Fry and Focillon all considered art to reside in an abstract, intrinsic property which could be perceived by sensitive viewers but was not amenable to scientific analysis. Indeed, for Bell (1961: 21), writing in 1915, one was only aware of it through 'personal experience of a peculiar emotion': this precluded any possibility of objective assessment. Individual artworks had extrinsic properties, too, notably subject matter and material constitution. Artistic form did not, however, partake of these. Fry, who adopted Bell's term 'significant form' in 1920, wrote of 'the extremely elusive aesthetic quality which is the one constant quality of all works of art, and which seems to be independent of all the prepossessions and associations which the spectator brings with him.' This, along with Fry's (1920: 197, 199) regretful admission that he could not 'get beyond [a] vague adumbration of the nature of significant form', draws attention to the subjective element in the formalist definition of art's separateness.[7] Experience of artistic form is not to be understood, nor judgements about it made, on the basis of normal concepts. 'To appreciate a work of art,' Bell wrote (1961: 25), 'we need bring with us nothing from life, no knowledge of its ideas and affairs.' Such form is a special kind of abstraction, present in but not confined to individual works. (It does, however, include colour; though how this might be possible in an abstraction is not adequately explained by any of the writers discussed here.) It is clearly difficult to argue for artistic autonomy with reference to a phenomenon whose existence and character is verifiable only on the basis of subjective emotional or, as Focillon seems to have thought, psychological experience. Certainly, the writings of the formalists bear this out. They boil down to intelligent and thought-provoking assertions, with which it is easy for the aesthetician seeking a sufficient definition of art to find fault (Collinson 1992: 149–50). In the context of this chapter, their importance, and whatever conviction they may be considered to carry, reside in their unqualified affirmation of art's complete separation from moral and social considerations, and their attempt to locate this in an ostensibly value-neutral phenomenon which, unlike Kantian beauty, was exclusive to, indeed synonymous with, art itself.

The formalism of Henri Focillon, while not as well studied as that of Bell and Fry, is surely the ultimate statement of what in the wake of these developments in aesthetics might be called 'art for form's sake' (Singer 1954: 348). Focillon published his treatise *The Life of Forms in Art* in 1934 (Focillon 1992), while professor of medieval archaeology and art history at the Sorbonne.[8] It is heavily influenced by the work of Heinrich Wölfflin, mentioned above as one of a group of late-nineteenth and early-twentieth-century scholars who appealed to form not as a means of defining art, but rather for understanding style in historical context. While *The Life of Forms* is Focillon's most theoretical work, his other studies of medieval art and (particularly) architecture consistently sought to distance the idea of the development of style – the aspect of art most obviously related to form – from ideology and socio-economic imperatives, thus manifesting sympathy not only with the Bell-Fry school of formalism but also the avant-garde, with which he felt an affinity (his father was a professional engraver). The book is chiefly worth considering for its very clear indication of the looseness of formalist arguments for artistic autonomy, and also the sympathetic link between nineteenth- and twentieth-century ideas about this autonomy which it indicates, as for example where it is said that 'the more a work of art is used for any specific purpose, the more it is despoiled of its ancient dignity,' and art is described as 'an affirmation of something that is whole, complete and absolute' (Focillon 1992: 31–2). Unlike Bell, Focillon does not attempt a structured definition of form. Indeed, he is Delphic on this point: throughout his treatise, form is identified with life, colour, structure, touch, line, matter, time and other things. He also states that form is never abstract, that it exists in artists' minds before it is transferred into works of art, and that it occupies a 'fourth realm' (by which he seems to mean a fourth dimension) 'distinctly not our own ... with its own laws, material and development' (Focillon 1992: 60, 101, 103, 122–3). Focillon does not speak of specifically artistic form, but he does believe that form finds its highest expression in art and architecture, with which he believes it shares a special relationship. His distinctive contribution was to conceive form-in-art as a non-biological life-force, self-generating and undergoing perpetual metamorphosis. 'Forms,' he noted, 'tend to manifest themselves [in art] with extraordinary vigor ... a work of art is motionless only in appearance' (Focillon 1992: 38, 41).

Focillon's beliefs about the special nature of form-in-art led him to posit a unique status for artists, who on his account belong to a separate race, endowed with the 'special privilege ... to imagine, to recollect, to think and to feel in *forms*' (Focillon 1992: 123, 143). Artists do not create form, of course, but they are the conduits through which it finds phenomenal expression. How this could be possible is veiled in obscurity: form's relationships to the human mind are described as 'inconstant' and not amenable to any 'ultimate definition' (Focillon 1992: 125). In essence, such aggrandisement of the artist apparently differs little from that found among nineteenth-century proponents of art for art's sake. While Focillon never claims that artists participate in form's 'fourth realm', it is reasonably clear that he considers them superior to their fellow men. That this notion here flows from the pen of a Sorbonne *professeur*, rather than an opinionated bohemian or aesthete, and is embedded in a substantial text dense with learned allusion and paradoxology, does not increase its philosophical credibility. The nature and acuteness of the claims for the sovereignty of artists contained in *The Life of Forms*, influenced, one assumes, by the author's personal links to the artistic fraternity, set Focillon apart from other formalists. However, in his elementary beliefs that art is form, and that form is unrelated to utilitarian and moral considerations, he is at one with them.

Like art history, aesthetics has now moved beyond formalism in its search for meaning in art. Little effort has been expended, however, in re-examining the semantics of art for art's sake. The idea that art is somehow Olympian, and that its nature is degraded if it is exploited for anything other than aesthetic experience, has persisted in the avant-garde, where abstract expressionism, neo-Dada and postmodernism have all selectively continued to subvert the usefulness of art through lack, absurdity or miscontextualisation of subject matter. The academic and social commentator Germaine Greer recently received a Plain English Campaign 'Golden Bull' award, which recognises (in the language of the Campaign website) 'the worst examples of written tripe' in the popular press, for stating that: 'The first attribute of the art object is that it creates a discontinuity between itself and the unsynthesised manifold.' This, as Greer complained, was simply a way of saying, with a nod towards Kant's *Critique of Judgement* (from which the term 'unsynthesised manifold' comes), that art is separate from everything else, physical or metaphysical (Greer 2006). That she did not use the term art for art's sake is hardly surprising, for, except in a negative sense, it has fallen into abeyance in post-War academic discourse. Its use by academics is now primarily historical, with reference chiefly to the Aesthetic Movement. It also has a popular currency: if asked, the man-in-the-street with an opinion on the matter will usually say that it expresses an elitist ideal of art's separation from commercial or political exploitation (though he might not put it in those terms). Ironically, art for art's sake has been annexed by commercial interests precisely because of its perceived advocacy of artistic distinction. The most pervasive example of this is surely its use (in the Latin form *ars gratia artis*) as a corporate motto by the American media giant Metro-Goldwyn-Mayer Inc. That it has become part of the iconography of capitalism in this way was parodied in the song 'Art for Art's Sake', released in 1975 by the British pop group 10cc. The song has the refrain 'Art for art's sake, money for God's sake' (www.lyricsdownload.com): with an irony surely intentional, it functioned to increase its performers' personal wealth, reaching No.5 in the UK singles charts. These popular and commercial uses of the term, like those reviewed at greater length above, all relate fundamentally to the idea of aesthetic autonomy which caught Benjamin Constant's attention in 1804.

Was it ever thus?

While the answer to this question must, unsurprisingly, be 'no', the matter should not be left at that. The concluding section of this chapter will glance at some early views about the distinctive nature of art which can be connected with the idea that it exists for its own sake. Despite the occasional, and typically superficial, invocation of art for art's sake by contemporary historians of pre-eighteenth-century painting and sculpture (e.g. Hochstrasser 2007: 271), it is normal to suppose that the idea of art's autonomy, whether as an aspect of beauty or form, was impossible before the rise of Idealism in German philosophy. The art of ancient, medieval and early modern societies is usually characterised as rigidly functional in its expression of devotion or power, its status as entertainment (e.g. Plato), or its value as an emotional stimulant and purgative (e.g. Aristotle). Art, together with architecture, is thought to have constituted a form of communication used in conjunction with speech and writing. The Platonic theory of forms, despite its exploitation by twentieth-century philosophers concerned with aesthetic ontology (in particular the so-called 'type-token' theory of Richard Wollheim), has no place for representational art, which Plato thought imitative and thus lacking reality. His denial of form to art did not, however, extend to buildings, architectural elements (e.g. columns), or other aspects of visual culture which might now be considered art. Insofar as this is true, Plato's metaphysics can be argued to admit art in the modern sense, although they do not give it a distinct ontological status (all forms being ontologically undistinguishable).[9] Medievalists, whose period of study is particularly vulnerable to stereotyping by non-specialists, have reinforced the nostrum that art was purely subservient to religious faith and secular power. For example, in a now-classic study published in 1898, Émile Mâle, Focillon's predecessor at the Sorbonne, claimed that all French art of the thirteenth century was a sort of text, designed to express the central tenets of Christian belief. He considered this true of later medieval art as well (Luxford 2003). Yet, as noted, Focillon himself sought to distance the development of art and architecture in this period from function. The formalist construction of aesthetic autonomy permits this. There is nothing which restricts Bell's 'significant form', Focillon's form-in-art, or the perception of either, to the post-Kantian period. All three formalists discussed above illustrate their arguments liberally with medieval, Renaissance and Baroque art, which, even if it cannot communicate its makers' idiosyncratic experience of form, clearly (according to their line of argument) demonstrates the fact of this experience. Against this, the conventional, uncritical objection that medieval and Renaissance people had no concept of 'fine art' in the modern sense, that *ars* for them meant skill rather than its products, carries no force. Such an objection is in any case unsatisfactory insofar as it presupposes a fixed modern understanding of 'art', ignores the fact that practical and philosophical theories about painting, sculpture, metalwork, etc., existed in the Middle Ages, and assumes an unjustified omniscience about pre-modern aesthetic experience.[10]

Thus any validity which formalist aesthetics brings to the idea of artistic autonomy is not temporally constrained. What about the earlier belief in art's separateness and artists' superiority predicated on Kant's conception of the aesthetic as a domain discrete from science and morality? As noted, this idea is premised on errors, particularly, that all art belongs to the category of the beautiful, that only artists can formulate judgements about beauty-in-art, and that such judgements can be made independently of the morality which is one of man's defining characteristics. Historically, such ideas, and such errors, could only have arisen at a given time, among a particular class of individuals. It thus seems fruitless to try to align them with beliefs about art pre-Kant, even if Whistler and Wilde did quixotically claim moral detachment for the great artists of the past (Singer 1954: 351). However, some correspondences between opinions expressed by such nineteenth-century proponents of art for art's sake on the one hand and medieval thought on the other are worth noting, if only to demonstrate that the two are not completely ideologically incompatible. The belief that artists were special by virtue of their relationship to art was also current in the Middle Ages. As Rudolf Berliner has shown – and he has been followed in his observations by the likes of Meyer Schapiro and Michael Camille – far from operating under strict patronal constraint, artists played a part in shaping devotional agendas through their pictorialisation of written dogma, and even invented new religious iconography for which they might be held responsible (Berliner 1945). (Had they lacked the freedom to invent religious subject matter, this responsibility would have fallen to others when a matter of misuse or misinterpretation arose.) They thus had a unique role in revealing divine truths. Medieval artists enjoyed prestige conferred by their ability to convincingly represent Creation, too (Berliner 1945: 266–7).

This esteem had also existed in the Ancient World, whose most highly skilled artists, known through texts like Pliny the Elder's *Natural History* and the *Description of Greece* by Pausanias, provided role models and objects of nostalgic reflection for medieval and early modern artists and architects. Such names as Apelles, Daedalus (with whom surpassing medieval artists in particular were wont to be compared), Phidias, Polykleitos, Praxiteles, Parrhasius and Zeuxis, were imbued with a nigh-peerless prestige among men and women of learning, especially during the Renaissance and early modern periods. In the seventeenth century, Peter Paul Rubens (1577–1640), whose own contemporaries associated him with Apelles on the basis of his artistic ability, gushed of his 'profoundest reverence' for 'Apelles ... Timanthes ... [and] the dignity of the ancients': 'I adore their footsteps', he wrote (Magurn 1971: 407). Like praise was directed at Michelangelo, whom, for example, Giorgio Vasari spoke of as quasi-divine, and Sir Joshua

Reynolds idolised, most memorably in the *Self Portrait* of 1780 in the Royal Academy, London, and the last sentence of his final *Discourse* (Reynolds and Wart 1997: 282; Vasari *et al.* 1996: II, 643). While artists never appear to have been accorded super-human status before the early nineteenth century, the origins of the perception that they were aloof due to involvement with art must be sought long before the turn of the nineteenth century (Barker *et al.* 1999).

Finally, a link can be suggested between a central tenet of medieval aesthetics and the identification of Kantian beauty with God found in the work of some nineteenth-century writers, notably Théophile Gautier, who we have encountered above as an effusive proponent of art for art's sake in the 1830s. In his *L'Art moderne* (1856), Gautier stated both that '*L'art pour l'art* signifies a work disengaged from all preoccupation other than with the beautiful itself' and that 'in its absolute essence the beautiful is God'. He went on to invoke Plato and Wincklemann in support of the divinity of beauty (Wilcox 1953: 376–7). He might as well have invoked St Augustine, and the line of medieval thinkers that followed in his broad wake. Ultimate beauty, according to Augustine, is identical with God: 'Late have I loved thee, beauty so ancient and so new!' he wrote in his *Confessions*, describing the recentness of his conversion. Eight centuries later, and in different terms, St Thomas Aquinas made a similar equation, describing the Second Person of the Holy Trinity as 'the art of the omnipotent God', the very type of beauty and its three conditions, proportion, integrity and clarity. Indeed, unsurprisingly, many medieval writers on aesthetics associated beauty with God, and, to the extent that art was considered beautiful – and the lavish use of aesthetic language in medieval texts about art provide abundant testimony that it was – it participated in divine beauty (Bourke 1960: 269–78; Collinson 1992: 123; Crouse 2003: 19; Eco 1988: 64–71). How Gautier understood God was clearly very different from the ways in which medieval thinkers comprehended Him (the authorities he appeals to, if nothing else, show this). But what he wrote is sufficient to demonstrate a belief at least that art aspires to divinity and at most that it partakes of it, a conclusion which can also be drawn from medieval thought. Thus, while the term art for art's sake is unquestionably post-Enlightenment in its origins and use, it is at least reasonable to inquire whether the ideas it represents have any parallels with the theory and practice of earlier centuries.

Conclusion

The modern ideas collected around the term 'art for art's sake' respond to the anxieties of a post-Enlightenment age. The need to claim for a single product of human endeavour a privilege which sets it apart from quotidian experience can ultimately be understood as part of a secularist response to the absence of transcendence offered by religion. For the champions of art for art's sake, be they pseudo-Kantians, aesthetes or formalists, the artist transubstantiates mundane matter at his or her workbench or easel as the Catholic priest does at the altar during mass, creating, or at least enabling the expression of, an aesthetic phenomenon which hand cannot touch or mind fully appreciate. From a religious perspective (and not uniquely a Christian one), it is relatively easy to construe the aesthetic in sacred terms; to apprehend artistic beauty as an aspect of a divinity which functions to no definable end in itself. Thus the core concept of art for art's sake, as opposed to the all-too-human accretions which have gathered upon it, possesses a much broader historical relevance than is usually supposed.

Acknowledgements

I thank my wife, Claire Luxford, for the benefit of her musicological expertise, and her willingness to discuss the content of this essay.

Notes

1 I retain the title allotted to my paper by the organizers of the 'Art for art's sake?' workshop held at the University of St Andrews, 1 December 2006.
2 For a lucid overview of some of the main ideas associated with art for art's sake see Jenkins, I. (1973–4), 'Art for art's sake', in P. P. Wiener (ed.) *Dictionary of the History of Ideas*, I: 108–11, New York: Scribner. A more recent but less informative summary is Morgan, H. (1996) 'Art for art's sake', in J. Turner (ed.) *The Dictionary of Art*, II: 530, London and New York: Macmillan.
3 On the term's origins see for example Egan, R. F. (1921) 'The genesis of the theory of "art for art's sake" in Germany and England', *Smith College Studies in Modern Languages*, 2: 5–61; Rosenblatt, L. (1931) *L'Idée de l'art pour l'art dans la littérature anglaise pendant la période victorienne*, Paris: H. Champion; Wilcox 1953; Bell-Villada, G. H.

(1996) *Art for Art's Sake and Literary Life: How Politics and Markets Helped Shape the Ideology and Culture of Aestheticism, 1790–1990,* Lincoln, NE: University of Nebraska Press.

4 Ruskin's remarks provoked a trial for libel: see Lambourne, L. (1996) *The Aesthetic Movement,* London: Phaidon.

5 For Pater's Aestheticism and the constraints placed upon him see also Donoghue, D. (1995) *Walter Pater: Lover of Strange Souls,* New York: Knopf, particularly Chapter 28, 'Art for art's sake'.

6 'Pure art' was, for example, a term of Victor Cousin's: Wilcox 1953: 369.

7 For differences between the formalism of Bell and Fry which cannot be discussed here see Jutras, P. (1993) 'Roger Fry et Clive Bell: divergences fondamentales autour de la notion de "Significant form"', *Revue d'Art Canadienne/Canadian Art Review,* 20: 98–115.

8 See also Luxford, J. M. (2004) 'Focillon, Henri-Joseph', in C. Murray (ed.) *Encyclopedia of Modern French Thought*: 222–4, London and New York: Fitzroy Dearborn.

9 See the essays Hanfling, O. (1992) 'The ontology of art' in O. Hanfling (ed.) *Philosophical Aesthetics: An Introduction*: 75–110, Oxford: Blackwell, in association with the Open University, at 80–82 (type-token theory); and Hursthouse, R. (1992) 'Truth and representation' in O. Hanfling (ed.) *Philosophical Aesthetics: An Introduction*: 239–96, Oxford: Blackwell, in association with the Open University, at 239–52 (analysis of Plato's theories).

10 On these questions see, for example, Eco, U. and Bredin, H. (transl.) (1986) *Art and Beauty in the Middle Ages,* New Haven, CT, and London: Yale University Press, especially 92–115; Kessler, H. (2004) *Seeing Medieval Art,* Toronto: Broadview, especially 45–64; Theophilus, Dodwell, C. R. (ed. and transl.) (1961) *De diversis artibus,* London: T. Nelson.

References

Adams, E. B. (1971) *Bernard Shaw and the Aesthetes.* Columbus, OH: Ohio State University Press.

Barker, E., Webb, N. and Woods, K. (eds.) (1999) *The Changing Status of the Artist.* New Haven, CT, and London: Yale University Press.

Bell, C. (1961) *Art,* second edn. London: Arrow.

Benjamin, W., Zohn, H. (transl.) (1969) *Illuminations.* New York: Harcourt, Brace and World.

Berliner, R. (1945) 'The freedom of medieval art'. *Gazette des Beaux-Arts,* 38: 263–88.

Bourke, V.J. (ed.) (1960) *The Pocket Aquinas.* New York: Washington Square Press.

Brake, L. (2003) 'Walter Pater (1839–94)', in C. Murray (ed.) *Key Writers on Art: From Antiquity to the Nineteenth Century:* 230–6. London and New York: Routledge.

Collinson, D. (1992) 'Aesthetic Experience', in O. Hanfling (ed.) *Philosophical Aesthetics: An Introduction:* 111–78. Oxford: Blackwell, in association with the Open University.

Crouse, R. (2003) 'Augustine (354–430)', in C. Murray (ed.) *Key Writers on Art: From Antiquity to the Nineteenth Century:* 18–22. London and New York: Routledge.

Dahlhaus, C., Robinson, J.B. (transl.) (1989) *Nineteenth-Century Music.* Berkeley and Los Angeles, CA: University of California Press.

Eco, U. (1988) *The Aesthetics of Thomas Aquinas.* Cambridge, MA: Harvard University Press.

Eliot, T.S. (1976) *Selected Essays.* London: Faber.

Focillon, H., Hogan, C.B. and Kubler, G. (transls.) (1992) *The Life of Forms in Art.* New York: Zone Books.

Fry, R. (1920) *Vision and Design.* London: Chatto and Windus.

Goehr, L. *et al.* (2001) 'Philosophy of Music', in S. Sadie and J. Tyrrell (eds.) *The New Grove Dictionary of Music and Musicians,* second edn: XIX, 601–31. London and New York: Macmillan.

Greer, G. (2006) 'The Plain English Campaign have given me a "Golden Bull" award. Well, they can stuff it'. (*The Guardian*) available at www.guardian.co.uk/commentisfree/2006/dec/04/1 (accessed: 8 January 2009).

Harrison, C. and Wood, P. (2003) *Art in Theory 1900–2000: An Anthology of Changing Ideas.* Oxford: Blackwell.

Harrison, C. and Wood, P. (eds.) with J. Caiger (1998) *Art in Theory 1815–1900: An Anthology of Changing Ideas.* Oxford: Blackwell.

Hauser, A., Northcott, K. (transl.) (1979) 'The *l'art pour l'art* problem'. *Critical Inquiry,* 5: 425–40.

Hochstrasser, J.B. (2007) *Still Life and Trade in the Dutch Golden Age.* New Haven, CT, and London: Yale University Press.

Luxford, J.M. (2003) 'Émile Mâle (1862–1954)', in C. Murray (ed.) *Key Writers on Art: The Twentieth Century:* 204–11. London and New York: Routledge.

Magurn, R.S. (ed. and transl.) (1971) *The Letters of Peter Paul Rubens.* Cambridge, MA: Harvard University Press.

Prettejohn, E. (2007) *Art for Art's Sake: Aestheticism in Victorian Painting.* New Haven, CT, and London: Yale University Press.

Reynolds, Sir Joshua and Wark, R.R. (ed.) (1997) *Discourses on Art*. New Haven, CT, and London: Yale University Press.

Schoenberg, A., Stein, L. (ed.), Black, L. (transl.) (1984) *Style and Idea: Selected Writings of Arnold Schoenberg*. London and Boston: Faber.

Singer, I. (1954) 'The aesthetics of "art for art's sake"'. *Journal of Aesthetics and Art Criticism*, **12**: 343–58.

Spencer, R. (1972) *The Aesthetic Movement: Theory and Practice*. London: Studio Vista.

Swinburne, C.A. (1912) 'Morris's life and death of Jason', in S.V. Makower and B.H. Blackwell (eds.) *A Book of English Essays (1600–1900): 349–61*. Oxford University Press.

Vasari, G., de Vere, G. du C. (transl.), Ekserdjian, D. (introd.) (1996) *Lives of the Painters, Sculptors and Architects*, II. London: David Campbell.

Wilcox, J. (1953) 'Beginnings of l'art pour l'art'. *Journal of Aesthetics and Art Criticism*, **11**: 360–77.

www.lyricsdownload.com/10cc-art-for-art-s-sake-lyrics.html (accessed: 8 January 2009).

6 | The logics of art: analysing theatre as a cultural field

DORIS RUTH EIKHOF

A considerable amount of creative industries research has been devoted to the analysis of a putative conflict between art and business, creativity and control, Muse and management (see, for example, Bilton 2007; Caves 2000; Davis and Scase 2000; DeFillippi *et al.* 2007; Hartley 2005; Howkins 2001; Jeffcutt and Pratt 2002; Lampel *et al.* 2000; Strandgaard Pedersen *et al.* 2006). Artistic endeavour, creativity and spontaneity have been portrayed as central but somewhat unruly inputs of creative production, with artists and creatives 'passionately involved in their work' (Howkins 2001: 125) and valuing 'independence' and 'non-conformist ways' (Davis and Scase 2000: viii). Management in the creative industries thus has to create structures and processes that allow artistic and creative talent to flourish and at the same time lead to profitable outputs (see, for example, Bilton 2007; Davis and Scase 2000; Hesmondhalgh 2007).

This perspective on artistic production is typical for many studies of management, business and organisation: it focuses on the transformation of input into marketable output by analysing organisational forms, processes of production and management instruments. From this point of view, central management issues in the creative industries seem to be high production costs, unknown product success and the fact that products are semi-public goods, i.e. consumption by one person does not necessarily restrict consumptive value for another consumer (see, for example, Caves 2000; Hesmondhalgh 2007; Howkins 2001), as well as the inclination of artists and creatives to disobey management logic and to prioritise art for art's sake over product success and company revenue (see, for example, Alvarez *et al.* 2005; Bilton 2007; Davis and Scase 2000; Eikhof and Haunschild 2007). However, from a sociological perspective, the creative industries are described as an 'economic world reversed' (Bourdieu 1983), with not only individual motivation, but collective structures and dynamics that are distinct and at times diametrically opposed to those of other fields of economic production. Attempts 'to grasp this anti-economy in economic terms' (Bourdieu 1983: 321) and to apply business or management concepts can thus offer only partial insights.

This chapter aims to explore the potential of a sociological perspective for our understanding of artistic production in the creative industries. In particular, it will employ a practice theory perspective to analyse the logics driving artistic production. This analysis draws on Pierre Bourdieu's theory of practice as an analytical tool and on his description of the cultural field for empirical insight and applies both to a study of German theatre. Bourdieu has researched what he calls 'the field of cultural production' as an area of specific social activity. His sociological perspective allows investigating artistic work practices first and foremost as social practices produced by agents in a certain social setting and only secondly as practices embedded in employment relationships, careers and management structures. Applying this perspective in order to gain insight into the creative industries is justified for at least two reasons. Firstly, and as commonly acknowledged in creative industries research, individual artistic practices are the central resource of the creative industries and both subject and object of any attempt to organise creativity. They are thus the obvious starting point for any investigation of (managing and organising) artistic or creative work. Secondly, as individual artists do not think or act in concepts of business, management and organisations studies, taking into account the wider social context of artistic production promises a deeper insight into artistic production.

Bourdieu describes the field of cultural production as characterised by three aspects and the chapter is organised around these. After a brief outline of the theoretical and empirical background, the following sections describe the belief in art for art's sake prevalent in theatre; how the theatre industry maintains autonomy from economic imperatives; and how theatre actors strive for artistic recognition and in doing so follow unexpectedly economic rather than artistic logics. I then discuss how these quasi-economic logics are reconciled with the belief in art for art's sake. The conclusion evaluates the contribution of such a sociological perspective on artistic production.

Theoretical and empirical background

In his analysis of society, French sociologist Pierre Bourdieu seeks to understand various manifestations of the interplay between structure and agency (for the following see Bourdieu 1983, 1984, 1990, 1993). Bourdieu considers two aspects of structure: the allocation of resources agents draw on, which he describes as different forms of capital, and the logics, 'rules of the game' that govern the use and accumulation of such capital. With respect to agency, Bourdieu understands individuals as producing social practices, i.e. any enactment that can be observed and attributed to an individual, and drawing on their capital portfolio in doing so. He asserts that agents aim to maintain or increase the quantity and quality of their resources in order to secure current, or advance to more, powerful positions in society.

Bourdieu's analysis of social practices demonstrates how in different areas of society, fields, different logics for the successful use of capital prevail. A field constitutes a complex network of positions. Agents try to advance their individual situation in these fields by obtaining more powerful, secure or influential positions. These 'position-takings' (*prises de position*, Bourdieu 1983: 312) are governed by field-specific logics. Logics determine what benefits the investment of capital will bring, i.e. what chances of advancement via position-taking an agent with a given capital portfolio has. Typical fields include, for example, business, politics, academia or culture. The creative industries, as they have been addressed in the past ten years (Hesmondhalgh 2007; O'Connor 2007), can be understood as constituting a subfield of what Bourdieu refers to as 'the field(s) of cultural production', 'the artistic field' or 'the cultural field'.[1]

Drawing on extensive research, Bourdieu (1983, 1993) describes three key elements of the field of cultural production:

1. The cultural field comprises a structure of positions and practices of agents geared towards taking those positions (*prises de position*, position-takings): depending on the capital they command, agents can be in more or less powerful positions within the field. Their social practices are geared towards either maintaining or improving current positions via strategic investment and accumulation of capital.
2. According to Bourdieu (1983: 317), the cultural field is 'based on a particular form of belief', the paradigm of art for art's sake. This belief is the central logic that governs social practices and position-takings.
3. The cultural field has gained a 'relative autonomy' (Bourdieu 1983: 319) from its environment. Outside the field of cultural

production, the allocation of capital is organised by economic principles, for instance market values, returns on investment. Although the cultural field is never wholly independent from these economic principles, the belief in art for art's sake as well as various features resulting from this belief mark the cultural field as a space of social practice distinct from others. Bourdieu (1983: 320) points out how the field of cultural production is the more likely to 'fulfil its own logic as a field' the higher its relative autonomy.

The following sections will analyse each of these characteristics for a particular creative industry or artistic field – German theatre. They are based on a series of studies into work and employment in the German theatre industry conducted between 2000 and 2003 in collaboration with Axel Haunschild (see also Eikhof and Haunschild 2006, 2007; Haunschild 2003, 2004). The analysis mainly draws on data from semi-structured in-depth interviews (cf. King 1994) with theatre actors, theatre managers and directors. Within this group, thirty interviews were carried out and analysed along categories such as career aims, work motivation, perception of work situations, flexibility and spatial mobility. Additional information was collected at premiere celebrations, gatherings after shows and other cultural events (e.g. readings). Findings were derived from several rounds of independent and joint interpretations of the empirical data and were contrasted with interviews with experts (representatives of the national employers' and employees' associations, the state-run work agency for actors and a state-run theatre school) and secondary sources such as interviews with theatre artists in newspapers and practitioner journals, statistical reports and information given on theatres' and intermediary organisations' websites.

The paradigm of artistic production: *l'art pour l'art*

Bourdieu (1984, 1993) describes the field of cultural production as centred on the idea of art as a greater good that needs no external legitimisation. Art is seen as an abstract quality, as a transcendental phenomenon represented only in humankind's doings, and accounting for more than the sum of all works of art. This 'particular belief' (Bourdieu 1983: 317) translates into an 'artistic logic of practice', a logic that drives individual practices in the artistic field and that is marked by the desire to produce art for art's sake, *l'art pour l'art* (Eikhof and Haunschild 2007). But *l'art pour l'art* is not only 'for art', it is at the same time essentially 'against economic reasoning', against measurement, comparison and translation into monetary values. Bourdieu points out that, very famous paintings set aside, the more well-established the commercial value of a piece of art or an artistic practice, the less its reputation within the cultural field and the less a 'true' artist's motivation to produce it (Bourdieu 1983, 1993).

The empirical data showed this particular belief in *l'art pour l'art* to be very prominent in German theatre. Actors tended to regard their job as a vocation rather than an occupation. They felt called to devote their production of work practices entirely to the production of theatre art as a greater good.

Being on stage every night, doing what you are best at and being rewarded with applause and, even, money – that is just the most magnificent thing ever. Everything else becomes less important compared to that. (Actor)

Most actors had wanted to become actors since they were children and many could not even imagine working in another occupation. This strong intrinsic motivation helped in overcoming disadvantages other employees would not want to cope with. Even the subordination of the most private and personal aspects of life to work was accepted with an explicit devotion to theatre.

One reason for breaking up with my wife was that I had to change places so many times. Still, I do not regret moving around that much. (Actor)

For theatre artists, the idea of being part of 'the theatre world' and sharing cultural rather than materialistic or economic values was central to their self-perception. In their eyes, 'being something special' (Actor), 'not being one of those grey, worn-out blue- or white-collar workers' (Director) justified extreme dedication, if not devotion, to work. What seems disadvantageous from an external point of view – long-term spatial mobility, for instance – was often not perceived as disadvantageous, but was seen as an opportunity to commit one's whole personality to the higher mission of *l'art pour l'art*. Without such intrinsic drivers of artistic work practices, artistic inputs could not only be expected to be pricier (Caves 2000: 3), it can also be doubted that the disadvantages and (employment) uncertainties that come with occupation as an actress or actor would be accepted at all.

To sum up, the belief in art for art's sake that Bourdieu described as particular to the cultural field in general was certainly a strong theme in German theatre artists' narratives of work and employment.

German theatre's relative autonomy: public funding and *Kunstfreiheit*

According to Bourdieu (1983), a second characteristic of the field of cultural production is its relative autonomy from other fields. The most immediate and relevant other is the field of power, in which economic paradigms such as markets, investment and return are central. In this neighbouring field, social practices are predominantly driven by economic logics of practice (Bourdieu 1983; Eikhof and Haunschild 2007). At the heart of the economic logic of practice lies an explicit market orientation. The particular belief of this field is that individuals gain benefits from exchanging goods and services via markets of various kinds. Consequently, practices produced following economic logics often involve attempts to measure quantity and quality of output in order to foster market exchange and to achieve cost efficiency. It is mainly this economic logic that the cultural field requires to be relatively autonomous from (Bourdieu 1983). Applying Bourdieu's perspective of relative autonomy to the German theatre industry, two features appear as particularly important.

The first feature is public funding. Nearly all German theatres of artistic significance are public theatres owned by cities or states and are publicly funded. This unique set-up[2] has its roots in the Age of Enlightenment, particularly in the writings of dramatist and philosopher Friedrich Schiller (1759–1808; see e.g. Schiller 1931, 2000). Schiller, a close companion of other founding fathers of German theatre such as Johann Wolfgang von Goethe, claimed '[the stage] is a great school of practical wisdom, a guide for civil life, and a key to the mind in all its sinuosities' and thus 'a standing theatre would be a material advantage to a nation' (Schiller 1931: 189 and 191). In Schiller's tradition, theatres – along with other cultural institutions – are still regarded as fulfilling cultural and educational functions similar to those of schools and universities in Germany today. This view is institutionalised in Article 5 (3) of the German constitution which establishes the state's obligation to publicly fund the production of art – and, consequently, theatre.

Supported by Schiller's tradition of thought and surprisingly unharmed by 200 years of changing political systems, German theatre developed from royal theatre groups at court and free citizens' theatres into an industry that now comprises around 150 publicly funded theatres (Simhandl 2001; Waidelich 1991). The respective cities or local states finance up to 95 per cent of these theatres' annual budgets via income tax (Pitz and Köhn 2001). At the time of the study, 2002/03, total subsidiaries for all German theatres amounted to €2,144 billion. Medium-sized and reasonably commercially successful theatres had annual budgets of €20–23 million, of which typically only 12–15 per cent stemmed from ticket sales and merchandising and the remaining 85–88 per cent were public subsidies. The most commercially successful public theatre, the Thalia Theater Hamburg, still earned as little as 23.4 per cent of its annual budget itself (all figures Deutscher Bühnenverein 2004).

Article 5 (3) of the German constitution is also at the root of the second feature relating to the relative autonomy of the theatre industry. Scarred by the experiences of the Third Reich, the current German constitution establishes the principle of *Kunstfreiheit*, literally: freedom of art. *Kunstfreiheit* protects the right of artists to produce art of any content as long as they do not violate other constitutional rights, especially that of human dignity. This constitutional right of *Kunstfreiheit* is highly relevant for the management of theatres. The responsibility for a theatre's artistic output lies solely with one artist, the theatre manager or '*Intendant*'. The German word *Intendant*, which does not translate into English, is particular to the field of cultural production: it denotes a position of artistic leadership, for instance at an opera, theatre or concert hall, and does not carry any connotation of management or administration (although an *Intendant*'s remit does include managerial and administrative tasks). An *Intendant* will be appointed and employed by the local city or state government first and foremost for their artistic reputation. As their brief is to lead the theatre in fulfilling its artistic and educational functions, the constitutionally guaranteed *Kunstfreiheit* limits the employing government's influence on how that brief is fulfilled. *Kunstfreiheit* thus grants theatres independence from their funders.

From the perspective of relative autonomy, the principles of public funding and *Kunstfreiheit* are crucial to the German theatre industry as a subfield of cultural production. The reference to and application of these principles marks theatre as a field of production that is – in its artistic or cultural essence – distinct from other fields of production. Like other industries, theatre produces experience goods that are purchased by consumers and that thus become subject to economic logics of market exchanges. But public funding and *Kunstfreiheit* make German theatres independent from the economic logics of the market, from consumers' tastes, purchasing decisions and powers. The empirical study revealed a number of indicators of this relative autonomy:

- In 2002/03, subsidies per ticket sold ranged from €62 to €190 across the whole industry (Deutscher Bühnenverein 2004), considerably freeing theatres from the pricing policy challenges experienced by for-profit organisations in the entertainment industry.
- Actors' narratives showed them to be almost solely concerned with the artistic content of their work. If finances were mentioned, it was with respect to individual income and not to theatres as (employing) organisations or the theatre industry in general.
- Actors and directors stated that they preferred to play for a small, but appreciating audience rather than for a 'theatre full of ignoramuses', without giving the economic implications of small audiences in large venues any mention.
- Actors' perceptions of theatre managers focus on the *Intendant*'s artistic leadership and their artistic advice to actors – despite the *Intendant*'s various and often publicly undertaken managerial and administrative tasks.
- Members of theatre management did mention budgeting and the existence of financial constraints but saw them as quasi-natural parts of their job. Without budgeting, they recounted, directors, costume and stage designers would happily let spending spiral out of control while pursuing grand artistic ideas. While some smaller theatres undoubtedly experience financial difficulties that impinge on artistic production (Briegleb 2005), larger theatres like those researched 'have definitely got no reason to whinge' (*Intendant* Ulrich Khuon in Briegleb 2005).
- At one of the theatres researched, the manager's contract came up for renewal and the city's Minister for Culture announced that for artistic reasons it would not be prolonged. Despite the fact that the *Intendant* had considerably overstretched the budget in his reign,

the ensuing heated public debate focused on artistic issues, indicating how not only theatre artists themselves, but also politicians, the media and the public recognise that theatrical production is judged by non-economic criteria.

The above examples illustrate how relative autonomy from the economic logic of product markets enables German theatre to concentrate on theatre as a production of art. Theatres can focus on fulfilling their artistic and educational function without worrying about the commercial viability of their products or their funder's artistic agenda. The role of public funding and *Kunstfreiheit* in securing this autonomy is illustrated in a quote from an experienced and influential *Intendant*: 'The truth is that I do not know any colleague who has let economic pressure influence, let alone dictate, their artistic programme' (*Intendant* Frank Baumbauer in Briegleb 2005). The Bourdieuan perspective of relative autonomy thus helps to pinpoint not only the importance relative autonomy has for daily production in theatre, but also those industry features that secure autonomy in this field.

Position-taking in German theatre: the accumulation of artistic prestige

Given that public funding and *Kunstfreiheit* shield German theatre to a large extent from market pressures, the artistic logic of practice should be dominating this field. However, a surprisingly economic theme emerged from theatre artists' narratives of work and employment: actors seemed to calculate work efforts and results very consciously and while, as demonstrated in section two, the logic of art for art's sake was important to them, certainly not all their practices could be interpreted as driven purely by a desire to produce art.

In order to understand why actors display such calculating rationales, Bourdieu's perspective of *prises de position* can be applied. Bourdieu describes how agents try to advance their position in a field. These position-takings require the investment and accumulation of those resources that are most valuable in a given field. In the field of cultural production, the most valuable resource is 'artistic prestige' (Bourdieu 1983: 320).[3] Artistic prestige is understood as a signal of an agent's capability to produce art that will be recognised and successful. In theatre, an actor's artistic prestige is ascribed and judged with respect to four areas:

1. *Roles and productions.* The quantity and quality of roles played and the reputation of the productions these roles were part of contribute to an actor's artistic prestige. Demanding lead roles in productions of high artistic reputation are more valuable as signals of artistic capability than support roles or roles in lesser known productions. Additionally, certain roles and plays are regarded as artistic milestones in an actor's career, such as Shakespeare's Lady Macbeth or Goethe's Mephisto.

2. *Appointments and employers.* Within the German theatre industry, theatres are explicitly ranked and referred to as 'A-house', 'B-house' or 'province' (see also Caves' (2000) observation on the stratification of labour markets in the creative industries). Although a theatre's reputation depends on the current *Intendant*, theatres such as the Burgtheater Wien or the Hamburger Schauspielhaus are generally regarded as A-houses and working for them will enhance artistic prestige. German actors are either employed as ensemble members on a one-year temporary contract or as freelancers for one production (see also Haunschild 2003, 2004; Eikhof and Haunschild 2007), which introduces additional ranking nuances: a history of freelance work with A-houses only is most prestigious, followed by ensemble employment for A- and B-houses. Working as a freelance for provincial theatres only contributes least to one's artistic prestige.

3. *Partners in a production.* The directors, theatre managers and fellow actors with whom an actor has worked in a specific production or at a theatre in general are also interpreted as signals of artistic capability. Working with renowned partners, for instance with a director whose production has just been voted 'Play of the Year' or with an actor or actress who has previously been recognised for his or her artistic work, enhances artistic prestige.

4. *Publicised evaluations.* Positive reviews in leading national newspapers and prizes and awards (e.g. Best New Actor, Best Actress) increase artistic prestige. Reviews in national newspapers such as *DIE ZEIT* or *Frankfurter Allgemeine Zeitung* represent the most influential and regularly publicised assessment of cultural production in theatre. Prizes and awards are often given by leading

journals in the field and at theatre festivals, and being a laureate can increase artistic prestige significantly.

The interviews showed that theatre actors did not define their success in monetary terms, for instance by the wages they can command, but by recognition within the field. Gaining artistic prestige can satisfy an actor's personal ambition to be recognised by peers and experts in the field and to achieve their goal of producing art. However, artistic prestige is also vital for staffing decisions: the more artistic prestige an agent possesses, the more capable potential employers will believe they are and the higher their chances of being cast for a play or as an ensemble member. Artistic prestige crucially influences whether an artist is given the chance to participate in the production of art for art's sake. However, to accumulate artistic prestige, actors have to participate in productions. Participation in productions is both the vehicle and the result of the accumulation of artistic prestige.

Participation in the production of art is linked to employment. A- and B-houses will recruit early-career actors from established drama schools based on degree shows and less reputed theatres will hire from less renowned drama schools. As a result, drama school auditions constitute the first important hurdle in the accumulation of artistic prestige. Once they have entered the theatre industry, actors will be hired on the basis of previous work. In Germany, actors will be offered contracts either as ensemble members or as freelancers (see Eikhof and Haunschild 2007; Haunschild 2003, 2004). Although ensemble members' employment contracts span the whole season, ensemble actors are not guaranteed to participate in every production. Similar to players in a football team, ensemble actors are selected for some plays and will be left out of others. This creates a strong competition for participation in productions and, as outlined above, for participation in prestigious positions, i.e. artistically renowned roles or with prestigious colleagues. Labour market competition both for ensemble contracts and freelance jobs is fierce, which further adds to the pressure of securing participation in prestigious production for all actors: a job in a prestigious production will not only secure the current position, but also make the future maintenance or improvement of that position more likely.

As a consequence, *prises de position*, maintaining or improving their positions in the subfield by securing current (employment) positions or advancing to more prestigious appointments, is the actors' main focus. Interestingly, these position-takings were not necessarily cast as enhancements of careers or securing of employment, but rather in terms of 'being able to play' or 'being part of the theatre world'. Interviewees would not speak about 'going to work' but simply of 'going in [to theatre]'; instead of 'working' they would almost exclusively use 'playing' and 'rehearsing'. Nevertheless, the interviews showed that although they are not cast in economic terms, position-taking and accumulation of artistic prestige are pursued explicitly and strategically:

If you want to work with a certain director, you have to actively seek contact with him or at least make sure that he – through third parties – gets to know about your interest. (Actress)

Actors consciously calculate the allocation of their creative resources …

If I'm shooting a film with a prestigious director in the morning and am scheduled to play a minor character in the nightly show the same day – I don't think twice about how to allocate my energies for that day. I'm sure the theatre manager won't like it, but that's just the way it goes. (Actor)

… and control the outcome of their efforts:

You are not only exposed to external judgement all the time, you also constantly monitor your own work … There is a low barrier to panic and you are always afraid that you will be cast for too little or too small roles – you are always afraid that theatre management and audience will not love you enough. (Actor)

These quotes are indicative of the input-output and investment-return calculations that underlie many actors' narratives and that are part of the economic logic of practice rather than the artistic one. In a similar vein, actors strategically chose with whom they surrounded themselves in the theatre canteen and at premiere parties. In addition, position-taking governed private life: actors reported buying flatpack furniture since it was easiest to move houses with and not wanting children or a permanent partner as such commitments would limit their spatial mobility and chronological flexibility. To sum up: due to the ensemble system, German theatre actors enjoy considerably more job security than actors in other countries. Nevertheless, their narratives often documented more strategic position-taking than a desire to produce art for art's sake.

Bourdieu (1983) points out that although paradigms and logic of practice in the artistic field are different from the economic logics of its environment, the mechanisms of position-takings are similar. In both the field of cultural production and its environment, positions are taken via the accumulation of resources or capital. Although the resource most crucial in the artistic field is artistic prestige and although the logic of accumulation may be centred on art for art's sake, the mechanism is still one of accumulation and thus lends itself to strategy and calculation – as the above reported findings of strategic *prises de position* and accumulation of artistic prestige illustrate. Bourdieu's insight into *prises de position* thus helps to explain the seemingly economic theme in actors' narratives of work and employment: the dominating principle in the field of cultural production is art for art's sake and thus anti-economic, but the art for art's sake principle requires those who want to participate in the production of art to acquire recognition as artists, and this recognition is achieved via strategic accumulation of artistic prestige and via strategic *prises de positions*. Such strategic and calculating practices are typical symptoms of the economic logic of practice. The actors' behaviour thus seemed economical when in fact it was the result of the position-taking that is indigenous and central to the artistic field.

Reconciling art for art's sake and position-taking

The previous sections have described how even in a field dominated by the belief in art for art's sake and shielded from market pressures, quasi-economic logics still play an important role. Theatre artists strive to produce art for art's sake and are subject to the quasi-economic logic of position-takings at the same time. Elsewhere we have demonstrated that when economic logic meets artistic logic in cultural production, the former tends to crowd out the latter (Eikhof and Haunschild 2007). What then is the relationship between the artistic logic and the quasi-economic logic of position-taking? Bourdieu (1983: 353) initially assumed that artists had to be oblivious to the quasi-economic logics prevailing in the artistic field, because 'lucidity would make the [...] artistic undertaking itself a cynical mystification' and thus damage the belief in art for art's sake which is the artists' central

motivation and creative resource. However, he did find some indication of such lucidity, and the awareness of tensions between art for
art's sake and the quasi-economic logic of position-takings did indeed
emerge as a key theme from the study of theatre, too.

All interviewees' narratives indicated some degree of consciousness
of and discomfort with the underlying quasi-economic rationale of
position-taking, which supports Bourdieu's suspicion of the negative effect of strategic position-taking on artistic motivation. Equally
prominent in the artists' narratives was a wide-spread strategy of
(self-)protection: denial. This finding became particularly obvious in
the discussion of a key vehicle of position-takings, networking. One
actor's statement was both indicative and typical: 'Oh yes, everybody
does it [strategic networking], but I don't, really. I'm not that kind.'
Such statements would typically contradict not only the interviewees'
own accounts of, for instance, how they got jobs or their colleagues'
claims about 'everybody else's' behaviour, but also participant observations at premiere celebrations that clearly showed the actors engaging in networking. The frequency and conviction with which such
statements were made despite contradicting evidence suggests that
(self-)denial is the central strategy to reconcile tensions between a
belief in art for art's sake and awareness of the quasi-economic logics of position-taking. To a remarkable extent, actors simply denied
seeing themselves and being seen as strategically acting, calculating
accumulators of artistic prestige. Instead, they emphasised the intrinsic satisfaction that came with their job.

The individual self-denial is complemented by theatrical human
resource management (HRM) practices. Formal HRM geared towards
ensemble actors was limited to recruitment, contract negotiations
and staffing decisions (see also Haunschild 2003). Staffing decisions
were officially communicated via notice board announcements listing
the cast for each play approximately three weeks before rehearsals
started. Apart from that, actors were provided with scripts and schedules and were expected to organise the remainder themselves. Any
additional HRM consisted of one-on-one talks amongst theatre managers, dramaturges (roughly: assistants of the *Intendant*), directors
and actors and was thus, as all interviewees confirmed, a decidedly
individual and idiosyncratic affair. Comparing different leaders they
had worked with, interviewees reported how it depended on the personalities as well as the artistic prestige and their own artistic prestige

in relation to that of the leader whether they would accept requests or suggestions in rehearsals or generally put in extra effort: 'Well, if it's *him* [*Intendant*], you'd do it' (Actor).

Crucially, such personalisation of HRM practices allows casting all decisions as personal artistic ones and thus integrating the quasi-economic logics of position-taking as represented in staffing decisions and recruitment into an artistic work relationship focused on art for art's sake. However, the individualisation of HRM and lack of transparent routines and clear-cut criteria also allowed for considerable evasiveness, crookedness and even outright dishonesty, as members of the theatre management described:

Working in theatre is at the same time social-democratic and dishonest. (Dramaturge)

Despite all leadership efforts to the contrary, the underlying tendency is dishonest, because openness is too strenuous and hurtful. (*Intendant*)

The general perception seemed to be that the tensions between art for art's sake and the quasi-economic logic of position-taking cannot be reconciled on a collective level, but have to be dealt with by each artist individually, depending on their artistic convictions, their ability to tolerate ambiguity or, failing this, their capacity for (self-) denial. Partly, artistic practices themselves seem to provide an escape from these tensions: by immersing themselves in art, theatre artists escape the irreconcilable tensions these practices are embedded in.

Conclusion

The aim of this chapter was to study German theatre from a sociological point of view and to analyse the logics driving artistic production. Applying Bourdieu's characterisation of the field of cultural production to the German theatre industry has highlighted that, like other artistic fields, German theatre is characterised by a 'particular belief' in art for art's sake. The production of art is regarded as needing no external legitimisation and artists understand themselves as following a calling to partake in the production of *l'art pour l'art*. The belief in art for art's sake can prevail as the field's central paradigm because public funding and the principle of *Kunstfreiheit* grant German theatre considerable autonomy from the economic imperatives of meeting business demands and surviving on the market. On the individual level participation in the production of art for art's sake requires continuous position-taking and accumulation of artistic prestige. Both activities constitute social practices that seem to be driven by economic rationales rather than an ambition to produce *l'art pour l'art*. In the constant accumulation of artistic logic and position-taking a quasi-economic logic of practice prevails in this field that is otherwise so well protected against economic pressures.

At first glance, these findings seem to resonate with a general theme of the creative industries discourse, the putatively conflicting relationship between business and art, between suits and creatives outlined in the introduction. Elsewhere we have analysed this putative conflict as the relationship between artistic and economic logics and have found that while product market pressures are suspended in the German theatre industry, tight labour markets force actors to act according to economic logics when marketing and selling their own labour power (Eikhof and Haunschild 2007). However, the sociological analysis undertaken in this chapter has revealed that actors' practices are not only driven by market-oriented economic logics, but also by the quasi-economic logic of position-taking. The latter is a logic indigenous and central to artistic production: artists are driven by the need to accumulate artistic prestige and to take positions that enable their occupants to participate in the production of art in the first place. But while the vehicle of position-takings may be unique (accumulation of artistic prestige as opposed to accumulation of economic and/or symbolic capital), the mechanism of position-takings is essentially the same as in the artistic field's economically dominated environment (accumulation of capital). These structural homologies result in synergies between the need to self-market and sell labour power on the labour market and the logic of artistic position-taking. Consequently, actors experience little if any need to reconcile artistic position-taking and economically driven labour market behaviour. However, both economic logics of labour markets and quasi-economic position-takings tend to contradict the belief in art for art's sake. Economic logic in particular is likely to crowd out artistic motivation. Extrinsic monetary rewards threaten to supersede intrinsic artistic motivation and thus active reconciliation is required (Eikhof and Haunschild 2007). Artistic *prises de position* and *l'art pour l'art* enjoy a similar relationship: the prosaic realities of position-takings cause such discomfort to the artistic conscience that denying the strategic activities of *prises de position* is a frequent reconciliation tactic. While economic logic and artistic position-takings can co-exist or even be complementary, their relationship with the artistic logic of art for art's sake is considerably more controversial.

The key contribution of the sociological analysis presented here is twofold. First, it has highlighted that what is commonly believed to be a clashing of art and business is more likely to be a *ménage a trois* between three logics influencing artistic production: the belief in art for art's sake, the quasi-economic logic of artistic position-takings and the economic logic of the market. The management of artistic production will thus not only face tensions between art and business or creativity and control. It will also have to be aware of artists' need to reconcile art for art's sake with artistic position-takings. Second, while such reconciliation of logics has previously been described mainly at the interface of organisational functions, for instance between cultural bureaucrats and creative workers in the BBC (Davis and Scase 2000) or between account managers and copywriters in advertising (Grabher 2002), this chapter has shown that different logics need to be reconciled at the individual level as well if artistic endeavours are to be pursued. The sociological analysis can be developed to research those points at which the fragile equilibria of the *ménage a trois* are in danger. It seems to be plausible, for instance, that the higher the relative autonomy of an artistic field the easier the reconciliation of art for art's sake and the quasi-economic position-takings for individuals.

Nevertheless, both theoretical reasoning and empirical data suggest that the latent conflicts between the three logics cannot fully be resolved, especially not in the way managerial approaches might prefer them to be solved in a user manual-like way. As an *Intendant* put it:

The basic schizophrenia in theatre is that you ask your actors to understand themselves as independent, creative and critical partners, while at the same time you expect them to dispose of their independence on the spot and at your discretion, whenever decisions simply have to be accepted as orders and have to be carried out. *(Intendant)*

However, as threatening as this basic schizophrenia may look from a managerial point of view, from a sociological point of view this symptom of artistic production has its cause in the same condition that makes creative industries what they are: the individual aspiration to produce art for art's sake.

Notes

1 Throughout this chapter, these terms will be used interchangeably.
2 A similar structure of publicly funded theatres exists in Switzerland and Austria, however.
3 In a more precise application of Bourdieu's concepts, artistic prestige would be understood as a symbolic form of incorporated cultural capital, i.e. a recognised symbol of an agent's artistic capabilities (see Bourdieu 1984). For ease of reading I will use the term artistic prestige throughout this analysis, as Bourdieu (1983) does.

References

Alvarez, J. L., Mazza, C., Strandgaard Pedersen, J. and Svejenova, S. (2005) 'Shielding idiosyncrasy from isomorphic pressures: towards optimal distinctiveness in European film making'. *Organization,* 12(6): 863–88.

Bilton, C. (2007) *Management and Creativity: From Creative Industries to Creative Management.* Malden: Blackwell Publishing.

Bourdieu, P. (1983) 'The field of cultural production, or: the economic world reversed'. *Poetics,* 12: 311–56.

(1984) *Distinction: A Social Critique of the Judgement of Taste.* London: Routledge and Kegan Paul.

(1990) *The Logic of Practice.* Cambridge: Polity Press.

(1993) *The Field of Cultural Production: Essays on Art and Literature.* New York: Columbia University Press.

Briegleb, T. (2005) 'Wer A ist, muss auch B sagen'. *Die neue Klassengesellschaft? Theater heute Jahrbuch 2005:* 4–18. Berlin, Friedrich-Berlin-Verl.-Ges.

Caves, R. (2000) *Creative Industries: Contracts between Art and Commerce.* Cambridge, MA: Harvard University Press.

Davis, H. and Scase, R. (2000) *Managing Creativity: The Dynamics of Work and Organization.* Buckingham: Open University Press.

DeFillippi, R., Grabher, G. and Jones, C. (2007) 'Introduction to paradoxes of creativity: managerial and organizational challenges in the cultural economy'. *Journal of Organizational Behavior,* 28(5): 511–21.

Deutscher Bühnenverein (Bundesverband deutscher Theater) (2004) *Theaterstatistik 2002/2003 Vol. 38.* Köln: DBV.

Eikhof, D. R., and Haunschild, A. (2006) 'Lifestyle meets market: Bohemian entrepreneurs in creative industries'. *Creativity and Innovation Management,* 15(3): 234–41.

(2007) 'For art's sake! Managing artistic and economic logics in creative production'. *Journal for Organizational Behavior,* 28(5): 523–38.

Grabher, G. (2002) 'The project ecology of advertising: tasks, talents and teams'. *Regional Studies,* 36(3): 245–62.

Hartley, J. (ed.) (2005) *Creative Industries*. Malden: Blackwell.

Haunschild, A. (2003) 'Managing employment relationships in flexible labour markets: the case of German repertory theatres'. *Human Relations*, 56(8): 899–929.

—— (2004) 'Employment rules in German theatres: an application and evaluation of the Theory of Employment Systems'. *British Journal of Industrial Relations*, 42(4): 685–703.

Hesmondhalgh, D. (2007) *The Cultural Industries*, second edn. London: Sage.

Howkins, J. (2001) *The Creative Economy: How People Make Money from Ideas*. London: Penguin.

Jeffcutt, P. and Pratt, A.C. (2002) 'Managing creativity in the cultural industries'. *Creativity and Innovation Management*, 11(4): 225–33.

King, N. (1994) 'The qualitative research interview', in C. Cassell and G. Symon (eds.) *Qualitative Methods in Organizational Research: A Practical Guide*. London: Sage.

Lampel, J., Lant, T. and Shamsie, J. (2000) 'Balancing act: learning from organizing practices in cultural industries'. *Organization Science*, 11(3): 263–9.

O'Connor, J. (2007) 'Cultural industries: a critical bibliography'. Unpublished mimeo, Leeds.

Pitz, C. and Köhn, M. (2001) 'Öffentliche Trägerschaft – aber wie?' *Die Deutsche Bühne*, 7: 26–9.

Schiller, F. (1931) 'The stage as a moral institution', in L. Thomas (ed.) *Gems of the World's Best Classics*. Chicago: The Geographical Publishing Co.

—— (2000) *Über die ästhetische Erziehung des Menschen in einer Reihe von Briefen*. Stuttgart: Reclam.

Simhandl, O. (2001) *Theatergeschichte in einem Band*. Berlin: Henschel Verlag.

Strandgaard Pedersen, J., Svejenova, S., Jones, C. and de Weerd-Nederhof, P. (2006) 'Editorial: Transforming creative industries: strategies of and structures around creative entrepreneurs'. *Creativity and Innovation Management*, 15(3): 221–3.

Waidelich, J.-D. (1991) *Theatermanagement/Theaterorganisation. Teil I: Problemaufriß und Geschichte des Theatermanagements bis zur Gegenwart*. Hagen: Fernuniversität.

7 | Turning rebellion into money: The Clash, creativity and resistance to commodification

STEPHEN LINSTEAD

Musicians are exemplary agents who, through their creative practice, demonstrate how one might act differently, and in so doing, rebut, at least to some extent, the exigencies of the capitalist system. The question is, though, how can this happen? In what sense might creativity emerge from the very social relations which perpetuate domination?

(Toynbee 2006: 71)

> No slimy deals, with smarmy eels – in Hitsville UK
> Lets shake'n say, we'll operate – in Hitsville UK
> The mutants, creeps and musclemen
> Are shaking like a leaf
> It blows a hole in the radio
> When it hasn't sounded good all week
> A mike'n'boom, in your living room – in Hitsville UK
> No consumer trials, or AOR, in Hitsville UK
> Now the boys and girls are not alone
> Now that Hitsville's hit UK
> (The Clash (1981) 'Hitsville UK'. Sony Music
> Entertainment (UK) Ltd. from the Columbia
> album *Sandinista!*)

Introduction

In this chapter I pursue the dilemma of commodification that creative artistes working in a commercial system experience, explored through critical themes in the work of UK punk band The Clash (Topping 2003). The critical themes present in their work are music as cultural resistance/revolutionary form; work, employment and opportunity; domestic fascism; urban dispossession and multiculturalism; and global politics and postcolonialism. The pursuit is ultimately inconclusive, as we might expect, but illuminates some of the dynamic and often excruciating tensions involved in commercializing creative resistance whilst producing perhaps the most musically complex, professionally influential, politically energized, commercially successful and artistically enduring body of work by any of the punk bands.

'Origination is perhaps more instinct than inspiration'[1]

Joe Strummer's words above capture a concern he had also raised in '(White Man) in Hammersmith Palais' with a thrust at emerging punk rock bands who were not concerned with learning about the underlying political dynamics of social relationships that energized their music, or new musical forms of expressing them, but were too busy 'fighting for a good place under the lighting' and 'turning rebellion into money'. In 'Death or Glory' Strummer also levelled his caustic pen at a situation where:

> … every gimmick-hungry yob digging gold from rock'n'roll
> Grabs the mike to tell us he'll die before he's sold
> But I believe in this and it's been tested by research
> He, who fucks nuns, will later join the church

The irony of course is that Strummer's band, The Clash, were seen by many to be the biggest villains in contributing to this situation, with editor Mark P.(erry) of punk fanzine *Sniffin' Glue* opining that 'Punk died the day The Clash signed to CBS' (which they did on 25 January 1977 for an advance of £100,000, and which, unlike the Sex Pistols, was to be their only label) (Perry 1977). CBS were the biggest and perhaps most conservative record label of the day and The Clash's struggle with the commercial demands of such a relationship ultimately took a toll on their creativity. Strummer was particularly torn between his ambition to make great music that would challenge people to question the way they thought and acted, and the need to be commercially successful in order to reach the widest possible audience – a tension that ultimately stretched him to the limit and arguably into hypocrisy. But at the time they signed to CBS the band only received an allowance from their manager, Bernie Rhodes, and continued for some period to live and work in surroundings that were close to the high-rise and squat culture from which they had emerged. Furthermore, as with all advances, it was in effect a loan against future royalty earnings that tied the band, not to the five albums they originally thought, but gave CBS options on up to as many as ten. But rather than being suppressed by this, the band unusually revealed the conflicts they had with the label (as in 'Complete Control' – a single critical of the very label it was released on, which was not the case with the Sex Pistols' song 'EMI'). Indeed, the band were as self-obsessed as any contemporary rap or hip-hop artists, as David Quantick (2000: 121) pithily notes, from the early 'Garageband' (whose argument was basically 'we are a garage band and defy the oppressor', a category that includes the critics and some of the neighbours) to the late and ironic 'We Are The Clash' (which by this time, with the loss of two original members and the musical interference of the manager, they manifestly weren't) they constantly wrote about themselves. This also meant that the band could not duck the contradictions they faced, and they took their political beliefs into real life (which in fact was where they originally came from) rather than leaving them within some abstract musical relation (as the Sex Pistols did).

Creativity, and the often ascetic conditions that it needed to flourish, were vital to Strummer, as was working to develop and maintain a line of political critique somewhere between the mood of the streets and the workings of the intellect. The dilemma that the group faced – that of needing to criticize the features of a commercial system that simultaneously elevated them to a position of international influence that would have otherwise been impossible, whilst threatening to sanitize and censor the very voice that had made them distinctive and popular enough to invite such treatment – was not essentially new, either to rock'n'roll or the arts more generally. Bob Dylan, who remained with the same CBS label as The Clash and Abba, had struggled over the same terrain publicly for years and by the late 70s was himself entering a creative crisis. But The Clash experienced it under a new set of conditions, and with a different set of resources both to sustain and challenge them. In this struggle they could, however, be romantic and pragmatic, self-mythologizing, manipulated and manipulating as well as resistant. They told lies to each other, they fell in love with romanticized aspects of the same America that they criticized, they were guilty of hypocrisy, they dumped their friends, they lost contact with their UK fans, and they admitted that they had publicly told some untruths about themselves. In this chapter then, I am going to examine the response of The Clash to the conflicts and contradictions of being creative and critical in a commercialized culture industry that commodifies artistes, and reflect on 'what there is to be learned' (Strummer, '(White Man) in Hammersmith Palais', 1978). The Clash were both important members and outspoken critics of the industry in which they worked and offer important insights into the fragile relations between creativity, commercialism and critique, and the potential significance of management approaches in this.

The commercial clash

The Clash were the most successful of the punk bands of the 70s – commercially, globally and musically, producing 'one of the most impressive catalogues in modern musical history' (Fletcher 2005: 4; Topping 2003). They are widely regarded as one of the most influential bands of the rock era, with Bruce Springsteen and U2 amongst those inspired.[2] They became one of the founding bands of punk in the UK, producing in their first album what has been regarded as '*the Great British punk statement*' (Fletcher 2005), and, after the demise of the Sex Pistols, its main spokespersons. They constantly articulated a vision personally and through the music media, and struggled – not without considerable self-contradiction – to stay in touch with that vision whilst 'staying aware' as Strummer often put it, developing it as their music, ideas and personalities, which were frequently not at one, matured.

In early interviews The Clash developed a Beatles-style John-Paul-George triumvirate (at that time they did not have a stable drummer) and established their rock personae and their personal mythologies based on their reconstructed biographies. Joe Strummer (rhythm guitar and lyrics) laid out the punk manifesto. The former public schoolboy turned hippie (who changed his name from John 'Woody' Mellor) declared that the hippie movement had failed as it was never revolutionary enough, as former revolutionaries grew bloated on the luxuries of stardom with a self-indulgence reflected in the form and content of their music (glam-progressive keyboardist Rick Wakeman became iconic of this). The Clash declared themselves to be anti-denim, anti-drugs, anti-*Top of the Pops*, anti-fascist, anti-racist, anti-violence and pro-creative. Mick Jones (lead guitar and music composition) was particularly concerned that their outspoken stance would produce expectations that they would fail to satisfy (which inevitably turned out to be true). Strummer's sometimes silly rhetoric was 'political' in that it was intended to produce a reaction, to wake young people up and make them think, because the band was also 'anti-ignorance', as he put it in an interview in *New Musical Express* in December 1976 (cited in Gilbert 2004: 127). Although their self-mythologizing was frequently inconsistent they developed a loosely coupled organic approach that encompassed design, fashion, art, literature, politics, film and music. 'The Clash' was about style and an approach to living as much as music, with a community of roadies, aides, advisors and friends who formed a sort of fluid academy where ideas and issues were discussed, challenged and hammered into shape as a matrix that informed their musical creativity.

The potential richness of this resource was augmented with an attitude of openness and accessibility to their fans that persisted as far as possible throughout their career – often bringing them into conflict with venues, security and hoteliers. Especially in the early days, this accrued them significant debt. Their enthusiasm for communicating with their fans, finding out about their lives and what they thought about the world, taking as many of them as possible back to their hotel bar after gigs to socialize and often putting several of them up on their floors, carried over into their live performances and gained them considerable reputation and influence in both youth culture and music on both sides of the Atlantic. Brilliant American critic Lester Bangs (2003) was totally won over by their integrity and resistance to the temptations of exploitative and degrading 'rock star' behaviour towards their fans.

They offered a bridge from classic rock'n'roll values that they never rejected, having a strong sense of history, to post-punk developments that ultimately outstripped them – and in Joe Strummer created an icon, although he rejected the appellation of 'spokesperson for a generation'. In the process they contributed to the (re-)politicization of popular music for a generation that had been too young to remember the 60s, raising questions over the persistence of global war and neo-colonialism; domestic fascism, the politics of the ultra-right and its resistance; work and exploitation; urban dispossession and multicultural diversity; and the potential of music as a revolutionary form.

But in working through these and other themes, in what was often an atmosphere of intellectual and interpersonal conflict, the band were always put together with the objective of being successful. They were formed in 1976 by Bernie Rhodes, a close friend, collaborator and rival of Malcolm McLaren, who wanted to manage a band that would be different and would turn his ambitious ideas into commercial success; guitarist Mick Jones, who wanted to be a rock star and befriended Paul Simonon (who looked good, wanted to be a cultural icon but had to be taught to play bass), ultimately recruiting him after he turned up to a friend's audition; and another guitarist Keith Levene (who stayed only until September 1976, later becoming a founder member of Public Image Limited). They persuaded Joe Strummer (an exciting front man with pub rockers The 101ers, who topped the bill when the Sex Pistols played their first gig, and wanted to make his mark on the world) to leave his band just as it was taking off. After some difficulty they co-opted drummer Terry Chimes, who played on their first recordings before being replaced temporarily by Rob Harper and then finally by Nicky 'Topper' Headon, who wanted to play great music with the best and expected to move on within a year, although Terry was to help the band out on subsequent occasions and even play Shea Stadium with them in 1982. The tensions and paradoxes of a working band between the audiences that inspired and consumed them, and the culture industry that commodified them, exploited them, somewhat belatedly rewarded them, eventually destroyed them and ultimately and perhaps hollowly honoured them by induction into the Rock'n'Roll Hall of Fame in 2003, were present, though not developed, from their inception.

Pop and creative subjectivities

People want to have fun. (Adorno 1941/1990)

> No fun my babe no fun
> No fun to hang around
> > (The Stooges 'No
> > Fun', 1969)

> I'm the all-night drug-prowlin' wolf
> Who looks so sick in the sun
> I'm the white man in the Palais
> Justa lookin' for fun
> > (The Clash '(White Man) in
> > Hammersmith Palais', 1978)

Viewing the popular music sector of the aesthetic economy from the perspective of the twenty-first century, where TV programmes such as *Pop Idol* and its derivatives make no secret of the motivations behind nor the power of the industry barons, and display on a mass scale the popular urge amongst both the talented and talentless happily to be commodified, it might be easy to assume that the traditional struggle between artistic integrity and commercial necessity is all but a historical relic. But if we look a little beyond the glaze of our TV monitors we find that not only are there still a significant number of bands and artists unwilling to sacrifice their artistic aspirations and political commitments for commercial success, but some are able to achieve a combination of both. In the work of such a band as the Arctic Monkeys, whose 2005 chart-topping success in the UK was built on downloads of their studio recordings made available to their fans at gigs and which the fans themselves put up on Internet sites, there is a clear sense of connection to a youth or street sensibility that speaks both with and to a particular social demographic. As Bob Dylan noted forty years earlier in 'Ballad of a Thin Man' (1965), all the commercial world can do in such a situation is observe and attempt to exploit such a mood – it will never really understand what is 'happening here'.

Historically, we also find that the artificial creation of celebrity is nothing new in principle – whilst The Monkees were perhaps the first obviously commercially manufactured pop band of the 1960s (whilst being composed of artists with genuine talent but little else in common) the UK's first open TV competition to create a manufactured individual pop star was a documentary aired in 1980 called 'The Pop Singer', an episode in Esther Rantzen's series *The Big Time* (1976–80). The competitive auditions were not televised but were won by ambitious Glasgow drama student Sheena Easton, who went on to become a transatlantic success (two UK top ten singles, a US No. 1, two Grammys and a platinum album; like Tom Jones and Engelbert Humperdinck she relocated to the USA, where she continues to record, perform and act). This programme was arguably merely a development of 1960s and 70s competitive talent shows such as *New Faces* or Hughie Green's *Opportunity Knocks*, whose origins lay in his radio series of the 1940s (BBC) and 50s (Radio Luxembourg). But this too is a social phenomenon outside music, as there have always been people who would do anything to be famous. Yet in the late 1980s such was the apparent dominance of the drive to become *entertainers of the masses* rather than musical *spokespersons for a generation* that it led rock music critics such as Lawrence Grossberg (1992) and Simon Frith (1988) to claim that rock – as comprised of distinctive musical voices of youth movements and marginalized social groups against the hegemonic commercial mainstream represented by pop – was dead.

If Walter Benjamin (1936/1969) was correct in arguing that the main function of popular culture was *distraction*, itself a means of perpetuating false consciousness, and Theodor Adorno's (1941/1990) critique and extension of this to popular music had some validity, then by the late 80s and 90s it could be argued that it was spectacularly successful (Miklitsch 1998: 12–14). Indeed Malcolm McLaren had argued presciently in the early 80s that the only available response to the dominance of radical right-wing politics on both sides of the Atlantic was to have a good time – a new sort of 'party' politics that was in essence no politics at all but Grossberg's (1992) 'passionate apathy' (although ultimately via the rave movement even this turning away from the political managed, however briefly, to express the mood of a 'luv'd up' generation in a way not seen for twenty years – see Reynolds 1998/2008). But although post-1987 in the UK the political leverage of left-leaning cultural genres was as low as it had been for decades, cultural hegemony is never total, and always requires maintenance – and meanwhile contemporary originality emerges as a site for resistance, whilst at the same time the awareness of historical continuity in forms of assemblage other than pastiche provides resources for the rediscovery of culture's potential to contribute to change in the socio-political landscape.

Rock music in this period continued to change but did not die, experiencing more of a cyclical turn (Peterson and Berger 1975) and since the turn of the millennium rock bands have achieved popular success through the rediscovery of the creative and ideological wellspring that was the post-punk era (1978–85). They have also adapted to the potentialities of new technological opportunities in performance, production, reproduction and distribution to create mass-popular options that update earlier advances made in that period (Reynolds 2005). Hirsch (2000: 357) argues:

One sign of a possibly countervailing force [to large-scale mergers in the cultural industries] is the increasing utilization of the Internet by musical groups and author 'producers' to release new materials without going through the more traditional routes of recording companies and publishers as their distributors.

But he does not note that in the music industry this is a natural technologically enabled development from the rise of the DIY movement and growth of independent labels that took place at the end of the 70s and early 80s, when new studio and reproductive technologies such as the photocopier brought some aspects of production, communication and distribution within the compass of both artists and fans and facilitated fan creativity.

If the popular underclass creativity of the punk era represented a break with the commercialized varieties of rock music available in the 70s, and for some bands at least a break with the traditional values of rock'n'roll, then post-punk could be said to have both radicalized and diversified these tendencies in terms of the technological and intellectual resources that informed it, and the socio-political, cultural and musical influences on which it drew. This, for some commentators at least, also eventually succumbed to a combination of creative entropy and commercial incorporation – indeed, punk *per se* was said to have lost its critical edge on the day (8 October 1976) that the Sex Pistols accepted their advance of £40,000 from an unsuspecting EMI. The twin evils that always bedevilled punk were its relations, or lack of them, to capital and new technology. Punk as a movement, swallowed up in its own reckless energy, tended not to think these relations through but to reject their relevance by not thinking openly about the economic and power relations in which bands were embedded and by making rigid stipulations about (for example) what sorts of instrumentation were acceptable and unacceptable. But the originators of punk were thoughtful about these issues even if the followers were not, and the history of music and the trajectories of celebrity were not anathema to all bands.

The clash of politics

... The punk stance in general [is] riddled with self-hate, which is always reflexive, and anytime you conclude that life stinks and the human race mostly amounts to a pile of shit, you've got the perfect breeding ground for fascism. (Bangs 2003: 275)

Whilst the band, especially Strummer, were always politically conscious, they were not originally adept at giving expression to their concerns. Much of the stimulus to The Clash's distinctive stridency on political issues came from their manager, Bernard (Bernie) Rhodes, a self-made entrepreneur of sorts with a colourful background in design in the 'mod' scene of the 60s. By 1974 he was contributing designs to Malcolm McLaren's projects including several iconic 'statement' T-shirts, discovering Johnny Rotten and creating 'a punk movement of value'. Rhodes does not talk much about his early past, but his recently launched website, www.bernardrhodes.com, gives a fascinating glimpse of the complex character he was and remains, and a flavour of the stimulating and creative effect he could have – on some people at least. Whilst Joe Strummer found his ideas and intellect energizing and necessary, Strummer's friend Richard Dudanski of The 101ers, invited to be the original drummer in The Clash, turned the offer down because 'he gave me a forty-five-minute socio-political spiel about the group. Bernie said it was all part of a bigger thing, all connected. I thought, no way am I going to work with this guy' (quoted in Gilbert 2004: 87; for other negative views of Rhodes in this period see also 65, 78, 89–95, 111–17).

Rhodes had a socialist, but somewhat Socratic, approach in that he constantly challenged his bands, and their members individually, to address what they stood for, to take a position on specific issues, and identify what made them different. He was critical, entrepreneurial, intellectually arrogant, and proud of his lower working-class background. He encouraged the band to read widely, giving them political, cultural and philosophical reading lists to stimulate their ideas, and instigated a routine of often aggressive social and political discussions as part of their rehearsals. With The Clash he introduced a regime that they themselves referred to as Stalinist, in that former friends who did not fit with the politically correct image for various reasons (such as class, in the case of designer Sebastian Conran, for example) were often suddenly cut from the circle and more or less written out of their history. This applied to those close to the band, like sound man/ producer Mickey Foote, friend and interim manager Caroline Coon, and even to members of the band in the case of Mick Jones and Topper Headon. Rhodes' confrontational and divisive style was also coupled with a need for control, and a consequent frequent lack of communication on important issues that led to an improvisational business practice – whilst he always had plans, he did not communicate them and kept the band guessing over practicalities, whilst challenging them to see the bigger picture. At one point he was sacked as manager, then brought back two years later when the band, but Strummer particularly, tired of the more mainstream business practices of the Blackhill group that had taken over their administrative management (much to their financial benefit, ironically). During Rhodes' absence the band released their masterwork, *London Calling*, produced by Rhodes' legendary but tragically unstable associate from the 60s, Guy Stevens, and this seemed to rankle with him. Rhodes eventually manipulated Strummer and Simonon into removing Mick Jones in an atmosphere of deteriorating relations, and he worked his way into co-writing credits on the band's final album, which he produced under the pseudonym Jose Unidos. He even referred to himself publicly as one of The Clash. Rhodes kept the band in a tension that was often creative, but ultimately proved destructive.

Rhodes provoked the band to write 'what you know about', 'an issue' and 'what's affecting you, what's important' whilst seeking to connect it to a bigger picture (Savage 2001: 232). This makes some sense of the puzzling fact that whilst they wrote dozens of songs that had a political message, they frequently claimed to be 'apolitical'. The late 70s were a time of realization of the impending failure of both the welfare state and the post-war form of traditional socialist politics, and the rise of an often extreme domestic political right wing, especially at working class level (see 'Something About England' on *Sandinista!* (1980) for a reflection on the sources of this). The Clash declared themselves against fascism and against racism (despite some misunderstandings of 'White Riot') but refused to be aligned with any political party (the Socialist Workers' Party, for example, who were keen to co-opt the punk movement) or with any pre-ordained political (such as anarchy) or subcultural (such as mod) positioning (see D'Ambrosio (2004) for a discussion of Strummer's maturing political position from pre- to post-Clash).

Boy meets/has problems with/breaks up with/laments girl songs were therefore out for The Clash unless they had wider resonance, and on the occasions when the band did write this type of song they were usually less than successful (with the spectacular exceptions of 'Train in Vain' and 'Should I Stay or Should I Go?' although in both cases these songs offer musical surprises). When Strummer met the band at their squat for his first rehearsal, Mick Jones began by playing 'I'm So Bored With You' (a girlfriend song). Strummer insisted that they rewrite it there and then to be 'I'm So Bored With the USA', a song about American cultural hegemony. They looked down one night from the balcony of Mick's grandmother's flat over the Westway and Strummer subsequently wrote 'London's Burning' (with boredom). They also wrote songs about themselves and the bands around them, which at the time were songs that bonded them with their audience, as the separation between audience and artist had been violently dissolved by punk. Where the Sex Pistols replaced this dissolution with an attitude of individualized aggression and mutual contempt (which carried some of the traditional essence of the word 'punk'), The Clash challenged their audiences to make up their own minds as individuals in order to reach (or 'grope for' as Strummer puts it in *Westway to the World*) something collective – a loose rather than party-political socialism and a sense of mutual respect. They embodied this collective by being surrounded by a group of 'supporters', including designers, roadies, friends and advisors, 'lads, liggers' and 'poseurs' and by opening their world to their fans, frequently inviting many of them back to their hotels when on the road and putting them up on the floor if they had travelled long distances or missed their last train or bus home (even sneaking them into gigs free in some cases, as they noted in 'Complete Control'). In retrospective interviews the band repeatedly recall this sense of being part of something *with* the audience, rather than playing *to* the audience.

Creative control

The Clash and Rhodes, who was fond of demanding 'complete control', had been assured that they would have artistic control over their output, but this was tested to the limit soon after they signed with CBS. CBS had no idea what a punk band should sound like, and their producers and engineers could not tell a good punk solo from a bad one (Gilbert 2004: 144–5). The recording of the first album was a matter of pulling the wool over the eyes of CBS whilst educating Basing Street Studios engineer Simon Humphrey, but on the second album CBS brought in heavyweight producer Sandy Pearlman (who had originated the term 'heavy metal') to make the band sound, in Joe's words, like Fleetwood Mac (Marcus 1994: 30). It took inspired but tragic legend Guy Stevens and brilliant unflappable Wessex Studios engineer Bill Price to repossess and develop the sound on *London Calling* with an increasingly substantial input from Jones, who was learning all the time. Furthermore, industry norms were at variance with the punk interpretation of 'control', so when the label released a single from the album without consulting the band (quite normal for the industry but against everything the band stood for), they were incensed. It looked as though the band had indeed 'sold out' to CBS, especially as the track 'Remote Control' was musically the softest and least 'punk' of the original songs on the album.

Rhodes was able to negotiate with CBS that a non-album track be released, with an associated tour, to compensate for the problems with 'Remote Control'. The song followed on from 'Garageland' (a response to a review by Charles Shaar Murray slamming an early gig) telling the ongoing story of the band, and their feelings of being 'conned' – the words emphasising the 'con' in control. It was unusual for artists to be allowed to release records with verses such as:

They said we'd be artistically free
When we signed that bit of paper
They meant let's make a lotta money
And worry about it later
Oohhh we'll never understand
Oohhh let me see your other hand

It was a powerful single, full of a passionate irony that was not lost on either the label or the band. The band were far from free of contradictions, but they were at least meeting them head on (Savage 2001: 488). Audiences loved it, but still puzzled about where or whether the con would or could end. Some critics such as Tester (1994) see The Clash only in terms of the rise and fall, the sell-out, the failure of a romanticized revolutionary vision of pop music as somehow capable of eluding the reach of the cash nexus that envelops it from its inception. Of course, The Clash do embrace the revolutionary ethos with a passion, but simultaneously Strummer blends this with a 'ferocious and self-reflexive irony' (Miklitsch 1998: 34). '(White Man) in Hammersmith Palais' demonstrates this lyrically, but as both Savage (2001: 488) and Miklitsch (1998: 35) point out, the music plays off against the words to suggest that behind the discursive problems of finding a language in which to resist or negotiate commodification (and one's own fetishization of the commodity one might become), and the risks of romanticizing and exoticizing the revolutionary potential and 'authentic' struggle of the Other in ways that the Other might not wish to embrace, there might be some human bond that gives cause

for optimism. As Strummer commented elsewhere, it isn't so much
a matter of articulating it, but physically *groping* for it through the
movement of the music and the energy of the words as much as their
meaning.[3] But the words are nevertheless intelligent and their semiosis
is mobile. Whilst lamenting that not only is he the only white guy in
an all-night black reggae concert, he appears also to be the only one
looking for politicized 'roots rock reggae' rather than The Four Tops
kitsch, which is what is served up. After romantically criticizing the
audience and the artists for turning away from their heritage, and criticizing the rest of contemporary white music for not being interested in
what that heritage might contain, he reflexively acknowledges that the
only space left is in fact *distraction* – the lonely 'drug-prowlin' wolf...
lookin' for fun' but really looking for meaning, and for hope. But at
the very moment that this irony comes home, the music subverts the
message by delivering a consummate fusion of punk and reggae that
allows its audience to *feel* the 'authenticity' of its attempted resolution
as it delivers some hope. The point here is that if the band *did* sell out
on one level, they also did much more, and as Miklitsch (1998: 35–6)
notes, the 'historical pulse of their music', coupled with the reflexivity
and often savage irony of their lyrics, opens up the estranging tensions between 'negation and affirmation, art and commodity fetish'
by embodying them in the juxtaposition and combination of musical
styles – punk, roots reggae, backbeat, dub, rock'n'roll, R'n'B, hip-hop,
rap, country and even rockabilly.

The second verse of 'Complete Control' alluded to the extent to
which both security and the forces of the law were intervening in the
band's relationships with their audience, but this was just the beginning of a process of increasing distancing. Yet the band did not enjoy
the trappings of fame immediately. After the second album, *Give 'Em
Enough Rope*, was not well received by punk purists, and the band's
first American tour, Bernie Rhodes was no longer on the scene so they
lost their rehearsal space and their assets were frozen. Highly suspicious of the record company, they found a cheap place to rehearse
in Pimlico, and travelled there by bus seven days a week to make
an album they weren't even sure would be released. Road manager
Johnny Green (Green *et al.* 2003) commented on the intensity with
which they worked and performed, not sparing themselves or with-
holding effort – even in their daily break to kick a football around.

Their schedule was such that they were forced to leave for another US tour immediately after recording and left the mixing to the producer and engineer. Their feet remained on the ground until well after the album's release in 1979.

> I should be jumpin' and shoutin' that we made it all the way
> From Camden Town station to 44th and 8th
> Not many make it this far and many say we're great
> But just like them we walk on and can't escape our fate.
> ('Gates of the West', *Cost of Living* EP 1979)

Prescient or not, after the later experience of playing Shea Stadium (supporting The Who in 1982) it was clear how much things had changed. Their performances were now 'mediatized' such was the size of the venue (Auslander 2006: 86). It was no longer possible for the band to stop playing and break up fights in the audience or engage onstage with invading fans, or even to ask the audience to stop fighting – although they were not so likely to start in those surroundings, and the artistes were too far away to get covered in the audience's spit. After the departure of Mick Jones, Bernie suggested that the band should try to get back to their roots, and the five-piece went on a busking tour of the country, playing acoustically in the streets and in car parks, asking fans if they could put them up on their floors. It was a remarkable step to take, and each member of the band reported it as a significant personal experience, despite its gimmicky appearance and the round of radio interviews that accompanied it. For Strummer the experience only increased the awareness of the gap that had opened up between where he was now and where the band had been; his sense of isolation as being the sole creative force and the pressure that this put him under both artistically and commercially (despite Rhodes' attempt to take Jones' place); and his acute awareness that ultimately, at the band's peak of popularity on both sides of the Atlantic, 'I couldn't believe that we turned into the kind of people we were trying to destroy'.[4]

Whatever a group is ... was the chemical mixture of these four people ... that makes a group work ... that's a lesson everyone should learn ... if it works don't mess with it. Do whatever you have to do to bring it forward but don't mess with it ... and like ... we learnt that *bitterly*. (Joe Strummer at the end of *Westway to the World*, Letts, 2001)

Opening out

Several of the people around the band have observed how they were often practically able to put their creativity to work politically in a way that was lower key than the causes they supported with other bands, and more inspiring at a grass-roots level. Johnny Green (Green *et al.* 2003) recalls Mick Jones responding to a request for an auto-graph by asking why the fan wanted him to be a star for them, on their behalf. 'Go and form your own band,' he said, 'I did.' This attitude was embodied in those parts of their recorded output that espoused *music as a revolutionary form* as in 'Clash City Rockers' – 'burn down the suburbs with a half closed eye, you don't succeed unless you try'; 'White Riot' where 'all the power is in the hands of people rich enough to buy it, while we walk the streets too chicken to even try it'; 'Hitsville UK' about the DIY music ethic; 'Radio Clash'; the sarcastic 'Capital Radio'; the multilevelled eco-apocalyptic 'London Calling'; and several songs that play with the idea of a simmering, incipient revolutionary reckoning about to explode, such as 'Sten Guns in Knightsbridge'. The social conditions of *urban dispossession and multicultural diversity* that fed this were documented at length, in particular with regard to the disillusion, boredom, lack of oppor-tunity and frustration that accompanied them, in both political and cultural terms – 'London's Burning' ('with boredom now'); 'Remote Control' and 'City of the Dead'. *Domestic fascism*, the complacency and hypocrisy that allowed it to flourish and the possibilities for its resistance appeared in 'White Riot', 'English Civil War' 'Hate and War', 'The Guns of Brixton' and 'Clampdown'; *work and exploit-ation* in 'Career Opportunities' (about a job Mick Jones had opening mail at the DHSS when letter bomb attacks were suspected), 'Janie Jones' (a London madam who provided disaffected white-collar work-ers with surrogate lives) and 'Magnificent Seven'; and an increasing number of songs addressing *global war and the consequences of neo-colonialism* – 'Tommy Gun' and 'Spanish Bombs' on international terrorism; 'Rock the Casbah' with its return to the music as revolu-tion theme; 'The Call Up'; 'Charlie Don't Surf', 'Ivan meets GI Joe', 'Washington Bullets' and the title of the *Sandinista!* album. The inter-national scope of the thought behind the music was however evident from the beginning, as the boredom of cultural entropy expressed in 'I'm So Bored With the USA' (and the invasion of TV detectives and

McDonalds) was connected to issues that remain of contemporary concern:

> Yankee soldier
> He wanna shoot some skag
> He met it in Cambodia
> But now he can't afford a bag
>
> Yankee dollar talk
> To the dictators of the world
> In fact it's giving orders
> An' they can't afford to miss a word
> I'm so bored with the U...S...A...
> But what can I do?
>   (from the album *The Clash*)

The lyrics sought to open out onto a world beyond localized anarchy, and encourage the questioning of connections, and one typical fan was significantly influenced:

> I never knew who the Sandinistas were or where Nicaragua was. The lyrics of Joe Strummer were like an atlas: they opened up the world to me and other people who came from blank suburbia. (Bono Vox (Sir Paul David Hewson), U2, in *The Future is Unwritten*, Temple 2007)

In contradistinction to Adorno's (1990: 9) arguments that 'pleasure always means not to think about anything, to forget suffering even where it is shown ... flight from the last remaining thought of resistance', The Clash wanted their audiences to react, to notice, to think and do something about it for themselves. At the same time the music made creative connections, respecting both great styles of the past and emerging movements of the future. On their first US tour the band were supported at their request by the great Bo Diddley (who was paid more than they were), and Strummer would go on stage each night to introduce him and put the young punk audience 'on manners', just as he did on a later tour when the support was hip-hop pioneer MC Grandmaster Flash. It was in these moments, as much as in the 'authenticity' or commitment of performance, that Strummer and The Clash demonstrated that 'lightning-conductor' awareness of the value within fleeting instants to create events that could change the consciousness of an audience. They distanced themselves from punk by looking backward with respect, forward with hope, outward with inclusivity and inward with a reflexivity that whilst recognizing the ironies and contradictions of the creative artist in a commercial system, resisted the inner colonization by the exteriorized commodity. And, as Strummer eventually and reluctantly realized, a final act of self-destruction might in the end be the only true creative option left to avoid a living death.

It's marvellous, the fact that they never besmirched themselves like Elton John or became cabaret like The Stones. (Caroline Coon in *Up Close and Personal* (Ridgway 2006))

Conclusion

Two important conceptual distinctions can be made in relation to *creativity* and The Clash. One is implicitly made by Joe Strummer himself, who prefers to use the term *origination* over creativity to refer to the activities of the band, lyrically and musically. However, this recognizes that Bernie Rhodes, as manager, was himself a creative individual, and that the designers, producers, engineers, roadies and friends that they surrounded themselves with were also, in different ways, creative. They formed in some cases technical and in others intellectual, discursive and inspirational elements in a matrix that was supportive of the band, but within which some of the creative elements (such as Bernie Rhodes) could conflict. The second then is the distinction between *conflictual* and *complementary creativities*. The experience of The Clash suggests that the process of management is itself a creative process, and when successful, it achieves positive complementarity between the various creative elements that go into making a focused creative group successful. But as Strummer also observes, the chemistry that makes this focused group work should not, in the process, be dissolved, and recognition of the fact that it is both fragile and ephemeral is an essential reflexive component of the creative organizing and managing process.

The question of the relation between commercialization and creativity is thus more complex and ambivalent than many commentators would have us believe. The idea of a DIY ethic is an important element of critique, and The Clash found themselves in the ironic position of espousing the ethic firmly, whilst being tied to a contract with one of the world's major and most conservative labels. This illustrates the sometimes stumbling ways in which artistes develop their vision,

turning their particular experiences into often prescient and sometimes prophetic work, and also the often equally stumbling ways that
corporations and their managers attempt to extend the late capitalist
commodification process into the commodification of critique itself.
Simple binary oppositions and cyclical reverses are not sufficient
here: too much is emergent, fragmented and non-hierarchical, authority is often elusive and swift on its feet, and much laughter is ambivalent. And whatever compromises The Clash made, they did have a
powerful influence on so many others – artistes, designers, journalists, critics, performers, ordinary people at all levels – who became
concerned about issues The Clash alerted them to, became informed
about situations they were unaware of, especially globally, and felt
empowered to do something. From the beginning the band struggled
with their contradictions as creatives who cared, and part of their
legacy today is the relative openness with which these contradictions
are confronted, if not resolved. As early as 1979 Joe Strummer, in an
interview with *NME*'s Paul Morley, lamented the fact that punk had
become a matter of style and form (despite the fact that The Clash
were self-consciously stylish, they rejected any alternate orthodoxy):

> Punk's now become 'oh yeah, he's got zips all over him sewed on by his
> mother and he's shouting in Cockney making no attempt to sing from the
> heart and the guitarist is deliberately playing monotonously, and they're
> all playing as fast as they can, so this is punk'. ... I don't want to see punk
> as another slavish attitude and image and everything is pre-planned and
> pre-thought out for you to slip into comfortably. (Strummer cited in Miles
> 1980: 35–6)

Comfort and complacency were the enemies of creativity, yet were
encouraged by a certain type of mainstream music. On the other
hand, commodification was voraciously neophilic and commercialization fed eagerly on the next new thing, to discard it rapidly when its
popularity waned, often without any of its more serious messages registering with its consumers. This continues to bedevil music that has
any kind of connection with a social and philosophical position, and
inhabits the contested terrain between subculture, style and meaning.
Yet as The Clash and their legacy indicate, the issues evolve, they need
to be addressed in the present, and the future remains not desolate,
but unwritten – for commercial interests, for originators, and for creative consumers and communicators.

Table 7.1. *The chart history of The Clash*

Date	A-side or *album title*	Theme	Highest chart position
18.3.77	White Riot	Urban dispossession and multi-cultural diversity (UDMCD)	38
8.4.77	*The Clash*		*12*
23.9.77	Complete Control	Work and exploitation (WE)	28
17.2.78	Clash City Rockers	Music as revolutionary medium (MRM)	35
16.6.78	White Man in Hammersmith Palais	MRM	32
10.11.78	*Give 'Em Enough Rope*		2 (USA 128)
24.11.78	Tommy Gun	Extremism – global war and neo-colonialism (GWNC)	19
23.2.79	English Civil War	Domestic fascism and resistance (DFR)	25
11.5.79	I Fought the Law (*Cost of Living* EP)	Outlaws – DFR	22
23.7.79	*The Clash*		*126* (USA only)
7.12.79	London Calling	Post-apocalyptic warning on global warming	11
14.12.79	*London Calling*	Regarded as their masterpiece	*9*
12.2.80	Train in Vain	Love – betrayal	27 (USA only)
8.8.80	Bank Robber	Outlaws – DFR	12
21.11.80	The Call Up	DFR/GWNC	40
12.12.80	*Sandinista!*	GWNC – overtly political and global triple album	*19*
16.1.81	Hitsville UK	MRM – global	56

Table 7.1. *Cont.*

10.4.81	The Magnificent Seven	WE	34
20.11.81	This is Radio Clash	MRM	47
23.4.82	Know Your Rights	DFR	43
14.5.82	*Combat Rock*	GWNC – much anti-US foreign policy material	2
11.6.82	Rock the Casbah	MRM (global)	30
20.7.82	Should I Stay or Should I Go?	Love – doubt	45 (USA only)
17.9.82	Should I Stay or Should I Go? (reissued 1991)	Love – doubt	17 (1)
2.10.82	Rock the Casbah		8 (USA only)
30.9.85	This is England	DFR	24
8.11.85	*Cut the Crap*		16
21.3.88	*The Story of the Clash*	Compilation	7
1.11.91	*The Clash*	Compilation	68

Notes

1 Joe Strummer, voice heard at the opening of Don Letts' (2001) film *Westway to the World*.
2 Springsteen, along with Elvis Costello and Dave Grohl (of Nirvana and the Foo Fighters), led a live band in tribute to Joe Strummer and indirectly The Clash at the 2003 US Grammy awards, the recording industry equivalent of the Oscars.
3 In the film *Westway to the World*.
4 In the film *The Future is Unwritten*.

References

Adorno, T. with the assistance of George Simpson (1941/1990) 'On popular music', in (1941) *Studies in Philosophy and Social Sciences*, IX(1). Republished in S. Frith and A. Goodwin (eds.) (1990) *On the Record*: 301–14. New York: Pantheon.
Auslander, P. (2006) 'Performance and the anxiety of simulation' in A. Bennett, B. Shank and J. Toynbee (eds.) *The Popular Music Studies Reader*: 85–91. London: Routledge.
Bangs, L. (2003) 'The Clash (1977)', in L. Bangs and G. Marcus (ed.) *Psychotic Reactions and Carburetor Dung*: 224–59. New York: Anchor Books.

Benjamin, W. (1936/1969) 'The work of art in the age of mechanical reproduction', in H. Arendt (ed.) and H. Zohn (trans.) *Illuminations*. New
York: Schocken.

D'Ambrosio, A. (2004) *Let Fury Have the Hour: The Punk Rock Politics
of Joe Strummer*. London: Nation.

Fletcher, T. (2005) *The Clash: The Complete Guide to their Music*.
London: Omnibus Press.

Frith, S. (1988) *Music for Pleasure*. Cambridge University Press.

Gilbert, P. (2004) *Passion is a Fashion: The Real Story of The Clash*.
London: Aurum.

Green, J., Barker, G. and Lowry, R. (2003) *A Riot of Our Own: Night and
Day with The Clash – and After*. London: Orion. (Originally (1997) *A
Riot of Our Own: Night and Day with The Clash*. Indigo.)

Grossberg, L. (1992) *We Gotta Get Out of This Place: Popular
Conservatism and Postmodern Culture*. New York: Routledge.

Hirsch, P. M. (2000) 'Cultural industries revisited'. *Organization Science*,
11(3): 356–61.

Letts, D. (dir.) (2001) *The Clash: Westway to the World* (film).
London: Sony.

Marcus, G. (1994) *In the Fascist Bathroom: Punk in Pop Music, 1977–
1992*. London: Penguin.

Miklitsch, R. (1998) *From Hegel to Madonna: Towards a General
Economy of Commodity Fetishism*. Albany, NY: State University of
New York Press.

Miles, B. (1980) *The Clash by Miles*. London: Omnibus.

Perry, M. (1977) editorial in *Sniffin' Glue* number 8 February collected in
M. Perry (ed.) (2000) *Sniffin' Glue: The Essential Punk Accessory*.
London: Sanctuary.

Peterson, R. A. and Berger, D. G. (1975) 'Cycles in symbol production: the case of popular music.' *American Sociological Review*,
40(2): 158–73.

Quantick, D. (2000) *The Clash*. New York: Thunder's Mouth.

Reynolds, S. (1998/2008) *Energy Flash; A Journey through Rave Music
and Dance Culture*. London: Picador.
  (2005) *Rip It Up and Start Again: Post Punk 1978–1984*. London: Faber
and Faber.

Ridgway, A. (dir.) (2006) *The Clash: Up Close and Personal* (film).
Nassau: Stormbird.

Savage, J. (2001) *England's Dreaming: Anarchy, Sex Pistols, Punk Rock
and Beyond*. London: Faber and Faber.

Strummer, J. and Jones, M. (1978) *Clash: The Words and Music to 20 of The Clash's Songs*. London: Wise.

Temple, J. (dir.) (2007) *The Future is Unwritten* (film). London: Film4.

Tester, K. (1994) *Media, Culture, Morality*. London: Routledge.

Topping, K. (2003) *The Complete Clash*. London: Reynolds and Hearn.

Toynbee, J. (2006) 'Making up and showing off: what musicians do', in A. Bennett, B. Shank and J. Toynbee (eds.) *The Popular Music Studies Reader: 71–84*. London: Routledge.

Infinite variety

Introduction to Part III

Caves' (2002) characteristic of 'infinite variety' refers to the variety of creative products that are available to the consumer and also the wide variety both within and between formats that compete for consumers' attention. 'We use it [infinite variety] to invoke either the universe of possibilities from which the artist chooses, or the array of actual creative products from which the consumers choose' (Caves 2002: 6). The 'infinite variety' of products available and the 'infinite variety' of facets within each creative product make market prediction difficult. While a creative product may be successful, it is generally difficult to ascertain what element or combination of elements led to its success (see also Eisbach and Kramer 2003; Moeran 2005). The criteria of choice for one consumer may not be the same for another even for the same product. As a result it is difficult for an industry to build on success by replicating 'successful combinations', although this does not prevent attempts at doing so, as sequels and franchises attest. Because of 'infinite variety' there is a large element of risk in any investment process with problems of evaluating likely returns on investment. Infinite variety also raises difficulties of replication and standardization of production and, with this, implications for economies of scale. This indeterminacy of infinite variety leads to a broad variety of business responses: investment decisions that spread risks through portfolio management where they are absorbed by offsetting hits and flops; production and/or distribution alliances and licensing; controlling costs through outsourcing and flexible specialization; decentralized production allied to a more concentrated and globalized distribution function; controlling production and creation through Fordist methods (e.g. the Hollywood studio system, 'manufactured' bands); controlling distribution; and 'controlling' consumption through influencing consumer choice (Alvarez and

Barney 2005; Cohendet and Simon 2007; Davenport 2006; Delmestri *et al.* 2005; Dempster 2006; Gander *et al.* 2007; Hirsch 1985; Negus 1998; Tschang 2005). All these strategies represent the search for, and imposition of, 'discipline', rules of the game, that will allow for the inherent indeterminacy of the creative process to become more known and through this more manageable.

The 'market' for creative products, however, is itself a 'creative' product, created through the interplay of individuals, inscribed with varying degrees of cultural and social capital, and the engagement of social networks (Keat *et al.* 1994). It is continually evolving. Innovation within genres through product differentiation may result in a fundamentally different form of category, a new genre, thus extending and transforming the market. Changing technologies identify or create new markets. Point of sale recording of music sales, for example, reinvigorated country and western in the USA, and, with the concretization of a 'direct link' between product and market, led to the creation of new market categories, e.g., 'new artists' (Anand and Peterson 2000). Thus a different technology, a different power/knowledge strategy, changed the discipline of the market in terms of how it became known and the rules that then applied as to how it might be managed. To this extent the 'market' or 'audience' may be seen as the function of a measurement artefact (Shimpach 2005) and, increasingly, marketers play a role in the commissioning of new music, and developing new and established talent. As Horkheimer and Adorno (1995: 125) lamented earlier, with the advent of the 'culture industry' the 'marked differentiation ... [of art forms] depend not so much on subject matter as on classifying, organizing and labelling consumers ... there is nothing left for the consumer to classify. Producers have done it for him.' While those involved in the creative industries engage heavily in identifying and segmenting audiences for markets, the 'infinite variety' of the creative process also places an onus on the audience. The 'audience' is not just the passive consumer of product. As was noted by Hirsch (2000) earlier, the product of the creative industries is 'dependent upon the end user (viewer, audience, reader, consumer) decoding and finding value within these meanings'.

The inherent unknowability of the creative process; whether there will be a worthwhile or tangible product as its outcome; whether there is a prospective audience or market and how the creative product is likely to be received, place strong demands on a sense of identity as one mechanism developed to deal with these uncertainties: be this an individual 'creative' identity, an audience identity, or the creation of brand identities (Cohen *et al.* 2005; Neff *et al.* 2005; Nixon 2006; Nixon and Crewe 2004; Wright 2005). A strong sense of 'artistic' identity helps sustain an artistic impulse or budding career while building an audience. An audience learns what to appreciate in responding to an artistic creation and builds up an identity associated with a particular creative product. Audience awareness thus involves an element of embracing a particular identity in response to, or appreciation of, the creative product. A 'brand' identity helps differentiate a product in an increasingly complex and oversupplied market, and the consumer learns, or is taught, what being associated with a particular design or brand means or implies (Shimpach 2005). Additional 'filtering' or mediation of products through audience 'education' is provided by critics and reviewers who have the power to promote and showcase certain products while ignoring or 'demoting' others. Such mediation introduces a further layer of complexity in relation to 'infinite variety'. Through all these processes individuals are disciplined. But what is the impact of the creative process on identity? How does being creative and appreciating creative endeavours construct a sense of identity and with what effect? In particular, how does identity link to the risks attached to creative products and strategies of risk allocation that are such an important element of the management of creative industry ventures?

These themes are debated and discussed in the chapters (Randall, Johnson and White) in this section, where the focus is on the nature of the 'audience' and factors that influence its creation and identity. Each author sees the audience as integral to the creative process and the 'reception' of the product integral to its production and meaning. As Caves (2002: 175) reminds us, 'creative goods are consumed in a social context, not by isolated hermits. The pleasure people get … depends on the presence of other people at the event itself and the shared residue of the memories of the experience.' The social nature of the consumption of creative goods raises a number of questions: what is the relationship between the familiar categories of 'producers' and 'audience'; what is meant by 'audience participation' and how this is created, informed and guided; and what is the relationship between 'audience' and 'market'?

It would be a very minimalist interpretation to conceive artistic appreciation as a simplistic perceiver → receiver model, where the 'intent' of the art is transmitted to the audience. Randall examines the role of the audience in the creative process, emphasizing its creative role and how much the 'receiver' brings to the process of communication and the implications this has for practice. The role of codes and the act of 'decoding' is an important part of the significance of the creative industries, with the ability to engage in this process an important element of an individual's cultural capital. People creatively construct creative meaning and there is a variety of interpretations open to them. Randall illustrates how, within a performance, there is simultaneously an objective content, an interpretive content (i.e. an interpretation sustained by the disciplines of the genre), and a subjective or experience content (the personal response of the audience member). What is taken to be significant, and how significance is interpreted through the role and activities of cultural intermediaries, is part of the creativity of all the participants in the process. Given this, a very linear interpretation of 'communication' is an inadequate model of the processes involved. This perspective, however, undermines the view of 'creativity' as just residing in the 'creator'; it also lies in the 'receiver'. As a result, it becomes difficult to engage in the binary divides of audience and artist, active and passive. Randall argues for a much more collaborative understanding of creativity and the importance of community in creative endeavour. Everyone, performer and audience, plays a creative role. Everyone 'performs'.

But the question arises as to the extent to which an audience has to be 'taught' its role. What are the links between participation and education? How are audiences educated into a range of permissible responses? Johnson takes up some of these themes in an examination of a production of an immersive, community-based, participant Museum Theatre. A lot of appreciation or 'consumption' of the creative industries takes place in a public domain. Theatre, for example, is a *social* act of producing and consuming, and it is this shared experience that characterizes it. It is part of an ancient dramatic tradition whereby 'reflection' is brought before a community (and informs community-based theatre) (Brining 2008). Because art is public, the 'ground rules' of the creative event are usually framed within an institutional context within which an event is read and understood. The context 'marks out' a theatre event and signals where and how an audience positions itself. The internal frames of the performance establish the dramatic conventions and the shared context of the audience generates the range of behaviours and practices. The 'rules of the game' exist through enactment. Johnson considers what happens when conventional understandings of roles are challenged, and the importance of creativity, as audience members attempt to make sense of a theatrical presentation or 'finish' the contribution. By examining the 'rules of the game' that inform various audience roles, Johnson explores how far interpretation and audience roles and expectations can be challenged and revised in exploring what an 'audience' is.

It is worth noting that producers are also consumers. One artist is an audience member for other artists and, as a producer, one's art might be directly or tacitly referential to the work of others. In many forms of creativity, the building upon – or reacting to – previous products, sometimes within genre and sometimes between (e.g. poetry inspiring a musical setting) is common. This process of taking inspiration is not merely a strategy of mimetic behaviour as is common in many industries, but is an interweaving of influence through consumption, (re)production and reconsumption.

White's chapter examines the dimensions of consumption in questioning the relationship between audience participation and the potential for market exploitation. In doing so he again examines the theme of community that informs Randall and Johnson's work. These issues are made more complex by the advent of new technology and especially the role of the Internet. While web 1.0 involved didactic space, web 2.0 is a participative space. 'Users' are now people formerly known as the audience. The size of the audience is immense, and the rules of this particular medium, the disciplines that sustain it, are currently in the process of being worked out. The rise of web 2.0, user-generated content and social networking sites building 'communities' through shared experiences, raise questions of when and how use value could potentially become exchange value, thus returning us again to the overarching theme of the nature of the market.

References

Alvarez, S.A., and Barney, J. (2005) 'How entrepreneurs organize firms under conditions of uncertainty'. *Journal of Management*, 31(5): 776–93.

Anand, N. and Peterson, R.A. (2000) 'When market information constitutes fields: sensemaking of markets in the commercial music industry'. *Organization Science*, 11: 270–84.

Brining, J. (2008) 'A reflection on policy and practice'. Paper presented at The Discipline of Creativity: Exploring the Paradox conference, 6 February, University of St. Andrews.

Caves, R. (2002) *Creative Industries: Contracts Between Art and Commerce.* Cambridge, MA: Harvard University Press.

Cohen, L., Wilkinson, A., Arnold, J. and Finn, R. (2005) 'Remember I'm the bloody architect!' *Work, Employment & Society,* **19**: 775–96.

Cohendet, P. and Simon, L. (2007) 'Playing across the playground: paradoxes of knowledge creation in the videogame firm'. *Journal of Organizational Behaviour,* **28**(5): 587–605.

Davenport, J. (2006) 'UK film companies: project-based organizations lacking entrepreneurship and innovativeness'. *Creativity and Innovation Management,* **15**(3): 250–7.

Delmestri, G., Montanari, F. and Usai, A. (2005) 'Reputation and strength of ties in predicting commercial success and artistic merit of the independents in the Italian feature film industry'. *Journal of Management Studies,* **42**(5): 975–1002.

Dempster A.M. (2006) 'Managing uncertainty in creative industries'. *Creativity and Innovation Management,* **15**(3): 224–33.

Eisbach, K. and Kramer, R. (2003) 'Assessing creativity in Hollywood pitch meetings: evidence for a dual-process model of creativity judgements'. *Academy of Management Journal,* **46**(3): 283–301.

Gander, J., Haberberg, A. and Rieple, A. (2007). 'A paradox of alliance management: resource contamination in the recorded music industry'. *Journal of Organizational Behaviour,* **28**: 607–24.

Hirsch, P. (2000) 'Cultural industries revisited'. *Organization Science,* **11**(3): 356–62.

(1985) 'US cultural productions: the impact of ownership'. *Journal of Communication,* Summer: 110–21.

Horkheimer, M. and Adorno, T.W. (1995) *Dialectic of Enlightenment.* New York: Continuum.

Keat, R., Whitely, N. and Abercrombie, N. (eds.) (1994) *The Authority of the Consumer.* London: Routledge.

Moeran, B. (2005) 'Tricks of the trade: the performance and interpretation of authenticity'. *Journal of Management Studies,* **42**(5): 902–22.

Neff, G., Wissinger, E. and Zukin, S. (2005) 'Entrepreneurial labour among cultural producers: cool jobs in hot industries'. *Social Semiotics,* **15**(3): 307–34.

Negus, R. (1998) 'Cultural production and the corporation: musical genres and the strategic management of creativity in the US recording industry'. *Media, Culture and Society,* **20**: 359–79.

Nixon, S. (2006) 'The pursuit of newness'. *Cultural Studies,* **20**: 59–106.

Nixon, S. and Crewe, B. (2004) 'Pleasure at work? Gender, consumption and work-based identities in the creative industries'. *Consumption, Markets and Culture*, 7(2): 129–47.

Shimpach, S. (2005) 'Working watching: the creative and cultural labor of the media audience'. *Social Semiotics*, **15**: 343–60.

Tschang, F. (2005) 'Videogames as interactive experiential products and their manner of development'. *International Journal of Innovation Management*, **9**(1): 103–31.

Wright, D. (2005) 'Mediating production and consumption: cultural capital and "cultural workers"'. *British Journal of Sociology*, **56**(1): 105–21.

8 | Communication, artists and the audience

CHRISTOPHER RANDALL

It was Professor Duby who, by pointing out the remote affiliation of the script with Low Greylag, made possible the first tentative glossary of Penguin. The analogies with Dolphin which had been employed up to that time never proved very useful, and were often quite misleading.

It seemed strange that a script written almost entirely in wings, neck, and air should prove the key to the poetry of short-necked, flipper-winged water-writers. But we should not have found it strange if we had kept in mind the fact that penguins are, despite all evidence to the contrary, birds.

Because their script resembles Dolphin in *form,* we should never have assumed that it must resemble Dolphin in *content.* And indeed it does not. There is, of course, the same extraordinary wit, the flashes of crazy humor, the inventiveness, and the inimitable grace ... The joy, the vigor, and the humor are all shared by Penguin authors; and, indeed, by many of the finer Seal *auteurs.* The temperature of the blood is a bond. But the construction of the brain, and of the womb, makes a barrier! Dolphins do not lay eggs. A world of difference lies in that simple fact.

Only when Professor Duby reminded us that penguins are birds, that they do not swim but *fly in water,* only then could the therolinguist begin to approach the sea literature of the penguin with understanding ...

(Le Guin 1982: 6)

Communication governs the relationships between artists, arts organizations and audience members. An awareness of how context, individual creativity and the anticipation of the reactions of others interact within the communication process allows us to reconsider how various participants in a given artistic event relate to each other and, as a result, to model new aesthetic, organizational and economic approaches to the arts.

This chapter is divided into two main sections. The first presents a brief survey of communication theory from the perspectives of

157

both cultural theory and information theory. The ensuing analysis synthesizes aspects of these theories to produce a model of human communication in which participants rely on continuous feedback and a wide range of biological and cultural contexts to construct, send and interpret messages. The foundation of this feedback system lies upon two complementary elements: the inherently creative act of interpretation and the use of multiple and overlapping contexts to anticipate and, to some extent, direct the interpretive activity of others.

The second section uses a series of examples to illustrate how feedback, individual creativity and context interact in the generation, marketing and reception of music. Particular attention is given to how the tension between individual creativity and attempts to control the content of a message affects the relationship between audience members, artists and arts organizations. The dynamic nature of audience/artist/art organization relationships revealed by these examples in turn suggests new approaches to audience participation and education, alternative organizational models for structuring the interaction between artists and audience members and an expanded definition of artistic practice itself.

Communication theory, information theory and a metaphor for human communication

Whether they are planning a concert, a gallery showing, a marketing strategy, a community outreach plan, an audience education programme or some other such event, it is vital for artists, arts organizations, marketers and everyone else involved in delivering an artistic product to consider the overall goals for the event, their methods of achieving these goals and the variety of effects these methods may have on the perception and reception of the artwork or event. Communication is central to interaction between participants in any endeavour and, in a broad sense, to all of that work which we call art. As such, an examination of the communication process is fundamental to an understanding of the relationships between artists, arts organizations and the general public.

Two of the most prominent strands of contemporary thought on the possibility and mechanics of communication arise from two distinct fields: literary (or cultural) theory and information theory. The works of Barthes and Derrida are, to a large degree, representative of contemporary cultural theory's general scepticism of the reliability or, at the extreme, even possibility of the communication of specific meaning from one person to another. Simply stated, the idea of communication as the passage of information from one person to another is considered highly problematic (Derrida 1996). Rather, meaning is conceived as being constructed by the individual reader, listener or viewer from within the context of his or her cultural, physical and emotional experience (Barthes 1977).

For example, a fourteen-year-old African-American girl from South Central Los Angeles, a thirty-year-old man from New Delhi who has been trained in Hindustani classical music and a forty-year-old British woman who remembers her first viewing of Kubrick's *A Clockwork Orange* all come from strikingly different cultural backgrounds. Clearly, a performance of Beethoven's *Symphony No. 9* will mean very different things to each of these people. Much of cultural theory, insofar as it is concerned with communication and meaning, highlights the creative activity of individuals as they construct their own interpretations and meanings for the work which they experience. Whether the music is understood as the irrelevant product of a dead white man, a fascinating exploration of alien musical structures, a representation of political power or something else entirely, the individual listener draws upon personal experience of his or her cultural milieu to imaginatively construct a unique set of meanings for the performance.

However, as a number of authors have argued, this individual creative agency does not preclude the possibility of widely shared meanings, or limitations on the variety of possible meanings, for a specific performance or work (Cook 2001; Juslin 2005). Broadly speaking, my hypothetical audience members share a number of contexts which, to some degree, limit the variety of possible interpretations. At the most basic level, they are all human and, as such, they share common means of sensing the performance. They will all experience the performance by hearing sound, seeing the performers as they play and feeling the vibrations of the sound waves as they pass through their bodies (all of this varying, of course, with the relative acuity of each sense in each person). The physical experience of the body is a powerful source for the contextualization and interpretation of meaning (Lakoff and Johnson 1999) and the profound effects of this biological limitation and shaping of meaning across all of humanity can be neither underestimated nor ignored (Mithin 2006).

In addition to biology, most participants in any artistic event will share some common cultural contexts, no matter how thinly or subtly. This is a far cry from saying that all participants will have similar backgrounds or interests or share some sort of subcultural identity. Rather, I am simply stating that at any event where a group of people gather of their own free will, the majority of those people will have some cultural experiences in common. These shared cultural contexts may be limited to such things as the knowledge that Beethoven was deaf, the location of the concert hall or the fact that the concert should finish before the city buses stop running. Regardless of how general they are, these shared contexts help provide space for the participants to communicate with each other (Small 1998).

In my previous sample of an African-American girl, an Indian man and a British woman, all share a legacy of British colonialism. This will undoubtedly affect their individual understandings of the music in multiple, possibly non-conscious ways but, most obviously, this shared cultural history allows these three participants to discuss their different perceptions with one another in English and, through their interaction, to refine and alter their understanding of the performance.

Figure 8.1 offers a preliminary model for the perception of intent and possibility of communication as suggested by the excerpt from Ursula K. Le Guin which opens this chapter. The existence of shared contexts allows us to perceive meaningful behaviour and to generate our own understandings of penguin behaviour, whether it be descriptions of joy, humour or otherwise. Disparate contexts unavoidably introduce variety into these interpretations, for example in the case of a scientist whose training leads him to dismiss Le Guin's description as an unwarranted anthropomorphization of penguin behaviour. Different personal, cultural, social, emotional and other contexts lead each of us to different interpretations, but shared contexts, both biological and cultural, are what make the act of interpretation possible in the first place.

Information theory provides a strikingly different approach to thinking about communication. Developed in the early twentieth century as a means of describing the transfer of information from one machine to another, particularly in regard to computers, the basic

Common understanding of penguin/human interaction

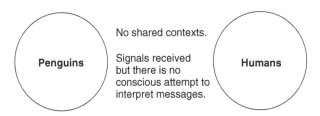

Ursula K. Le Guin's metaphor for penguin/human communication

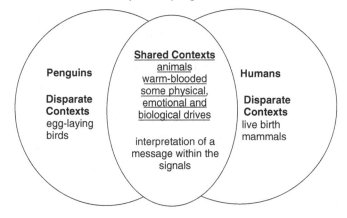

Figure 8.1 Shared and disparate contexts of penguin/human interaction

model of information theory (Figure 8.2) has been used by many theorists as a metaphor for human communication (Cohen 2005; Eco 1976; Shannon and Weaver 1949). It should be noted that information theory, particularly at the basic level discussed here, is not expressly concerned with inter-human communication. It is designed, rather, to model the transfer of information within formal, electrical or mechanical systems.

One must be careful here to acknowledge the limitations of this metaphor. As Umberto Eco (1976) takes pains to point out, this diagram models 'the process which takes place before a human being looks' at it (Eco 1976: 33). It is a model for the communication of

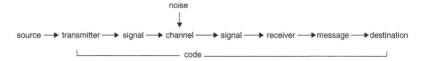

Figure 8.2 Model of a system for the transmission of non-signifying stimulus

stimuli which have no significance in and of themselves. A code – a strictly defined set of rules – is used by one machine, the transmitter, to translate stimuli into a form which can be readily transmitted to and deciphered by another machine, the destination. The machines in this system share the code fully. While noise can interfere with or corrupt the signal, there are no ambiguities in the code itself which might allow for a variety of interpretations at the destination. Within the system, there is no attempt or even ability to distinguish between noise and signal. There is no human involvement at this level and no decision to be made between multiple possible meanings. Indeed, there is no meaning here, only stimulus.

Obviously, this model is inadequate to describe human communication. In the first instance, the stimuli which pass between humans are usually perceived as being loaded with various degrees of significance. The sound of a low C on the viola, a splash of colour on canvas, an abrupt inhalation of breath; each of these is bursting with a variety of potential meanings. And we are not even aware of which stimuli might or might not be regarded as significant by others. The blink of an eye, stress on a particular word, a rise in pitch at the end of a phrase – which of these, intentional or otherwise, are part of the message and which of these should be dismissed as noise? In human communication, the source does not have full control over which signals are sent and the destination is not always certain how to distinguish between those stimuli which are significant and those which are irrelevant.

This uncertainty is one manifestation of a second inadequacy of this model: humans have no universally and absolutely shared codes with which we can transform and decipher information. Language may at first seem to be a good analogue for a code but it is under constant negotiation and renegotiation as slang, neologisms and foreign words pass into and out of use and accents, dialects and common usage vary. And since no two people have fully congruent fluencies or understandings of language, it is too ambiguous and variable to take on the function of a mechanical or formal code. Human language is too full of misunderstandings, misinterpretations, contradictions and outright lies to allow for something as definitive as a code to serve as a metaphor for communication.

In addition, the transmission of information in one direction alone, from source to destination, does not adequately describe human interaction. This is again due, in part, to the fact that, unlike machines, humans have no universal and fully shared codes. Rather than being born with a set of explicit instructions, we must learn to communicate. And we can only do this by interacting with each other. We send signals, we receive signals, we interpret the behaviour of others, we make mistakes, we revise our own behaviour and assumptions and try again. Human communication is not a one-way process. It is a continuous feedback loop.

Finally, the image of a direct connection between a source and a unique destination suggested by this model is misleading. While much human communication is directed from one person to another, art in particular is often part of a very public display and marketing or audience outreach programmes are almost by definition targeted at groups of people. In a public setting, then, the signal will reach numerous destinations and the speaker may not even be certain who the message might touch. Audience members will use their mobile phones to send photos and snippets of music to friends around the world, fans will bring friends and loved ones along to a show, and students will attend concerts, plays or showings to fulfil course requirements. No one can fully predict the reach of even a single performance. With these deficiencies in mind, it is possible to devise an alternative metaphor for the communication of potentially significant stimulus, i.e. for human communication, which incorporates aspects of both literary and information theory (Figure 8.3).

While several elements of the non-signifying stimulus model remain, this model attempts to incorporate the multivalence and ambiguity of human communication as it is experienced in our daily lives. The multiple arrows are nothing more than a reminder that, whatever a participant's original intent (or lack thereof) may be, a large portion of human signals and messages will be perceived by many people and not just one.

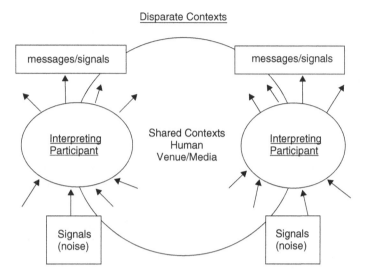

Figure 8.3 Metaphor for the communication of potentially significant stimulus

A more drastic change is my conflation of outgoing message and signal into one package. This is an acknowledgement of the sender's lack of complete control over which stimuli the perceiver will view as significant and which will be dismissed. This is particularly relevant in the case of art, as the sender may not have a clear or conscious intent to send a message at all. My description of this model as a metaphor for *potentially* significant stimulus is an additional reminder of this lack of control over the perceptions and interpretations of other participants.

In regard to incoming stimuli, it is only a signal which is perceived. Whether or not that signal might contain some kind of message is an interpretive decision on the part of the perceiver. Likewise, whether or not that signal has been corrupted by noise is another interpretive decision, as the difference between a potentially meaningful signal and noise is not always self-evident. Finally, if there are no shared contexts by which the perceiver can interpret meaning in the signals, they will either be disregarded as irrelevant or interpreted in a way that is radically different from the original intent (much as a human being might interpret the behaviour between two penguins as signifying love).

This model is limited in both scope and purpose. In particular, the omission of a transmitter and a receiver prevents an examination of the effects of different technologies and media on the transmission of stimuli. I do not mean to dismiss the importance of such considerations but I know of no simple way to disentangle the method of transmission from the message/signal, the contexts within which it is operating, or even from the participants themselves. To represent such a hybrid thing as method/technology/media as a single and distinct graphic, e.g. a transmitter or receiver, would be a gross simplification. It is, however, far beyond the scope of this chapter to fully explore the relationships between these different aspects of the communicative process.

Perhaps the most substantial difference, for my current purpose, between the two models is the elimination of a code and its replacement with shared and disparate contexts as the means of translating, transmitting and interpreting messages/signals. As there are no comprehensive and reliable codes for the translation of information between human beings, the inclusion of a code, even as a metaphor, would be deceptive. Rather than the translation and transmission of information from one participant to another, we are faced with the inherently creative role of each participant in a dialogue as he or she interprets a multitude of incoming signals. This creativity is also put into practice when, in an attempt to communicate with others, each of these same participants fashions a set of signals into what he or she hopes will be perceived as a coherent message.

Finally, the lack of clear directionality within this model and the abandonment of 'source' and 'destination' emphasises the fact that communication cannot be encapsulated within a single utterance. It consists, rather, as a feedback loop in which participants take turns listening to and speaking with each other.

Intent to communicate and the creativity of all participants

The metaphor of shared contexts as fields within which communication occurs allows for two fundamental elements of our lived experience of art: first, intent on the part of artists to communicate and, second, creative interpretations of, and uses for, art on the part of other participants in arts events.

To the extent that an artist is consciously working within a set of contexts, he or she has a generalized expectation of how the work might be understood by people who share, to varying degrees, those contexts. An artist's awareness of cultural, physical and emotional contexts may be fragmentary and incomplete but there is always some conscious awareness of context, whether it be of the gallery or performance space; the media of expression or presentation; the reasons for the creation of this particular work or event, etc. The generalized expectations may be explicit, as in the case of much film and television music. They may also be internalized as part of the creative process in the form of decisions by the artist: this is good, that is bad, this line works, that sound doesn't, this marks a beginning, etc. These are exactly the same decisions that audience members make as they creatively construct their own meanings from their perceptions of the work. And all of these decisions are mediated by cultural, physical and emotional experiences and contexts, many of which are shared to different degrees by large numbers of people.

As a simple example, a composer's choice of instruments, tempo and harmonic, melodic or rhythmic structures will influence whether a performance is interpreted as part of a religious ceremony, as a work to be contemplated with focused attention, or as a dance piece that demands a physical response. An artistic director's decision to perform the same piece in a night club, concert hall or cathedral may strengthen or undermine these interpretations of the piece or perhaps add an aspect of irony to the performance. And a marketer's choice of advertising media, images and language will suggest different social and cultural contexts through which an event may be experienced. This might be exemplified by a choice to pass out flyers to university students to advertise a hot DJ at a local club versus a decision to target locally registered Tories to 'hug a hoodie' and attend the same gig as a means of understanding contemporary youth culture. All of these people are relying on a variety of cultural contexts to express and construct a multitude of meanings.

As for the audience, to the extent that each participant has his or her own unique set of experiences through which to understand an event, each individual will construct his or her own meanings and uses for a particular work or performance. Returning to Beethoven's ninth symphony, an academically trained musician may choose to understand the piece as one statement in a centuries-long dialogue on the limits of symphonic form. As a resident of a member nation of the European Union, this same musician may also view the symphony, in particular the 'Ode to Joy' theme, as a statement of a pan-European quasi-nationalism. And, as a sometime student of contemporary musicology, this hypothetical musician may further choose to understand Beethoven's ninth as a culturally encoded expression of an ideology of male dominance. A variety of cultural contexts enable a variety of interpretations, even within a single person.

What does all of this mean for attempts to educate, or even identify, an audience? In part, it means that the designers of such programmes need to consider the extent to which they wish – and are able – to 'educate' an audience by emphasizing or establishing a limited set of contexts as a means of suggesting and reinforcing specific interpretations of an artwork in contrast to the possibility of inviting people – artists, performers and members of the public alike – to 'participate' by sharing their diverse experiences and understandings of the work and exploring a wide range of meanings.

However, far more important than the distinction between 'education' and 'participation' is the recognition that it is the dialogue between creative individuals which makes such outreach and marketing programmes possible. Clearly, participants in this dialogue play different and often highly specialized roles. Regardless, it is a mistake to casually divide participants into explicit groups, such as artists and audiences, and assign them contrasting qualities, such as active and passive, creative and receptive, professional and amateur or knowledgeable and ignorant, for the continuous feedback loop of communication is constantly blurring the lines between those who speak and those who listen.

A series of examples will demonstrate the operation of feedback within the dialogue between composers, performers and audience members and how multiple contexts, and the fluid identities which are tied to them, defy the categorization of a discrete audience. As I am a musician, these examples are drawn primarily from the music world. When considering the role and effects of dialogue in other arts and media, my arguments and conclusions may not be fully applicable.

Communicative feedback in the production of, reaction to and use of music

Critical reactions to the premiere of Leonard Bernstein's *Mass* provide a good example of how shared and disparate contexts allow numerous participants to react creatively to the messages/signals of others and to carry on a dialogue without engaging in a specific education programme. Premiered in 1971 for the opening of the Kennedy Center in Washington DC, the piece was criticized by some as either blasphemous or banal and praised by others as a realistic and moving expression of faith. Despite the varied and intense reactions, however, almost all of the critics justified their views by pointing to one feature of the piece, Bernstein's mixing of rock, popular music, Broadway-style song and numerous other musical styles with a religious ritual in a secular concert hall.

In interviews and personal notes, Bernstein himself made it clear that he felt both the mixture of musical styles and the religious nature of the piece to be essential aspects of its character (Sheppard 1996) and, judging from the reactions of critics, he communicated this successfully to listeners. While Bernstein could not fully determine the variety of interpretations other participants in the musical dialogue would generate from the performance of the piece, his skill as a composer and sense of broadly shared cultural contexts were strong enough for him to direct, consciously or otherwise, a large number of audience members, critics, musicologists and theologians to focus their continuing conversation on a set of relatively limited topics: the nature of faith, the role of music in religion and the use of pastiche as a compositional device (Sheppard 1996). In essence, Bernstein used a variety of tools, including musical cues drawn from a range of styles, expectations aroused by the religious nature of the text and the historical, cultural and political associations attached to the performance space, to emphasize a limited number of contexts within which the piece operates.

But despite Bernstein's success in focusing attention on the multiplicity of the piece and the centrality of faith, both his inability to fully control a message and the creativity of others in interpreting the work are demonstrated in the varied reactions of audience members to the *Mass*. While the Catholic publication *Commonweal* gave a positive review which described the *Mass* as 'the ultimate "People's Mass"', a review in the journal *Sacred Music* accused Bernstein of appealing 'to the hedonistic instincts of the masses' and described the piece as a work of 'cultural schizophrenia' (Sheppard 1996). Such commonplace disagreements about the meaning of a given work of art are the ultimate illustration of the artist's lack of control over the creative activity of other participants and the unavoidable intrusion of disparate contexts into any dialogue.

More to the point of the current argument, however, is that no one needed to be taught how to understand the *Mass* in order to participate in this dialogue. Theologians, magazine reporters and Washington's cultural elite all have very different educational backgrounds, beliefs and life experiences. In other words, they work in a wide range of disparate cultural contexts. And yet all of them felt qualified to speak up in reviews and interviews. Bernstein was a Jew who set a Catholic ritual to secular music and gave it a theatrical staging in a public concert hall. If people can intelligently interpret and react to such a complex and potentially confusing piece of art without recourse to some authoritative guide, then they can respond similarly to almost any artwork.

As a second example of the creativity of all participants in an artistic dialogue, feedback in the communication process and the difficulty of separating the roles of artists from audience members, let me draw on my own experience as a composer. In early 2007, guitarist Paco Bethencourt-Llobet asked me to write a piece for his band. The group, Electroflamenko, is a somewhat eclectic fusion of flamenco guitar, a classically trained singer, electric bass, a rapper, samples and digital effects on a Kaos pad, flamenco dancers and live video. My own background includes playing electric bass in metal and latin-jazz bands as well as training in both Western and Hindustani classical music. It was similarities between Hindustani and flamenco rhythmic practice, as well as the sounds of some flamenco scales and Hindustani *raags,* which first inspired my friend to ask me for a piece. These sounds presented a shared, if weak, musical context.

At that point, I knew that the band usually played in nightclubs and that they wanted a piece which could be performed in that setting. While I had heard recordings of their music, I did not initially understand precisely how the band worked. In particular, I had to be taught a number of flamenco rhythmic patterns and how they function within the music. I also worked with Francisco Sologuren, who uses samples in place of percussion and to provide additional effects, in order for me to get a clear sense of what was possible with his machines and how, in the absence of music notation, I could give him instructions to enable an effective performance. Finally, I needed to see the dancers in action to better understand how they were relating to rhythm, harmony and melody. Some of this work was done in conversation with individual performers. Most of it, however, was done by attending and observing band rehearsals and shows.

In other words, before I could fulfil my role as a composer, I first had to be a listener and observer. And it was through listening, watching and conversing with the band members – the feedback loop of human communication – that I began to make sense out of and share the contexts within which their music-making occurred.

Though all of the instrumentalists read notation, the band as a whole learns and rehearses music primarily through aural and oral communication. They also treat songs as malleable, rather than fixed entities, varying the number of repeats, for example, to allow time for the dancers to add steps or the rapper to play with the rhythm of his lyrics. With limited rehearsal time and a large set to practice, the band also cannot afford to spend too much time on any one song.

With these factors in mind, I set to the task of writing a song. Being aware of how the band works, the piece has no static structure. The beginning of the piece is improvized in the style of a Hindustani *alaap* while the main body of the song is made up of two sections which draw on both Hindustani and flamenco structures and can be repeated as the band likes. When I first presented the piece to the group, I gave short notated excerpts to the singer, guitarist and bassist and then proceeded to sing through the various sections of the music. I also clapped rhythms for the dancers and recited Hindustani rhythmic *solfège* to the sampler-cum-percussionist.

In essence, I had become a performer and it was the band's turn to listen. And this process did not end with just one presentation of the material to the band. They played the music back to me and, where it was not what I was looking for, I changed the notation or sang my ideas back to them again. Through this interaction, they also came up with material which was compelling enough to keep in the song. In this way, my own concept of the music changed. It was through such musical dialogue that we created and reinforced shared contexts for making and understanding music.

But the piece is not yet finished. Whenever they play a show, the band examines the crowd for signs of what is resonating with the audience and what is not. This assessment is a regular practice and they may well drop a repeat if they think the song went on too long or add more improvizations at the start if they want to emphasize the

Hindustani aspects of the piece, all depending to a large degree on how they interpret the crowd's reactions.

Everyone who dances to the music, claps with the rhythm, sings along, smiles, laughs or otherwise is sending out signals and messages to the whole room. Whether those signals are intended for the band or for a lovely lass or lad on the dance floor is another issue. *Everyone is performing.* Everyone is part of the feedback loop of communication at that moment and, whether they are aware of it or not, they are playing a part in shaping the music.

Finally, as a demonstration of the multiple, overlapping and fluid contexts within which dialogue occurs, I offer the example of networking Internet sites, such as Myspace.com. Myspace and similar networking sites present a complex intertwining of public, private, social, economic and cultural spheres, all operating within a technological context which is shared by their users. For many people, these sites serve as means to establish and maintain contact with friends, family and acquaintances. For musicians, such sites present an opportunity to advertise their shows and recordings. Often, it is difficult to discern a clear dividing line between these different behaviours or functions. The result of this ambiguity of purpose is that the content of any given page will reflect the multiple cultural contexts which that individual member moves through in daily life. You may follow a link from a site devoted to bee-keeping and end up on the site of a fan of medieval metal who makes mead out of honey. And who knows, maybe you'll pursue a further link to the site for the band Sunn O))), sample one or two of the songs on their page and decide you like them.

Are you part of an identifiable audience? The multivalence of links on such networking sites and the overlapping contexts within which they operate prevent any real 'targeting' or 'identification' from taking place. The most anyone can do is offer clues to the contexts within which he or she is working. There are no discrete, static audiences; there are, rather, multiple participants in multiple, simultaneous and overlapping dialogues.

It is the ease and speed with which participants communicate that makes networking sites, and the Internet in general, such a difficult environment for traditional marketing strategies. Artists active on the Internet employ the usual stylistic markers, such as hair, clothing, make-up, slang, colour, artwork and references to other artists, in order to craft an image/message which they hope will be easily understood by and appeal to potential audience members. Artists also create links to 'friends' which they use to promote their recordings and concerts in much the same way as a traditional mailing list. In comparison to non-web-based practice, however, the ease of personal interaction on the web brings the fundamental features of communication to the fore. The inherent creativity of each participant in the dialogue, the ultimate lack of control of any one person over the content and use of a message and the continuous feedback from multiple online sources force (or enable) artists and arts organizations to spend as much time listening to audience members as speaking to them.

Working within the dialogue

An awareness of how the inability of anyone to fully determine how others will interpret their messages, the creativity of each participant in a dialogue and the influence of constantly shifting contexts, identities and roles affects the communication process and can open up new means for expanding and strengthening the dialogue between artists and the communities they are a part of. A few examples suffice to illustrate this.

Newgrounds.com is an example of a website which exploits the communicative free-for-all of the Internet to enable people to create, interpret and recontextualize artistic products at will. Newgrounds is a for-profit company which administers an online community of video game developers, film makers, musicians and fans who create, use and respond to materials posted on a cluster of websites. The rapid feedback enabled by online communication is used by Newgrounds to encourage interaction between artists, listeners, viewers and game-players. In part, this is achieved by Newgrounds' limited editorial control over the films, games and music available on the site. The only circumstances under which Newgrounds staff bar material from the site are to limit extreme pornography, prevent copyright abuse and close down links to viruses or other malicious software. All other editorial decisions, such as which games and films appear on the front page and how long material remains available on the site, are based on the number of times a particular item is downloaded and how highly it is rated by community members. (The rating of a film or game is measured by a strict voting system.) Forums linked directly to each game, film and song also encourage interaction by allowing users and artists to communicate with each other on a one-to-one basis. As a result, Newgrounds users have a great deal of input into what is seen and heard on the site. They are also able to effectively and clearly interact and communicate with artists. All of the community members are in constant dialogue and, as a result, all of them take part in shaping the products of that dialogue.

In addition to using feedback to support dialogue between creators and users of content, Newgrounds also facilitates communication between artists. A prime example of this is the fact that music can only be submitted under a Creative Commons licence, rather than a traditional copyright, with the specific intent of allowing the music to be used by other members of the community in their own creative work. In effect, this allows artists to listen and respond to each other through their artwork. The dialogue which takes place contains all of the elements of the communication model proposed in Figure 8.3, but it is largely transferred into the realm of art, rather than language.

Finally, the method for submitting content to Newgrounds includes a 'buddy' system which provides an easy means for artists to contact each other and effectively encourages the kind of collaboration which I experienced with Electroflamenko. Indeed, several stable groups of authors are identified by their 'collab' title, rather than the names of the individual artists. Ultimately, Newgrounds is not an online gallery which simply provides space for individual artists to display their work to others. It is, rather, a community which fosters dialogue between artists and the people who view and use the products of artistic activity.

Southwest Chamber Music, a group of performers based in Los Angeles, offers a real, as opposed to virtual, example of how a simple change in concert programming can take advantage of the interpretive creativity of all participants and the feedback loop of communication. When presenting a new piece of music, the ensemble will often play it once just before the interval and then again immediately afterwards. In part, this allows the audience members to familiarize themselves with the musical language of the piece while giving them a second chance to listen for important aural cues within the music. Given the fact that many audience members are unfamiliar with much of twentieth century and contemporary art music, such repeated performances allow the ensemble (and through them, the composer) to build or reinforce shared musical contexts with the audience (much as

I and Electroflamenko built shared contexts for our music-making).
However, by separating their performances with the interval,
Southwest Chamber Music also encourages audience members to dis-
cuss the music and share their perceptions of and reactions to it.

The ensemble's novel programming device is, in effect, a realization
of the communication model proposed in Figure 8.3. By playing the
piece twice with a significant time span in between, the musicians
emphasize the alternation of all participants, including themselves,
between listening and speaking roles. The interval leaves space for the
creativity of each listener to come to the fore, as he or she discusses
various interpretations of the music with others. The interaction
between audience members during the interval also brings a wide
range of cultural and emotional contexts into play, as each individual
brings a different set of experiences into the dialogue. The multivalence of communication also comes into play here, as signals are moving in many directions and between numerous participants. Finally,
the second performance gives the musicians a chance to respond to
their interpretations of the first run-through, as well as the audience's
reaction to it, by adjusting how they play the piece a second time,
much as Electroflamenko change their performances.

In terms of arts organizations themselves, the communication process
might lead to a model similar to the collectives popular amongst many
contemporary artists but with the inclusion of members of the local
public as explicitly active participants. The opportunities for showing, viewing and discussing new work afforded by such an arrangement might be compared to the *fin-de-siècle* salon or late-Renaissance
Italian academy. With careful consideration of the barriers to inclusion
which operate in these earlier examples, such artist/public collectives
could have a wider reach into the community. This kind of structure
would almost necessarily be organized around a physically localized
community and could be as anarchic as the folk-music sessions which
are common in many pubs across Britain or as planned as a series
of studio or gallery visits in which members of the public are openly
invited to question art works, artists and the role and purpose of the
arts in general, both as a prelude to, and as an ongoing part of, the
creative process. In this latter case, audience members would not be
criticizing finished products, as might be the case in a gallery opening
or a concert. Rather, they would be instrumental in shaping, from the
start, the dialogue within which the artistic process takes place.

While these three examples are limited in scope, they illustrate how an awareness of the communication process, in particular the creativity of all participants and the feedback loop of communication, can suggest alternative aesthetic, social and economic behaviours on the part of all participants in an artistic dialogue. The ease with which various participants in a dialogue change their roles from speakers to listeners and back; the ongoing nature of a dialogue in which a single utterance or act is only one part of a larger process; and the tension between anticipating how others will react and the inability to control either the creative activity of other participants or the contexts within which they interpret signals, all work together to blur the boundaries between artists, arts organizations and audiences and open up new regions to a wider artistic dialogue.

References

Barthes, R. (1977) 'From work to text', in S. Heath (transl.) *Image Music Text*: 155–64. London: Fontana Press.

Cohen, A. J. (2005) 'Music cognition: defining constraints on musical cognition', in D. Mell, R. MacDonald, D. J. Hargreaves (eds.) *Musical Communication*: 61–84. Oxford University Press.

Cook, N. (2001) 'Theorizing musical meaning'. *Music Theory Spectrum*, 23(2/2): 170–95.

Derrida, J. (1996) 'Semiology and grammatology: an interview with Julia Kristeva', in P. Cobley (ed.), A. Bass (trans.) *The Communication Theory Reader*: 209–24. London: Routledge.

Eco, U. (1976) *A Theory of Semiotics*. London: Macmillan.

Juslin, P. N. (2005) 'From mimesis to catharsis: expression, perception and induction of emotion in music', in D. Mell, R. MacDonald and D. J. Hargreaves (eds.) *Musical Communication*: 85–115. Oxford University Press.

Lakoff, G. and Johnson, M. (1999) *Philosophy in the Flesh: The Embodied Mind and its Challenge to Western Thought*. New York: Basic Books.

Le Guin, U. K. (1982) 'The author of the Acadia Seeds and other extracts from the Journal of the Association of Therolinguists', in *The Compass Rose*. New York: Harper and Row.

Mithin, S. (2006) *The Singing Neanderthals: The Origins of Music, Language, Mind, and Body*. Cambridge, MA: Harvard University Press.

Shannon, C. and Weaver, W. (1949) *The Mathematical Theory of Communication*. Urbana: University of Illinois Press.

Sheppard, W. A. (1996) 'Bitter rituals for a lost nation: Partch's *Revelation in the Courthouse Park* and Bernstein's *Mass*'. *Musical Quarterly* 80(3/4): 461–99.

Small, C. (1998) *Musicking: The Meanings of Performing and Listening.* Hanover, CT: University Press of New England.

9 Art or honesty? Breaking the rules of the game with immersive museum theatre

PAUL JOHNSON

A museum visitor arrives at a museum with a certain set of expectations of that visit, whilst a member of a theatre audience attends a performance with a different set of expectations. Expectations of types of interaction or participation; the balance between education and entertainment; even whether the individual can wander at will and leave at any point, or should sit down and remain seated for the duration. The growing field of museum theatre has developed a range of models of practice, modes of interaction between visitor/audience member and performer that are becoming recognised and widely accepted (see Hughes 1998 for an account of the standard model of museum theatre practice). Much of the early research on theatre programmes in museums centred on the importance of not upsetting the audience/visitor by unduly challenging the expectations of a museum visit through the use of live performance or theatre as an interpretative tool – the theatre was carefully constructed and constrained to operate broadly within the expectations of the museum visitor (see for example Bicknell and Mazda 1993). At times, however, a museum or a theatre company might for various reasons wish to work against or unsettle those expectations, and this chapter discusses just such a case in the immersive museum theatre work of Triangle, resident theatre company at the Herbert Gallery, Coventry.

Triangle Theatre

Triangle has developed a remarkable method of engaging young people with theatre work involving explorations of history, location, artefacts and narrative through immersive participatory performance, and this chapter analyses a project developing this work for a more general audience. One defining feature of Triangle's immersive museum theatre work is that almost all parts of it are carried out 'in role' through extended improvisations and much of the development and subsequent publicity for the piece this chapter focuses on, *Chico Talks – The Pollard Trail* (Triangle 2006), was also carried out in role, including through a number of websites and blogs.

The work grew out of the more traditionally educational focus of the venue, working on projects involving young people. For example, the *War is Over* project (2005) ran over a month-long period with 21 sixteen-year-olds and 150 ten- and eleven-year-olds and explored issues related to the end of the Second World War, such as celebration, commemoration and remembrance. The framework used was that of the 'Whissell and Williams Training Regime', a fictional quasi-governmental agency responsible for training recruits to, in this instance, celebrate the end of the war. The twenty-one youths were 'trained' first so they could go on to work with the younger children to explore the theme creatively. The training was in effect actor-facilitator training undertaken entirely in role, much as the work with the younger children would also take place within a fictional framework. Previous projects had explored evacuation (*Coventry Kids in the Blitz*, 2004) and life on the home front (*The Whissell and Williams Home Front Training Camp*, 2003), involving schools, the Herbert, the Coventry Transport Museum and Coventry Cathedral, amongst other partners. Within the immersive world created, partner organisations were also in role, with for example the Cathedral as the Ministry of Faith and the Transport Museum as the Ministry of Transport. The work is immersive in that the participants and the actor-facilitators remain in role throughout, and everything can become part of the fictional world created. As there is not one predetermined narrative which is acted out, but merely a framework in which an almost limitless range of activities can be undertaken, the work is also loosely structured and allows for digressions and creative responses from the participants.

This creation of a fictional world for young people to engage with is not in itself particularly new, and can be seen in, for example, Dorothy Heathcote's 'Teacher in Role' and 'Mantle of the Expert' techniques, where the teacher or the pupils take on roles to facilitate the exploration of a particular topic (Heathcote 1995). Similarly Augusto Boal's forum theatre allows for the embodied exploration of oppression, and more importantly allows participants to try out ways of challenging or changing that oppression (Boal 1992). With forum theatre, however, there is a clear division between in role and out of role, often with a signifying item of costume or a prop used to distinguish clearly between these two states. Although the drama presented should reflect a real-life situation, there is no possibility for confusion between the two as the participants are told they are being shown a play, and then are able to replay the various scenes to try out different solutions to the oppressions shown. This is very different from the work of Triangle, which is more unusual still in that the process of development of the material is also undertaken in role. Hence as well as the eventual delivery of the product, so the performance itself is in some ways developed by the fictional characters that would normally be thought of as being 'contained' within it.

Frames and rules

Museum theatre, like the techniques of Heathcote and Boal, operates largely through a series of 'rules of the game', through which performers and spectators understand what is expected of them. Following Goffman (1986), one way of thinking of this is in terms of a set of frames, which Jackson and Leahy (2005: 310), when discussing the educational efficacy of theatre and theatre techniques in museums, identify as the external frame, the performative frame and the internal frames of the performance. The external frame is the broad context within which the participants engage with the event. For museum theatre this would be the frame of the museum as an institution. The performative frame is 'that which marks out the theatre event itself as theatre', and furthermore provides the audience with cues as to what sort of audience they should be, for example whether sitting to watch a traditional play or following the action around in a promenade performance (Jackson and Leahy 2005: 310). Finally the internal frames operate within the museum performance much as in any dramatic performance, and indicate character, narration, place, etc., through a range of dramatic conventions. A comparable set of frames could be envisaged for museum visiting more generally, with the external frame being the same in both cases and an interpretative frame replacing the performative frame. These frames guide the behaviour of the visitor, or response of the audience: the frame through which the activity is viewed determines what it is that is seen. A person in a white coat might be seen very differently through the institutional or performative frames, either as a curator or a 'mad scientist', and someone putting on a white coat might signify a change of character if viewed through an internal performance frame, if, for instance, actors were playing numerous characters.

The frame is created through a complex interaction between the horizon of expectation of the visitor/audience member, the material circumstances of the location (objects and their arrangement, lighting, architecture, text, etc) and the action of the performers, facilitators, curators, and so on. The frame analysis can also be reconsidered in terms of a set of 'rules' through which visitors interact with the museum. One advantage of reconfiguring this frame analysis in terms of a set of 'rules of the game' is that it clarifies that this is information that needs to be explained, either explicitly or implicitly, and understood or negotiated, however imperfectly and provisionally, in order to reach a shared understanding. The rules of the game are enacted, and exist through their enactment, rather than existing extant of that enactment.

One of the ongoing, though lessening, resistances to museum theatre comes from the potential or perceived inconsistency between the rules of the game for museums, and those for museum theatre. As Jackson and Leahy (2005: 305) argue, the use of drama in UK museums is 'still relatively constrained by practical, professional and philosophical factors' and:

The resistance to theatrical performance implies a disavowal of the performative nature of museum displays and indeed museum visiting, while distrust of the fictionalising effect of museum theatre is based on a refusal to acknowledge the role of the subjective, the arbitrary and the expedient in the construction and narration of history in the museum.

So when visiting a museum, regardless of whether or not theatre is used as an interpretative technique, a frame is used by the visitor, and the institutional rules of the game for the visit are not changed substantially by the introduction of dramatic techniques. While there might be fundamental disagreement as to how closely dramatic interpretation in traditional museum theatre should either follow material evidence or instead extrapolate from the known for the sake of narrative or performance reasons, part of the conflict comes from attempting to understand both sets of activity through the same frame (interpretative or performative), or using the same rules of the game, whereas for the museum and for theatre, whether immersive or not, the rules of the game are strikingly different. So although the institutional frame does not change, and the interpretative and performative frames fulfil similar broad functions, the particular details of those frames, as well as the internal frames, may be quite different. For example, the spatial rules for the museum might involve diffusion and separation of visitors, whilst for theatre a concentration and cohesion of audience might be required. Museums might generally encourage visitors to flow through the space, whilst museum theatre might require the 'clumping' of visitors. Similarly, the duration a visitor spends at any part of a museum might be highly variable and determined by the interests of the individual visitor, whereas museum theatre might exist for a specified period, and might only be able to be accessed at that time. Finally, traditional museum curatorial devices are generally passive and respond to the visitors' interrogation of them, while in contrast museum theatre interpretation has the potential to turn the tables and interrogate the visitors. As well as the genuine philosophical discussion that needs to be had surrounding the legitimacy of fiction in interpreting material collections, equally important is a means of establishing appropriate rules of the game for whatever types of museum theatre are used.

Tessa Bridal, in her book *Exploring Museum Theatre* (2004: 5) argues that:

Museum theatre begins with *content-based educational performances*, typically shorter than those in theatre venues and frequently interactive, performed *in formal and informal theatre spaces*, both within the museum and as outreach, *by trained museum theatre professionals for museum theatre audiences of all ages* and for school audiences.

This definition is clearly utilitarian rather than aspirational, and Triangle's work sits outside Bridal's definition in at least three key ways: in terms of content, educational aims and duration.

Though it may be accepted, as Eilean Hooper-Greenhill (1992: 3) states, that 'knowledge is now well understood as the commodity that museums offer', it remains the case that there is less agreement as to what the precise nature of that knowledge should be. Clearly though, if museums offer knowledge, not objects, then interpretation, understood as part of the process of production of knowledge from objects, becomes increasingly important. This move from object-content to interpretation-content can be taken further so that the objects (almost) vanish and we are left instead with the act (and acting) of interpretation.

Chico Talks

Chico Talks is in some ways atypical of Triangle's usual immersive museum theatre work, and was created in response to a collection of clown objects and ephemera discovered in the Herbert archives. These objects were used to develop a project in the Hillfields area of Coventry, where Irving Pollard, otherwise known as Chico the Clown, had lived. As Triangle describes it, the 'project is a journey into the life of a clown who lost his memory and voice in the Coventry Blitz and carved his way back to health through recreating the puppets he lost in the explosion which traumatised him' (Triangle 2006). This bio-graphical, narrative account does not give a satisfactory description of the piece, and audience members expecting a comfortable retelling of local history are unlikely to have their expectations fulfilled.

The performance of this 'journey' took place over ten days in August 2006. The CMP Soc (named after the Coventry Musical Play Society (1924–75), and inaccurately self-described as 'Britain's biggest histor-ical re-enactment company' (CMP Soc 2006)) recreated the 'life and times' of Pollard in a daily programme consisting of performances at fourteen venues in Hillfields. One way in which this differs from more traditional museum theatre work is that the CMP Soc, which developed, publicised and performed the work, consisted entirely of fictional characters created by the members of Triangle. This created an unpredictable and challenging set of relationships between audi-ence and performers, between history and creativity, and between art and honesty.

In attempting to establish the various rules of the game in oper-ation here it is worth looking at some conflicting definitions. The International Council of Museums, in Article 2 of its Statutes, defines a museum as an institution 'which acquires, conserves, researches, communicates and exhibits, for purposes of study, education and enjoyment, material evidence of people and their environment' (ICOM 2007: Statutes). The International Museum Theatre Alliance describes museum theatre as a 'specific kind of interpretation that employs fictional activity to communicate ideas, facts and concepts' (IMTAL 2006: Definitions). Kurt Zarniko, the character created for the *Chico Talks* project, describes the immersive museum per-formance methodology developed by the CMP Soc as investigating the 'museum's process of regeneration, conservation and pillage by exploiting performative phenomena such as disappearance, absence and object-relations' (CMP Soc 2006: Blog). Whilst it is perhaps a little dangerous to take the writings of a fictional character too seriously, it is clear that those involved in this immersive museum theatre work are far less concerned with the transmission of ideas, but are instead interested in performative responses to those ideas.

The first live experience on the Pollard Trail was titled *Pollard's Theatre*, and varied greatly from performance to performance in terms of form, if not function. Located in a church hall, a small fairground-type box office took money, mobile phone numbers – used later in the performance to text instructions to the audience – and photographs of the visitors, all of which contributed to the feel of wandering in on some rather strange local society. This is very different from the accepted model of museum theatre, where, in *Exploring Museum Theatre* Tessa Bridal (2004: 40) comments that:

In order for a performance to be successful, both the audience and the actors need to feel at ease. We can help audiences understand our expectations by telling them what those expectations are, and we can support performers by allowing them to take action where necessary.

This model of museum theatre is fundamentally pedagogic, with the intention of the museum theatre actor being able to convey as clearly as possible the information to the museum visitor. To facilitate this communication clear ground rules are established, with performers even 'taking action' to maintain this. The opening of *Chico Talks* did not set the audience at ease, but rather signalled that things were possibly going to be difficult, certainly confusing, and that audience members would not be allowed or able to passively receive neatly packaged and palatably presented local historical facts.

This prologue was followed by an introductory lecture by the director of the fictional CMP Soc, Lance F. S., played by the Triangle Artistic Director. Throughout, the distinction between fictional and non-fictional events, objects and persons began to be undermined. The artefacts presented were treated as authentic, at least as authentic as the characters presenting them. The rules of the game have not been made clear to the audience at this point. In terms of frame analysis it is unclear whether this activity should be viewed through the institutional frame of the Herbert, from which the objects gain their presumed authenticity; or through a performative frame, as it is reasonably clear that some form of performance is taking place; or through an interpretative frame focusing on the objects; or whether it should already be viewed through one of the internal frames which are used to establish performance conventions. The performers set up a distinction between what is happening at this point as real, and the performance that is about to begin, as fiction. However, the characters are so clearly exaggerated that most audience members will view this through a performative frame, and this may then cause them to question the authenticity of the artefacts shown to them, and indeed the authority of the institutional frame itself. As an opening then, there is a clear dichotomy between the low-key form taken, and the extremely exaggerated characters used to inhabit that form. One consequence of this was audience desensitisation towards those characters, which enabled the audience to handle the later, more formally challenging sections.

The second part of the opening was a performance by the CMP Soc of *Alf's Button*, a 1920s play in which Irving Pollard played the lead in 1946. This was clearly signed as moving to viewing through a performative frame, which again suggested that what had come before was not performance, even though clearly it had been. Here there was a threefold overlapping of actor, CMP Soc member and *Alf's Button* character. This section used deliberately 'bad' performances, with Lance F. S., the director, shouting instructions from amongst the audience, and pulling ropes over pulleys to create the required 'magical' effects on stage. For the audience there was a clear conflict in how to read the performance, as a well-performed comedy or a badly performed rehearsal. Additionally there was a difficulty in how to respond – if the performance was laughed at there was the very real risk of offending Lance, who appeared to be working hard at producing an effective piece of theatre.

Following the performance of *Alf's Button* there was a 'cup of tea' session with the company, and at this point the role of the audience began to change significantly from spectator to participant. Sitting round a table at the top end of the church hall, being offered tea and then bullied to pay a subscription contribution towards it, broke down the separation between audience and spectator and made them participants in the creation of this fictionalised reality. The audience were required to define their own rules of the game – rules that would then be challenged at various other points. Throughout the day these rules are refined, redefined, or challenged outright, most clearly with the final *Pollard Effekt* section where it was made explicit that a movement would be made beyond what was previously established as acceptable interaction between performers and audience.

Within interpretative museum theatre traditionally, the 'fiction' serves to convey the 'facts', interpretative facts relating to the material objects in the collection. Within immersive museum theatre, the fiction, itself presented as fact, develops through a web of performative interactions developed by a deliberately subjective response to the material objects. As Zarniko (CMP Soc 2006: Blog) states:

Productions are based around carefully structured realities shared by members of the CMP Soc. Performers and performative installations encourage, facilitate and pursue unpredictable strategic interactions with the general public. So far the CMP Soc has created a complex network of affectively ambiguous encounters between the historical and the everyday, between the politically correct and the anachronistic.

Throughout the piece there were a number of ambiguous encounters between actors, the core audience and the general public. Following 'the cup of tea' discussed earlier was a procession from the church hall to the ruined St Peter's church, for a re-creation of Pollard's wedding. The audience were given flowers to process behind a vintage car borrowed from Coventry Transport Museum, which carried the happy couple. As the procession travelled the short distance between the two churches a number of children ran out from the houses lining the route and asked the character whether they 'could come to the church' that day. The rather grotesque nature of the characters combined with the unusual activities that they were engaged in meant that they could not have been taken as anything other than fictional characters, but the young residents of Hillfields were quite happy to interact with them in what appeared to be a very genuine manner. They were quite able to understand the rules of the game, at least for that short section.

A slightly more difficult interaction came in a section called *Tipper Territory*, involving the ritualised return of a bottled finger to a site overlooked by some tower blocks scheduled for demolition. This is a controversial development, and there was clearly some resentment at the theatre company coming in and using it as a location. During the performance a number of objects were thrown out of windows in the tower block, creating a real sense of apprehension amongst the participants. A final example of the interaction was in the section *Shandin, a song of loss*, where members of the CMP Soc performed a Kurdistan folk song in a Kurdistan café, and a number of the regulars at the café would join in and add additional verses.

The various exchanges with the residents of Hillfields also presented the opportunity for action completely outside of the existing or established rules of the game. For instance, for those who came across the performance without seeing any of the publicity material, there was no obvious connection with the Herbert Museum, and so the institutional frame or rules would be entirely lacking. It is a distinct possibility that other sets of rules might then be invented to govern the interactions, for instance the rules appropriate to the café, or perhaps ironic or humorous rules invented by the young people.

The final section of the piece, the *Pollard Effekt*, was prefaced with dire warnings that the CMP Soc could not be held responsible for anything that happened to the audience if they agreed to take part in it. As throughout the day the lines between fiction and reality had become increasingly blurred, it was difficult to know how to take this warning. The nature of this final section indeed moves almost entirely from the communication of information to a subjective performative experience, as the development through the day goes from object-content, to interpretation-content and then finally to experience-content.

With such an atypical process for developing the performance material, the creation of audience expectation is unusually complex. An unusually narrow subjective (fictional) perspective is used to create the identity of the performance event, a perspective that in many ways is misguided or even self-delusional. The rules of the game that usually exist in live performance, or even those particular conventions pre-existing for interpretative museum theatre become unreliable and untrustworthy, and either audience members are required to construct new rules, or risk having their expectations frustrated.

The way in which audiences respond to theatrical performance and to museum visiting appear to be so different only when the standard model of each is considered. *Chico Talks* offers a valuable example of how un-theatre-like and how un-museum-like museum theatre can be. When measured against the standard model of museum theatre *Chico Talks* perhaps falls short – the educational outcomes would be difficult to measure, there was little consistency of experience for the visitors and if imagined as 'outreach' it perhaps did little to bring new visitors into the museum. In terms of the International Museum Theatre Alliance definition of communicating ideas, facts and concepts it would again be difficult to identify even what those facts might be, let alone whether they were communicated or even 'true'. The piece demanded a great deal in terms of time and space, for performers and audience. What *Chico Talks* achieved, however, was for the relatively small number of visitors/audience members who took part in it to completely reconsider the rules of the game for theatre visiting, museum visiting, and for their own creative engagements in those activities. As the piece moved so far outside of the institutional frame (and for some audience members was perhaps never seen through that frame at all) the challenge to create a set of rules for engaging with it became a genuinely creative act. The audience members contributed to the piece not only as spectators or witnesses, not only through the creation of performance content such as the ritual of returning the finger, but even more through the shared creation of the means and mode of interaction: the very rules of the game.

The various identities created by the performers of *Chico Talks* existed in a range of virtual and real spaces. Zarniko himself read an early version of this chapter, and in *Pollard's Blog* (CMP Soc 2006) responded that at 'CMP Soc we are making a case for manipulating meaning, images and identity in ways that are not cynical, but transparent and playful'. Performers in immersive museum theatre might be seen to be in an unusually powerful position, as the audience might appear unaware of the rules of the game. In fact, the rules of the game are so fluid that the performers are left in an incredibly exposed position, and must trust in the audience to take part in the shared creative process of establishing and re-establishing the rules throughout the performance. Perhaps the only unchanging rule is that everything takes place within the immersive fictional space. Not all audience members responded well to this, but frustration and disappointment can be the result of any creative endeavour.

Zarniko also claims that 'CMP Soc's museum performance may be distinguished by its adherence to and immersion in an intermediate reality that begins internally with the performing subject and becomes transitional in the negotiation with external actuality' (CMP Soc 2006: Blog). As part of this process the adherence to historical accuracy, normally such a key component of interpretative museum theatre, becomes undermined. The fictional reality is presented with the same conviction as the evidence from the material collection, leading to an uncertainty and unreliability becoming apparent when examining the work against standards of historical accuracy and fidelity. When the work is measured against its own standards of authenticity, with an audience engagement developed responsively, it provides an effective paradigm for a more autonomous and creative form of museum theatre.

References

Bicknell, S. and Mazda, X. (1993) *Enlightening or Embarrassing: An Evaluation of Drama in the Science Museum.* London: National Museum of Science and Industry.

Boal, A. (1992) *Games for Actors and Non-actors.* London: Routledge.

Bridal, T. (2004) *Exploring Museum Theatre.* Walnut Creek, CA: AltaMira Press.

CMP Soc (2006) website. Available www.cmpsoc.kk5.org (accessed 22 January 2009).

Goffman, E. (1986) *Frame Analysis.* Boston, MA: Northeastern University Press.

Heathcote, D. (1995) *Drama for Learning: Dorothy Heathcote's Mantle of the Expert Approach to Education.* Portsmouth, NH: Heinemann.

Hooper-Greenhill, Eilean (1992) *Museums and the Shaping of Knowledge.* London: Routledge.

Hughes, C. (1998) *Museum Theatre: Communicating with Visitors through Drama.* Portsmouth, NH: Heinemann.

International Council of Museums (ICOM) (2007) website. Available www.icom.museum (accessed 22 January 2009).

International Museum Theatre Alliance (IMTAL) (2006) website. Available: www.imtal.org (accessed 22 January 2009).

Jackson, A. and Leahy, H.R. (2005) '"Seeing it for real...?" Authenticity, theatre and learning in museums'. *Research in Drama Education,* **10**(3): 303–25.

Triangle Theatre (2006) '*Chico Talks – The Pollard Trail*'. Available www.triangletheatre.co.uk (accessed 22 January 2009).

10 | *User-generated content and the participative market*

GREGOR WHITE

According to the December 2008 Internet Activity Index, half of the people using the World Wide Web are accessing social media content, constituting by far the most popular activity of web users (OPA 2008a). It is an activity that is increasingly indicative of the Internet's direction of travel, and shows that accessing, sharing and producing video, music and entertainment media is becoming definitive of the medium. If people are not accessing media, they are probably using email or VOIP telecommunications like Skype (30.4 per cent), shopping (14.2 per cent), or accessing search services (6.7 per cent) (OPA 2008a). These are activities that individuals would probably be doing generally, if they were not doing them online. So why should online activities still feel novel when we watch TV, go to the cinema, socialise, communicate, shop and learn every day? These kinds of social activity are fundamental to society building and help define the nature of our communities. They are formative in our relationships and our values. These activities, and the artefacts produced, have an intrinsic, social significance. Our sense of identity and community is predicated on them. Such activities and artefacts can be regarded as the user-generated content of every community; the by-product of social activities where individual community members are both users and creators. Artefacts generated in this way are the product of established interests and traditions generated in response to dynamic technological and procedural practices that are agreed as being of value to the community. The relationships between activities, the technologies that support them, and how the artefacts are used, constitute much of contemporary experience and define and confirm meaning and value of the culture to itself.

In light of this, value judgements about user-generated content must consider the role of digital media content created by the community not in terms of quality or proficiency, but rather how such content helps fledgling online communities define themselves through shared and negotiated meaning, and how this in turn creates new forms of engagement, audiences and markets that are born of participation and supported by participative communities. In making judgements about value we must draw upon assumptions about the changing nature of online community activity, trends in media production and Internet usage, and in particular think about the relationships within communities and how they rely upon shared value systems.

User-generated content (UGC) is a specialist term that has migrated into common usage and is generally agreed to describe any, and all, digital media content generated by users for the purposes of self-expression and sharing ideas. It is specific to content published exclusively on the Internet outside of the media publishing industry as opposed to information and media produced by professional content creators for mainstream distribution. The phrase offers insight into the complexity of the social and information environments where UGC gains meaning and value.

UGC and the web

Unpacking the term UGC implies that individual users are not the passive viewers, listeners or readers we might associate with traditional forms of media consumption, but are active in creating content and are in possession of specialist expertise and technology that allows them not only to access online materials, but to actively contribute to it. There are without doubt technological and intellectual barriers to accessing internet services, most of which, though rudimentary, can appear bewildering and insurmountable to the uninitiated. That there are those who seem to have been initiated into these secrets raises suspicion and distrust, leading some to question the individual's commitment to the real world. Because active participation in online communities is not public there is a tendency to think of these communities as constituted from those other or different to ourselves.

The reality is, however, that this group amounts to a significant proportion of the developed world. Current estimates of global internet users are in the region of 1.4 billion, rising daily. A large proportion of this number will participate in online environments both through consumption and production of media content. The 2006 report by Pew Internet reported that 35 per cent of the adult internet user population were publishing their thoughts or creations online, rising to 57 per cent of teenage users (Lenhart 2006). The 2007 Organisation for Economic Co-operation and Development (OECD) report, 'Participative Web and User-created Content', suggests European Community participation to be around 30 per cent of the adult population. Figures from Asia show 8.7 million Japanese bloggers and 7.2 million social network members; 50 per cent of Korean internet users publish personal homepages or blogs; and 43.2 per cent of Chinese internet users use bulletin boards, blogs, social networks and instant messaging (OECD 2007: 10). New online technologies offer access to media production tools and techniques at previously unimagined levels. As of December 2007 Technorati was tracking 112.8 million English language blogs (Helmond 2008). The China Internet Network Information Center reports 72.82 million Chinese blogs or self-publishing sites for aspiring authors. Video uploads include the sublime to the ridiculous on YouTube, with reported traffic levels of 65,000 uploads and 100 million downloads per day (van Grinsven 2007). Sophisticated documentaries and films have resulted in user-generated advertising making its way into mainstream broadcast. Current TV and Current.com, a hybrid UGC video post/news aggregator, straddles the internet protocol television (IPTV)/cable divide by publishing high-quality content and encouraging high journalistic standards.

The demographic of the community is as diverse as its activities, with different subgroups enjoying different activities. Users between twenty and thirty years old are more likely to blog and file share, whereas teenagers will share content through instant messaging services and video posting. Each group and subgroup identifies with particular technological or communications environments and user communities. The role of the UGC artefact as a social device with a community-driven filtering function allows individuals with shared values or concerns to find each other and has contributed to the functionality and appeal of social network sites such as MySpace and Facebook.

The emergence of participation as a description of online activity is associated with the wider platform development referred to as Web 2.0, which encompasses developments in new forms of online services in response to the rapid market contraction in 2001, or the bursting of the dotcom bubble. New social networks such as MySpace and Facebook characterise Web 2.0 applications along with collaborative spaces such as Wikipedia and YouTube, news aggregators like Digg and Technorati and blogging sites like Blogger and BlogSpot.

The OECD report (2007) explicitly presents a technology fundamentally different:

The concept of the 'participative web' is based on an internet increasingly influenced by intelligent web services that empower users to contribute to developing, rating, collaborating and distributing internet content and customising internet applications. As the internet is more embedded in people's lives users draw on new internet applications to express themselves through 'user-created content'. (OECD 2007: 4)

The terms 'participative web' and 'Web 2.0' became conflated at the O'Reilly Media Web 2.0 Conference in 2004. The conference was hosted by O'Reilly Media whose charismatic Chief Executive Officer Tim O'Reilly has been a supporter and advocate of open-source community development and a proselytiser of emergent technologies. (As well as a number of annual conferences, O'Reilly is also host to the annual FOO (Friends of O'Reilly) camp where guests meet with the agenda of how to encourage technological and ideological innovation on the web. Andrew Keen's 2007 polemic 'The Cult of the Amateur' described the participants as '[Tim] O'Reilly and his San Francisco acolytes ... a mix of graying hippies, new media entrepreneurs and technology geeks' (Keen 2007: 13).) The spirit of the group was aspirational. They plotted to democratise the web and liberate the user experience from the didactic model of Web 1.0, and user knowledge from the tyranny of expert knowledge. Concurrent to this thinking was the emergence of a number of highly successful new platforms that exploited the rapid spread of domestic broadband services in North America, Europe and Asia, as well as software and development techniques that supported enhanced interaction allowing users to upload as well as download, to create what O'Reilly describes as an 'architecture of participation' (O'Reilly 2004). In coining the phrase, O'Reilly makes reference to Linus Torvald, Linux OS Project Co-ordinator, and Larry Lessig, founder of the Centre for Internet and Society at Stanford University, both of whom refer to systems architecture in drastically differing fields, politics and software operating systems, as a means of supporting and predicting effect. The suggestion was that the systems architecture of Web 2.0 has made a participatory web inevitable.

Table 10.1. *Top ten most popular UK websites (Alexa 2008)*

UK ranking	Site	First offered	Global ranking	UGC/ social network
1	Google UK	2004	38	*
2	Facebook	2004	6	*
3	YouTube	2005	2	*
4	Yahoo	1995	1	*
5	Windows Live	2005	3	*
6	Google	2004	4	*
7	EBay UK	1995	97	*
8	BBC Headline Ticker	1996	—	
9	MySpace	2003	5	*
10	Bebo	2005	120	*

* indicates content sharing or social networking features.

Over the following years O'Reilly's vision of Web 2.0 became a reality. Of the current top ten visited sites in the UK, seven made their first public services available between 2003 and 2005; nine offer social networking or UGC upload services or both, and six also appear in the global top ten.

The growing popularity of these sites matched the growing public awareness of the success stories of Web 2.0 applications. The mainstream reception of UGC and the participative web was marked in *Time* magazine's selection of 'You' as 2006 Person of the Year. 'You. Yes, you. You control the Information Age. Welcome to your world' (*Time* 2006: front cover). Managing Editor Richard Stengel explained the idea behind the choice in that issue's editorial:

… that individuals are changing the nature of the information age, that the creators and consumers of user-generated content are transforming arts, politics and commerce, that they are engaged citizens of a new digital democracy. From user-generated images of Baghdad strife and the London Underground bombing to the 'macaca' moment that might have altered the US midterm elections to the hundreds of thousands of outpourings of hope and poetry and self-absorption, this new global nervous system is changing the way we perceive the world. And the consequences of it all are both hard to know and impossible to overestimate. (Stengel 2006: 4)

Stengel's hyperbole matches the mood of the moment, reflecting the FOO Camp vision of Tim O'Reilly and his band of hippies, geeks and entrepreneurs. In the Person of the Year issue, *Time* highlighted a number of individuals who personify or typify the Web 2.0 citizen and the nature of participation and practice in the new online environment. They are participants in social networks and blogs, creating their own content and recommending and rating the content of others, and they represent the constituency of the participative web. Those featured included Lane Hudson, a citizen journalist, who uploaded amorous emails from Florida representative Mark Foley to a congressional aide, resulting in Foley's resignation and withdrawal from the congressional elections; Ali Kurdishid, photographer, who came to public attention through images posted on Flickr; Megan Gill, social network super-user; Lee Kelley, military blogger (individual entries on his blog 'Wordsmith at War' have recorded over 200,000 hits); and Shekar Ramanuja Sidarth, who tracked the election campaign of Virginia senator George Allen. Sidarth's video recording of the senator's personal racial attack on him has become known as 'the macaca incident'; its posting on YouTube led to public outrage and Allen issuing a hasty apology. The issue also featured Waz and Lenny, who post an online cookery show; Harriet Klausner, a librarian who has reviewed more books on Amazon than any other user; Tila Tequila, and Smosh. The issue continued offering a name and face for every form of online participation or content creation (*Time* 2006).

Of particular interest here is Leila's story, subtitled 'The Real Lonelygirl' (Grossman 2006). This introduces a phenomenon that can offer insight into how user-led innovations in media production and distribution are built on participatory communities with shared values which become apparent in online social networks. Leila is a young video blogger with the username ppppanic who shares her problems and desires with likeminded individuals in a teen blogging community on YouTube. What they do represents the way that groups have re-purposed UGC and content-sharing sites in order to create social spaces. This is a phenomenon paradigmatic of participation in Web 2.0 communities in that it is user led, media based and it supports community value creation through user participation. YouTube was neither conceived nor designed to be a social network. These functions rose from user participation and the architecture of the platform and it prospered because it fulfilled a specific social need of its constituency. Leila describes the 'feeling of togetherness' with other video bloggers as 'a beautiful thing' (Grossman 2006: 32). This socialisation and inhabitation of YouTube is peculiar to asynchronous applications. These websites are not information kiosks or shops. They are sign-posted locations where individuals and groups who have common identities or motivations can find each other and share ideas and experiences. They are social in as much as user knowledge is based on participation, emerging conventions and trust. Users communicate by publishing their own content and viewing the content of others.

Bree, aka Lonelygirl15, was a teenage girl much like Leila who started posting a video blog in June 2006. She told of her boy problems and school work in video messages posted two or three times a week. After a few episodes the content changed tone as she disclosed that her parent's strict religious beliefs stopped her from 'doing things that other kids did' (Davis 2006: 238). The inclusion of footage that increasingly suggested Bree's home life was less than normal led to an emotional episode entitled 'My Parents Suck ... ' posted on 4 July 2006, which saw the average total hit rate of 50–100,000 per post matched in the first two hours, ultimately reaching nearly 900,000 hits. Subsequent episodes regularly received between 300,000 and 800,000 hits. The particular significance of the Lonelygirl15 phenomenon was not the number of hits ('Evolution of Dance', posted by judsonlalpply on 6 April 2006, is the most often viewed YouTube posting, having been watched more than 111.2 million times as of January 2009) but that Lonelygirl15 was not a girl named Bree and her webcam, but an actress named Jessica Rose and the product of co-creators Ramesh Flinders, Greg Goodfried and Miles Beckett. Like all media successes Lonelygirl15 was part plan, part luck. The producers of Lonelygirl15 had an insight into audience expectation that was more sophisticated than traditional TV productions, and although Rose proved difficult to convince that the project was serious, her casting was central to its success. In Jessica Rose and the character of Bree, the producers had identified the kind of personality, content and events that appealed to the YouTube community. She could be perceived as one of their own. The audience started to speculate about Bree's faith, where she lived and her relationships. They would start to leave messages offering personal advice or enquiring about her situation.

Her character is also deliberately crafted to target the web's most active demographics. Nerds geek out on the idea that this beautiful girl lists astrophysicist Richard Feynman and poet E.E. Cummings as heroes. Horny guys respond to the tame but tantalising glimpses of her cleavage. Teenage girls sympathise with her boy troubles and her sometimes stormy relationship with her strict parents. Early on viewers started emailing to offer advice and sympathy. Others wanted to talk dirty and discuss mathematical equations. (Davis 2006: 238)

In response to the participation of the audience, scriptwriter Flinders was able to write the Lonelygirl15 scripts around the subjects that were engaging the community, tapping into the community response as a way of ensuring continued viewer participation. On Friday 3 August 2007, LG15 Studios marked a new partnership with social network MySpace by showing the finale of Lonelygirl15 exclusively on MySpaceTV. Known as '12 in 12', twelve videos were uploaded over the course of twelve hours resulting in the highest ever one-day views of the series. On 16 July 2007, episode one of Kate Modern was shown on Bebo, MySpace's direct competitor in the teen social network space. Kate Modern is a sibling show to Lonelygirl15, part of what is now referred to as the 'Breesphere'. However, this show is openly explicit in its fiction and in its collaboration with its audience, allowing viewers to suggest storylines and interact with the story through associated media elements and an alternate reality game (ARG). As the latest iteration of a new media format, and given the benefit of hindsight, Kate Modern has a number of advantages over Lonelygirl15. If the creators of Lonelygirl15 had known how successful the show would become, and that the audience would happily play along with the fiction, they might have taken the opportunity to offer product placement opportunities, multi-platform delivery premium subscription and layered access models and to exploit the advertising potential. Kate Modern does not miss any of these opportunities and, while it may not have the mystique of Lonelygirl15, LG15 Studios employed upward of twenty people on two continents and has not, as yet, entered 'mainstream' television drama production. And yet, the funding keeps flowing in from technology and production investors (Buckman 2008).

A UGC 'community'

The story of LG15 Studios is not typical by any means. Most of the UGC success stories have used social networking sites as a direct marketing

tool and will move into mainstream media markets to exploit their
online following. What Kate Modern represents is the emergence of
a new form of media production and distribution that appeals to the
teenage generation that is alienated from traditional broadcast television. By engaging with the architecture of the technology and the aspirations of the community, EQAL, the company established by Beckett
and Goodfried to continue producing Kate Modern, has developed a
medium that appeals to its constituency, and a track record of success
in engaging an elusive demographic in a monetised media environment that has proved problematic to television producers and television advertisers. By creating media that comes directly from its target
audience, the creators of Lonelygirl15 have tapped into the processes
of negotiating meaning shared by the teen video blogging community,
and by using the vernacular of the community, they have created value
in the exchange of meaningful content through fundamental features
of the participative web. The only assumption that is true of participatory media is that users will find ways to use content sharing to project
their social identities and develop a shared cultural language through
the community's cultural output. Thus as Sharpe and Salomon (2008)
note there is a limited usefulness in reducing social networks to relational mapping between individuals. 'Social networking makes little
sense if we leave out the objects that mediate the ties between people'
(Engeström 2005 in Sharpe and Salomon 2008: 18). The 'object' is the
reason people affiliate with 'specific' others rather than just anyone.

The development of a shared language and a practice of cultural
production can be identified as having a significant role in the development of community in online societies. An understanding of this
can help us to understand the relationship between participation and
the creation of meaning, and the function of UGC in the online community. While describing a group as 'users' has a shorthand value in
identifying an activity as particular to a technological and systematic
environment, if we were to describe them as active participants in a
community of shared practice (self-publishing) we can better understand the value and meaning of the content they produce. The concept
of a community of shared practice also offers a theoretical framework
to apply to these judgements.

Much of the thinking around productive social practice has been
developed from the work of Russian psychologist Lev Vygotsky
whose development of learning theories was based on the study of
object-centred activities. The two main strands to emerge from his

work are Activity Theory, developed by Alexei Leont'ev and currently led by Yrjö Engeström (Engeström *et al.* 1999) and educational theories around communities of practice, currently led by Jean Lave and Etienne Wenger (Lave and Wenger 1991). Leont'ev and Engeström's Activity Theory presents the object as the medium of social activity transformed by social practice into a unit of cultural exchange made significant by its specific cultural content.

In activity there does take place a transfer of an object into its subjective form, into an image; also in activity a transfer of activity into its objective results, into its products, is brought about. Taken from this point of view, activity appears as a process in which mutual transfers between the poles 'subject-object' are accomplished. (Leont'ev 1978: 50)

Engeström (1999) describes how individual practice becomes significant to the community through the the socialisation of this subject-object.

The central issues of activity theory remain the object – that is what connects my individual actions to the collective activity. However, the projected outcome is no longer momentary and situational; rather it consists of societally important new, objectified meanings and relatively lasting new patterns of interaction. (Engeström *et al.* 1999: 31)

In this way we can identify UGC as the objects around which social practice on the Internet is mediated, and the development of online culture as the motive for the emergence of social behaviour in UGC environments. Vygotsky (1981: 163) proposes that shared language is deployed formatively between adult and child, initially as a means of communication and shared action, which becomes internalised as a means of thought and action control. In this way the child enters his culture through the acquisition of social and communal rules and values, mediated by the active use of social instruments. The instrument becomes the communication tool through being imbued with significance within the community of shared practice. Engeström has developed Activity Theory to present the view of the 'meaningful object', where cultural objects become the carriers of meaning in specific cultural environments. He describes interaction with these objects as culturally transformative and socially evolutionary.

The object refers to the 'raw material' or 'problem space' at which the activity is directed and which is moulded and transformed into outcomes with the help of physical and symbolic, external and internal mediating instruments, including both tools and signs. (Engeström 1990: 79)

Wenger (1999) identifies the explicit elements of practice in the codified cultural output of the community, its symbolic language and the implicit elements in its hermeneutics. He does not define practice as manual or mental activity but as activities that, when conflated in the creation of social or cultural products, become meaningful. This is true of cultural production in general, where any understanding of practice involves simultaneous engagement with both the intellectual underpinning of the practice and its reification through practice. The extent of the community's understanding of both elements renders the practice more or less meaningful and in turn more or less valuable. While Activity Theory presents entry into social or cultural practice as mediated by object-centred activity, the community of practice literature proposes that the hermeneutics of specific practices impart procedural, and therefore meaningful, value to the objects of social or productive activity. In their 1991 book *Communities of Practice: Legitimate Peripheral Participation,* Lave and Wenger detail the knowledge dynamics of specialist groups, and in particular, the construction of meaningful artefacts through a process of mutual engagement and community participation. Wenger (1999) offers a useful approach to understanding the internal dynamics that generate the meaningful artefacts, which in turn, define a community of shared practice through commonly held values. 'The concept of [social] practice connotes doing, but not just doing in and of itself. It is doing in an historical and social context that gives structure and meaning to what we do. In this sense practice is always social practice' (Wenger 1999: 47).

The greater the investment in the practice, the higher the products are valued. The significance of the social nature of online UGC communities is that it offers an access point to a community of practice that enables meaning and value to develop around the content. Once again it is object-centred participation that ensures the persistence of the practice. This phenomenon is what Wenger refers to as 'reification' where 'understanding is given form. This form then becomes a focus for negotiated meaning' (Wenger 1999: 59). The product of the community, in this case online media content, becomes the point around which relationships are formed and culture is developed and communities become dynamic.

The sharing of individual and group identity forms the underlying currency of participative online social networks. Even the minimum of information the individual is obliged to reveal when participating in a social network locates him or her within a specific user group, regardless of whether a real name or username is used, likes and dislikes are listed, or whether an image is posted. All these decisions start to build a picture of the individual as a social network citizen, a socialite or a 'lurker'. What is central is that social groups and individuals find each other. Publishing personal details as well as embedding media content in profiles allows this to happen, just as in the 'real' world where individuals deploy a range of visual and behavioural clues to demonstrate particular social affiliations, or attend events where they find people who share their sensibilities. Online social networks cannot afford such subtleties, hence the lists of favourite books, heroes and villains, hobbies and activities, etc. The more active the individuals, the more explicit the mores and aspirations of the groups, and the easier they are for others of like mind to find.

Communities and markets

That users can embed media, rate users and recommend content, establishes support for the forms of exchange that are emerging as participative markets. The constitution of online communities shows that a core community of active users is the driver of UGC publication. In January 2007 Second Life claimed over 880,000 active users from a community of 2.5 million residents (OECD 2007: 12) and YouTube claimed a daily upload total of 50–60,000 against downloads of more than 100 million (OECD 2007: 20). Technographics figures for 2007 published by Forrester Research show this proportion of active to passive users is consistent across UGC communities and types.

This distribution mode of active and passive participants in market communities has been identified as essential in supporting market dynamics, in both on- and offline markets and across diverse communities. In his 2001 book *The Tipping Point*, Malcolm Gladwell introduces 'the law of the few' to explain how some markets respond to the stimulation of particularly active participants with expert or specialist knowledge and how the application of specialist knowledge can transform products from local to global commodities and see

Table 10.2. *Percentage of consumers using blogs or user-generated content (Li and Bernhoff 2008: 20)*

	United States	United Kingdom	France	Germany	Japan	South Korea
Read blogs	25%	10%	21%	10%	52%	31%
Comment on blogs	14%	4%	10%	4%	20%	21%
Write blogs	11%	3%	7%	2%	12%	18%
Watch user-generated video	29%	17%	15%	16%	20%	5%
Upload user-generated video	8%	4%	2%	2%	3%	4%
Listen to podcast	11%	7%	6%	7%	4%	0%

sales rocket. He introduces three kinds of specialists. 'Connectors' are individuals with extraordinarily active networks of friends and contacts who collect people 'naturally and instinctively' (Gladwell 2001: 41) and actively maintain relationships. 'Mavens' are knowledge holders, slightly obsessive individuals who derive pleasure from playing inside games with market values and prices. Also referred to as 'price vigilantes' (Gladwell 2001: 60), they are also disposed to share their insight with others. 'Salesmen' (Gladwell 2001: 70) are identified as critical to the tipping process where ideas or products tip from niche markets or communities into mass-market commodities. Gladwell presents these individuals as actors in raising awareness, drawing on the analogy between the spread of knowledge and epidemiological behaviour or viral infection, but focused on traditional mass-marketing and the conversion of niche products into high-demand products. Conversely, in *The Long Tail*, Anderson (2006) analyses new models for retail markets and suggests that products do not need to tip to become viable in online retail environments. He argues that specialist knowledge expressed through recommendations, and accessibility to specialist knowledge through social features of content site membership, will drive consumers into new markets or 'further

down the long tail' (Anderson 2006: 119). He proposes that the negligible retail and distribution costs of online outlets will offer greater
diversity of products and greater liquidity in traditionally niche interests. Where high street retailers are dependant on high-volume sales
of limited stock to be cost-effective, online retailers can offer an
almost limitless stock of products because of negligible storage costs.
However, the economics of the retail sector are not matched on the
production side. Although small numbers of sales can justify the storage of digital files they cannot support professional production costs,
resulting in the niche market becoming dependent on UGC products
to enhance the viability of niche media and encouraging community
participation in the filtering function of specialist recommendations.

Although there are different community effects in these different
market scenarios, both are dependent on active participation by the
consumer to connect supply with demand. The difference in Gladwell's
traditional markets and Anderson's online market is that the form of
participation described by Anderson is not simply a case of commodity transaction, but the commodification or monetisation of social
dynamics of individual and group expertise offered by online technologies. This kind of participation is transparent to marketers and
offers target demographic 'eyeball time' to advertisers, where participants exchange valuable attention time for a sense of community and
the chance to be entertained. It offers market solutions that work with
the community in the same way as LG15 Studios did, to establish new
models that address the specifics of online consumerism and exploit
the architecture of the media, that are defining a new market.

Under these conditions, economies have mutated and flourished in
a variety of ways through the dissolution of the link between producer and consumer. Products and solutions are developed through
participation in collaborative and iterative design and development
projects such as the Wikipedia contributor community that deploy
'mob' or 'crowd' action and knowledge to produce equivalent output
to those of smaller teams of highly skilled experts. Similarly, community activities may result in innovative solutions for online use or
services that may or may not make the transition to mainstream culture. New media audience and market models, as well as their administration and legislation, have evolved and been developed through
the participative behaviour of the online community. This form of
engagement with online markets has changed the nature of online

retailing through increasing the diversity of community participation. The growth of niche sectors in the retail economy, driven by the accessibility of specialist content, was established by the success of peer-to-peer file sharing communities supported by distributed expert opinion which acted as a guide to new content. The increasing demand for digital media and the portability offered by new formats, alongside improved accessibility to broadband services, make the digital media market the largest and most dynamic on the Internet and the driver for many of the market, licensing and intellectual property innovations in recent years. The volatility of these markets is evidenced by the transition from widespread media piracy, through the crisis in confidence in the music industry and the development of new media formats, to the relatively secure and steady states offered by iTunes and other hardware-affiliated formats. Alongside technological innovations, this period has witnessed the emergence of new market dynamics and new forms of consumer behaviour and the transparency of the producer/consumer relationships.

Intrinsic to the technology that supports the Internet and World Wide Web is the accessibility to user data. Every computer with access to the Internet has a unique identity or internet protocol (IP) address, making it possible for Internet Service Providers (ISPs) to record and analyse every website visit and subject search entered by web users. Beyond the IP address individual user identity cannot be verified, and published user data is anonymous to a large extent. Privacy, however, is not the concern of the market. The data generated by ISPs is of enormous value to anyone interested in the demographic make-up of individuals or groups of users in relation to online behaviour and media consumption habits. Once again it is through active participation that data aggregators can build up user profiles with a level of sophistication and personalisation that canvassing or viewer surveys cannot replicate.

Evidence of the effectiveness of online marketing can be found in the Online Publishers Association (OPA) Europe report (2008b). It predicts the UK will be the first of the world's major economies to see TV spending overtaken by the Internet and that spending on internet advertising in 2009 in the UK will increase by 31 per cent against a 1 per cent rise in spending on TV ads. Given the functionality of search engines involving the typing in of the subject of interest, it is no surprise to find that 65 per cent of online advertising is associated with search activities (OPA 2008b). As a result of developments in internet services and technologies, the way users find what they are looking for has also radically changed. The efficiency and efficacy of search engines such as Google and tools such as PageRank and AdSense are deployed to tailor advertising at an individual level. These technologies not only ensure that the individual conducting a search finds a suitable site and has a satisfactory experience, but they also use the vast collection of user data to build sophisticated ranking systems. PageRank describes itself as a model of user behaviour:

PageRank relies on the uniquely democratic nature of the web by using its vast link structure as an indicator of an individual page's value. In essence, Google interprets a link from page A to page B as a vote, by page A, for page B. But, Google looks at considerably more than the sheer volume of votes, or links a page receives; for example, it also analyses the page that casts the vote. Votes cast by pages that are themselves 'important' weigh more heavily and help to make other pages 'important.' Using these and other factors, Google provides its views on pages' relative importance. (Brin and Page 1998)

Google deploys its AdSense software to target advertising, matching interests and search habits. The software automatically crawls the content of the pages viewed and matches advertisements based on relevance to the content of pages viewed. Other forms of interaction also can be monetised to different extents, from the banner advertisements that are familiar from the first form of web advertising to less discriminating pay-per-click models. All of these software tools are dependent upon participation in the form of surfing and searching, and the ways in which surfing habits conform to user profiles, to initiate the marketing and advertising responses. In this way, the architecture and functionality of the platform not only support users in social behaviour that encourages shared meaning and exchange value in content output, but also record and analyse these activities in order to monetise the dynamics of interaction, resulting in an environment and community fundamentally compatible with a participative market.

Conclusion

The online world was built on 'doing' and 'sharing' by the giants of interactive media Norbert Wiener and Vanevar Bush (Parker and Jordan 2001: xviii), who envisioned machines that could record and disseminate knowledge and technologies that would help users innovate and create. Tim Berners-Lee shared their vision in developing the protocols that would become the World Wide Web (Berners-Lee 1989 in Parker and Jordan 2001: 210). The internet and web technologies have always been participative and supported specialist community activities and information sharing. Ideologically, they were conceived as technologies that would allow everyone to participate and share in the sum of human knowledge for the common good, encouraging meaning making through consensus as a driver for participation. The activists who replaced the academics as the driving force behind the expansion and adoption of internet and web technologies envisioned a utopian space where they could act out their social, political or environmental visions and encourage participation through the organisational and social potential of the technology.

The building blocks of the market models that currently exist online were put in place before computer technologies existed. Establishing exchange systems that were dependent on shared notions of cultural meaning that act to confirm communal values and community identity has always underwritten specialist markets. Exclusive communities whose cultural output is scarce drive the market for luxury goods. The accessibility of the Internet and the easy reproducibility of digital media means that the cultural output of online communities should be judged in the context of open sharing and exchange. UGC is not created or shared in order to be regarded by the cool, critical eye or ear of the audience but functions to identify the creator as part of a community and as a beacon to others to join in. UGC has hybridised the language of television, radio and the press and develops its own vernacular. The Internet functioned as an open exchange system making an individual's content anyone's content, resulting in online content becoming everyone's content. The communications industry response has been to try to shackle online distribution and peer-to-peer file sharing. Content sharing has been long established in online communities and the use of licensed content in the production of new content or UGC mash-ups is taxing the minds of copyright holders. The solutions to these challenges are shaping new legislation, commodities and dynamics of online markets. Many solutions are being driven by communities. User-led innovation applies the wisdom of the crowd to create legal, retail and media solutions that best address specific demands. Participation in online markets supports a range of emerging consumption models that are changing the nature of media production and distribution beyond recognition and creating new consumer and market behaviours.

Transactions within these markets are predicated on a shared sense of value, both extrinsic and intrinsic, of a commodity that varies widely in its relationship with its community. Those who understand how to listen to communities and to exploit the movement of content rather than the acquisition of content will be best placed to exploit the participative market. Uniquely, the participative market knows what you like because it knows who you are. And it knows who you are because you told it so, through where you go and what you do and the company you keep. The more you do, the more transparent you become. The more you become part of a community the things you do make meaning for the community and value for the market.

References

Alexa Internet (2008, 14 April) 'UK Top 100 Websites', available: www.alexa.com.

Anderson, C. (2006) *The Long Tail*. London: Random House.

Berners-Lee, T. (1989) 'Information management: a proposal', in R. Parker and K. Jordan (2001).

Brin, S. and Page, L. (1998) 'The anatomy of a large-scale hypertextual web search engine'. (*Stanford University Infolab*), available: http://infolab.stanford.edu/~backrub/google.html (accessed 13 January 2009).

Buckman, R. (2008) 'Lonelygirl gets popular with investors'. (*The Wall Street Journal Digital Network*, 17 April), available: http://online.wsj.com (accessed 13 January 2009).

Davis, J. (2006) 'The secret world of Lonelygirl'. *Wired* **14**(12): 238.

Engeström, Y. (1990) *Learning, Working and Imagining: Twelve Studies in Activity Theory*. Helsinki: Orienta-Konsultit.

Engeström, Y., Miettinen, R. and Punamaki, R.-L. (1999) *Perspectives on Activity Theory*. Cambridge University Press.

Gladwell, M. (2001) *The Tipping Point:. How Little Things Can Make a Big Difference*. London: Abacus.

Grossman, L. (2006) 'Power to the people'. *Time*, **168**(26): 32.

Helmond, A. (2008) 'How many blogs are there? Is someone still counting?' (*The Blog Herald*, 11 February), available: www.blogherald.com (Accessed 13 January 2009).

Keen, A. (2007) *The Cult of the Amateur: How Today's Internet is Killing our Culture and Assaulting our Economy*. London: Nicholas Brealey Publishing.

Lave, J., and Wenger, E. (1991) *Situated Learning: Legitimate Peripheral Participation.* Cambridge University Press.

Lenhart, A. (2006) 'User-generated content'. (*Pew Internet & American Life Project*, 6 November), available: www.pewinternet.org (accessed 13 January 2009).

Leont'ev, A. N. (1978) *Activity, Consciousness, and Personality.* Englewood Cliffs, NJ: Prentice-Hall.

Li, C. and Bernoff, J. (2008) *Groundswell: Winning in a World Transformed by Social Technologies.* Cambridge, MA: Harvard Business Press.

Online Publishers Association (OPA) (2008a) 'Internet Activity Index', available: www.online-publishers.org (accessed April 2008).

(2008b) 'Industry News Headlines', available: http://www.opa-europe. org/ (accessed 9 January 2008).

O'Reilly, T. (2004) 'The architecture of participation'. (*Oreilly.com*, June) available: www.oreillynet.com/pub/a/oreilly/tim/articles/architecture_of_participation.html (accessed 13 January 2009).

Organisation for Economic Co-operation and Development (OECD) (2007) *Participative Web and User-Created Content: Web 2.0 Wikis and Social Networking* report.

Parker, R. and Jordan, K. (2001) *Multimedia: From Wagner to Virtual Reality.* New York: Norton.

Sharpe, D. and Salomon, M. (2008) *User-led Innovation: A New Framework for Co-creating Business and Social Value.* Eveleigh, NSW: Smart Internet Technology CRC.

Stengel, R. (2006) 'Now it's your turn'. *Time*, 168(26): 4.

Time (2006). 'Person of the year' issue, **168**(26).

van Grinsven, L. (2007) 'On-line editing tools nurture new video makers'. (*Reuters UK*, 2 February), available www.uk.reuters.com (accessed 13 January 2009).

Vygotsky, L.S. (1981) 'The genesis of higher mental functions', in J.V. Wertsch (1979), *The Concept of Activity in Soviet Psychology.* Armonk: Sharpe.

Wenger, E. (1999) *Communities of Practice: Learning, Meaning, and Identity.* Cambridge University Press.

The motley crew

Introduction to Part IV

Caves' (2002) identification of the 'motley crew' recognizes the collective nature of creative production, involving the development and maintenance of both creative teams and those providing technical, managerial or support activities, each having diverse specialist skills, diverse interests and different expectations of the final product. Creative production also stresses the importance of co-ordination of activity within a finite time frame (Caves' *time flies* property). All these factors combine to raise a number of organizational and management issues. How are creative individuals and the creative process managed? How does the discipline of production required for the successful co-ordination of activity impinge on the creative process, the organization of creative work and creative talent? How does creativity relate to the demands of production and productivity, and concerns with efficiency and control? What are the constraints on creative work and what are the compromises that are forced on it and with what effects by commercial demands and scarcity of resources?

While there is no 'style template' for the creative industries – film, for example, is different from music production – there are certain characteristics of the productive process that result from its 'motley crew' nature (Banks *et al.* 2000; Davis and Scase 2000; Henry 2006; Jeffcutt and Pratt 2002; Oliver and Roos 2003). There are recognized difficulties of managing the creative input, especially where the product is dependent on the co-ordination of diverse skilled and specialist workers, i.e. where there is a multiple production function (Bilton and Leary 2002; Blair *et al.* 2001; Kavanagh *et al.* 2002). Caves (2002) cites the often idiosyncratic behaviour of artists making the control of labour difficult. However, it is important that we do not fall into stereotypes when thinking about the people involved. Being creative is not necessarily removed from being pragmatic, and achieving something new often entails marshalling resources, organ-izing money and materials and making a sufficient return to enable the next creative endeavour. Equally, many people involved in the administration of the arts have a creative bent and can contribute to creative outcomes. Hence, the units of analysis are not simply 'crea-tives' in the motley crew who need to be managed by non-creatives. Rather, the questions of people management entail understanding the variety of creative, productive and routinized tasks and ensuring that people's skills are employed, ideally in a way that both gives them some fulfilment and is productive for the organization, audience and other stakeholders such as funders. The impact of the web now also means that there are multiple entry points into some markets and into parts of the creative industries. As we have seen, the end consumer and clients are also part of the creative process. There are thus multi-ple points of management.

First, a review of terminology. 'Management' refers simultaneously to the activity, the role and the person. In one sense, management encompasses the activity of organizing and co-ordination and in this sense everyone, artists and creatives included, engages in manage-ment as a necessary part of 'managing' elements of work and activity. Management also refers to the activity of directing. Its role signifies the authority to give orders as to what should be done, with the expec-tation that these will be followed, and, concomitantly, the ability to apply sanctions should these not be done. Again, some creative roles have this as their basis. The final sense of management is as a discrete part of economic activity where the power of ownership is devolved to a cadre of personnel. Here the power to direct is exercised in the intent of securing surplus value or profit. Some creative roles have this as part or all of their function. The power exercised in this role may be complemented by an artistic ability or talent, and this for-mal power is supplemented with authority. Authority may be ceded on the grounds of institutionalized expectations of hierarchy and/or the grounds of superior ability or talent, such that the directing role appears 'natural'. Some roles in the creative production process may not involve a creative element at all. In this case, authority may well be lacking, with power exercised through the economic function of ownership.

Our chapters in this section (Warhurst, Julier and Donald *et al.*) discuss all these various aspects of management and managing in relation to the motley crew: the relative neglect of management in considerations of the creative industries; various attempts that have been adopted in trying to 'discipline' the workforce; and how creative industries raise different understandings of management in the execution of their practice.

As has been discussed, the creative industries are characterized by the indeterminacy of labour and the indeterminacy of outcome. The indeterminacy of labour is a function of labour power (i.e. although labour is contracted, the actual nature and degree of effort remains within the control of labour itself and the requisite amount of effort has to be secured) and is thus not specific to the creative industries. However, the labour market for the creative industries is unusual, in that there is a chronic oversupply of creative talent providing a reservoir and pool of potential labour, both of non-professional and professional workers who, with the exception of the 'A' rated celebrities of each profession, are paid well below other service-related professions. The sector is characterized by self-employment, portfolio careers and multiple jobs, often where, through under-employment and low pay, creative workers bear the costs of artistic conception and production as people compete for contracts and places in productions (Antcliff *et al.* 2007; Baines and Robson 2001; Barnatt and Starkey 1994; Lash and Urry 1994; McRobbie 2002; Starkey *et al.* 2000; Storey *et al.* 2005). The importance of freelance labour emphasizes the importance of the ability to favourably negotiate terms and conditions, or employ agents who can secure this. It is for these reasons that there has been a focus on 'employment relations' rather than 'work relations' both as a means of securing output and in the discussion of the creative industries generally (Caves 2002).

For Warhurst, the neglect of production in the creative industries and, more specifically, the role of management, is partially attributable to the emphasis that has been placed in the literature on the consumption of creative products and its significance, rather than on their production. He sees this as stemming from the claims that the creative industries herald a discrete development in the economy, claims that he questions, as he does whether the creative industries pose distinct managerial and organizational issues. Claims about the changing model of the economy, and that creative work has to be managed differently as a consequence, have important implications for the claims made about the nature of management. Within a 'new' model of management, 'traditional' hierarchical models are challenged. However, as Warhurst reminds us, a lot of 'creative' labour is 'routine' and under strict managerial control. Rather than seeing different models of management as reflecting a 'development' of the economy, Warhurst sees them as reflecting the difference between managing in emerging versus mature markets, or between micro or small companies and medium-sized enterprises; differences that are well recognized in the managerial literature.

Nonetheless, the 'management' of immaterial labour is problematic. While there are underlying understandings and ways of working that underpin any production process, work organization in the creative industries generally relies on indeterminate skills, i.e. there are difficulties of definition and description (and consequently of measurement). Production is maintained through tacit understanding and knowledge of processes rather than through codified knowledge. Those within the field function as a 'community of practice', where the emphasis is on tacit, collective knowledge and mastery of a body of knowledge through practical expertise in situ (Lave and Wenger 1991). Work organization functions through varying degrees of self-regulation, and the values, skills and expectations that control work organization remain somewhat independent of formal organization. As a consequence, managing creatives and creative production has an ambiguous relationship with systems and rules. Much creative production takes place within what is termed 'loose/tight' control, that is, delegated responsibility for producing marketable creations that trusts to professional judgement, with little interference beyond time and budgetary constraints, where the latter are generally strictly controlled. While there is loose regulation of day to day work, there is tight control through budget, targets, plans, release dates, etc.

While there is a tendency to highlight the 'creative' labour of the creative industries, it must not be forgotten that there are also attempts to introduce the routine systematization of labour, especially where there is a large client interface, as in advertising, design or architecture. While there is a discourse of creativity, there is simultaneously an audit culture, with different inscription strategies attempting to gauge and construct effort, identifying that which relates to 'work time' and that which relates to 'brand value'. A large element of labour in the creative industries also involves retaining clients and getting new clients, with the implications that this has for client-based, deadline-oriented roles and long unsociable hours. In discussing some of these issues, the chapter by Julier focuses on management approaches to labour in the design industry. The view of creative labour heralding a new management style is challenged by Julier, as it is by Warhurst. He argues that design incorporates the 'myth' of individual creativity resistant to management techniques, but illustrates how, through moves to systematize control and accountability, the reality of the design studio conveys a different message. It is through such processes of systematization that the 'studio' evolves into the 'office'. These moves are the result both of the underlying imperatives of valorization and also systematization coming from institutional pressures. Yet within this imperative for control there is also a need for flexibility, and Julier examines the 'creative' use of bureaucratic systems to support space for creativity.

Within the creative industries, and outside of corporate hierarchies, there is generally a less clearly defined management structure and under-played managerial identities (Cummings 1965; Lash and Urry 1994). The management function of co-ordination and control tends to be more closely integrated with a professional, expert, creative role. As such, management relies on authority rather than power; managers are rarely in a position of 'ordering' others to be creative. Rather, the focus is on building a conducive environment and facilitating the creative process. Job roles and reporting mechanisms remain rather loosely defined with an emphasis on the importance of mutual adjustment, reciprocity and negotiation in tasks and goals. Work is also structured to reduce the formal managerial role. In exploring the nature of management practice at music festivals, Donald *et al.* discuss the implications of this different style of management. Again the dilemma for management stems from the unknowability of the creative process and the need for this to be rendered known in the process of organizing. The collective nature of the creative process introduces several complexities: what might be seen as an efficient decision-making process; the emphasis, in an ensemble nature of production, of the importance of continuously relating; and the importance of focusing on objects in order to stimulate dialogue for the formation of ideas in a heterogeneous group. As a consequence, in their questioning of the nature of management knowledge and practice, the authors question some of our conventional interpretations of what is understood by management. They stress the importance of recognizing the different ways of knowing, again eschewing conventional antitheses that force false choices between a deterministic or an 'anything goes' management scenario. In doing so they argue for a new language of discussing management, one that emphasizes preparation, practicing performance, creating value and performing; themes that explore the possibilities of creativity within discipline.

References

Antcliff, V., Saundry, R. and Stuart, M. (2007). 'Networks and social capital in the UK television industry: the weakness of weak ties'. *Human Relations*, 60(2): 371–93.

Baines, S. and Robson, E. (2001) 'Being self-employed or being enterprising? The case of creative work for the media industries'. *Journal of Small Business and Enterprise Development*, 8(4): 49–62.

Banks, M., Lovatt, A., O'Connor, J. and Raffo, C. (2000) 'Risk and trust in the cultural industries'. *Geoforum*, 31(4): 453–64.

Barnatt, C. and Starkey, K. (1994) 'The emergence of flexible networks in the UK TV industry'. *British Journal of Management*, 5(4): 251–60.

Bilton, C. and Leary, R. (2002) 'What can managers do for creativity? Brokering creativity in the creative industries'. *International Journal of Cultural Policy*, 8(1): 49–64.

Blair, H., Grey, S. and Randle, K. (2001) 'Working in film: employment in a project based industry'. *Personnel Review*, 30(2): 170–85.

Caves, R. (2002). *Creative Industries: Contracts Between Art and Commerce*. Cambridge, MA: Harvard University Press.

Cummings, L. (1965) 'Organizational climates for creativity'. *Academy of Management*, 8(3): 220–7.

Davis, H. and Scase, R. (2000) *Managing Creativity: The Dynamics of Work and Organization*. Buckingham: Open University Press.

Henry, J. (2006) *Creative Management and Development*. Milton Keynes: Open University Press.

Jeffcutt, P. and Pratt, A.C. (2002) 'Managing creativity in the cultural industries'. *Creativity and Innovation Management*, 11(4): 225–33.

Kavanagh, D., O'Brien, C. and Linnane, M. (2002) 'Art, work, and art work'. *Creativity and Innovation Management*, 11(4): 277–85.

Lash, S. and Urry, J. (1994) *Economies of Signs and Space*. Thousand Oaks, CA: Sage.

Lave, J. and Wenger, E. (1991) *Situated Learning*. Cambridge University Press.

McRobbie, A. (2002) 'Clubs to companies: notes on the decline of political culture in speeded up creative worlds'. *Cultural Studies* 16(4): 516–31.

Oliver, D. and Roos, J. (2003) 'Dealing with the unexpected: critical incidents in the LEGO Mindstorms team'. *Human Relations*, 56(9): 1057–82.

Starkey, K., Barnatt, C. and Tempest, S. (2000) 'Beyond networks and hierarchies: latent organizations in the UK television industry'. *Organization Science*, 11(3): 299–305.

Storey, J., Salaman, G. and Platman, K. (2005) 'Living with enterprise in an enterprise economy: freelance and contract workers in the media'. *Human Relations*, 58(8): 1033–54.

11 | *The missing middle: management in the creative industries*

CHRIS WARHURST

Introduction: a second industrial revolution?

A radically different new economy is said to have emerged, driven by creativity. As Prime Minister of the UK, Tony Blair even proclaimed this creativity to herald a 'second industrial revolution' (cited in H. Blair *et al.* 2001: 174) and the UK government has been at the forefront of policy initiatives to develop the creative industries based on their assumed job creation (Pratt 1999). Moreover, the creative industries provide demonstration effects that reverberate wider; their model of production representing 'a long wave of change affecting every sector of the economy' according to Tom Bentley, a former UK government adviser.[1] Consequently, the creative industries are a model to which other organisations are said to have to adapt or die (Coy 2000; Florida 2002).

Three key claims thus underpin this new economy. Firstly, that creativity is becoming more prevalent, so that the creative industries provide for significant job growth. Secondly, that this creativity has to be managed differently. Thirdly, that these new jobs are at the vanguard, influencing the way other jobs are to be managed.

Paradoxically, however, the evidence to support these claims is, as Oakley (2004: 68) acknowledges, 'small to non-existent'. In particular, Leadbeater and Oakley (1999: 12) signal that there is a 'missing middle', with little known about creative work. This gap in understanding exists, Oakley noted in 2004, because the claims made for the creative industries are largely under-researched. Richard Florida's influential *The Rise of the Creative Class* is usefully indicative here. It has many interesting things to say about creativity, cities and class. Nevertheless, despite a section on 'Work' containing five chapters, most of the evidence presented concerns orientations *to* work rather than *of* work. There is little real indication of how creative work is managed.

This chapter has two purposes. First, drawing upon secondary data, it attempts to plug the gap in understanding by highlighting some of that evidence that does exists in relation to the management of creativity in the workplace. Second, it highlights how the lack of understanding has arisen and tentatively indicates how it might be addressed. Before these comments, the chapter critically evaluates the three claims made of the new economy. It starts, however, with an outline of the assumptions and expectations about the creative economy and its model of management.

The creative economy and its new model of management

In 1997, the Labour government established a Creative Industries Taskforce of government ministers and business leaders. Two Creative Industries Mapping Documents emerged in 1998 and 2001 (DCMS 1998, 2001) and a Creative Economy Programme was initiated in 2005 that pulled together industries such as architecture and design; film, television, video, radio and publishing; music and the performing arts; software and computer gaming; advertising; crafts; and even the art and antiques trade; promoted not just for their cultural influence but their economic value, as stated by government minister Tessa Jowell.[2] By 2003 these industries were claimed to be providing 1.1 million jobs, although this figure would rise to nearly 1.9 million if an estimated 770,900 creative jobs in organisations outwith the creative industries were included. Moreover, employment in the creative industries was stated to be growing faster than for the economy as a whole (3 per cent compared to 1 per cent) (DCMS 2004).

Influenced by academics such as Florida, UK policy-makers came to believe that the old economy had been displaced by a new economy driven by ideas and creativity (Oakley 2004). As such, radical change is said to have occurred: 'an epochal change in the history of production' according to one CEO cited in Byrne (2000: 46). This new model of production comprises 'corporate ecosystems' or networks of suppliers, manufacturers and distributors, many of which, previously competitors, are now collaborators on projects, sharing and exchanging ideas, competences and skills. Enabled by ICT, the structures, practices and relationships of the new firms are 'intentionally ephemeral ... predicated on constant change, not stability, organised around networks, not rigid hierarchies, built on shifting partnerships and alliances' (Byrne 2000: 46; see also Florida 2002).

The dominant assumption is that the intangible nature of intellectual assets requires and results in an abandoning of traditional, hierarchical organisational structures and practices. Because firms need ideas to survive and these ideas are intangible – 'the stuff inside employees' heads' (Coy 2000: 41) – firms' dependence on creative workers increases. Management and creative labour are presented as in 'fundamental tension', and creatives difficult to manage (DTI/ESRC 2003). Because creativity, Florida states, 'cannot be turned on and off at will' (2002: 5), the best firms simply hire talented people and let them get on with it. He even goes so far as to claim that Karl Marx was partly right: workers do now own the means of production: 'because it is inside their heads'. Howkins (2001) makes a similar point: people with ideas have more power not only than people who work with machines but the people who own them. Whereas the workers of the twentieth-century company were employees, those emblematic of the twenty-first century are 'free workers' (Knell 2000; 'free agents' in US parlance, Pink 2001) and to be treated 'as if they were the owners of the enterprise' (Byrne 2000: 48).

Florida (2002: 106–7) draws back from the excessive claim that the creative economy is populated by a growing army of free agents. Most creative workers, he points out, are employees. He equally rejects the 'company as oppressor' view; in the new 'no-collar' workplace the emphasis is on informality, collegiality, high autonomy and self-managing teams. This heady mixture of flexibility, intangibility and autonomy results in a dramatic shift in the nature of management, with a 'new order in the workplace', Florida asserts (2002: 5). The key management task becomes attracting, retaining and motivating the creative workers through enhanced terms and conditions of employment. The consequence is that employers find themselves 'in a war for talent', according to one IBM executive cited in Coy (2000: 42). To win this war, firms are exhorted to provide these workers with loosened dress codes, working time flexibility, ambient work environments and lots of 'perks', such as subsidised food, tickets to sporting events, dry-cleaning and free massages. Opportunities for self-expression, not managerial direction, are required. Work and life become blurred, and 'fun' has to be the 'adhesive, tying talent to an organisation', Knell (2000: 21) claims. The result is a twenty-first century 'welfare capitalism', with firms providing support services to employees. The enviable jobs of these workers are exemplified in a US profile of the 'typical internet worker' (from *Industry Standard* cited in Campbell 2000: 18):

He works 10 hours a day, makes more than £70,000 a year, doesn't bother to take holidays, dresses as he pleases [and] has never been happier ... There is also a reasonable chance that his employer will arrange his dry cleaning, allow him to bring his dog to work, offer him free massages and give him stock options.

This model of management is not confined to the creative industries but, Florida claims, is being adopted as the standard in other industries: 'this way of working has moved from the margins,' he states, 'to the economic mainstream' (2002: 13). If artists, musicians, scientists and professors have long determined their own working hours, work wear and work pace, other workers are now able to do likewise as creativity comes to pervade other workplaces. Traditional, hierarchical forms of management and control are crumbling under the demand for the mixed soft control of peer recognition, intrinsic motivation and self-management:

Companies of all types, including large established ones, are adapting to this change by striving to create new workplaces that are more amenable to creative work. In this they have no choice. Either they will create these kinds of environments or they will wither and die. (Florida 2002: 13)

Caves (2000) even goes so far as to say that the biggest impact of the creative economy may not lie with the expansion of the creative industries per se but in the way that the creative industries model is now being rolled out elsewhere. Thus to the claims that the extent of creativity is expanding and the number of creative jobs growing, and that this creativity demands a new and distinct form of management, is added the further claim that this management is being adopted by other workplaces. If true, there could be little doubt about the assertion of economic transformation – which is why it is so important to interrogate the claims being made.

Evaluating the claims

The first claim is that creativity is now more important to the economy, with rapid growth in the number of creative jobs. To return to the policy context, the UK government defines the creative industries as 'those industries that have their origin in individual creativity, skill and talent and which have a potential for wealth and job creation through the generation and exploitation of intellectual property' (DCMS 2001: 5). Such definitions are consistent with well-known expositions of the creative economy (Florida 2002; Howkins 2001) in which creative ideas are said to be the key asset in economic success – intellectual work creating intellectual value.

In one sense, therefore, creative industries are being defined by a particular form of labour centred on content origination (Pratt 2005) – or the creation of 'meaningful new forms' in Florida's (2002: 68) words. Unfortunately, the mainstream creative industries literature says little about the work involved in this content origination. Bilton (2007), for example, offers only folksy anecdotes about work in the creative industries, an approach that Florida also occasionally adopts, as will become evident later. Moreover, it is not clear that labour can be a robust distinguishing feature. Though the intensity will vary according to content and contexts, all human labour contains both creative and non-creative elements – whether art, music, plumbing or gardening (Smith and McKinlay 2009).

An additional organising or defining characteristic is therefore offered by Howkins and Florida. The former utilises a sectoral approach in which fifteen sectors are identified, ranging from R&D through to software, film, video games, architecture and art, linked in part by their products falling within the framework of intellectual property law (copyright, patents, trademarks and designs). Such a definition can only bring all the different (and often not very creative) jobs together under one heading by treating the products as the *de facto* responsibility of the collective labourer. However, as Hesmondhalgh (2007a) points outs, whilst the music industry has creative output created by some ground-breaking recording artists, much of its input, for example that of CD manufacturing workers, is routine labour. To argue therefore that a single form of labour exists across a sector would stretch credulity. Florida, by contrast, defines a creative economy through commonality amongst a set of occupations in which people 'add economic value through their creativity' (2002: 68). This approach produces a 'super-creative core' consisting of scientists, university professors, poets and architects, for example, and a secondary group of creative professionals in knowledge-intensive industries such as financial services and healthcare. The advantage of occupational classification is that it escapes the obvious objection that sectors include a wide variety of forms of labour. Nevertheless, many of the same categorisation problems reappear. It is difficult to see the logic of any grouping that includes scientists and poets other than they are, in Florida's words, both 'purveyors of creativity' (2002: xxvii). This definition is so loose that it inevitably expands to include more and more of the labour force – even secretarial labour, according to Florida, as well as his own house cleaner.

The UK government admits that definitions are problematic. Its cat-egorisation draws on the Standard Industrial Classification (SIC) and Standard Occupational Classification (SOC) (DCMS 2002). Many of the same objections made about Howkins and Florida can be made about this categorisation. Moreover the UK government admits that robust data is lacking – and there is certainly methodological wobble in its job statistics: practically it is difficult to map creative employ-ment against SIC and SOC codes (see DCMS 2003, 2004),[3] differ-ent job totals are offered for the same year (cf. DCMS 2001, 2004), downward revisions to previous figures are made (DCMS 2004) and the subcategories of jobs that are covered shift in content and else-where are simply broadened (DCMS 2002, 2004), whilst suggestions are made that hitherto non-included jobs might be included (DCMS 2001). Ultimately, any 'scientific' definition is shunted aside by prag-matic opportunism, with 'a *de facto* definition based simply on those activities for which the [Department for Culture, Media and Sport] has responsibility', the government concedes (DCMS 2002: 9). The outcome of this approach, however, is that the range of jobs included is extremely heterogeneous and beneath the surface many, again, are not creative. Reflecting on attempts to define, categorise and thereby measure the creative industries, Pratt (2003: 6) suggests that: 'Most definitions of the new economy are so wide and all encompassing that even if there were anything going on it is likely that it would be swamped by the noise of contradictory activity.'

Whilst these attempts to measure the extent of creativity within the economy lack either consistency or coherence, what is interest-ing, and often overlooked, is that despite claiming the creative indus-tries to be an important source of job growth, government data does not support this claim. By its own calculations, overall employment in the creative industries has fallen: it is stagnant in television and radio, down 10 per cent in publishing and *down 3 per cent over-all* in the UK. After the widely reported aggregate annual growth of 3 per cent over 1995–2003, from 2003 five of the ten industries that are stated to provide creative employment in the UK actually shed jobs, with another three reporting zero job growth. Put bluntly, after a decade of expansion, the number of businesses in the creative industries peaked in 2002 and has dropped back to 1997–8 levels (DCMS 2005).

Such data, along with the definitional problems, makes it difficult to sustain the claim that more jobs are now creative. Moreover, recognition that there is much heterogeneity of workers within the creative industries also suggests that the second claim – that there is something new and distinct about management in the creative industries – might also be open to question. In other words, if the sums are wrong, what about the claim made about management?

As noted above, the categorisations used often envelop not only putative creative workers but also more routine workers. This range shouldn't be surprising. As the UK government recognises, creative industries involve production chains. These production chains, ranging over origination, manufacture and exchange (see also Pratt 2005) are characterised by divisions of labour separating, most basically, conception and execution work, with the former derived from creative, high-skill, high-value-added workers and the latter undertaken by routine, low-skill, low-wage workers. In this respect, UK research of the fashion industry provides evidence of the residual tight control of workers by management at the low-value-added end of the production chain. As one fashion designer states in Banks (1999: 4): 'To be quite honest the worst thing is having to deal with the machinists – that sounds terrible – but that's where you really have to start being the boss, it's like, you know, organising tea breaks and fag breaks.' The imperative for this managerial intervention arises from the need to control labour costs within the manufacturing process – which can be as high as 50 per cent of total garment cost in the UK. Consequently, production is measured in 'standard minute values' which have to be controlled by managers, with a dual strategy focused on reducing labour content in production and off-shoring that production to low-wage countries (Hines 2001a, 2001b). Researching such practices in clothing manufacture is long-established academic territory (see, for example, Elson and Pearson 1981). The goalposts are not being shifted here; clothing manufacture *is included* as part of the designer fashion creative industry (DCMS 2004).

Florida (2002) uses the example of IT workers to support his account of creative workers. Parking the point that the IT industry also encompasses a range of very different occupations, some involved merely in data processing work (see Warhurst *et al.* 2006), even the high-value-adding creatives in this industry are not immune from tight managerial control, as Barrett (2004) reveals in her turn-of-the-millennium case study of Webboyz. This Australian internet software company started small, created around a kitchen table. The creatives were young and 'nerdy', whose iterative work was to develop new software, and had, as Florida would suggest, task and time autonomy. As the CEO explained, the company would 'take a programmer, sit them down in front of a computer and say, "come up with a product"' (Barrett 2004: 784). Unfortunately, as the company grew and the market became more competitive, this self-management proved too chaotic and soon had a commercial discipline imposed upon it. New senior mangers were employed – 'the suits' – and the company became 'more conservative and conventional' (Barrett 2004: 781) and a combination of worker autonomy with timely direct control by managers was imposed. 'Generally, the staff are left to do their own thing and gently steered from time to time', the CEO stated, but 'around deadline time this changes – we get the whip out and start cracking it, and the company becomes a different place' (Barrett 2004: 788).

Such developments are not unique to Webboyz. Research of twelve software companies in Germany by Mayer-Ahuja and Wolf (2007: 89) reveals similar outcomes with the bursting of the dotcom bubble in 2001. Following massive job losses, the management of the remaining workers within the companies was tightened. Egalitarianism was replaced by hierarchy: 'collective muddling through' displaced by 'clearer distribution of functions'. A deepening division emerged between creatives and managers, with the creatives' autonomy restricted: 'channelled ... by the newly established hierarchies, stricter controls and the subsumption under economic imperatives', state Mayer-Ahuja and Wolf (2007: 98).

Given the managerial practices and developments noted above *within* the creative industries, particularly in Florida's exemplar IT industry, it might seem curious to now turn to the third claim that the creative industries have demonstration effects that go *beyond* the creative industries to shape management in mainstream firms. Doing so, however, is useful, for it starkly highlights the analytical superficiality in mainstream commentaries, and how assumptions, expectations and anecdotes substitute for evidence of this management.

Florida cites the adoption in the Western economies of Japanese management practices as evidence of the increased drive for using the creativity of workers. IBM is offered as an example of a creative factory because it revived its slogan of 'THINK' and claims to now want its employees' minds, not just manual labour (2002: 52–3). Florida also offers a personal anecdote of how he trusts his cleaner not just to clean his home but to rearrange and suggest ideas for decorating it. His hairdresser too has reconfigured her work so that she can be more creative – although examples of how she does so are not offered (2002: 76–7).

Leaving aside the more critical accounts of Japanese management both in Japan and as adopted elsewhere that suggest that scientific management is far from absent in these workplaces (but see, for example, Danford 1998; Elger and Smith 1994), Florida's anecdote is self-defeating in that it reveals that both his cleaner and hairdresser have become self-employed in order to '*get away from* the regimentation of large organisations' (Florida 2002: 77),[4] suggesting that the alleged new and distinct management of creativity is not being diffused more widely, at least as evidenced by these cases.

It is not being argued here that no change has occurred to management within mainstream firms over the past twenty years (though attributing any change to the causal influence of the creative industries would be methodologically difficult). Rather it is the substance of this change that needs to be examined in more detail. As has been pointed out elsewhere (Warhurst and Thompson 1998), over the 1980s and 1990s management of 'mainstream' firms such as those in the auto industry did experiment with new organisational practices such as quality circles and team-working as ways of trying to lever ideas out of routine workers' heads about how production processes could be improved. Such experiments were borne of management's recognition of the tacit knowledge held by workers about work – their 'knowledgeability'. As we stated, there was 'increased emphasis on cognitive and behavioural abilities geared towards multi-skilling, problem-solving and decision-making' (Warhurst and Thompson 1998: 6). The problem was, however, that these experiments were limited in scope and longevity, so that much management today remains traditional, with organisations working lean and mean, not smarter. More recently, governments have exhorted firms to become ideas-driven as part of that other, overlapping 'new' economy – the knowledge economy (DTI 2004; EC 2004) – and academics have claimed that 'knowledge management is part of everyone's job' (Davenport and Prusak 2000: 107). Again, however, the evidence of systematic workplace change is weak. At best an 'exclusive' knowledge economy is being pursued focused on developing graduate labour to the detriment of a more 'inclusive' approach that might draw in routine workers and draw upon their knowledgeability (Warhurst 2008). The outcome is that any putative knowledge management for these workers often has striking similarities to scientific management (Thompson *et al.* 2001). Again, the goalposts are not being shifted by including discussion of management within the knowledge economy – there are clear overlaps in the claims made about the knowledge and creative economies, and Florida (2005) has made it clear that he sees very little, if any, ontological difference between the two.

The three claims about the creative industries seemed to be confounded, therefore. A key reason for this reality shortfall is the tendency to confuse management in *emerging* industries with that in *mature* industries. Whilst the kind of longitudinal research undertaken by Mayer-Ahuja and Wolf (2007) might be difficult, there is existing historical evidence that ought to feature in analysis of the creative industries. To return to Florida's IT industry example: as it emerged in the 1960s, computing work was autonomous, complex, varied, highly skilled and creative, with individualistic workers. Thirty years later, with a mature industry, this work had been rationalised: 'subject to ... a scientific management of the mind' (Kraft and Dubnoff quoted in Beirne *et al.* 1998: 146). This development has been driven by advances in technology, management-imposed bureaucratisation and market pressures. Although obstacles remain and informal worker creativity can never be wholly stripped out, standardised, routinised and repetitive work is common in the industry, with many workers executing others' conception elsewhere in the production chain (*ibid.*). Such research would suggest that far from 'mainstream' firms becoming more like those in the creative industries, the opposite can occur. To emphasise this possibility, assessing the future of the UK fashion, music, new media and graphic design industries, Banks

(1999) notes that as these industries mature, he detects a 'generational shift', with the new firms 'becoming more mainstream, formal and businesslike' (Banks 1999: 5). In other words, these industries are converging on the putative 'old economy' model.[5]

If the evidence to support the claims is weak, it is not because evidence of management doesn't exist. There is clearly some research on work, organisation and management in many of the occupations and sectors now lumped together as the creative industries. This research is, however, overlooked in mainstream creative industries literature; the reason lies in the legacy of debates about the cultural industries.

Moving from claims to an evidence base

A key reason for the shortfall between the claims and the available evidence is the conceptual approach taken to the creative industries. This approach marginalises analysis of production in favour of consumption and makes understandable why so little attention is paid to the management of creativity, either by policy-makers or mainstream creative industry academics.

In this approach, there is a widespread consensus that creative (and cultural) industries[6] are characterised by a distinctive kind of creativity that has considerable implications for markets and management. Movies, television, music, theatre and visual arts produce outputs whose commodity status is inextricably linked to their aesthetic characteristics. These goods have been variously described as cultural, non-material, experiential or symbolic (du Gay and Pryke 2002). Lawrence and Philips (2002) argue that the aesthetic quality of entertainment and fashion products – from novels and theatre to designer sunglasses and running shoes – means that cultural industries are defined by their mode of consumption rather than production. As such firms compete in the symbolic realm, management is about the manipulation of meaning in relation to consumers rather than the organisation of production and workers. In such accounts work is decentred, and meaning, cast as 'identity', is no longer derived from production but from consumption (Warhurst *et al.* 2008). Watching particular television shows and listening to particular genres of music are acts of self-expression and self-definition (see Frank 2002 for further commentary).

Production is acknowledged in this approach but a different argument about creative distinctiveness and cultural goods is offered in

both mainstream creative industries literature as well as that aim-
ing to be more critical (for example Caves 2000 and Hesmondhalgh
2007a, respectively). In both, it is accepted that creativity is in various
ways part of the currency of exchange, leading to a higher degree of
uncertainty of outcomes for firms in the creative industries. The huge
failure rate in these industries is described by Caves as the 'nobody
knows' dilemma. The solution is over-production or the spreading of
risks through large catalogues of products, with the premise that the
one success will recoup – and much more – the expenditure laid out for
the many losers cast onto the market. For Caves, emphasis on the role
of contracts between companies and creatives also helps resolve the
uncertainty allied to the nobody-knows principle. Each industry has
developed standard contracts that are open-ended enough to reward
success but punish failure by non-renewal and other measures. For
Hesmondhalgh, companies attempt to control the risks by exercising
control over the reproduction, distribution and marketing of creative
products, what he terms these products' 'circulation' (2007a: 24). In
both cases, it is the indeterminacy of outcomes rather than of labour
that is assumed to absorb the attentions of firms: in other words, the
management of market uncertainty, not creatives in the workplace, is
the concern. As a consequence, it is no surprise that Lampel *et al.*'s
(2000) review of the literature finds that there are few empirical studies of cultural industries that focus on how creativity is managed and
organised at work.

This conceptual approach is thus not only unable to answer but
also fails to pose the questions about Leadbeater and Oakley's missing middle – 'how do creatives work?', 'what makes them tick?' (1999:
12); or, to reframe these questions, what happens between conception and consumption in the creative and cultural industries? As
Frank (2002: 31–2) wryly notes, 'convinced that the really important
moment of production was not in the factory or the TV studio but
in the living room and on dance floors as audiences made their own
meanings from the text of the world around them, the cult studs generally left questions of industry alone … they weren't interested in
noticing it as a matter of principle'. Instead, assumptions, expectations and anecdotes substitute for evidence, and, as with many other
claims for new economic shifts (see Warhurst *et al.* 2008), emphasis
within these claims is placed not just on work and management being
transformed but also thereby improved.

One of the key industries and one that is said to epitomise the shift to the creative economy – and indeed, as such, was a central feature of 'Cool Britannia' (Cunningham 2003) – is the music industry. This industry, however, is also a good example of how such approaches miss the key moments of management through which musical product makes it to the market, as Box 11.1 reveals.

Box 11.1 *Moments of musical management*
The stereotypical image in popular music is one of independently minded, uncontrollable artistic geniuses. These artists work in the musicians' equivalent of the garret scribbling away new lyrics and working up new sounds. They are difficult characters whose egos rail against corporate attempts to manage their creative output (see for example Hewitt 2008). Whilst there may be some truth that some artists are capable of being musical trend-setters, and can achieve considerable market success, record companies cannot be certain about which artists and what records will sell. The portrayal is one of a tension between creativity and commerce. Some artists have the 'X factor', in the wake of which the companies have to follow and hope for the best. If the boss of Universal, David Joseph, is as indicative as he suggests, the espoused record industry maxim seems to be, 'If you sign quality, the commerce will follow' (quoted in Gibson 2008: 1).

Investing considerable resources into signed artists and supposedly unable to manage them, but needing to ensure a return on their investment, companies are said to have two strategies: to over-produce in the hope that those artists that do sell well will more than cover the costs of those who do not and/or to terminate the contracts of artists who are deemed actual or potential market failures (Hesmondhalgh 2007a; Hirsch 1972). Both situations do occur. In the UK, the 'majors' have large artist repertoires and around 200 albums are released each week but only about 10 per cent are profitable (Davis and Scase 2000). Companies regularly terminate artists' contracts – both artists who are established and emerging – as Mariah Carey and Joe Lean and the Jing Jang Jong demonstrate, respectively (Thompson *et al.* 2007; Salmon, 2008 respectively).

Such occurrences, however, mask the management of those artists by the companies and, as a consequence, perpetuate the analytical missing middle. In reality record companies have key management moments embedded in the labour process of creating popular music product. Firstly A&R (Artist and Repertoire) departments have the task of signing and preparing artists for recording and forming a profitable joint venture with the company. As one American A&R executive remarked about his job: 'I sign them, and then as long as they are with the company, I kind of work with them on all aspects of their career … I'm like a manager – so I'll make suggestions about songs, albums, videos, everything' (quoted in Bowe *et al.* 2001: 346). Secondly, in the studio, artists' recordings are moulded by producers imposed by the company; some producers even co-write and perform on their artists' recordings. To quote one of the very few commentaries on producers by Peterson and Berger (1971: 99): 'Performers have usually chosen the material that they want to record, but … producers diplomatically exercise the final judgement on what is recorded.' Producers are now more prominent figures and their input into artists' sounds is becoming more visible: 'Major labels have teams of 15 people working on one track', said one high-profile producer, Diplo (quoted in Fox 2008: 7). Highly sophisticated and structured, such moments of managerial intervention by record companies reveal both the music *industry* and its *commerce and creativity nexus*. As Barfe (2004: xix) wryly notes about both points, 'the record business [is] where the monetary and the military have joined forces with the musical'. This closer look at music production suggests that the artistic genius on the stage or CD cover is not so much the essential input factor of creative production but rather a carefully factored output of a process in which management and artistic practice are neither as separate nor as opposed as commonly espoused.

In order to advance and so better understand management within the creative industries, production has to be present in the analysis; models of management cannot be simply read off conception and consumption. In addition, that analysis requires more of the empirically grounded workplace-centred research that is now beginning to emerge (see for example Eikhof and Haunschild 2007). Such research provides the necessary and rich, systematic accounts of the missing middle of management across the putative creative industries and occupations.

Recasting Leadbeater and Oakley's (1999) questions, this research needs to focus on the *management process* of creative labour and, consequently, how this labour is organised, controlled, regulated, monitored, rewarded and disciplined. What is disappointing, though explicable given the current approach to creativity noted above, is that there was once a wealth of such studies that centred on occupations that now feature in mainstream creative industries literature. For example, the scientists identified by Florida as emblematic of the new creative economy of the twenty-first century existed in the mid-twentieth century, and Burns and Stalker made much the same points about them then in their classic *The Management of Innovation* as is made now: they were a distinct group, they were growing in number, they had superordinate power based on their knowledge and ideas, and they were difficult to manage. Using detailed case studies, Burns and Stalker revealed how these 'scientist[s] with a touch of genius' (1961: 176) could not be, and were not, unmanaged – quite the contrary. Senior management had to turn these scientists' ideas into money – in today's parlance, to go from 'molecule to market'. This task hinged on managers being able to identify and ensure the 'point' at which the design side handed over to the production side (1961: 178) so that a product could be feasibly manufactured for sale. To this effect, a managerial discipline came to be imposed on the company laboratories: ideas were to be encouraged, but only those that were deemed practical and profitable. It is these types of studies which are required again. Indeed these older existing studies could and should have been used to plug much of the gap in evidence that exists about putative creative work as highlighted by Leadbeater and Oakley.

Conclusion

This chapter opened by outlining the claims made about creativity and the new economy and how this creativity is requiring and driving new forms of management. It is something of a paradox therefore to learn that little is actually known about the management of creativity because there is a 'missing middle', to use Leadbeater and Oakley's (1999) phrase, in understanding. The research-derived evidence that might fill this gap has, instead, been substituted by assumptions, expectations and anecdotes. This chapter has sought firstly to offer some of that evidence and map it against the claims being made and, secondly, to suggest why the gap in understanding has arisen and how it might be addressed.

With regard to the first task, the chapter outlined and evaluated the three claims of a shift to a creative economy, and found those claims to be weakly evidenced. With regard to the first claim, it was pointed out that it is difficult to determine if creativity is becoming more pervasive, with definitions and categorisations being empirically and methodologically muddled. Moreover, even accepting the definitions and categorisations offered, the huge expected expansion of creative jobs has not occurred. In terms of the second claim, it was pointed out that the wide variety of jobs 'umbrella-ed' by the creative industries nomenclature makes it difficult to discern a particular and distinct form of management across these industries. In addition, and in relation to this variety of jobs, it is clear that within the creative industries there is as much residual scientific management of workers as the expected self-management by workers. With respect to the third claim, evidence of any causal diffusion of the assumed form of management within the creative to mainstream industries is absent, either substituted by anecdotes or overlooking counter-evidence, some of which would indicate that there is the potential for some of the newer creative industries, as these industries mature, to adopt the management characteristic of other and older industries.

In offering an explanation for the weakness of these claims, it was suggested that a key problem lies with the conceptualisation of the creative industries. This conceptualisation privileges consumption, creating very limited awareness of the production within creative industries. The analytical leap from creative conception over production to consumption subsequently negates adequate analysis of the management of workers, whether putatively 'creative' or otherwise. Consequently, it should not be surprising that so little understanding exists of how creatives work, despite claims that how they are managed heralds economic transformation and represents an economic imperative for policy-makers.

That the claims made about the creative economy are unsupported, even contradicted, by evidence as a result of the conceptual myopia does not mean that analysis of the creative industries should be abandoned, consigned as merely the misguided rhetoric of policy-makers looking to spin the next big idea or the outcome of evidence-lite analysis by high-profile-seeking academics. Instead it signals the need for better analysis of the jobs and management of those jobs categorised as creative. This better analysis requires empirically grounded research that takes account of the wide variety of jobs and the dynamism of the occupations and industries within which these jobs are located. This analysis would also benefit from the insights gained through longitudinal or historical analyses. Folding this range and type of research into analyses of the creative industries would help make the missing middle complete, overcoming the current lack of understanding and so also perhaps temper some of the wilder claims made about the management of creativity.

Acknowledgements

I would like to thank Cliff Lockyer and Eli Dutton of the Scottish Centre for Employment Research for their contributions to the research project from which this chapter emerges. Some of the material is also drawn from Thompson *et al.* (2007).

Notes

1 In the Foreword to Florida and Tinagli (2004: 8).
2 In the Foreword to Work Foundation/Department for Culture, Media and Sport (2007).
3 A full list of creative industries' 'corresponding' SIC and 'best-fitting' SOC codes can be found in DCMS (2003: 8).
4 My emphasis.
5 See Warhurst *et al.* (2006) for similar arguments about the IT industry specifically.
6 As Pratt (2005) notes, the cultural and creative industries are used interchangeably in current policy discourse – even though the two have different origins (see Hesmondhalgh 2007b).

References

Banks, M. (1999) 'Cultural Industries and the City: findings and future prospects'. Paper presented to *Cultural Industries and the City* conference, Manchester Metropolitan University.

Barfe, L. (2004) *Where Have all the Good Times Gone?* London: Atlantic Books.

Barrett, R. (2004) 'Working at Webboyz: an analysis of control over the software development labour process'. *Work, Employment and Society*, 38(4): 777–94.

Beirne, M., Ramsay, H. and Panteli, A. (1998) 'Developments in computing work: control and contradiction in the software labour process',
in P. Thompson and C. Warhurst (eds.) *Workplaces of the Future*.
London: Macmillan.

Bilton, C. (2007) *Management and Creativity*. Oxford: Blackwell.

Blair, H., Grey, S. and Randle, K. (2001) 'Working in film: employment in
a project based industry'. *Personnel Review*, 30(2): 170–85.

Bowe, J., Bowe, M. and Streeter, S. (eds.) (2001) *Gig: Americans Talk
About Their Jobs*. New York: Three Rivers Press.

Burns, T. and Stalker, G.M. (1961) *The Management of Innovation*.
London: Tavistock.

Byrne, J.A. (2000) 'Management by Web'. *Business Week*, 21–28
August: 44–52.

Campbell, D. (2000) 'Net workers log on to American utopia'. *Guardian*,
21 September: 18.

Caves, R. (2000) *Creative Industries*. Boston, MA: Harvard University
Press.

Coy, P. (2000) 'The creative economy'. *Business Week*, 21–28 August:
38–43.

Cunningham, S. (2003) 'The evolving creative industries'. Unpublished
mimeo, Queensland University of Technology.

Danford, A. (1998) 'Work organisation inside Japanese firms in South
Wales: a break from Taylorism?' in P. Thompson and C. Warhurst
(eds.) *Workplaces of the Future*. London: Macmillan.

Davenport, T.H. and Prusak, L. (2000) *Working Knowledge*. Boston,
MA: Harvard Business School Press.

Davis, H. and Scase, R. (2000) *Managing Creativity*. Buckingham: Open
University Press.

Department for Culture, Media and Sport (DCMS) (1998, 2001) *Creative
Industries Mapping Document*. London: DCMS.
  (2002) *Regional Cultural Data Framework: A User's Guide for
  Researchers and Policymakers*. London: DCMS.
  (2003, 2004, 2005) *Creative Industries Economic Estimates Statistical
  Bulletin*. London: DCMS.

Department of Trade and Industry (DTI) (2004) *Creating Wealth from
Knowledge*. London: DTI.

Department of Trade and Industry/Economic and Social Research Council
(DTI/ESRC) (2003) *Creativity, Technology and the UK's Creative
Industries: Where Next?* Available: www.esrc.ac.uk (accessed 15
January 2009).

du Gay, P. and Pryke, M. (2002). *Cultural Economy*. London: Sage:.

Eikhof, D.R. and Haunschild, A. (2007) 'For art's sake! Artistic and economic logics in creative production'. *Journal of Organization Behaviour*, **28**: 523–38.

Elger, T. and Smith, C., eds., (1994) *Global Japanisation*. London: Routledge.

Elson, D. and Pearson, R. (1981) '"Nimble fingers make cheap workers": an analysis of women's employment in Third World export manufacturing'. *Feminist Review*, 7: 87–107.

European Communities (EC) (2004) *Facing the Challenge*. Luxembourg: Office for Official Publications of the European Communities.

Florida, R. (2002) *The Rise of the Creative Class*. New York: Basic Books.

(2005) *Cities and the Creative Class*. London: Routledge.

Florida, R. and Tinagli, I. (2004) *Europe in the Creative Age*. London: Demos & Carnegie Mellon Software Industry Centre.

Fox, K. (2008) 'Meet the new sonic revolutionaries'. *Observer*, review section (6 April): 6–7.

Frank, T. (2002) *New Consensus for Old*. Chicago: Prickly Paradigm Press.

Gibson, O. (2008) 'Bang! And the duds are gone'. *Guardian*, media section (21 July): 1.

Hesmondhalgh, D. (2007a) *The Cultural Industries*. London: Sage.

(2007b) 'Cultural and creative industries', in T. Bennett and J. Frow (eds.) *Handbook of Cultural Analysis*. Oxford: Blackwell.

Hewitt, P. (2008) *Paul Weller: The Changing Man*. London: Corgi.

Hines, T. (2001a) 'Globalisation: an introduction to fashion markets and fashion marketing', in T. Hines and M. Bruce (eds.) *Fashion Marketing*. London: Butterworth-Heinemann.

(2001b) 'From analogue to digital supply chains: implications for fashion marketing', in T. Hines and M. Bruce (eds.) *Fashion Marketing*. London: Butterworth-Heinemann.

Hirsch, P.M. (1972) 'Processing fads and fashions: an organization-set analysis of the cultural industry systems'. *American Journal of Sociology*, 77: 639–59.

Howkins, J. (2001) *The Creative Economy*. London: Penguin.

Knell, J. (2000) *Most Wanted*. London: The Industrial Society.

Lampel, J., Lant, T. and Shamsie, J. (2000) 'Balancing act: learning from organizing practices in cultural industries'. *Organization Science*, 11(3): 263–9.

Lawrence, T.B. and Philips, N. (2002) 'Understanding cultural industries'. *Journal of Management Inquiry*, 11(4): 430–41.

Leadbeater, C. and Oakley, K. (1999) *The Independents: Britain's New Cultural Entrepreneurs*. London: Demos.

Mayer-Ahuja, N. and Wolf, H. (2007) 'Beyond the hype: working in the German internet industry'. *Critical Sociology*, 33: 73–99.

Oakley, K. (2004) 'Not so cool Britannia: The role of the creative industries in economic development'. *International Journal of Cultural Studies*, 7(1): 67–77.

Peterson, R.A. and Berger, D.G. (1971) 'Entrepreneurship in organisations: evidence from the popular music industry'. *Administrative Science Quarterly*, 16: 97–106.

Pink, D. (2001) *Free Agent Nation*. New York: Warner.

Pratt, A. (1999) 'Cultural industries: the first steps and the roads ahead'. Paper presented to *Cultural Industries and the City* conference, Manchester Metropolitan University.

   (2003) 'A "third way" for the creative industries?' Unpublished mimeo, London School of Economics.

   (2005) 'Cultural industries and public policy: an oxymoron'. *International Journal of Cultural Policy*, 11: 29–44.

Salmon, C. (2008) 'Lean times for the Jing Jang Jong'. *Guardian*, 24 July: 4.

Smith, C. and McKinlay, A. (2009) 'Creative labour: content, contract and control', in A. McKinlay and C. Smith (eds.) *Creative Labour*. London: Palgrave Macmillan.

Thompson, P., Jones, M. and Warhurst, C. (2007) 'From conception to consumption: creativity and the missing managerial link'. *Journal of Organization Behaviour*, 28: 625–40.

Thompson, P., Warhurst, C. and Callaghan, G. (2001) 'Ignorant theory and knowledgeable workers: interrogating the connections between knowledge, skills and services'. *Journal of Management Studies*, 38(7): 923–42.

Warhurst, C. (2008) 'The knowledge economy, skills and government labour market intervention'. *Policy Studies*, 29(1): 71–86.

Warhurst, C. and Thompson, P. (1998) 'Hands, hearts and minds: changing work and workers at the end of the century', in P. Thompson and C. Warhurst (eds.) *Workplaces of the Future*. London: Macmillan.

Warhurst, C., Lockyer, C. and Dutton, E. (2006) 'IT jobs: opportunities for all?' *New Technology, Work and Employment*, 21(1): 75–88.

Warhurst, C., Thompson, P. and Nickson, D. (2008) 'Labour process theory: putting the materialism back into the meaning of services', in M. Korczynski and C.L. MacDonald (eds.) *Service Work: Critical Perspectives*. London: Routledge.

Work Foundation/Department for Culture, Media, and Sport (2007) *Staying Ahead: The Economic Performance of the UK's Creative Industries*. London: DCMS.

12 | Playing the system: design consultancies, professionalization and value

GUY JULIER

Two graphic designers sit at their workstations.

They have just completed their electronic timesheets, accounting for every six minutes of work done each day between 9 and 5 for the last month or so. It's a shame that the time they put in on projects outside these hours is not accounted for. The design firm they work for would be charging their clients a lot more if they did. But they can't.

They are now discussing how they are going to get the pitch they are preparing ready for tomorrow morning. All the efficiency and tracking procedures for processing design projects which were recently put into place in their twenty-strong firm are bypassed when it comes to getting a short pitch done. And in any case, these will only be used for a) explaining to their clients how they process projects and b) trying to figure things out if something goes wrong.

Not that it matters to these individuals. They rarely see their end clients. Clients don't come to their studios any more. There isn't much to be seen except for rows of computers – unlike the old days of drawing boards and model-making rooms. In any case, the design firm's meeting room is too small to accommodate a client visit which might include marketing managers from several departments. They – that is the account handler and the firm's 'star' designer – go to them these days. If there is a client visit, then they try to jazz the studio up, make it look more creative.

Thankfully the pitch presentation in hand is not very creative. The two designers will probably trawl through some graphic design magazines for ideas and then turn the job around quickly. This will be saved for a more prestigious project, something that will keep the firm's profile up, like a competition brief or a creative solution that'll get them a design award nomination. And they'll get some help from freelances for this.

Introduction

The above is a composite account of designers' experience of their day-to-day activities. It testifies to many of the demands of alienated labour within the creative context of a design consultancy. There is the tension between accounting billable hours and the need to retain or win clients within tight work schedules. Designers recognize the need to balance creative input against the prestige of a particular job. While creativity may be the prime currency of the design firm, it is difficult to evidence this beyond the material results of labour, that is, the actual physical designs themselves.

Such dry calculations amongst these designers may seem anathema to many contemporary accounts of creative work. This chapter springs from the observation that just as notions of creativity and the promotion of 'creative industries' within national and regional government policies have been in their ascendency, in line with certain ambitions of the so-called 'New Economy', so greater regulatory systems have been introduced into their practices. The result is designers encountering an increased prominence of report writing, accountability or structured workflow systems within their everyday labour. This chapter therefore pursues the messy, mundane and humdrum world of design in contrast to more widespread conceptions of creativity as being 'spontaneous' or resistant to ordering and management. In doing so, it views design practice as being deeply embedded in micro-economic systems of studio organization as well as the macro-economic world of professional and commercial value.

Traditional conceptions of creativity foreground its individualism as an assertion of freedom, a freedom apparently resistant to systemization, measurement, bureaucratization or audit. Within the design industry this myth is generally supported. (The fragmentation and heterogeneity of the design profession mean that it is unlikely to adopt stringent norms of training, practice or ethical conduct.) Yet the demands of clients and pressures on organizing creativity in the complex environment of the design studio conspire towards varying levels and usages of systemization. Balancing the need to manage creativity while maintaining its 'mystique' and hence, symbolic power, is a recurrent challenge.

The aim of this chapter is to critically analyse the relationship between ideas of creativity and the organization of the creative process within contemporary design consultancies. Since the 1980s, design has been in its ascendance, both as an increasingly prominent sector within the creative industries and as an object of consumer and business fascination. This chapter begins by situating design within wider discourses of the New Economy, and considers the role of art and design education and design's professional institutions in underscoring certain notions of 'creative freedom'. Given the rapidity of design's growth and its fragmentation and volatility, the establishment of professional norms of practice has been tricky, if not doggedly resisted. However, the demands of making the design studio work efficiently (particularly in the context of economic pressures) and those of clients who want to buy both 'creativity' and to understand exactly what they are paying for, mean that design studios are often required to employ the stringent systemization and accounting of their processes. However, this chapter reveals the ways by which this systemization itself is frequently subverted in order to obtain other values, either within the internal power relationships of the design firm or in order to harness a stronger brand value in the eyes of its external audience. Ultimately, the polarization of creativity and its management plays, I argue, a discursive role through which everyday identities and practices in the design consultancy are imagined and played out.

Creativity and design in the New Economy

The ascendance of creative industries discourse since the 1990s has often been accompanied by an optimistic championing of individual freedom as their human bedrock. 'Individuality' figures as the first of Florida's key 'creative class values'. This is taken as a collectively understood given, with minimal page space devoted to explaining the significance of this assertion, and thus maintaining its mystique (Florida 2002: 77–8). Individual creativity is set in contrast to collective action that is believed to dampen such endeavour (Montuori and Purser 1995). Equally, Thiel (2005) identifies a number of authors who maintain a romantic notion of creativity. It is seen as fulfilling inner necessities (Caves 2000), of 'doing what you love' (Amabile 1996) and being linked to personal identity (Helbrecht 1998). Creativity fulfils Schumpeter's ideal type of the entrepreneur, dedicated to upsetting or undermining norms rather than adapting to them: a type that is, again, vigorously championed by Florida (2002: 31–2).

Within this, the management of the self is assumed to be somehow intrinsic as it is folded into the 24-hour, 'art is everything' lifestyle (Eikhof and Haunschild 2006). Being outside the frame of traditional systems managerial control then becomes a key issue to some authors (e.g. Caves 2000; Scase and Davis 2000; Howkins 2001; Sutton 2001; Jeffcutt and Pratt 2002; Alvarez *et al.* 2005). Creative work is assumed to engage improvizational networks and attitudes as against more 'humdrum' activities such as business, law or accountancy where interactions are more routine and therefore predictable (Caves 2000).

These issues find their place within a wider rhetoric of the New Economy. Business studies academics Scase and Davis (2000: 23) claim that the creative economy is at the 'leading edge of the movement towards the information age [as its] outputs are performances, expressive work, ideas and symbols rather than consumer goods or services'. In support of this notion, books such as Howkins' *The Creative Economy: How People Make Money From Ideas* (2001) or Ray's *The Cultural Creatives* (2001) set out a business agenda in which creativity and creative people are the frontiersmen of this new economic landscape.

Meanwhile, within the creative industries, the design profession has become emblematic of these moves. In her study of London-based fashion designers, McRobbie (1998; 2002) shows how their working patterns were typified by the requirement to network, to be visible and available for virtually twenty-four hours and to work on a flexible, project-by-project basis. These patterns of labour resonate with the emergent entrepreneurialism of the New Economy. Equally, arch-supporter of New Economy thinking, the American magazine *Fast Company*, has made claims that business leaders should not only understand design but work creatively as if they were designers (Breen 2005). In short, much writing connects creative work to the individualistic, entrepreneurial world of the New Economy. This has attendant qualities of resistance to professional regulation and control and the foregrounding of a creative lifestyle and milieu that supports an 'other' conception of labour as being intrinsic, fulfilling and vital.

As within all creative industries, and as others have argued (eg. Hesmondhalgh 2000; Banks *et al.* 2002), it is important that attention is paid to specific contexts in which creativity is enacted. This means understanding the day-to-day actions, environments and discourses in which they take place. Design practice gives rise to particular systems of value, tensions in its professional demarcation and educational background and in its relationships to its outside world.

Within the culture of design there is a degree of reflexive fashioning of the self for this process. The mediation of design has not been neutral in the creation of this. Contemporary international design magazines such as *Blueprint, Domus, Icon* and *Experimenta* place a strong emphasis on the work of individual designers. Their brief is mostly to represent the most cutting-edge of design practice that underlines uniqueness, difference and non-conformity. Equally, professionals at sector conferences are presented with a constant 'fashion parade' of young and not-so-young turks who embody the creative capital of their labour. Thus, for example, Cape Town's annual 'Design Indaba' features a three-day conference in which a stream of famous creative personalities simply talk about what they do. Its emphasis is on authorship and conspires to build a global and almost mystical sense of belonging amongst its delegates. One attendee described it as 'the closest thing to a religious experience I've known' (quoted in McGuirk 2008).

Equally, art and design education, particularly in the UK, has a long history of encouraging individualism where the emphasis is just as much on developing the creative personality as the skills to support this. Frith and Horne (1987) state that:

Constant attempts to reduce the marginality of art education, to make art and design more 'responsive' and 'vocational' by gearing them towards industry and commerce, have confronted the ideology of 'being an artist', the Romantic vision which is deeply embedded in the art school experience. (Frith and Horne 1987: 30)

They were speaking of British art and design education's wilful determination to remain separate and different from mainstream regulatory frameworks; in other words, its refusal to be instrumentalized toward national economic goals.

In support of this process, educational policy underpins the fashioning of the creative individual. Angela McRobbie (2007) talks of the 'Los Angelisation of London' (or it could be of Leeds, Luton or Lincoln) that bears all the hallmarks of the Blair period. Blair's 'go it alone agenda' is mirrored in the creative economy, she argues. This is:

... bound up with deeper social transformations which involve re-defining notions of selfhood and which encourage more expansive forms of self reliance. These new more flexible forms of selfhood are institutionally grounded in education and through pedagogical styles as well as the transformation of the curriculum. (McRobbie 2007)

The ethic of 'self-reliance' corresponds 'with styles of working on a project-by-project basis'. Thus, by extension, design education neatly fits in with a wider political agenda of selfhood wherein more self-reliant, flexible approaches to labour are promoted. The fashioning or profiling of the self becomes an important aspect of this process.

The self is therefore imbricated into a promotional culture in McRobbie's terms. She goes on to identify the importance of the 'single big hit' that the design graduate aims for: the attention-grabbing, media-recognizable creative outcome that will work for personal launching. Hence, typically, the design graduate will offset the drudgery of a routine design job while the one personal project is developed that will buy them the big break and release them from that routine. Here the emphasis, again, is on individual profile.

Some views of creative labour in the design firm differ starkly from this account of this individualist, authorial designer. Indeed, design is invariably a collaborative, team-based activity (Morris *et al.* 1998). Product designer Geoff Hollington has suggested, in the context of increasing multi-disciplinarity and teamworking of designers, that the era of the individual star designer is over. A typical larger design consultancy may bring 'together materials, manufacturing, software and "futures" specialists, with the big ideas flowing from that chemistry' (Hollington 1998: 63). Arch-symbol of the mythical, individual genius designer, Philippe Starck, who has become a brand himself, is singled out as the last great 'designer hero'.

By contrast, in this new order of complex, collaborative teamwork, the rhetoric of creativity and innovation is contigent upon their management. And the larger the creative organization becomes, the greater the need for the management and systemization of its processes (Banks *et al.* 2002). Teams demand a level of agreed organization and normative procedures. This may not be inflexible. For example, Anthony *et al.* (2006) suggest that, like American football plays, innovation and creativity can be pre-planned, strategized and mapped in order to field and respond to rapidly changing business challenges and scenarios. But in the design firm, and more widely within the design industry and its institutional structures, the rhetoric of 'being creative' – something that is deeply embedded into the history, representation and education of design – and the actual day-to-day management of the design firm have to be reconciled. The next section reviews some of the structural resistances to systemization that are inherent in the design industry.

Professionalization and diversity

In addressing the vexed question of design's uneasy relationship with management, Thomas Lockwood, President of the American-based Design Management Institute, assesses how design can be measured. He quotes veteran designer Hartmut Esslinger ('Businesspeople are from Mars, and designers are from Venus'). He notes how designers tend to underline their importance with anecdotes and quotes (such as 'good design is good business') rather than with numbers. 'Creativity resists quantification', he observes (Lockwood 2007: 90–1). He goes on to map out ten criteria by which design can be evaluated and thus 'sold' to clients. These range from straightforward sales impacts, through improvement of time to market and development process, the establishment of patents, return on investment and cost savings, to the building of brand image and corporate reputation. According to Lockwood, such measures are not to be taken together. Rather, they should be used as appropriate to the design process in question.

Indeed, the breadth of such measurements given by Lockwood underlines the very diversity of the design industry itself. Just as the design industry has grown, so its base has widened, spawning ever new specialisms and approaches. The growth and increasing heterogeneity of design has in turn produced ever more complex challenges as to its valorization and professional frameworks. How the worth of design practice is costed and how this should be carried out becomes a harder question to answer as new forms and arrangements of design practice constantly emerge.

Globally, the design profession has seen exponential growth over the past two decades. A number of examples bear this out. The European design market grew at around 25 per cent between 1982 and 1989 (NDI 1994: 10). By 1994, the Netherlands Design Institute was predicting a growth of the European design market from $9.5 billion to $14 billion by 2000 (NDI 1994: 9). Country-by-country data appears to bear out this prediction. The independent design profession in France is relatively new, with 53 per cent of organizations operating for fewer than ten years. Sweden has seen a rise of 272 per cent in the number of firms between 1993 and 2002 (Bruce and Daly 2006). This growth should be taken within a broader framework of the ascendancy of cultural production since the 1990s (Lash and Urry 1994). According to a 1998 European Commission report, 'cultural employment' – that is, work in advertising, design, broadcast, film, internet, music, publishing and computer games – grew by 24 per cent in Spain (1987–94) while employment in Germany of 'producers and artists' grew by 23 per cent (1980–94) (cited in Hesmondhalgh 2002: 90).

This development of the design industries is matched by rapid growth within the education sector in recent years. In the UK, the number of first-year design students has risen by 35 per cent, from 14,948 to 20,225, between 1994 and 2001 (Design Council 2004). Of the 30,000 annual graduates of design in Europe during the 1990s, 30 per cent were trained in the UK. The years 1993–8 saw a 12 per cent rise in design degree applications and in 1998 a 63 per cent rise in students sitting the GCSE examination in Design and Technology (Design Council 1998: 24). There was a rise of 108 per cent in the number of postgraduate design qualifications available between 1994 and 2001, indicating substantial growth at the more advanced end of design education (Design Council 2004). By the end of the 1990s, there were 62,000 students specializing in design in higher education, where over 900 courses were available (CITF 1998). Growth in design education has also been a more global affair, however. China, for example, saw a 23 per cent increase in enrolment on art and design degree courses between 2003 and 2004. A further 1,200 design schools are planned, to add to the 400 that have opened in China in the last two decades (Rigby 2007). Enrolment on design degrees in Sweden grew from 2,000 to over 7,000 during the ten years up to 2003 (Nordic Innovation Centre 2004).

Despite, or more probably *because of* this sectoral growth, design has remained relatively untouched by norms in both its professional and educational spheres. The newness of the industry combined, as we shall see, with its diversity and instability conspire to rule out standardized procedures or 'codes of conduct'. Wherever design is practised, professional organizations are established to promote and safeguard the activities of designers. For example, the UK sports the Chartered Society of Designers and the Design Business Association, as well as numerous regional groups such as the South Coast Design

Forum, the Cornwall Design Forum, the West of England Design Forum, and so on. But their chief focus is on the general promotion of design, rather than on the generation of self-regulatory norms or 'best practice' models. They do not lead to their establishment as normative bodies overseeing and validating professional and educational processes. The American Institute of Graphic Arts publishes 'Standards of Professional Practice' that its members sign up to. This covers broad business ethics issues such as responsibility to clients and to other designers. However, it doesn't lay down any minimum expectation of educational achievement to practise or stipulation of levels of continuing professional development required. The Society of Graphic Designers of Canada publishes a broadly similar Code of Ethics and Professional Conduct for Graphic Designers, as does the UK-based Chartered Society of Designers.[1] However, membership of such organizations is not a prerequisite to professional practice, although it may accord some status and recognition with clients.

The norms of these organizations exist in a 'light touch' way that do little to standardize professional and educational procedures. In this respect, design may be understood to exist as a 'minor' profession in relation to a 'major' profession such as architecture (see Schön 1991, chapter 2). In the USA, Canada, New Zealand, Australia and the UK, as in many other countries, the architecture profession is standardized by registration or licensing requirements from a recognized institution. In the UK this is the Royal Institute of British Architects and, in the USA, the American Institute of Architects. Norms of content and quality assurance in architectural education are under approval from its respective registering body. More rigorous codes of professional practice and conduct are enforced than we have seen in design.

The discussion as to whether design should have more stringently defined and applied professional norms has frequently been exercised (e.g. Peters 2007). However, a fundamental difference between architecture and design is that the former deals with a singular medium (buildings) whereas the latter is distributed across a range of outcomes (at the most basic these being products, interiors, fashion, textiles and visual communication). Each design medium has its distinct technologies, size, type and distribution of clients, speed of development, modes of distribution, relationship with legal frameworks such as patent and trademark law, support networks and so on.

As the design profession has grown, so it has spawned increasing numbers of subspecialisms. In 2006, British Design Innovation (BDI) – a UK design industry monitoring company – identified 25 design subdisciplines. In addition to activities such as 'branding and graphics' or 'multimedia/new media' it also specified such approaches as 'design and innovation management', 'social responsibility', 'high-end consumerism', 'internal communications' and 'product testing' (BDI 2006). While the majority of work undertaken by design firms remained in the more traditional disciplines that are medium based, its survey was designed to recognize new skill-sets that were emerging in design, particularly in service and proposition creation. The latter, then, is a reflection of a trend in the design practice to move beyond 'visual translation of client strategy'. BDI classified this typology – which occupies roughly 70 per cent of UK design activity – as the work of the 'design agency'. But it also identified two other typologies. Occupying about 20 per cent of national design activity was the 'design studio' that is a production-led, mostly graphics-related practice that sees projects through to execution. But an increasing third sector, making up about 10 per cent of activity, was that of the 'strategic design consultancy'. Here the emphasis is much more on how design can be used, for example, within corporate planning or in policy development to gain competitive advantage or deliver public services more effectively. The physical output of the design firm may shift from design specifications, for example by way of corporate identity guidelines or technical drawings, to the production of the actual artefacts themselves through to strategic reports and audits.

If the process and outcomes of design have become increasingly diverse, so the employment patterns of designers are by no means homogenous. There are some 185,000 designers currently working in the UK. There are an estimated 12,450 design consultancies employing 60,900 designers, 348,300 non-designers and an additional 47,400 self-employed designers. Design businesses employing less than four people make up 84 per cent of the total, while about 6 per cent employ more than 250. A further 77,100 designers work in-house in 5,900 businesses with more than 100 employees (Design Council 2004).

Furthermore, the structure of the design industry is highly responsive to economic fluctuations that affect not only overall turnover but also its employment structure. Economic slowdown from

2001 – marked by the NASDAQ share index fall, the dotcom crash of 2001 and uncertainty following 9/11 – combined with a growth of foreign competition-conspired to cut overall turnover in the UK design industry by more than 30 per cent during the following five years (BDI 2006). However, within this decline the tendency was toward the creation of more small-sized design firms – those employing between one and five people moved from 34 per cent to 54 per cent of the total design firms between 2000/01 and 2002/03 (Design Council 2004). At the other end of the scale, the number of design firms employing more than fifty grew throughout this period (BDI 2007).

In such a context of flux, it is therefore impossible to talk of the 'typical' design firm. The design industry is typified by its heterogeneity. This is in terms of the mediums it works in, its range of clients and the kinds of intellectual and manual labour it engages. The range of business types and sizes that designers are employed in is another factor. Finally, its responsiveness to business climates makes it a precarious and unstable profession.

In view of these factors, the idea of stable, fixed, industry-wide occupational formulae is foreign. The following two sections discuss various attempts to regulate and valorize creative labour within the design firm. The primary research for this is drawn from two workshops,[2] several supplementary interviews, informal discussions and design consultancy visits. These engaged some fifteen designers working in a range of disciplines (graphic design and visual communication, digital media, interior and exhibition design, product design, urban design) and employment contexts (large-, medium- and small-scale consultancies, freelances and in-house designers). They represent a snapshot of experiences and observations that reveal the dilemmas of an industry that sits on the edges of professional normative structures.

Managing and measuring creative labour in the design firm

The design process has traditionally been represented as a linear activity (e.g. Archer 1965; Cooper and Press 1995; Lawson 1997; Design Council 2007). In this version, typically, the designer receives the design brief. A design specification is created that researches and details the problems and provides a list of outcomes to address them. A broad outline of the solution is created. This concept design is invariably evaluated through market testing and discussion with clients. A detailed design is then developed that specifies dimensions, production issues, cost factors and so on. This is then prototyped and tested before final delivery to the client.

Theoretically, the design studio would be laid out to reflect this sequence with specialist departments or sections. The development of a design project would then be physically evidenced as it passed through the respective stages. The growth of design consultancies in the 1980s saw what I have termed a 'neo-Fordist' configuration of large-scale design firms (Julier 2007) where throughput of design projects was arranged thus. Moreover, their very size was posited as part of their selling power for clients.

Alongside this physical structuring of the design firm through office layout, comes a bureaucratic system to ensure its efficiency and cost-effectiveness. The use of computer-based timesheets and work-flow systems – supported by programmes such as Oracle Workflow, co.efficient or HighOrbit – help to allocate, quantify, cost and monitor the distribution of tasks within a design firm. However, this in itself has to be managed, not only in terms of getting design projects through the system as regards budget and time, but also in terms of interfacing with a client's need to be kept 'in the loop' as projects develop. Thus, in the latter case, for example, one informant reported there being as many people in her fifty-strong graphics firm working as 'traffic managers' as strategic consultants. In other words, there were just the same number whose job it was to co-ordinate tasks between individual designers and departments as those engaged in harnessing new workstreams for the firm. Another informant working as a junior designer in a large-scale branding consultancy spoke of weekly resource meetings where client managers, the accounts team, project managers and design directors look at how many staff are needed for projects, whether supporting freelances need bringing in, and checking that they are not going over budget. In this context, the work of designers becomes that of focused creative practice within regimes of the unitization of time and tasks.

There is little evidence of any standardization of such management or bureaucratic measures, however. The diversity of, and self-conscious differentiation of design firms from one another, means that each adopts its own specific way of organizing itself. One detailed but significant feature unites them, though: what has now become the tool of the trade for designers – the computer – is also where the timesheets are filled and the individual's workflow progress is managed.

Regimes of systemization are, however, invariably subverted by the very demands of the design industry itself. Informants unanimously talked of needing to work outside the billable '9 to 5' timeframe. Labouring past the 'official' close of the working day was not deemed as chargeable to the client as it pushed margins on projects too high. And yet, this was often necessary for the project to be completed. This phenomenon was also put down to computerization. Formerly, the working day might be limited by access to specialist external tooling where models or prototypes might be made, to typesetters or in their early days, the presence of a computer technician. Nowadays, product testing, for example, may be modelled through software packages; typesetting is carried out by graphic designers themselves, and so on. The designer's tasks may at times therefore become disembedded from the need for co-ordination with other employees' temporal regimes. The only thing limiting creative labour time is the designer's willingness to work overtime. Whilst there may be unitization of creative practice, at least in (management) theory, the reality is often that there is seepage of creative labour time outside this structure.

This spilling-out of creative labour time – the 'long hours' culture of design practice (Business Ratio Plus 1998) – may be partly explained by commercial pressures within the design industry. The design process has been made more efficient by the streamlining of the creative processes through their more structured management as well as through computerization. But these efficiencies have been handed onto clients rather than kept as revenue-producing developments for design firms. Further commercial pressures are created by a more exigent client base which has become more demanding commissioners of design services. Added to this has been the growth of foreign and home competition for clients amongst the design sector itself. Lamenting the continued need for undertaking unpaid pitching for commissions, one informant, a director of a leading exhibition design firm, noted:

[In London] we're in the global epicentre of creativity but it drives the competition. And that's the problem: because the competition is so high it's forcing all the conditions down because there are so many of us chasing work and clients can do that to us.[3]

While industry-wide norms of practice may be absent, aside from a general processual sequence, as in any business in the knowledge economy, time has to be accounted for. This impels the unitization and alienation of creative labour that may seem at odds with traditional or mainstream conceptions of it. This is a slippery task, however, as 'creativity demand' outstrips the rationality of bureaucratic systems. In the next section, we shall see how, though, the bureaucratization of creative labour interplays with questions of value.

Locating and valorizing creativity

The account of the design sequence given at the beginning of the previous section is relatively traditional. It describes a neo-Fordist linear system where projects are moved through the design firm and out the other end. Developments in the way that design is practised, in particular in terms of the client relationship, may, however, challenge such a clean conception.

Firstly, creative ownership over a project may be lost as it passes through the various sections of a design firm. This situation may be exacerbated when the project is iteratively returned by a client for modification. This is increasingly the case where information and communication technologies allow the client to view its development more frequently. A design may be emailed to a client at more stages for its approval or comment. Additionally, given a high volume of projects passing through a design firm (particularly a large-scale one), then designers working on a commission may change in different sections each time it moves through.

Secondly, because of complications in ascribing creative ownership, creativity in the design firm has become more generalized. In traditional, linear arrangements, the location of the 'creative' work is clearly focused into the concept design stage, as is also found in architectural offices and advertising agencies. Coupling these issues with a more general observation of the rise of 'creativity' as a desirable and sellable quality, claims to it begin to fall more evenly across employees of the design firm.[4] A copywriter of a branding and communications design firm described the resultant effect as follows:

Client handlers, media buyers, account handlers – everybody is a *de facto* creative person these days. Creative decisions are being made all along the way and it makes it that much harder for us more traditionally creative people to surround ourselves with mystique in order to make it hard for other people to find out what you do and measure what you do.

Thirdly, designers are, by and large, involved in more complex everyday working contexts and relationships. Many have shifted from designing things or environments to undertaking more strategic roles with clients. Historical economic reasons account for this. The design boom of the 1980s was typified by an 'anything goes' sensibility. Most clients were using designers seriously for the first time and were relatively uncritical of the results. However, the economic recession of the early 1990s forced designers to spread their offers and look for new ways of engaging clients. Hence they widened the range of design disciplines on offer – providing more integrated services of graphic, product, digital media and interior design. But through this integration, many repositioned themselves as consultants, offering, in particular, brand and product strategy. With the growth of branding as a central driver of design practice (Moor 2007) so a project may be more tightly orchestrated across different design platforms such as interior, product and graphic design.

Furthermore, as we have already noted, there is the tendency for design firms to assume a more strategic role with clients wherein, for example, the clarification of a design brief becomes part of the design firm's offer. Client companies have also begun to adopt in-house designers who carry out the more focused production end of design. Plenty of examples of more 'ordinary', craft-based design still exist – designers who do brochure layouts or resolve technical, production issues. But the role of many design consultants has moved to the provision of more intangible services of 'imagineering', identity development, creative brainstorming, or product and service strategy. As a result, for those offering more complex services than technical resolution, the locus of 'creativity' has become more nebulous. The role of 'creativity' as a value to clients has risen while, simultaneously, more professionals, not necessarily just designers, lay claim to its authorship. If creativity has shifted beyond the visual solution, then locating and valorizing it is a more complex job.

The struggle for creative ownership is an important facet of the everyday life of the design firm as it relates closely to its internal and external systems of recognition. The generalized rhetoric of 'creativity' and 'innovation' in the contemporary economy resonates with the importance accorded to these 'for gaining a reputation', and is regarded as 'the lifeblood for the continued existence' of a design firm (Reimer *et al.* 2008).

Internally in the design firm, individuals or teams might vie for creative recognition by bidding for extra allocation of time to particular projects in order to make their mark. Being seen as part of a team that produces particularly innovative work was important for several informants in terms of their views on career progression. Thus, the use of systems that allocate unitized time to creative labour may not be strictly rational. It is subverted in order to achieve promotional ends. The apportioning of time in the studio to projects may be undertaken within the framework of a computerized workflow system of a large practice. But this process of apportioning time and therefore importance to competing demands of different design projects subsequently becomes a bargaining tool for the prioritization of projects and different levels of creative intensity. It is a means by which individuals maintain their capital within the studio hierarchy, their perceived value and possibility of recognition and promotion within the firm or externally, in terms of their name recognition through, for example, the design media. Nixon (2003) describes the delicate balancing that goes on between management and the environment of the advertising agency in order to safeguard 'creative' value. Equally, for the design firm, internal management is seen to involve attuning the need for turnover and throughput with the maintenance of creative ambition and worth amongst employees (e.g. Jones 2008).

This may not necessarily be self-seeking, however. In terms of the design firm's external orientation, the promotion, performance and evidencing of creativity is a crucial element where accounting systems may be employed, subverted or ignored. One informant spoke of her graphics firm employing a pointing system for *pro bono* design work such as for charities or design competitions. Non-chargeable work would be assessed against criteria that stressed the project's potential to deliver opportunities for the development and diffusion of creative abilities. Equally, it is noteworthy that many of the designs that have gained the international reputation of firms such as Ideo and Seymour Powell are, in fact, concept work, undertaken without a client.

The importance of maintaining creative reputation is also played out in other ways. By sharing computer files, clients can regularly view and comment on the development of a design project at a distance.

However, it is still important for representatives of the design firm to 'perform' their creativity through face-to-face meetings with their clients. This performance is often undertaken by the firm's 'star' designer who personifies the design consultancy's creative prowess. At the same time, the client audience for this has grown. The last decade has seen a shift toward 'concurrent design'. This is where marketing, sales, distribution and production strategies for a product are developed alongside each other. This contrasts with the sequential and linear neo-Fordist model of design. As a result, the client meeting may well involve large gatherings of representatives of different departments of the client's business. Hence, it has become more customary for the designer to visit the client than the other way round.

When the client does visit the design studio, this is another opportunity to show off the firm's creativity. The studio tour is part of this and, indeed, an informant expressed how the studio would be prepared for this: evidence of confidential work relating to other clients would be hidden, while obviously creative work such as drawings, mood boards or models may be self-consciously displayed. Design studios increasingly look like any other office environment as work has shifted from the drawing board to the computer interface. But efforts have to be made to disabuse clients of any views that make the designer's labour seem mundane or bureaucratic.

The importance of meetings may also contribute to a number of other factors in client retention, including understanding the client's needs, building relationships or 'chemistry' with them and maintaining a good reputation. In an in-depth survey of design consultancies and freelances, all of these features figured above price in terms of their importance in winning business. Half of UK design consultancies and freelances rely on personal recommendation for winning new business; 5 per cent say that they do not target new clients at all (Design Council 2005: 43, 52). The design industry is highly reliant on soft, informal relationships. This is particularly important where client retention is highly valued.

Given the breadth and heterogeneity of the design industry, it is perhaps difficult to draw generalizable conclusions concerning the ways that creativity is accounted for and valorized within the design firm. However, it is clear that there is a constant negotiation between the management of creativity and creativity's symbolic value. Creativity occupies a fundamental role in the differentiating and selling of professional services. Given this, it also retains considerable currency in the structuring and internal power struggles of the design consultancy.

Conclusion

While designers may express frustration at the increase of form-filling as part of their everyday working practices, they seem pragmatic enough to know that the systems themselves can be used creatively to negotiate or eke out value for themselves. Some disciplines of the creative industries – such as architecture and landscape architecture – are bound by much stricter systems of norms with regards to such things as registration, codes of conduct or continuing professional development requirements. The design profession, by contrast, constantly resists signing up to systems of registration or codes of conduct. For designers, systemization works in more subtle ways.

Du Gay (2000) reveals the wider polarization that has evolved around bureaucratization and entrepreneurialism in academic and business discourses. And within the design industry itself, these oppositions of bureaucracy/systemization/management and creativity/freedom/enterprise are, in themselves, as much discursive as they are operational. They allow a language by which designers can position themselves and give credence to practices. Designers may *appear* to disembed themselves even from their own norms of work as a way of giving value to their creative capital. At the same time, the relationship between an ethos and a practice of bureaucracy may be severed (Armbrüster 2002). The public face or ethos of a design firm may be that of unrestrained creativity while the actual everyday practice may be a lot more humdrum. Routine design practice may be dressed up as something 'other'.

It seems that systemization in the design firm does not fully drive its practices into a form of 'virtualism' (Carrier and Miller 1998) whereby abstracted systems and understandings then frame the modus operandi. The creation of systems by which design is carried out within the firm serves only loosely to guide the design process. This is already tacitly known, usually, and designers are far too flexible to be tied down to the application of abstracted structures into practice. Turnover of employees in design firms is rapid and they also rely significantly on hiring in freelances when either there is pressure to turn round extra work quickly or when there is a need for specialist technical or creative skills. Any systemization is quickly learnt, as are ways to 're-use' it. Its secondary functions are important, however. Within the performance of 'being a designer', systemization works for the valorization processes. This may be for legitimating and explaining otherwise tacit processes to clients. It exists as a fallback, 'checks and balances' system, in case the informal processes don't work. It is used to 'weed out' or promote certain potential projects that strengthen the intangible value of a firm. It is also used internally as a tool in order to prioritize certain pieces of creative work over others.

These observations must be seen within the framework of professionalization. The design industry has historically been caught between claiming professional status and resisting any normative structures. There is no compulsion for designers to conform to any professional body. Confirming Bourdieu's (1984) notion of 'cultural intermediaries', designers are constantly involved in 'needs' production. There is a recurrent emphasis on communicating their value to attract new clients or, more frequently, to retain clients. Systemization assigns a certain level of professional legitimation to what is otherwise a fairly unstable activity that is constantly looking for affirmation and acceptance.

The reconfiguration of the design firm as office rather than studio is about the changing technologies but also about changes in the kind of work and client relationships. It has become incrementally emptied of form. It has become progressively dematerialized. The visual and material evidence of progress, output and deliverables seeps away to be replaced by more abstracted measurement systems. Designers calculate their processes and inputs both to develop and promote their value as cultural intermediaries. Identity at work is reconfigured as creative play is subordinated to creatively playing the system.

This chapter has traced the linkages between the everyday practices within the design firm, their relationship to an external environment of client expectation and the professional, business, institutional and educational background to the culture of design in the age of 'disorganized capitalism' (Offe 1985; Lash and Urry 1987). As the design process has become increasingly complex and clients more demanding, so the locations and claims to creativity have become more diverse. At the same time, processes have become far from 'disorganized'. Indeed, creativity has been organized and managed through highly structured

frameworks. However, this shares the same tendency toward fragmentation, improvization and differentiation with the wider economy.
Far from mustering a homogeneous system of professional practice,
designers constantly invent their own logics as to the management of
creativity. This may be aimed as a positivistic tool to help them to 'get
the job done' (on time). At the same time, it may be used to underwrite
professional status and to 'make reasonable' the value of design.

Notes

1 These codes of conduct are available through the organizations'
respective websites: www.aiga.org, www.gdc.net and www.csd.org.uk
(accessed 14 April 2008).
2 'Counting Creativity: Understanding the Systemization of Design
Practices' within the Arts and Humanities Research Council 'Nature
of Creativity' programme, 2006–7. The results of this project appear
in Julier, G. and Moor, L. (eds.) (2009) *Design and Creativity: Policy,*
Management and Practice, Oxford: Berg.
3 This rhetoric of looming crisis in the creative industries was underlined
in the *Cox Review of Creative Business* (2005). This report, commissioned by the UK government, laid stress on the growing threat of the
development of creativity and innovation outside Europe and the USA.
There was only a five- to ten-year window of opportunity left before
Asia and Latin America begin to dominate in innovation, it claimed.
Following on from this the UK Design Council launched its 'Keep
British Design Alive' campaign – a web-based consultation on how the
design sector could respond to the Cox report.
4 A similar 'struggle for ownership' of creativity is reported in advertising
and marketing firms (see Banks *et al.* 2002).

References

Alvarez, J.L., Mazza, C., Strandgaard Pedersen, J. and Svejenova, S.
(2005) 'Shielding idiosyncrasy from isomorphic pressures: towards
optimal distinctiveness in European film making'. *Organization,*
12(6): 863–88.
Amabile, T.M. (1996) *Creativity in Context: Updates to the Social*
Psychology of Creativity. Boulder, CO: Westview Press.
Anthony, S.D., Eyring, M. and Gibson, L. (2006) 'Mapping your innov-
ation strategy. *Harvard Business Review,* **84**(5): 104–13.
Archer, L.B. (1965) *Systematic Method for Designers.* London: Design
Council.

Armbrüster, T. (2002) 'On anti-modernism and managerial pseudo-liberalism'. *Ephemera*, 2(1): 88–93.

Banks, M., Calvey, D., Owen, J. and Russell, D. (2002) 'Where the art is: defining and managing creativity in new media SMEs'. *Creativity and Innovation Management*, 11(4): 255–64.

Bourdieu, P. and Nice, R. (transl.) (1984) *Distinction: A Social Critique of the Judgement of Taste*. Cambridge, MA: Harvard University Press.

Breen, B. (2005) 'The business of design'. *Fast Company*, 93: 68.

British Design Innovation (BDI) (2006) 'The British Design Industry Valuation Survey – 2005 to 2006' (report). Brighton: BDI.

(2007) 'The British Design Industry Valuation Survey – 2006 to 2007' (report). Brighton: BDI.

Bruce, M. and Daly, L. (2006) 'International evidence on design: near-final report for the Department of Trade and Industry' (report). University of Manchester.

Business Ratio Plus (1998) *Design Consultancies*. London: ICC Business Publications.

Carrier, J. and Miller, D. (eds.) (1998) *Virtualism: A New Political Economy*. Oxford: Sage.

Caves, R. (2000) *Creative Industries: Contracts Between Art and Commerce*. Cambridge, MA: Harvard University Press.

Cooper, R. and Press, M. (1995) *The Design Agenda: A Guide to Successful Design Management*. Chichester: Wiley.

Creative Industries Task Force (CITF) (1998) *Creative Industries Mapping Document*. London: British Government, Department of Culture, Media and Sport.

Design Council (1998) *Design in Britain 1998–99: Facts, Figures and Quotable Quotes*. London: Design Council.

(2004) *Design in Britain 2003–04*. London: Design Council.

(2005) *The Business of Design: Design Industry Research 2005*. London: Design Council.

(2007) *Eleven Lessons: Managing Design in Eleven Global Companies: Desk Research Report*. London: Design Council.

du Gay, P. (2000) *In Praise of Bureaucracy – Weber, Organization, Ethics*. London: Sage.

Eikhof, D. and Haunschild, A. (2006) 'Lifestyle meets market: Bohemian entrepreneurs in creative industries'. *Creativity and Innovation Management*, 15(3): 234–41.

Florida, R. (2002) *The Rise of the Creative Class: And How It's Transforming Work, Leisure, Community and Everyday*. New York: Basic Books.

Frith, S. and Horne, H. (1987) *Art into Pop*. London: Routledge.

Helbrecht, I. (1998) 'Bare geographies in knowledge societies – creative cities as text and piece of art: two eyes, one vision'. *Built Environment*, 30(3): 191–200.

Hesmondhalgh, D. (2002) *The Cultural Industries*. London: Sage.

Hollington, G. (1998) 'The usual suspects'. *Design*, Summer: 62–3.

Howkins, J. (2001) *The Creative Economy: How People Make Money From Ideas*. London: Allen Lane.

Jeffcutt, P. and Pratt, A. (2002) 'Managing creativity in the cultural industries'. *Creativity and Innovation Management*, 11(4): 225–33.

Jones, P. (2008) 'The real value of team spirit'. *Design Week*, 3 April: 18.

Julier, G. (2007) *The Culture of Design*, second edn. London: Sage.

Lawson, B. (1997) *How Designers Think: The Design Process Demystified*. Oxford: Architectural Press.

Lash, S. and Urry, J. (1987) *The End of Organized Capitalism*. London: Polity.

(1994) *Economies of Signs and Space*. Thousand Oaks, CA: Sage.

Lockwood, T.L. (2007) 'Design value: a framework for measurement'. *Design Management Review*, 18(4): 90–7.

McGuirk, J. (2008) 'Design Indaba'. *Icon*, 59: 81–4.

McRobbie, A. (1998) *British Fashion Design: Rag Trade or Image Industry?* London: Routledge.

(2002) 'Clubs to companies: notes on the decline of political culture in speeded up creative worlds'. *Cultural Studies*. 16(4): 516–31.

(2007) 'The Los Angelisation of London: three short-waves of young people's micro-economies of culture and creativity in the UK'. (*Transversal*) available at http://eipcp.net/transversal/0207/mcrobbie/en (accessed 9 January 2008).

Montuori, A. and Purser, R.E. (1995) 'Deconstructing the lone genius myth: toward a contextual view of creativity'. *Journal of Humanistic Psychology*, 35: 69–112.

Moor, L. (2007) *The Rise of Brands*. Oxford: Berg.

Morris, L., Rabinowitz, J. and Myerson, J. (1998) 'No more heroes: from controllers to collaborators'. *Design Management Journal*, 9(2): 22–5.

Netherlands Design Institute (1994) *Design Across Europe: Patterns of Supply and Demand in the European Design Market*. Amsterdam: Vormgevingsinstitut.

Nixon, S. (2003) *Advertising Cultures: Gender, Commerce, Creativity*. London: Sage.

Nordic Innovation Centre (2004) 'The Future in Design: The Competitiveness and Industrial Dynamics of the Nordic Design Industry' (report). Oslo: Nordic Innovation Centre.

Offe, C. (1985) *Disorganized Capitalism*. Oxford: Polity.

Peters, M. (2007) 'Control quality to restore faith'. *Design Week*, 25 October: 23.

Ray, P. (2001) *The Cultural Creatives: How 50 Million People Are Changing the World*. New York: Random House.

Reimer, S., Pinch, S. and Sunley, P. (2008) 'Design spaces: agglomeration and creativity in British design agencies'. *Geografiska Annaler B*, 90(2): 1–20.

Rigby, R. (2007) 'Can design inject some creativity into China's karaoke economy?' *Design Council Magazine*, 3: 22–9.

Scase, R. and Davis, H. (2000), *Managing Creativity: The Dynamics of Work and Organization*. Milton Keynes: Open University Press.

Schön, D. A. (1991) *The Reflective Practitioner: How Professionals Think in Action*. London: Basic Books.

Sutton, R. I. (2001) 'The weird rules of creativity'. *Harvard Business Review*, 79(8): 96–103.

Thiel, J. (2005) *Creativity and Space: Labour and the Restructuring of the German Advertising*. Aldershot: Ashgate.

13 | *Organising creativity in a music festival*

JANE DONALD, LOUISE MITCHELL
AND NIC BEECH

One strand of thought holds that creative industries are so different to commercial and public service activities that the management
and organization theories that have largely been developed in those
contexts are inapplicable. In this chapter we explore this idea and
seek to reveal the relevance of general management for organizing
musical events. We start by reviewing managerial literature and in
particular the work of Fayol (1949). Our perspective is that Fayol
has been somewhat misrepresented and that sections of his formu-
lation are worthy of consideration, and on this basis we devise a
framework of management practice. We then explore the issue from
another literature; that concerned with music and management
(chamber and orchestral music) and that which seeks lessons from
music (extemporization in particular) for management. We conclude
this section of the chapter with a revised version of the framework
for management practice. Following this we illustrate the framework using empirical material gathered from the organization of an
international music festival.

The festival we focus on, Celtic Connections, is run by Glasgow
Concert Halls (GCH) which operates a number of music and arts
venues in Glasgow. The aims of GCH are to produce and promote
top-class cultural and educational events, incorporating music and
entertainment, through which 'we hope to bring the extraordinary
into the everyday and enrich the lives of people in the city'. Celtic
Connections is a festival that links artists with connections to the
celtic diasporas (both ancient and modern) and promotes their performances to audiences in Glasgow over three weeks every January.
It started in 1994 and has grown to attendances of over 100,000
people. The festival is recognized not only as the premier Celtic festival in the UK but also as one of the largest winter music festivals of its
kind in the world, and it has brought hundreds of artists to Glasgow
from every part of the globe.

The argument presented in this chapter is that management of festivals requires an understanding of, and empathy with, creativity, in which a balance has to be struck between creative processes and organizing processes. Our purpose in this chapter is to propose a reformulation of the characterization of management practice which potentially reduces the perceived gap between creating and organizing.

A framework of management practice

Classically, management has been regarded as a role and a set of practices that stretches across organizational functions and hence has a generic nature. For Fayol (1949) management is one of the core organizational activities alongside technical activities (production of services and goods), commercial activities (purchasing and selling), financial activities (gaining and using capital), security activities (protecting property and people) and accounting activities (stocktaking, costing and providing balance sheets). Each of these activities entails rendering the unknown known in the sense of discovering information and making it useful as organizational knowledge. Traditional production entails setting schedules, determining input and output levels and knowing timescales and deliverables. Commercial activities entail negotiation, and hence a degree of uncertainty. However, effective commercial activities set contracts and service level agreements such that what one can expect, at what price, is determined. Similarly, the financing of organizations entails uncertainty, but the financial operations seek to analyse and mitigate risk. Security activities, such as health and safety, have become increasingly professionalized and great effort goes into ameliorating risk and hazard. Accounting activities centre on the gathering and provision of information for decision making and developing knowledge of the costs and benefits of activities. So, in each organizational activity, one meets uncertainty and seeks to make it known such that risk is reduced and progress towards organizational goals is produced.

Fayol analysed the management practice that he observed and saw it as comprising five elements. First, it incorporates *planning and forecasting* – taking a view of the future and planning for it. Secondly, it is necessary to *organize* – to establish social and material structures that are oriented towards goals. Third is the activity of *commanding*, which for Fayol means ensuring that people are clear on what is needed and maintaining goal-oriented activities. Fourth is *co-ordination* – the unifying or 'harmonizing' of activities so that they work effectively together, and last is the activity of *controlling*. This entails ensuring that rules are working, that activities are in line with plans and, where necessary, they are brought back into line. This 'planning, organizing, commanding, co-ordinating, controlling' view of management can be regarded as rendering the unknown known. The ethos is one of developing a clear idea of what should happen and then making sure that it does happen.

As well as being one of the founding fathers of management, Fayol is also one of the most criticized. He is often paired with Taylor and it is assumed that his attitude is Tayloristic. However, Parker and Ritson (2005) have argued that this is a misrepresentation and a mis-understanding of Fayol. They explore his original work and show that there is much that is a precursor of, and is congruent with, current understandings of management. Certainly, Fayol's categories of man-agement can be seen in many modern iterations (for example, Hales 2001, 2002). But Parker and Ritson's point goes beyond this. Critical perspectives on Fayol suppose that he wanted to reduce and restrict freedoms and activities of workers through the *urge to know*. That is, his conception of management entailed developing knowledge of people and processes so that they could be closely and restrictively controlled. This flies in the face of some versions of modern manage-ment, but as Parker and Ritson show, it also flies in the face of what Fayol actually said.

In his work experience Fayol saw considerable conflict and was focused on matters such as education and the development of an *esprit de corps*. He thought that harmony within an organization was a great strength and achieving this should be a concern of man-agement. This type of management would entail both policies that enabled the fair co-ordination of effort at the organizational level and skilled interpersonal relations that achieved harmonious outcomes on an individual level. He did not believe that people worked only for money and extrinsic reward and his thinking was in line with the conception of providing both extrinsic and intrinsic rewards. In other words, there was a degree of personal significance associated with the value of work. Fayol did not see management as a singular and top-down activity, but rather as an activity that occurs throughout an organization's hierarchy. He believed that in order for such dispersed management to be effective, management training in some form needed to be available to all workers. Unlike Taylor, Fayol frequently used organic and biological metaphors when talking about organization. Such metaphors underpinned his approach to planning:

The act of forecasting is of great benefit to all who take part in the process, and is the best means of ensuring adaptability to changing circumstances. (quoted in Parker and Ritson 2005: 185)

He regarded planning as a process that enabled organizations to sense and adapt to their environments. It was not a deterministic conception, but was a contingency approach.

It is arguable that Fayol's formative conception of management is applicable, therefore, not only to modern management, but also to management in the creative industries. Hales (2001) reviews the study of managerial activities. In common with Fayol, Hales emphasizes activities such as: planning and scheduling, directing and monitoring work, technical specialisms and maintenance or co-ordination of processes. However, Hales, building on the work of Mintzberg (1973), placed greater emphasis on symbolic actions such as acting as a figurehead, communicative measures, problem solving and political action such as networking and negotiating. The other area that Hales gives emphasis to is innovation, and there is a common argument that this is a requirement in current organizations. Therefore, it is possible to synthesize a framework of generalized management practice that would incorporate the following:

- **Planning** in order to become sensitized and adaptable to the environment
- **Organizing** in an organic way to meet macro goals whilst enabling alteration and development at the micro level, and co-ordinating activities
- **Creating, negotiating and using meaning** through acting as a figurehead, 'commanding', consulting, negotiating and networking
- **Managing performance and outcomes** through problem solving, 'controlling' and rewarding

At this point we should acknowledge that this synthesis could appear to be managerialist in serving the perceived needs of the organization without acknowledging diversity of interests and power inequalities between various stakeholders. This is not the intention, and it is clear that each of these activities takes place within a context of the organization, the industry and economic setting as well as social and political contexts which will favour some positions and outcomes over others. At its extreme managerialism can be thought of as being content to exploit workers and other stakeholders overtly or covertly. Hence, we must apply further questions concerning the way that the managerial activities outlined above are conducted: what (or whose) purposes are being served? How are power dynamics operating? What are the intentions of the actors?

Given this generic framework of management practice, which entails seeking and using knowledge, our next question is how this relates to managerial activity in creative settings, and we will discuss this in the next section.

Management and creative settings

It has been argued that the management of arts, creative and cultural products entails a set of challenges that are somewhat different to management in other sectors. In particular, there is a need for skill in 'building creative systems to support and market cultural products but not allowing the system to suppress individual inspiration, which is the root of creating value' (Lampel *et al.* 2000: 263). Zan (2005) considers the distinctiveness of creative industries as a setting for managerial activities. He sees this sector as being populated by professional organizations that have a 'substantive-aesthetic' culture. This means that what Fayol would term technical activities (production of goods or services) are carried out by professionals who expect a higher degree of autonomy that would be common in many capitalistic or public sector organizations. Although Fayol acknowledges the intrinsic value of work, according to Zan, the significance and value of productive work to those who are regarded as being the creative people in creative organizations is heightened. And hence Fayol's concern for the establishment and maintenance of productive systems is likely to be reduced in order to give sufficient freedom to enable creativity. So, as Zan puts it, one cannot afford to be 'hyper-specialised' in management, but must be more broadly based in perspective and approach to organizing activities. Secondly, Zan argues that there is a great danger with simplistic applications of the managerial knowledge. Whilst there might be a 'managerial logic' that increased knowledge leads to increased control and hence to increased performance, it is arguable that creative organizations being too focused on control or assuming that certain types of communication will motivate workers are over-simplifications. For Zan the idiosyncratic nature of artistic activity evades codification and generalization. Therefore, managerial knowing needs to be of a different type. Rather than a determined, reductive form of knowing, there is a need for a form of knowing that is both liberating and able to set a framework within which performance can happen.

One way of approaching this has been the use of improvization, and particularly jazz improvization, as a metaphor for elaborating, organizing and managing activities (Hatch 1999), the idea being that management might learn something from those it purports to manage. Although jazz has been particularly popular in management and organizational writing, it is worth noting that improvization also exists, or existed, in many other musical forms, including Western music, until about 1800, where for example, in much keyboard music the bass part was improvized by the performer rather than being highly scripted by the composer (Bailey 1993). According to Montuori and Purser (1995) two key processes were highly significant in the increased codification (which we could see as an attempt to *know*) and control of music and a corresponding curtailment of improvization and extemporization. The first factor is referred to as the 'cult of genius', and this led to a desire to hear the score performed exactly (and fully) as the composer intended. This far-reaching cultural change was combined with a development of copyright laws and consequently musical performance became more controlled and constrained. Whilst it was possible to add emphasis, emotion and expression within the score, extemporization outside it was discouraged or disallowed. As Higgins (1991) has argued, improvization became regarded as an aberration because it constituted a lack of score at a time when musical aesthetics began focusing on the score and its correct performance.

There are parallels between this way of thinking and the deterministic conception of management that has been falsely associated with Fayol. The clearer the codification of what should be done, the better one is able to judge how good a performance is, and hence the more one is able to take corrective action. However, there is some evidence in the management-music literature that striving for greater certainty and the application of standard management techniques may not be appropriate. For example, Maitlis and Lawrence (2003) explore the failure of a major British symphony orchestra to produce an effective artistic strategy. They relate this to failures in a division of labour to allocate tasks appropriately, a failure to take responsibility, a degree of in-fighting and politics and a lack of strategy. Although Maitlis and Lawrence produce a sophisticated reading of this situation and see the problems as a dysfunctional politico-discursive construction of strategizing, one might reflect that these failures also chime with Parker and Ritson's reading of Fayol. Better management might have achieved more effective plans, greater co-ordination between roles and responsibilities might have overcome the division of labour problems and a better *esprit de corps* could have ameliorated the politicking. We must ask, however, whether it is that such management techniques were badly applied, or whether they were simply not the right ones to have been pursuing.

The proponents of improvization as a lesson for management would propose the latter. The management failure in the orchestra was not just because they were not doing things well enough, it was also because they were not doing the right things. Montuori (2003) provides a conceptualization of improvization that holds forth some potential lessons for such managerial situations. Montuori rejects dichotomies such as order/disorder or knowledge/ignorance. He suggests that views of improvization that see it as purely intuitive, disordered and removed from structure are mistaken. In fact, improvizations, whether in jazz or baroque keyboard music, start in a certain place and end in another. There is a degree of freedom on the way but it is not that 'anything goes'. For Montuori, improvization is a form of dialogue. This dialogue is multifaceted in that it connects what goes before with what comes after in the performance; in a band there is a dialogue between a soloist and the supporting musicians, and there is also a dialogue between the performer and their forefathers and mothers. Musicians pick up and reference phrases that others have used and form styles of improvization that relate to others they admire. If it is possible to form a 'style' then there is an element of rule-following (or rule-creating and following) about the activity, otherwise it would not be possible to differentiate between an example of this style and one of another. In addition, musicians are often immersed in the technical aspects of music including melody, harmony, counterpoint and so on. When improvizing they make use of such technical knowledge even if they are choosing to break certain traditional rules. So, the dialogue is in the moment between choices in style, references to those who have gone before, the technical 'rules of the game' and those around them. This dialogic approach contests both the view that creative activities are so distinctive that structure will crush them and the view that management is the answer. Zan (2005) argued that there is a great danger in the application of simple management rules, and Montuori's argument does not disagree with this. However, there is an implicit subtext in much of the pro-improvization-management literature that management rules are inherently simple and that management is anathema to creativity. Montuori draws attention to the idea that management practice does not need to be only the imposition of order and structure, but also incorporates challenge and extemporization. Sophisticated management practice is not just about a simplistic form of knowledge that equates to control. Rather, it can be postdichotomous (Beech and Cairns 2001), in that a process of knowing incorporates both following and changing traditions, using patterns and challenging them, playing from the score and extemporizing.

This position may appear to be paradoxical; however, perhaps that is exactly what management in creative industries should be concerned with. As Rehn and de Cock (2008) have argued, to attempt to explain creativity, or provide a model of creativeness is ontologically paradoxical because creating the new cannot be contained in the already existent. We cannot generalize or systematize creativity because creativity is precisely that which has uniqueness from that which existed before, including generalizations and systems. The postdichotomous, extemporizing approach does not seek to 'solve' such a paradox. Indeed, any paradox that can apparently be solved is consequently not a paradox. Rather, the approach is to live with, and play with the co-existence of contradictions. Hence, extemporization is both a use of, and escape from, structure. Similarly, management is both a process of knowing and an embracing of unknowing.

The 'both and' approach proposed here is opposed to the more common 'either or' view, but if it is genuinely 'both and', then it needs to learn from both managerial and creativity-exclusive-of-management forms of knowledge. Sicca (2000) studied the organization of chamber music and identified certain facets which appeared to be distinctive

from other forms of organizing. First, *reputation* played a highly significant role. For example, there were various attempts to develop an
innovative project which ran into difficulties. The innovation finally
worked when a particular violinist with an outstanding international
reputation joined the project. This gave the project credibility both to
other musicians and to organizers. In Sicca's view, he managed to create 'the best possible aesthetic contract between performers and public'
(2000: 149). From our perspective, this reputation effect is interesting
because it can be seen as a non-structured structure. The reputation
overcomes the normal hierarchical organizational structures that govern decision making. It goes beyond the organization to (apparently)
incorporate the public (and even if this claim might be contested, it was
taken as true within the company). Hence, the normal structure that
would have produced the answer: 'do not do this project' was over-
turned. However, it would be wrong to say that reputation has no structure whatsoever. There are some rules of that game, even if they are not
codified. For example, reputation comes from artistic success, critical
approval, the winning of prizes and performances that have become
seen as iconic. It also relates to commercial success to some degree, for
example, having been able to draw large crowds to performances.

A second distinctive feature is that of *value*. For Sicca (2000) the
value in the production of chamber music is not reducible to financial
or commercial success. Rather, it is in the meaning that is created in
the production process. Chamber music is a collective act and value
is produced as behaviours move towards 'reciprocal harmonization',
which renders the score 'speakable'. In other words, as the performances develop, they are based on forms of communication between
performers, some of which is actually spoken (e.g. agreements on
interpretations and so on), and others are tacitly developed. The 'aesthetic contract' with the audience is fulfilled when this communication includes them. Hence, value is creating a performance that acts as
a communication of ideas and emotion. This understanding of value
draws our attention to its ephemeral nature. If tacit understandings are
disrupted for some reason, then value is vulnerable. Repetition provides
an example of this. The repeating of a piece from a previous performance can enhance value as the overt and tacit meanings are well-formed
and resonate. Indeed, they can be enhanced because of positive associations with a previous successful performance. However, repetition
can equally devalue if it is felt to be a short-cut or laziness in programming or indicative of a lack of development. Hence, like reputation,

value is something that does not appear to be amenable to some managerialist tools such as 'added-value' programmes and audits.

A third feature that Sicca sees as distinctive is *listening ability*. The listening ability in performers is particularly important and they have to first listen to themselves in order to be 'in tune' with their colleagues. This quality of listening changes communication because it is not merely a matter of sending and receiving messages: 'this is what qualifies the work of an ensemble, when the sending of information is particularly strong, the result may be a reconstruction of the inner self' (2000: 153). In ensemble playing there is a dialogue both with others and with the self so that at one moment one is effectively accompanying one of the others and at another leading the music. This necessitates a radical dialogue which is communication between A and B, and through which A and B can themselves become transformed. We can relate this concept to Montuori's understanding of dialogue in which there is communication between players, with the composer and with the audience such that there is the possibility of them experiencing things differently and potentially being different.

Above we proposed a framework for management practice incorporating *Planning; Organizing; Creating, Negotiating and Using Meaning; and Managing Performance and Outcomes.* Having reviewed some of the ideas and potential lessons from creative settings, and music in particular, we can now adapt this framework to incorporate ideas from creativity:

Preparation

- the setting including social 'structures' such as reputation
- the score where extemporization starts and finishes

Practising performance

- listening to the self and others
- a dialogic construction of performance

Creating value

- creating 'reciprocal harmonization'
- establishing the aesthetic contract (including the audience)

Performing

- playing from the score
- using overt and tacit knowing
- extemporizing

The experience of managing Celtic Connections

It has been argued that the challenge of managing creativity is amplified when we are concerned with festivals (Snowball 2005) as they are at one time both forms of organization and fundamentally dispersed and disorganized. Festivals are processes and social sites, by and through which individual and group creations are co-ordinated as a means of bringing a more-or-less coherent product to the market. Festivals have been seen to be increasingly important in this role. Not only are they becoming more frequent and popular, they are also now playing a role in defining genres of music and art, rather than merely reflecting extant genres (Paleo and Wijnberg 2006). Hence, festivals are ways of organizing disparate products, such as musical, dramatic or artistic performances, under a banner which is beneficial for the producers of the art, because they gain access to a bigger market, as well as for the organizers. However, as the producers of the art are not employed by the festival organization the process of organizing is more akin to a temporary network (Starkey *et al.* 2000) than a traditional organization. (The exception to this is that the artistic director, whose role spans organizer and performer, is part of the GCH team all year round.) Whilst there might be some shared cultural assumptions between producers, they also operate in competition with each other, to a degree, and they do not report to a management structure in the festival-organizing company. Therefore, we see this as a productive empirical site for illustration of a postdichotomous approach to management which incorporates structure and non-structure, playing from the score and extemporization, not as competing opposites but as concurrent stimuli for action.

In the following section some selections from interviews with members of the senior management team are used to illustrate the concepts developed in the literature review above.

Preparation

The appointment of a new artistic director for the festival is clearly a significant strategic decision that will have an impact on the development of the festival and on internal processes of organizing. In this sense, it is part of the process of developing the social structure for performance. In this case, when the last appointment was made, there was time pressure on the decision and there were about six key names that were being discussed by the senior management team.

CEO: We knew and we needed to find an artistic director pretty quickly, and we needed to find somebody that would put new fire into the artistic side of what we were doing. We needed somebody we could work with, we also needed someone who was prepared basically to get on with it.

One senior manager invited the eventual Artistic Director, a highly successful musician, in to 'have a chat … just a cup of tea'. This was somewhat disconcerting for the Director of Sales and Marketing who would be the host of the 'cup of tea', but who had not yet fully agreed the nature of the role or the basis for a contract. The initial meeting went very well as the soon-to-be Artistic Director and the Director of Marketing knew each other and, although very informal, it was clear that there would be a good match with the festival and GCH. However, at the end of the meeting,

SENIOR MANAGER (SM2): […] off he [the Artistic Director (AD)] went, [SM1] thought, 'Yeah, yeah, job done'. But of course there's so much more we need to talk about. So then we had to wait till [SM3] was in to discuss the role.

This uncertainty became an opportunity:

MIDDLE MANAGER (MM1): […] because we realised we had an opportunity really to clarify the roles and in a small team like that working under festival conditions you all have to overlap, but there should be a purpose to each person's role.

Following this, the team started to codify some of the ideas and role definitions.

SM2: You wrote job descriptions. I remember because you wrote a job description for yourself and for [AD] and for the team. And looking back that seems quite funny now, because did we not have everything sorted.

But,

MM1: We had the strands, the themes for activities: education, entertainment, and we had these job descriptions, because I think we thought, 'well, we've got to give some sort of – '

SM2: – We've got to look like, particularly in front of [AD] […] we don't want to look like we haven't thought about this.

MM1: Exactly, yeah.

sm2: Which we *had* thought about the important stuff. Actually we'd done the thinking on what was important for the festival but it was just really quite open.

So, the dialogue with the Artistic Director was itself part of the process through which the roles and frameworks for action were developed, and taking actions, such as having meetings arranged at short notice, stimulated and crystallized thinking.

sm2: So we met [AD] and then he phoned me the next morning [...] and we went and got a cup of tea and he just wanted to talk through some more things.

mm1: I think that kind of worked. And then that night he phoned and he said, yeah, he'd take the job. Although obviously in between I had to make phone calls to make sure they were happy.

sm3: That's right, because we'd agreed we wouldn't agree anything while [...] somebody was away and we'd agreed we wouldn't do it until they came back. So actually I don't think really we would have done anything if they'd said 'I think this is a terrible idea'.

ceo: I was in Hong Kong I remember when it actually went through because I remember being phoned up by Radio Clyde when I was in Hong Kong. It seems quite comical now in some ways [...] There was lots of strategic thinking wasn't there!? [laughter amongst the group]

Although there is an implied self-critique of a lack of strategic thinking, this example shows a degree of flexibility and extemporization which brought about a very successful strategic change. A process of dialogue led to a number of names being in contention, but then one senior manager taking an initiative tipped the balance into action. Others on the list were also talked to, and it was through this conversational process that roles became developed and an understanding reached. This did not resemble a traditional version of managerial control, hence the joking self-criticism, but it did show a set of practices that resemble the thinking outlined in the literature above. A social structure was developed, rather than being imposed and rather than having a singular 'score' to play from, there was a degree of extemporization as different members of the management team played roles in developing the dialogue.

Practising performance

The practising performance group of activities includes processes of listening to the self and others, as Sicca (2000) emphasizes, and developing performance through dialogue. In the following example, the senior team are discussing how musicians are approached to play at the festival. In some cases it is a formal approach via agents and managers, but in many it is less formal and more dialogical.

SM2: So again it's all about ... I guess it's all back to what [the CEO] was saying about relationships and I think what [MM] says about artists' trust in [AD]. And then some artists trust other artists. So one of the things I thought was really interesting, what you [MM1] and [AD] do, is [AD] doesn't seem to always make the approach to somebody. Quite often he'll use another artist to make the approach to the next artist. It's that kind of ... so it kind of goes through a chain of 'you must play Celtic Connections, we had a great gig'.

So here there is a sense of dialogue extending beyond those who are within GCH. The reputation is grown via word-of-mouth and decision making: who to book from GCH's perspective, and whether to play from the musicians' perspective, is influenced by the discursive activities of people within the broader community, but outside the control of the organization. This is the inverse of the experience of another festival recounted by the CEO:

One of the key things actually from other festivals that I've worked on is the mutual respect and understanding between the core and the periphery [of the organizing team]. It's absolutely crucial to get right. To use an example, I used to work in the City 1 office of the City 2 festival and we did the programme planning from City 1 because that's how they did it in those days, and yet in July suddenly you had to move to City 2 and command a team of people you didn't know. It caused absolute hell. It was, 'Who do they think they are?' Being from City 1 didn't help either, as you can imagine. It was really difficult. You had a core team of twenty people who had worked in City 2 all year round, with visits from the director, but I would turn up, trying to make things work in very much the same kind of way you do, and not knowing how it worked, not knowing the people, not really fitting into the system was ghastly [...] so I was technically a member of the core but I felt like a member of the periphery and I wasn't, I hadn't been exposed to those values and ethos that everybody else had.

In this case, the absence of a dialogic connection meant that people felt differentiated from each other and this perpetuated and amplified what might be regarded as natural differences. Hence, the ability to listen to the self and others becomes limited, and trust and informal mutual influence more difficult to build and maintain.

Creating value

Creating value is about producing reciprocal relationships in which
there is a degree of harmony and an aesthetic contract which is concerned with the experience of creative quality along with financial or
commercial quality. In the following data extract the interviewees are
discussing a change in the organization of volunteers. Many festivals
rely on volunteers to help with activities ranging from picking up lit-
ter to aspects of staging. At Celtic Connections volunteers play an
important role in looking after musicians. Traditionally, a volunteer
would be associated with a particular venue and would be there to
help the venue manager, welcome the musicians and help with communicating any needs that they have. The new idea was that volunteers would be associated with musicians rather than venues, so that
from a musicians' perspective, they would be helped to find their way
around their festival performances with a person that they would get
to know and rely on.

INTERVIEWER: How does it work such that you can construct a festival
that is really effective when you can't ultimately determine what the artist
will do?

MMI: That's interesting. I think the artists, musicians have to trust the
festival. I think it's very interesting having [AD] on board because he is
a musician and he's a very well-respected musician and I think the artists
trust him. They trust his judgment. But also I think that the artists at the
end of the day, if they're happy I think you've had a really successful festival and I think that they're the top of the tree. Unfortunately a few years
ago they weren't. They were the last to be thought of and, you know, it was
dreadful. I get embarrassed thinking of things, you know, but for some
reason they were the last to be thought of and I think the wrong people
were being looked after.

INTERVIEWER: Who was being looked after?

MMI: People like, you know, MCs or hosts of venues were put on the top
of the tree, they were put at the top of the tree and I just felt that the relationships were upside down. I think that looking back, well now I think
the musicians really trust us and they know they're my main concern. I just
need to make sure they're all happy and they've got everything they need
and [...] this year we changed the systems of how we use the volunteers,
for example, and what they do. They used to be looking after a venue, so
they each used to have a venue and make sure there were riders there and
everything was happening. I thought it would be nicer for the volunteers

to see the scope of the festival so they could bounce round the different venues. Stage managers didn't like it so much because they had a little bit more to do, but we just didn't have the luxury of having so many bodies to do that as well. So, one person was assigned an artist so they would follow that artist around even if they did one gig or five gigs but that was their one contact. They got in contact maybe a week beforehand saying, 'Hi, my name is Amy, I'm going to look after you, here's my mobile number'. They met them at the hotel if they were coming in trans-Atlantic. They made sure their rooms were booked, checked in, all that sort of stuff.

It was much nicer for the artists as well, you know [...] They had a lovely time [...] 'Person X is going to take care of me when I go to Glasgow.'

SM2: It was so much better for us from a media point of view. We could then just say 'right, we need that artist' and instead of trying to track them round the venues we could just go straight to the person.

In this example, value is created for the musicians by altering the mode of organizing volunteers such that the experience of both volunteer and musician is a longitudinal pairing. This has the advantages of allowing them to get to know each other, to feel comfortable and that they have a place in the festival, and to move to new venues without having everything being new. Hence, the organizing activities add to the potential for a relaxed and successful artistic performance.

Performing

We have characterized performing as both playing from the score and extemporizing, the use of overt and tacit knowing. In organizing processes this is typically an ensemble effort and in the following extract members of the management team discuss how they have come to share aspects of an overall task by having particular roles. However, the roles are somewhat fluid and different people help out, passing the baton of activity between them:

CEO: I think, actually, what's changed over the last few years is that we're kind of all involved in most of the relationships. You know, the programming is very much now involved with the relationship with the audience. I used to regard the sort of fundraising side of it as my job, the sort of public body fundraising. But now I go to the Arts Council, and I take [AD], and we'll do stuff all together which is actually making it simpler rather than more complicated. We don't all do everything, but I recognize the fact that you [MM1] and [AD] have a lot to say with the relationship with the Scottish Government or the Arts Council. And [SM2] recognizes that you as programmers have a lot to do with the relationship with the audience which is ostensibly … that's the relationship you manage. You know, I tend to feel that I manage the organizational relationships, but I can't do that on my own. I need input and sparkiness from you. And I think we're all kind of involved in all the relationships that we have, and for example we had a dinner last night with [main sponsor] and we all went. We've never had a meal all together before.

I mean that relationship, on a high level, is managed by [SM2] and at an administrative level is managed by [MM2] but we've all got a bit of it. It seems to me […] I've never thought about this before but it seems as if we kind of shared the relationships a little bit more than we did before.

MM1: Absolutely, yeah. They work better if you share them too, so in the past I think you sometimes feel a sense of responsibility, say, towards a sponsor because you think, 'Well, that's within the old-fashioned kind of line management structure, and I should present this and look after it.' But actually when you're a bit freer with it the sponsor loves more than anything to meet the person who knows the artists. That's the exciting bit, and they like to be able to have input into how the staging looks for the concerts they sponsor.

In the next extract, the team are discussing the performance of organizing and the balances involved in decision making. In this particular example, perhaps ironically, the organizing performance is to decide to cancel a concert, but the following quotations show how different players took up supportive roles that enacted some rules of business about when a venture is not going to work, but also incorporated values and emotions associated with a creative venture.

CEO: My job is trusting other people to do things, very largely.

SM2: Maybe if we worked in another industry where we weren't constantly on the move […] so we do quite often have to react on a kind of – it doesn't mean we don't have piles and piles of statistics to look at, but there's also something about the business, about enhancing life through entertainment that also relies on a kind of – gut experience. And you do sometimes just have to, when we talk about the budget we always talk about taking the jump, and it does feel like a jump because we don't absolutely know how audiences are going to behave because we have programmed things that are risky. Because they've got to be unknown, and we've just –

CEO: – But you wouldn't do it if you knew what was going to happen. That's the sort of edge that keeps us here. That's the edge that you don't know. In other words a computer could be a festival programmer. It's the sparky bits and the bits you get, or that [AD] gets by having a conversation with somebody who met somebody in Brazil that knows about these people, it's that kind of thing. So we empower [AD] to make that judgment and we don't say, 'OK, in order to programme this event you need to fulfil these eight criteria.' We just say, 'Go and make it sparkle. You've got the sparkle dust, go and do it.'

MMI: Because you know the ones that will come and see you and go, 'This just doesn't feel right.'

CEO: Yes, that's right. Well, a classic example was you had that concert, we did cancel a concert and you and [AD] were really worried about it. [AD] rang me up and said 'I don't know what to do', and all that. Actually he knew exactly what to do.

MMI: We were both standing together ...

CEO: I thought you probably were. But he knew what to do and the reason he was not taking that decision was he was beating himself up about it and saying, 'We should have done this, we should have done that.' Yeah, fine, maybe you should have, but we haven't. That's fine, thank you, move on. And he knew exactly what to do.

MMI: Yes, it just felt ...

CEO: All I did was give him permission to know that. If you like.

MMI: Yes, which was great.

SM2: But that was all anybody could have done because it was clearly not going to work.

CEO: But all I did was to tell you what you already knew. The fact that I listened to what you were telling me and said, 'OK'.

MMI: That's great that we can have those conversations actually...

Conclusion

In this chapter we have argued that management practice has often been misunderstood as a will to control, constrain and direct. There have been management authors who have conceived activities in this way, but we have argued that it is easy to (mis)perceive the management literature through the lens of a stereotypical version of controlling management. It is not surprising, therefore, that management might be seen as antithetical to creative ventures such as music making. However, we have argued that management can be re-read as entailing greater fluidity, empathy for creativity and performance.

J. Donald, L. Mitchell and N. Beech

Based on an analysis of some of the music and management literature we have proposed a view of management practice as entailing
preparation (establishing social structures and the 'score'), practising
performance (listening to self and others and establishing dialogue),
creating value (by establishing reciprocal harmonization and an aesthetic contract) and performing (playing from and beyond the score).

Taking the managerial activities of organizing a musical festival
as an example, we have illustrated these four aspects of practice and
indicated that it is neither possible nor desirable to pursue a 'control
and constrain' agenda. Rather, effective organizing entailed listening, trusting, giving permission and sharing roles, along with making
tough decisions such as cancelling a concert. We are not proposing
an 'either or' argument. In rejecting the 'control and constrain' perspective we are not proposing an 'anything goes' replacement. Rather,
we see managing and organizing as complex balancing acts that are
a series of experimental steps forward. As each step is taken there
is a need to sense how things are going and to take the next step in
order to keep balance. In reality this entails a focus on dialogue, giving voice to interested and sometimes challenging people, from artists and the artistic director to volunteers, and acting in concordance
with the twin values of achieving musical quality and organizational
success.

References

Bailey, D. (1993) *Improvisation: Its Nature and Practice in Music.* New
York: Da Capo Press.
Beech, N. and Cairns, G. (2001) 'Coping with change: the contribution of
postdichotomous ontologies'. *Human Relations,* 54(10): 1303–24.
Fayol, H. (1949) *General and Industrial Management.* London: Pitman.
Hales, C. (2001) 'Does it matter what managers do?' *Business Strategy
Review,* 12(2): 50–8.
(2002) 'Bureaucracy-lite and continuities in managerial work'. *British
Journal of Management,* 13: 51–66.
Hatch, M. J. (1999) 'Exploring the empty spaces of organizing: how impro-
visational jazz helps redescribe organizational structure'. *Organization
Studies,* 20(1): 75–100.
Higgins, K. (1991) *The Music of Our Lives.* Philadelphia: Temple University
Press.

Lampel, J., Lant, T. and Shamsie, J. (2000) 'Balancing act: learning from organizing practices in cultural industries'. *Organization Science*, 11(3): 263–9.

Maitlis, S. and Lawrence, T.B. (2003) 'Orchestral manoeuvres in the dark: understanding failure in organizational strategizing'. *Journal of Management Studies*, 40(1): 109–39.

Mintzberg, H. (1973) *The Nature of Managerial Work*. New York: Harper and Row.

Montuori, A. (2003) 'The complexity of improvisation and the improvisation of complexity: social science, art and creativity'. *Human Relations*, 56(2): 237–55.

Montuori, A. and Purser, R. (1995) 'Deconstructing the lone genius myth: towards a contextual view of creativity'. *Journal of Humanistic Psychology*, 35(3): 69–112.

Paleo, I.O. and Wijnberg, N.M. (2006) 'Classification of popular music festivals'. *International Journal of Arts Management*, 8(2): 50–61.

Parker, L.D. and Ritson, P.A. (2005) 'Revisiting Fayol: anticipating contemporary management'. *British Journal of Management*, 16(3): 175–94.

Rehn, A. and de Cock, C. (2008) 'Deconstructing creativity', in T. Rickards, M.A. Runco and S. Moger (eds), *The Routledge Companion to Creativity*. London: Routledge: 222–31.

Sicca, L.M. (2000) 'Chamber music and organizational theory: some typical organizational phenomena seen under the microscope'. *Studies in Cultures, Organizations and Societies*, 6: 145–68.

Snowball, J.D. (2005) 'Art for the masses?' *Journal of Cultural Economics*, 29: 107–25.

Starkey, K., Barnatt, C. and Tempest, S. (2000) 'Beyond networks and hierarchies'. *Organization Science*, 11(3): 299–305.

Zan, L. (2005) 'Future directions from the past: management and accounting discourse in historical perspectives'. *Advances in Strategic Management*, 22: 457–90.

Ars longa

Introduction to Part V

For Caves (2002), *ars longa* refers to the durability of cultural products and the extraction of economic rents that this permits. It raises the question of how rents may be extracted from a creative product such that there is a (long-term) return on investment. In one sense this topic returns to the original question of how creativity is recognized, not in the sense of how it is recognized within the immediate context of practitioners as being innovative, but how is it recognized and evaluated within a broader context, i.e. how is it taken up or adopted, rather than being left to languish (Baumann 2001). What defines or determines the durability of a product? What are the evaluation processes and the institutional supports that are necessary to sustain durability? In a broader sense, *ars longa* also raises the issue of the nature of value, or what constitutes 'worth', and how this relates to economic value or worth (Hutter and Throsby 2008; Throsby 2001; Towse 1997). Although inter-related, the two are not synonymous, and it is the interplay between them, the processes of evaluation and exchange, how creativity becomes recognized and rewarded, that lies at the foundation of *ars longa*. *Ars longa* raises the underlying tensions between the relative weight of commercial success and artistic merit, as the interplay between economic and symbolic capital (arts for art's sake) is played out. Is value decided by artistic endeavour or 'grubby' commercialism? Is it registered by peers through acclaim, or clients through the market: high art or high street (Whitely 1994)? What is valued and how is this ascribed? What are the organizations and institutions that support assessment? And what are the impacts of valuation processes on creative endeavour?

As Luxford (Chapter 5) notes, Kant maintained that the issue of money distinguished between art and craft. It is a hierarchy of valuation that maintains itself today. There is 'higher' and 'lower' art with value ascribed in relation to degrees of exchange and commercialization. It is the distinction between, for example, alternative music and chart music. The former is more 'authentic', more 'in touch'. It aspires to a pinnacle. It is in contrast to the process of objectification, the making of things that enter the market place. However, as we have seen in earlier sections, art's relationship with money is ambiguous. As Dixon (Chapter 3) reminds us, 'art' is maintained through its 'otherness'. It is that which is distinct from the painful existence from which art wishes to escape. Art is not that which is a task or a trouble; that which one is constrained to perform. It is a pleasure in itself, created and produced out of nothing. Art is not labour, work or craft and leaves no traces of the pain and trouble that go into its production, the work and labour that constitute its construction. Through this process of division and distinction, 'art' gains an independent existence, secure through this exteriority. This distinction or separation, however, is integral to the ability to secure monetary value.

In essence, within the creative industries *ars longa* is achieved through control of intellectual property rights and the various contractual relationships that secure this. Contracts may be written to ensure future product through option clauses and long-term commitments. There may be an exclusive right to future product on pre-agreed terms or an obligation to supply future work within prescribed times. Mergers and acquisition strategies stress the importance of back catalogues (film and recordings), film libraries and backlists (publishing). There may be a focus on the benefits of subsidiary rights (e.g. film rights, videos, concert tours) as a means of developing different income streams and exploiting niches: the successful novel spawns the paperback, film, the 'novelization' of screenplay/film, TV broadcast and film soundtrack. There are licensing spin-offs through merchandise, etc. For the modern world, 'value' lies in 'property' (Towse 2002).

In contrast, in the medieval world, 'ars' signified artifice or performance, not 'art' or product. It encompassed both performance and composition. That which was extolled was the skill and practice inherent in the production of that which was displayed, rather than the product per se. Objects were not to be set aside to be fetishized and collected. Rather, the emergence of the 'object' to be revered and collected reflects a number of historical processes. Following the removal of art from Church control (as it was mainly religious, the Church governed its production and sale) from the end of the sixteenth century to the beginning of the seventeenth, there is the emergence of dealing in art, with this as an independent trade, both sustained by the growth of thriving centres of trade and commerce and the rise of an affluent bourgeoisie. Artists themselves gained greater control of art sales. Rules for the trading of art allowed a role for 'middle' men, and with this, the rise of the function of an intermediary – the dealer. Artists also acted as dealers. Differentiation within the art market sees art produced, not for its own purpose, but for financial gain. Artists work *for* a market and for dealers. As part of the artistic guild, dealers are artists, but also employ artists, indicating what is to be produced. A further differentiation produces the professional dealer, in time to be supplemented by a broader range of personnel that populate the field of art: the artist, the dealer, the collector and the connoisseurs (Marr 2006). The differentiation of the institutional sphere becomes reflected in the spatial differentiation of artists' studios, dealers' galleries and private collections. This institutional development of a creative field illustrates how a division of labour permits the 'by-product' of the financial assessment of art, those with this expertise: the professional art dealer. This differentiation both permits, and is sustained by, the activity of analyzing pictures, 'training one's eye', and with this, the emergence of connoisseurship.

What this brief historical excursus shows is that value or distinctiveness of a creative product is not intrinsic to the goods themselves, but is produced by social practices that construct 'art' as being special, a relationship of distinction that is inscribed and reactivated in each act of consumption (Bourdieu 1984, 1993). The 'value' of art requires a process of constructing cultural goods as valuable, to be sustained by those involved both in its production and consumption. Art derives its value from the institutions within which it is promoted and exhibited. And institutions invest heavily in criteria that add to their authority as arbiters of taste, shaping and reshaping public tastes (Anand and Jones 2008; Anand and Watson 2004). But what are the processes whereby cultural/creative products are ascribed value? And who 'counts' as a generator of meaning?

Any evaluation system requires a standard or discipline from which to assess something as being creative and 'worthy'. In business, the evaluation mechanism is achieved through the market: a product sells or it does not. While this is also true of the creative industries, evaluation in the arts also relies on more elaborate mechanisms and social networks that bestow worth, which then may or may not translate into the creation of economic value (Bourdieu 1993). How successful are the signals used to predict indicators of success that act as proxies for the market (Kim and Mauborgne 2000)? While market selection has the benefit of registering a 'direct' relationship between producers and consumers, it raises the underlying tension between commercial success and artistic merit. (While a YouTube upload can attract, for example, 42 million viewers, does this instil greater legitimacy? Or does creative activity without the provenance of being made in the 'right' context immediately lose any claims to artistic value?) Alternative evaluation criteria, peer selection (where selectors and selected are part of the same group) and expert selection (based on specialized knowledge as means of shaping selection) each raise problems (Wijnberg and Gemser 2000). Peer selection is criticized for reinforcing the importance and privilege of a group of producers, while the expert's certification powers, their ability to 'manage and control' values and knowledge rather than simply 'purvey' them (Caves 2002), raises criticisms that the critic becomes more important than the artist and that there is 'removal' of any evaluation by the 'average' consumer. With the rise of web-based consumer feedback and commentary, however, the role for the critic is under challenge (Bielby *et al.* 2005).

The multiple meanings of art render a single evaluation criterion suspect. However, we live in an audit society; evaluation criteria are demanded. There are obvious difficulties of assessing, quantifying and measuring intangible outcomes of 'art', as public policy in culture and the arts testifies. Criteria chosen have included social engagement, economic impact, a cultural consciousness and identity, and tourism. In the UK, while the 1990s saw the emergence of a social inclusion agenda, the turn of the century has seen a greater emphasis on the economic and the cultural being harnessed together. The contested nature of value and evaluation continues (Hesmondhalgh and Pratt 2005).

Our three chapters in this section (González, Parker, and Gulledge and Townley) add to the debate, both questioning the understanding and meaning of value, raising different perspectives on what is meant by 'adding value' (Donald *et al.*, Chapter 13). The chapters illustrate how monetary value is highly dependent on other value structures. González, in her discussion of the design object, *Juicy Salif*, a lemon squeezer, identifies the various dimensions of value other than simple functional value. Moreover, she demonstrates how a lack of functional value of a 'utilitarian' design item does not necessarily impact negatively on monetary value. Her consideration of some of the deeper 'hidden' dimensions of the valuation process and sources of meaning illuminates the importance of symbolic and systemic value systems that inform use and exchange value. Parker's essay also considers how value is embodied. She reminds us of the primary role of the subjective in appreciation and aesthetic experience, and in this interrogates the disembodied commodity fetishism that creates value. For Parker, valuation is an act of positioning. It sets up relationships to the past and to the future and, as such, emphasizes the role memories and remembering play in their links to value. The process of remembering and remembrance is linked with aesthetic experience informing how we relate to value. Echoing González, we see that the 'valuing' process is an encounter with our own selves and the traces of our own past.

Gulledge and Townley's chapter places the question of value in its broader institutional context. Their aim is twofold: to provide a framework for discussing the range of agents and interests that populate the production and consumption of creative products, 'the creative field'; and to discuss how agents' actions and practices are informed by different understandings of value, or 'what is at stake'. The example used is that of book publishing. Adopting an approach based on Bourdieu's concept of a field and the capitals that sustain it, the authors illustrate the importance of the institutional supports that function to maintain different understandings of value. In order to claim value creative goods must appeal to a field's institutional logics; here editorial and market logics, which each make differing demands and requirements. Through this, books come to be valued by actors involved in production and editorial work and by those involved in the book markets and, ultimately, valued by consumers. If a book is to be successful over time, a book's value must be 'translatable' for the purposes of a variety of agents. The longevity of value, and sustainability of a product, requires that it functions in both logics and also that it works for the various agents in the field.

In bringing these different discussions of value forward, the authors remind us of the underlying themes of 'inherent unknowability' and 'infinite variety' that have informed our discussion of the creative industries. Both remind us of the disciplinary acts of division and defining that create 'creative value'.

References

Anand, N. and Jones, B.C. (2008) 'Tournament rituals, category dynamics and field configuration: the case of the Booker Prize'. *Journal of
Management Studies*, 45: 1036–60.

Anand, N. and Watson, M.R. (2004). 'Tournament rituals in the evolution
of fields: the case of the Grammy Awards'. *Academy of Management
Journal*, 47: 59–80.

Baumann, S. (2001) 'Intellectualization and art world development: film in
the US'. *American Sociological Review*, 66(3): 404–26.

Bielby, D.D., Moloney, M. and Ngo, B.Q. (2005) 'Aesthetics of television
criticism: 'mapping critics' reviews in an era of industry transformation' in C. Jones and P. Thornton (eds.), *Research in the Sociology
of Organizations: Transformations in Cultural Industries*, 23: 1–43.
Greenwich, CT and London: Jai Press.

Bourdieu, P., Nice, R. (transl.) (1984) *Distinction*. Cambridge, MA: Harvard
University Press.

Bourdieu, P. (1993) *The Field of Cultural Production: Essays on Art and
Literature*. New York: Columbia University Press.

Caves, R. (2002) *Creative Industries: Contracts Between Art and
Commerce*. Cambridge, MA: Harvard University Press.

Hesmondhalgh, D. and Pratt, A. (2005) 'Cultural industries and cultural
policy'. *International Journal of Cultural Policy*, 11(1): 1–12.

Hutter, M., and Throsby, C.D. (2008) *'Beyond Price: Value in Culture,
Economics, and the Arts'*. Cambridge University Press.

Kim, C. and Mauborgne, R. (2000) 'Knowing a winning business idea
when you see one'. *Harvard Business Review*, 78(5): 129–37.

Marr, A. (2006) 'Art for art's sake: was it ever thus?' Paper presented at
The Discipline of Creativity: Exploring the Paradox conference, 1
December, University of St. Andrews.

Throsby, C.D. (2001) *Economics and Culture*. Cambridge University
Press.

Towse, R. (ed.) (1997) *Cultural Economics*. Cheltenham: Edward Elgar.

Towse, R. (2002) 'Introduction', in R. Towse (ed.) *Copyright in the Cultural
Industries*. Cheltenham: Edward Elgar: xiv–xxii.

Whitely, N. (1994) 'High art and the high street: the "commerce-and-culture" debate', in R. Keat, N. Whitely and N. Abercrombie (eds.) *The
Authority of the Consumer*. London: Routledge.

Wijnberg, N. and Gemser, G. (2000) 'Adding value to innovation: impres-
sionism and transformation of the selection system in the visual arts'.
Organization Science, 11(3): 323–9.

14 | Juicy Salif *as a cultish totem*

LAURA GONZÁLEZ

In the mainstream Spanish film *All Men Are the Same* by Manuel Gómez Pereira (1994), three flat-sharing bachelors hire a young maid to help with the cleaning. She falls in love with the handsome one but, feeling betrayed, she decides to leave her job and steal some of their property. She picks up a strange, menacing, spaceship-looking object placed on top of the TV and the rest of the storyline develops around her putting the object back or taking it depending on the mood of her relationship with the main male character. What she stole was a lemon squeezer. It was not, however, any lemon squeezer: it was Philippe Starck's *Juicy Salif*.[1]

I approach the analysis of this object from the point of view of a fine art practitioner – a sculptor. The account I will provide of *Juicy Salif* comes from a particular position in relation to objecthood and the subject. This is not the first time this object has been extrapolated from its field, however. The knowledge generated around Starck's lemon squeezer is shared, almost in equal measure, between the subject areas of product design and computing, the latter exemplified by organizations such as the Association for Computing Machinery (ACM 2006), the conference Designing Pleasurable Products and Interfaces (ICDPPI 2003; Russo and de Moraes 2003), the fields of Human-Computer Interaction – HCI – (Hassenzahl 2004; Norman 2004) and Captology – Computers As Persuasive Technology (Stanford University 2005; Khaslavsky and Shedroff 1999). The relationship between *Juicy Salif* and art, as we will see later, is not all that tenuous.

French interior and product designer Philippe Starck conceptualized *Juicy Salif* for the medium-sized Italian kitchenware company Alessi, which has manufactured the lemon squeezer since 1990. Alessi was set up in the 1920s outside Milan, as a business to produce household goods in metal. Since then the company has evolved to become, in the 1980s, a popular example of postmodern high design and of Italian design, with its important craft tradition and its intellectual links (Lees-Maffei 2002: 38). In addition, Alessi's emphasis on the concept of family, through the centralized running of its business and its manifest product 'families', is, as will be seen below, one of its key Italian characteristics. Alessi, as Grace Lees-Maffei indicates (2002: 41), is known for its technical innovation in relation to style, materials and function, which is achieved through small production runs, and versatile processes rather than investment in technologically advanced equipment. This investment in innovation differentiates Alessi's products from those of its competitors, so when it commissioned Starck, a 'star' personality and a controversial designer (Lloyd and Snelders 2003: 241), to create a range of products including a lemon squeezer, the framework was set for a culturally relevant object with value beyond its function and immediate context.

With *Juicy Salif,* Starck subverted the way manual lemon squeezers look, to the delight of Alessi. My investigations into the appearance of citrus juicers has led me to categorize them into six distinct groups according to form, action and delivery of juice:

1. Hand juicer: by pressing and twisting a lemon half against a solid ribbed cone, the pulp of the fruit is crushed and the juice is delivered (sometimes filtered through a strainer) into a tray or shallow bowl which may be separate.
2. Citrus press: by placing half of the fruit into a jaw and then pressing it with a cone, it delivers juice directly into a glass.
3. Citrus reamer: used to extract smaller amounts of juice, the reamer works through twisting its flute-shaped end into a half fruit.
4. Wedge squeezer: by placing a fruit wedge into the squeezer and pressing with the handle, a small amount of juice is delivered directly into the glass.
5. Citrus trumpet: this tool is screwed onto the whole fruit and through squeezing its outer rind, juice flows out of the spout of the trumpet.
6. Tabletop citrus juicer: through pressing fruit, usually through a handle, it delivers juice directly into a glass.

To use *Juicy Salif,* one would have to put a glass underneath the head, in between the three legs that keep the product upright. The glass, of course, would have to be of a particular size, as the squeezer does not have mobile parts. A citrus fruit, cut in half, would be hand pressed or rotated against the ribbed head and juice would trickle down through the grooves, directly into the glass. *Juicy Salif* thus combines the twisting action of the hand juicer with the extraction power of the reamer and the wedge squeezer (which may be used more for party drinks like cocktails rather than cooking food); the direct glass delivery of the citrus press and the trumpet; and the kitchen presence of the tabletop juicer, as its disproportionate legs make storage in common kitchen cupboards complicated. Still, it does not fit comfortably into any of those categories, and its shape is more reminiscent of popular culture references related to sci-fi than of any squeezer. Added to this is the fact that, as a lemon squeezer, its performance leaves a lot to be desired. So, if it is not as efficient as its rival products, how can *Juicy Salif* be evaluated? What brought Starck to create something that would not fulfil its intended function? Why is this lemon squeezer a market success and a recognized design icon? What do viewers, owners and users get out of it? This is what this chapter aims to explore.

One could evaluate this object's success simply by its economic value exemplified by its market performance, which is outstanding. It may also be argued that what makes a poorly performing object become valuable in economic and cultural terms, what rewards Starck's own brand of creativity and Alessi's innovative vision with a following *en masse,* is clever promotion, sophisticated marketing strategies and the right kind of early adopters. Yet that would not account for its significance and iconic status. Citations in research papers, appearances in the media, market research involving product owners and data on designers influenced by this object show that it has a cult following beyond the design milieu. Two main debates dominate the discussion around the meaning, conceptualization, production, marketing, consumption and influence of this object: those concentrating on its (lack of) functional value and those focusing on its symbolic value, a type of value related to kinship and culture, and not instantly measured in terms of money. For both, the way *Juicy Salif* manifests itself is a reference point, as no other lemon squeezer looks like it. Even if it comes at a performative cost, its impact and significance are seen to be derived from its outward aspect. This object has even been exhibited in contemporary art galleries, certifying its contribution to culture and truly converting it into an object of contemplation, unfit to squeeze lemons. It is this, its physical appearance and the connotations it arouses in viewers that makes it what it is: a valued and valuable object.

I will specifically explore the psychodynamics of *Juicy Salif*'s seduction; the psychological aspects this object brings out in people, both individually and as social groups, as it is in the particular relationship it establishes with its users, owners and viewers that its cult status and value lies. I will argue that the reason for this attribution of value derives from its power of seduction, its capacity to lead astray, not least from its perceived function. This, however, will not be approached through historical or purely economic contexts, but rather, through relational and subjective aspects. Here, I do not seek the truth about seduction (which, as we will see, would deceive me, anyway); or, indeed, an interpretation, which would kill it; or, again, its representation, which would be a flawed and false undertaking, if not impossible. I will start by exploring the functional and symbolic value of *Juicy Salif*. I will then attempt to reconcile these debates, which often seem in opposition, with the help of Jacques Lacan's Object (a) (1986), the object at the centre of his psychoanalytic theory of desire and his *Discourse of the Analyst* (1991). As Lacanian psychoanalysis is concerned primarily with the subject's desire and her rapport to objects, and is a relational practice, this framework seems appropriate for an analysis of *Juicy Salif*. The new conceptualization that will ensue will help us understand this object's value in a new way.

Functional value

The debate around the usability (and non-usability) of *Juicy Salif* is at the centre of many studies about this product's function. Beatriz Russo and Anamaria de Moraes (2003) from the Laboratory of Ergonomics and Usability in Rio de Janeiro, performed tests with this object, exploring usage, cleaning ease, work surface appearance after use and product aesthetics. The tests found that a majority of participants noted the high effort demand, inefficiency, dirty work area and instability of the product. Russo and de Moraes also explored ownership of *Juicy Salif* by gathering a sample group and looking at their reasons for buying the product, their usage frequency and the product's durability. Twenty-eight per cent of participants stated they had never used this lemon squeezer for its proper function: they purchased it as a decorative, aesthetic and status-bearer object; they used it as a display item, a function which is also integrated in the design, as its measurements make its storage in cupboards difficult. The tests concluded that, although the product is easy enough to clean, its durability is not satisfactory. Height – 29cm – , stability, the diametre of its head – 14 cm – and the materials used – gold or plated aluminium – were its main problems.

Beth Preston (2000) explores philosophical aspects of the term 'function' as is attributed to things. She argues for two distinct types: *proper function* (an item's disposition to perform based on historical selection, e.g. a chair is for seating) and *system function* (an item's disposition to perform within a system, e.g. in order to change this light bulb, I stand on a chair). She reveals the complexity of function by looking at the notions of misuse and malfunction, both of which are, of course, relevant to *Juicy Salif,* and concludes that function has a dynamic character: multifunction and function changes are a constant in material culture. A lack of consideration of ergonomic factors, Russo and de Moraes (2003: 147) argue, is what motivates the malfunction of this squeezer, which may dangerously slip into consumer dissatisfaction, a view endorsed by John Heskett (2003: 58) and, to a certain extent, disproved by Marc Hassenzahl (2004). Peter Lloyd and Dirk Snelders (2003: 251), however, take this object's functional peculiarity further: its intended function (to squeeze lemons) differs from its actual function (to be displayed); its proper function is different from its system function (Preston 2000). So, what is its function? What is *Juicy Salif* for?

Lloyd and Snelders (2003) start their study with a quote by design thinker Adrian Forty, from his book *Objects of Desire* ('no design works unless it embodies ideas that are held in common by the people for whom the object is intended') (Forty 1986 in Lloyd and Snelders 2003: 237) and set out to explore whether personal creativity is a determinant of success. Their enterprise crosses ours, as *Juicy Salif* is their case study. They attribute the product's successful sales at an average rate of 50,000 units per year since its launch in 1990 (Lloyd and Snelders 2003: 238) to consumer misuse as much as to the designer's creativity and the ideas present in a particular society (in the case of this object, Western European and North American societies in the late 1980s and 90s). According to them, Starck himself may have adopted the object's system function retrospectively, taking the focus out of its performative limitations and into its visual manifestation:

The *Juicy Salif* lemon squeezer [1990–1] is the biggest success of all. Strange, because it's a difficult object. Now it's well known, but when it wasn't, you thought, 'What is this?' A lot of people told me, 'This object is stupid because electric zinzinzin costs half and works better'. … Yes, it's true. There are one hundred electric things that work better. But sometimes you must choose why you design – in this case not to squeeze lemons … Sometimes you need some more humble service. (Starck 1997)

This is not a very good lemon squeezer: but that's not its only function. I had this idea that when a couple gets married it's the sort of thing they would get as a wedding present. So when the new husband's parents come round, he and his father sit in the living room with a beer, watching television, and the new mother-in-law and daughter-in-law sit in the kitchen to get to know each other better. 'Look at what we got as a present', the daughter-in-law will say. (Morgan 1999: 9)

This identification of *Juicy Salif*'s proper function as a conversation starter (Norman 2004: 112) or 'social lubricant' (Lloyd and Snelders 2003: 251) contributes to its acquisition of artistic status. Two additional factors add to this perception. First, the fact that Alessi, the commissioning and manufacturing company behind the lemon squeezer, treats its designers 'like gods' (Lees-Maffei 2002: 43–5), differentiating their intellectual and cultural role from the more practical responsibilities, which are left to a technical team which interprets the designer's sketches (Lees-Maffei 2002: 43–4). Second, Starck's designs have been 'literally and figuratively – placed on pedestals' (Whitely 1994: 131) in shop displays (Julier 2000: 70–1), design museums and, more importantly, art galleries and museums (see, for example, Sala Rekalde, Spain, in 1997; Philadelphia Museum of Art in 1998; Marble Palace at the State Russian Museum; Centre for Contemporary Art at Ujazdowski Castle, Warsaw, in 2002; Groninger Museum, the Netherlands; Centre Pompidou in 2003). *Juicy Salif* has even been included in an Art History timeline at the Metropolitan Museum in New York (2006). The tenth anniversary edition of *Juicy Salif*, gold plated, takes its artistic status to the extreme, as its precious material is incompatible with the citric acid of the fruit.

Nigel Whitely's account of the relationship between high art and the high street further explores this aesthetization of design through display in shops and museums: 'It is a change from the idea of the importance of "primary" function – how well the product works or mechanically operates, and value for money – to "tertiary" function – the product's perceived status and pride of possession value' (1994: 131). It is this shift in function from primary (its capacity to squeeze lemons in relation to a competitive price – its proper function) to tertiary function (what it means to people – its system function) that constitutes the main argument around the symbolic value of this lemon squeezer.

Symbolic value

The second debate surrounding *Juicy Salif* concerns its symbolic value, which assesses its worth in relation to notions of culture and kinship. In contrast to its functional value, symbolic characteristics are not obviously translatable into exchange mechanisms and money, although this is not to say they fall outside the market or contemporary capitalist processes.

Juicy Salif's symbolic value is directed by Alessi's approach to design. As Lees-Maffei (2002: 44) and Julier (2000: 77) point out, the company carefully crafts ready-made meanings and cultural associations to enhance the symbolic value of its products. Through its self-published literature (Alessi 1994, 1998; Scarcella 1987), marketing strategies and the Museo Alessi (Alessi 2004), it controls a dominant part of the public perception of its output, giving to its objects what Lees-Maffei calls *italianità:* a particular design heritage based on craft (Lees-Maffei 2002: 38–43), and a highly persuasive concept of family (Lees-Maffei 2002: 52–5). A photograph used in most Alessi publicity, publications and on the website, shows male members of the family from different generations – who, of course, control the company – holding *Juicy Salif* in various positions, some very creative, brandishing it as a trophy and prudently avoiding holding its main body, a pose that would convert it into a menacing weapon. The playfulness of this portrait, together with the relaxed attire and attitude of the younger Alessi family members, counteracts the traditional image of corporate business. The control of the family, however, is intense, centralized and goes to the extent that it is usual for Alessi's name to appear in the products, instead of the designer's, with Michael Graves being the only exception (Lees-Maffei 2002: 54).

Another family – fictional, this time – brandishing this lemon squeezer can be found in the card game *Unhappy Families* (2005). The Concretes represent a particular stereotype: they are culturally knowing, as exemplified by the visual and textual references in the cards and the booklet of character profiles: architecture, stainless steel, black, retro classics, Mercedes, cashmere, Mies van der Rohe, minimalist spaces and Barcelona are mentioned as the family's predominant identity conferrers and are used as a means of distinction (Bourdieu 1986) from other social groups, showing the family's knowledge of what constitutes a design icon. In the four cards that make the Concrete family, three Alessi objects appear: Michael Graves' kitchen timer, Alessandro Mendini's Anna G corkscrew and *Juicy Salif.*

The roles of producer and consumer are blurred, as the production of the object is only completed when meaning and value are attributed, through 'identification and decoding' (Lloyd and Snelders 2003: 244). At the time *Juicy Salif* was made, Alessi's products were typically gifts: the object bestows the owner (and the buyer of the gift) with specific 'cultural capital' (Bourdieu 1986: 12, 39, 53–4), a symbolic characteristic that can be used as currency, as in the Gómez Pereira film referred to above. The maid, by stealing *Juicy Salif*, aimed to take more than a lemon squeezer. As Julier (2000: 70) mentions, Philippe Starck's lemon squeezer is a 'token good', an affordable intimation (or imitation) of high life that evidences the discerning capabilities and connoisseurship of the consumer. Contemporary culture has numerous examples of these types of objects on the streets – think of Jonathan Ive's ubiquitous iPod – and in the media – for example Carrie Bradshaw's weakness for Manolo Blahnik's shoes in HBO's *Sex and the City* (2005). The concept of 'token good' has a debt to Thorstein Veblen's 'conspicuous consumption' – the demonstration of leisure time, cultural understanding and economic status through goods – a concept he contextualized within the leisure class (Veblen 2004). Annechen Bahr Bugge (2003) looks at cooking as a manifestation of identity with reference to Norwegian society. She identifies three main discourses: the health discourse, the national discourse and the gourmet discourse, framing the latter within a conspicuous cooking practice and the need for 'expensive design equipment and technological aids in brushed steel' (Bugge 2003: 7). She cites Alessi as the best-established company for kitchenware in Norway (2003: 7); Scandinavia is, indeed, the third-largest market for Alessi, after Italy and Germany (Lees-Maffei 2002: 51).

Veblen's 'conspicuous consumption' and Julier's 'token goods' ultimately relate to Marx's 'commodity fetishism', arguably his major contribution to the field of political economy. This concept signals the complicated relationship between objects and people. He defines commodity as: 'in the first place, an object outside us, a thing that by its properties satisfies human wants of some sort or another' (Marx 1995: 13). However, he also warns us that: 'A commodity appears, at first sight, a very trivial thing, and easily understood. Its analysis shows that it is, in reality, a very queer thing, abounding in metaphysical subtleties and theological niceties' (1995: 42). Commodities have two types of value associated with them: use-value – what satisfies the human need – and exchange-value – a quantitative measure that converts a product into a commodity by relating it to other commodities (Osborne 2005: 12–14). It is this latter value, an *ideal* and *social* one, that appears to be natural to the object; it contains the *metaphysical subtleties and theological niceties* and makes commodities contradictory, riddle-like, obscure to interpretation. To relate it back to the two debates around *Juicy Salif* that occupy us, use-value would normally be associated with issues around its function (to squeeze lemons), whereas the symbolic debate would turn around the exchange-value of the product. Moreover, according to Marx, objects, being distanced from their productive base, adopt special faculties or powers beyond their exchange-value, namely the powers that enable human relations (Marx 1995: 42–50): this is 'commodity fetishism'. Marx's use of the term fetishism in his coining of 'commodity fetishism', is radically different to Sigmund Freud's conception, who understood it as a psychological condition of a subject, whose desire transforms the significance of particular objects (Osborne 2005: 11). To understand Marx, we must return to the definition of fetish pre-Freud and pre-Enlightenment, and to the understanding of commodity as value rather than a physical object. For Marx, the fetish character of commodities is inherent to them insofar as they are commodities. In that sense, commodities are not fetishized by individual consumers – that may be consumer fetishism (Osborne 2005: 11). 'Commodity fetishism' is a product of the social relations of production characteristic of capitalism.

Marx's conception of value can be put in relation to the functional distinctions made by Whitely (1994) and Preston (2000) as outlined above. The primary or proper function of design objects is related to its use-value, whereas the meaning of objects for people or tertiary function would normally be part of its exchange-value. This type of value could also be linked to Preston's system function in the case of *Juicy Salif*, if we take the viewpoint that the object is a lemon squeezer, rather than a conversation starter. My own experience of buying *Juicy Salif*, though, is a testimony of how use/exchange-value and proper/system functions can switch places and provoke misunderstandings. When I worked in Central London, I could imagine no better pleasure than visiting Selfridges department store during my lunch hour. As at the time I was researching Starck's approach to kitchenware design, this was a perfect excuse for me to spend time at the Alessi counter, mainly handling *Juicy Salif*. One day, I was ready to buy it and I asked a shop assistant for a boxed product. To my surprise, I had to endure a long and hard conversation as she tried to save me money and sense, by convincing me to buy a more affordable and more efficient lemon squeezer, a glass one, which she claimed was also good looking. Only my assertion that I did not want it to squeeze lemons brought her silence. At the time, Alessi's item retailed at around £40, because it offered something more than a squeezer. Its potential to start conversations and become the centre of attention (which is what I was purchasing), is what differentiated *Juicy Salif* from all the other similar products in the shop, what made it desirable. The shop assistant and I had different use-values in mind.

Mariëlle Creusen and Jan Schoormans (2005) taxonomize what they see as the six different roles that product appearance may have in consumer choice: functional – exhibition of functional features; ergonomic – display of consequences of use; categorization – a product's differentiation from its category; attention drawing – capture of consumer attention in store; aesthetic – possibility of aesthetic appreciation; and symbolic – enablement of associations (2005: 75). Although the last four are the most evidently represented, Starck's lemon squeezer embodies all of them, even if tangentially, as, for example, one can easily imagine what would happen if it was put to use. Donald Norman (2004) studies designs that provoke emotions and distinguishes three levels of processing in the affective system: visceral or pre-conscious level; behavioural or use level, and reflective or cognitive level. *Juicy Salif*, he explains, scores 'zero for behavioural design' (Norman 2004: 115) as the pleasure and effectiveness of use are likely to provoke negative emotions. Starck's design, however, scores highly on the reflective and visceral levels because it provokes the generation of memories, giving the owner a degree of personal satisfaction and stimulating the creation of self-image. Its appearance is enticing (Norman 2004: 114–15). Norman owns an anniversary edition of the lemon squeezer, which, as he confessed, is proudly displayed in his entrance hall (2004: 115). To their owners – such as myself and Norman – *Juicy Salif* expresses specific characteristics related to their personal goals (Khaslavsky and Shedroff 1999: 47). As Starck himself puts it: 'The *Juicy Salif* – a byword for over-design, the parvenu's gewgaw – is more cultish totem than juicer' (McGuirk: 2006).

After reviewing all the taxomomies around this object – my own, related to different kinds of squeezers, Preston (2000) and Whitely's (1994) around function, Marx's value (1995), Creusen and Schoorman's on product appearance (2005) and Norman's study of levels of processing (2004) – we can now turn to explore directly why *Juicy Salif* has become a design icon. One possible reason why it is successful in embodying diverse symbolic characteristics is located in its polysemic nature, the possibility of containing different and often contradictory meanings within its manifestation. Julier alludes to its in-between characteristics: its 'neither male nor female' attributes (2000: 68), its 'strangely transsexual aspect' (2000: 67), the fact that it only half-works, its cultured but low-brow characteristics, its display function competing with its singularity and its commodified yet unmarketable quality (2000: 67–85). Lloyd and Snelders (2003: 250) mention its possible metaphorical associations: 'We have the idea of permanence, the idea of "a past future", the possibility of irony, the idea of instability, and of sex. A sexy, Soviet statue; a morality tale for the overspending consumer: beware of fixed, top-heavy systems, for they may be toppled.' These interpretations are all plausible, as Lloyd and Snelders (2003: 238–40) explain, because they are narratives that are personal and/or embedded into public consciousness and this is precisely what *Juicy Salif* taps into: 'The mere fact that the product exists says more about the people that buy and use the product than the original intentions of the designer' (Lloyd and Snelders 2003: 244). For them, the product 'offers up its secrets' (Lloyd and Snelders 2003: 245), and its misfunctioning adds to this process of forming a relationship. This, they argue, opens up the personal creativity of the consumer (Lloyd and Snelders 2003: 252), as can be seen in the playful meaning-making narrative they construct around *Juicy Salif.*

This polysemy both in its metaphorical qualities and its in-between characteristics is directly related to the object's appearance, or the way it manifests itself through form and material. A key consequence of the characteristic way *Juicy Salif* looks – the possibility of making associations with rocket ships, squids (Lloyd and Snelders 2003: 241–43) and arachnids – has been its cultural significance, cult following and creative impact evidenced through its inspiration of objects, publicity campaigns, film plots and props and, of course, other kitchen utensil designs.[2] The link between the two, however, is not clear.

How is it that this polysemy, this multiplicity of symbolic frameworks makes us, as individuals and groups, ascribe meaning and give value to this object, which, arguably, is simply a lemon squeezer? A psychoanalytic viewpoint, with a Lacanian slant, may help us shed some light onto the matter. Its focus on the psychodynamics of desire and the relation between subject and object, its ontology as a clinical practice – which can be put in relation to a design practice – and the importance of the gaze within it make it a suitable intellectual territory in which to situate an analysis of Starck's design icon.

Juicy Salif as seductive object

Psychoanalysis is a body of knowledge within the field of psychology that focuses on the functioning and behaviour of the mind and its treatment. It was first theorized and practised by Sigmund Freud at the turn of the twentieth century. After Freud's death, psychoanalysis split into many schools, the more relevant being Ego psychology, object relations and Lacanian analysis. In the seminar teachings that constitute the core of his writings, French psychoanalyst Jacques Lacan promoted a 'return to Freud' (Lacan 1975), to reading his texts and following him *à la lettre*, something, he claimed, other schools of thought within psychoanalysis had not done. Lacan's ideas, however, were also influenced by phenomenologists such as Maurice Merleau-Ponty, structuralists – in particular Claude Lévi-Strauss – and Swiss linguist Ferdinand de Saussure. These influences account for his search for structure within topology (see for example, his conceptualization of the three orders as a Borromean knot, Lacan: 1974–5), and for the importance he attributes to language within human experience – best exemplified by his famous statement: 'the unconscious is structured like a language' (Lacan 1998: 48).

Lacan's major contribution to the field of psychoanalytic practice and theory is, arguably, his conceptualization of Object (a). Object (a) is a complex concept, in flux throughout Lacan's work and linked to many aspects of his theory. This algebraic formula, normally left untranslated, refers to the little other (*autre*, in French), which in Lacanian theory relates to reflexivity, identification and the Ego, as opposed to the big Other, the radical alterity of language and the law. Object (a) is the cause of desire: not the object to which desire is directed, but that which provokes desire. Object (a) is *unspecularizable*, it resists symbolization and has no representation or alterity. Object (a) evolves from earlier formations such as Freud's *das Ding* (Lacan 1992) and Plato's *Agalma*, a precious object Alcibiades believed to be hidden in Socrates' body. Desire is paramount to Lacan's thought: in its unconscious form, it is 'at the heart of human existence and [is] the central concern of psychoanalysis' (Evans 1996: 36); Object (a) mobilizes this force. Paradoxically, Object (a) is also the object of anxiety. It is a lack, a void, around which the drives, partial aspects through which desire is realised, circle. As such, obtaining it and satisfying desire is impossible. Attempts, however, are made through partial objects, which stand in for Object (a). Object (a) is at the centre of clinical psychoanalytic practice and is also key to what can be termed the *Discourse of the Artefact*,[3] as will be seen below. Object (a) it will be claimed, is an object of seduction.

This last term, however, is a slightly contentious one. If I asked my readers if they had ever been seduced, I suspect I would get an almost unanimous positive answer. However, if I asked them to give me a definition of seduction, chances are it would take some time to find an agreement. Indeed, it is quite common to find divergent positions and inconsistencies in its conceptualization. Its complexity, contradictions, devious uses of the word, confusing definition and imprecision seem to be the only points of agreement between the different approaches taken by, amongst others, cultural commentators, film theorists, consumption theorists, captologists (those who study computers as persuasive technology) and psychoanalysts.

Etymologically, the term seduction comes from the Latin *se* (apart) and *ducere* (to lead). Its verb form is defined as 'to lead astray from right behaviour' by the Concise Oxford English Dictionary (1964). It is also 'to err in conduct or belief'. Seductive behaviour is often considered 'in contradiction with moral law' and tends to be related to sexual matters. Rex Butler defines it as 'the getting of another to do what we want, not by force or coercion, but by an exercise of their own, though often mistaken or misguided, free will' (Butler 1999: 71). Jean Baudrillard understood seduction as a reigning principle: 'everything is seduction and nothing but seduction', he said (Baudrillard 1991: 83). He sees seduction as opposed to production and belonging to the realm of appearances: 'To seduce is to die as reality and reconstitute oneself as illusion' (1991: 69). For him, seduction is dual, a matter of two; and it involves a duel, a challenging play or game. Seduction is relational, reversible, ambiguous. One can never be sure it really happens. Seduction and desire are not discrete terms, but continuous with each other (Tortajada 2004: 230). To follow a Lacanian structure, they seem to relate to each other as if part of a Möbius strip, a topological surface with one single side and only one boundary component. As the two sides are continuous, a crossover from inside to outside and back is possible. However, when one passes a finger round the surface of the Möbius strip, it is impossible to say at which precise point the crossing has taken place. To paraphrase Slavoj Žižek, seduction is not a simple reverse of content, 'we encounter it when we progress far enough on the side' of desire itself (Žižek 1991: 230). Baudrillard (1999: 111) further links seduction and desire: 'only the subject desires; only the object seduces'. Seduction, in and through Object (a), seduces desire and then moves on.

What makes our object of study culturally valuable is its ability to seduce, to lead consumers and viewers astray from what may be considered right behaviour (buying a cheaper, more efficient lemon squeezer, for example). Thus, *Juicy Salif* stands for Object (a) and actualizes it; it is its manifestation – although not its representation – and as such it incites desire in the viewer, user or owner. This is due to its appearance, and the playfulness of its function, a 'leading astray' characteristic as we saw above. *Juicy Salif* is seductive because of its ambiguous functional and symbolic value. In this case, function and form, however twisted and strange looking, follow seduction.

The idea of characterizing this lemon squeezer as a seductive object is not new, however. In their paper *Understanding the seductive experience* (1999), Julie Khaslavsky and Nathan Shedroff, exponents of captology, look at *Juicy Salif* and extract eight characteristics which, they argue, make this object seductive. These crystallize many of the qualities we have been discussing:

(1) They say that it entices by diverting attention. This is mainly due to the object's appearance.

(2) It delivers a surprising novelty. Its function, its purpose is ambiguous.

(3) It goes beyond the obvious needs and expectations of a usual lemon juicer. Offered as a kitchen utensil, it is also an object of contemplation.

(4) It creates an instinctive response, for example curiosity, interest, aversion, confusion, distress or fear. It squeezes lemons but can be brandished as a menacing-looking weapon.

(5) It espouses values or connections to personal goals.

(6) It also promises to fulfil these goals. According to Khaslavsky and Shedroff (1999), the subversive approach, the elegance and simplicity of this lemon squeezer's conception incites in the consumer a desire not only to possess the object, but also the values that helped create it, including innovation, sophistication, elegance and originality. To users, it speaks as much about the designer as about themselves.

(7) It leads the user to discover something deeper about the experience of juicing lemons. Through the obliteration of its function and the elevation of its status and that of its owner, as argued earlier, it makes an ordinary object extraordinary. Through transforming the experience (its peculiar shape makes the user adopt a specific body posture), it makes a common process different.

(8) *Juicy Salif* constantly renovates these promises and validates the original emotions and values every time the object is utilized, shown or talked about.

Baudrillard (1991), I suspect, would challenge Khaslavsky and Shedroff's (1999) attempt at systematizing seduction. These eight seductive characteristics mainly describe the reception of seduction from the point of view of the seducee. The seductive experience they refer to is that of the desiring subject, whose attention is diverted, has emotions, values, goals and squeezes lemons. The seducer object and 'its destiny' – to quote Baudrillard (1999: 111) – together with the relational aspects between object and subject, have not been addressed by this model.

Baudrillard (1991: 83) warns us that seduction will seduce everything, including attempts to study it. It will resist efforts at systematization whatever the approach. In his words, 'seduction is eternal

and its mastery, impossible' (Baudrillard 1988: 74). His answer to
seduction's power is reflected in the peculiar writing style used in his
study, which embodies seduction, rather than comments on it (Butler
1999: 101). Another answer to seduction's pervasiveness is to focus on
the study of its practices rather than on the phenomenon itself, or its
processes. Seductive practices call seduction into play instead of just
identifying and naming it. Even though studying seduction itself may
be problematic, if not impossible, we can recognize and study seductive
objects. Moreover, Rex Butler (1999: 107) argues that, from an analysis of the examples used by Baudrillard in *Seduction*, it can be concluded that music and literature are 'themselves seductive'. If we also
consider Baudrillard's later interest in objecthood, and his attempts to
relate this, and his theories around gaze, to the themes he developed in
Seduction (1991), one may argue that objects of contemplation can be
added to the category of things seductive *in themselves*.

Psychoanalysis is also a seductive practice, as explored, for example,
by Baudrillard (1991: 53–9) in his discussion on seduction as psychoanalysis's lost object; by Danuza Machado in her interview with Alex
Potts (Kivland and Du Ry 2000: 3–8) and in the clinical discussions
of Clapham (1997) and Weatherill (2000). To evidence this assertion
within the theoretical framework of Object (a) and desire, we must
now turn to explore Lacan's *Discourse of the Analyst* (Figure 14.2).
This discourse traditionally complements three others: those of the
Master, the University and the Hysteric (Lacan 1991), even though,
in Seminar XVII, Lacan suggested a fifth, the Capitalist Discourse,
left largely unexplored (see, for example, Declercq 2006). The theory of the Four Discourses examines different relationships within
structures of various social bonds, or situations of power. All four
discourses contain the same elements:

- Object (a), the object at the heart of clinical practice
- A Master Signifier, or a signifier outside the chain of signification
  (S_1), something that may not make sense
- The barred subject or subject of speech (S)
- The signifying other, or the place from which one speaks, know-
  ledge (S_2)

These four elements are then placed in relation to each other
(Figure 14.1). Each discourse is created from clockwise or anti-
clockwise rotation of the core elements, starting from the Master's

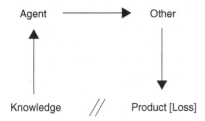

Figure 14.1 Structure of the Four Discourses

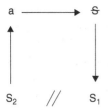

Figure 14.2 The *Discourse of the Analyst*

discourse. The four elements can take four different positions, each with a specific role: knowledge, the agent, the other and product or loss. So how does the *Discourse of the Analyst* work?

In the *Discourse of the Analyst*, the discourse 'that structures the conditions under which questions and answers circulate' (Adams 1991: 83), Lacan places Object (a) as representing the analyst in the commanding position. The analyst is the patient's object of desire. Thus, this is how the analysis relationship takes place: the analyst interrogates the divided subject (S), the patient or analysand, from a position of (assumed) knowledge (S_2). Her division shows through 'slips of the tongue, bungled and unintended acts, slurred speech, dreams' (Fink 1995: 135). These constitute the symptom, the master signifier (S_1), which also represents the end of an association, something that stops the analysand's speech, a signifier that is lost and does not make sense. This is what is produced in analysis, but also what is lost in the process: through analysis, this signifier is first, isolated; second, questioned and connected to other signifiers in a dialectic relationship (that is, made sense of in relation to knowledge or S_2); and third, got rid of (Žižek 2006).

Seduction and desire are essential to the practice of analysis, as Lacan demonstrates. But a seductive element is also present in our relation to certain objects, notably those found within the gallery space. The argument I would like to put forward is: if certain artefacts – such as *Juicy Salif* – can bring Object (a) into being and are its manifestation (as argued above) they therefore occupy, in the gallery space, shop display or any other privileged enclosure, the position the analyst occupies in the consulting room. Although Lacan did not explicitly form a *Discourse of the Artefact,* he thought about the object and suggested a possible relationship to the subject similar to that facilitated by analytic practice, as shown in his Seminars, especially VI (Lacan 1958–9), XI (Lacan 1986), XVII (Lacan 1991) and XXI (Lacan 1973–4). The artefact takes the position of the analyst, something not thought about in many psychoanalytic studies of cultural objects, since the common position is to 'analyse' the work. This means that we, viewers, in the right conditions and context, adopt the position of the analysand, with the object revealing our symptom, something of ourselves we might not have known about. Since Lacan, the mechanics of 'artefact as analyst' have been worked through by a number of theorists and practitioners: for example, by Parveen Adams, in her contextualization of Mary Kelly's *Interim* show (1991), and Robert Samuels, in his examination of Lacan's interest in art, especially Aragon's poetry and Holbein's *Ambassadors* (Samuels 1995). More recently, displays confronting viewers in this particular social bond have been held at the Centre for Freudian Analysis and Research in London, and have been discussed in the talks accompanying the exhibitions and the subsequent journal publication (Kivland and Du Ry 2000). However, the proposition that the place the analyst and the artefact occupy, that of Object (a), is the place of the seducer changes the framework and understanding of the social bond between subjects and objects, making it active. Seduction unfolds from the artefact, whether in the form of an analyst (for the analysand) or *Juicy Salif* (for the viewer/user/owner). As a result, a turning point for the subject can take place, similar to that represented by the psychoanalytic act – its practice, rather than the psychoanalysing of objects, authors or intentions. And I concur with Danuza Machado: that is a moment to celebrate (Kivland and Du Ry 2000: 7).

Conclusion

Juicy Salif has originated innovation in the relationship between its form and its function. Its 'household icon' status (Heskett 2003: 58) is affirmed by Alessi's careful product marketing strategies and the debates around its functional qualities and symbolic value. However, both debates cannot be separated; part of this lemon squeezer's symbolic qualities derive from the fact that its 'good looks' come at a performative cost: 'high ratio of price to functionality' (Julier 2000: 69), loss of material (gold or aluminium plating), high effort in squeezing lemons and cleaning the juicer (Russo and de Moraes 2003: 147) and spilt liquid.

As a best-selling design icon, *Juicy Salif* cannot be evaluated by its effectiveness in squeezing lemons. That, as we have seen, may not be its real function after all. Starck wanted to create something more, something that would make users, viewers and owners experience the object in a different way, both from the point of view of its performance (squeezing lemons with *Juicy Salif* is different than with any other juicer) and its aesthetic. With *Juicy Salif*, Starck used three distinct strategies to get to his client group: polysemy – users, viewers and owners are given the opportunity to attach meaning to an object that can hold many; extension of creativity into its consumption – demonstrated in the misuse of the product (Lloyd and Snelders 2003: 251–2); and, crucially, seduction – a relational situation in which the object leads astray and reveals something about themselves that users, viewers and owners might not have known about. Innovating a household product in this way, by altering both its functional and symbolic aspects, is not easy to accomplish and requires a high level of skill. *Juicy Salif* manages to fulfil this and, with a relatively affordable price and strong manufacturing, marketing and distribution framework provided by Alessi, it reaches a wide audience. Starck's creativity has been recognized and rewarded by his peers, his client group and the market. But, even though Alessi commissioned a star designer, the success of this object could not have been accurately predicted. While this chapter has given some thought to how it connects with people, why *Juicy Salif* works is partly a mystery. There's always something that escapes.

Seductive characteristics are crucial for the creation of design icons. *Juicy Salif* provides a challenging but pertinent case study for research into these, the interaction with seduced viewers, users and owners, the value(s) – in the broader sense of the term – in both sides of the relationship, and how these relate to the contemporary late capitalist context. Although Khaslavsky and Shedroff's (1999) study on seduction begins to pinpoint some of the factors that may have led consumers astray from buying a more economic, manageable and effective product, a study of its characteristics in a relational context, through the psychoanalytic Object (a) and an emerging *Discourse of the Artefact*, may help to better understand why this disproportioned, menacing-looking, inefficient lemon squeezer is one of Alessi's best selling products, a design icon, a cultish totem.

Notes

1 For an image of *Juicy Salif* and a summary account of the commission and conceptualization in the words of its manufacturer (Alessi), as well as for other products by this designer, the reader could, in the first instance, refer to Starck (2000).
2 Starck sketched ideas for *Juicy Salif* on a tablemat of the restaurant Capraia Isola. The drawings, reproduced in Lloyd and Snelders (2003), clearly show the connection with rockets, arachnids and spaceships. Apart from the Manuel Gómez Pereira film mentioned above, *Juicy Salif* appeared in the 2004 film *Team America: World Police*, amongst others.
3 Here, the term *artefact* has been used with the same meaning as that of *object* in the earlier part of the text. The change in noun is propitiated by a wish to avoid confusion between *object* and the psychoanalytic Object (a), which, as seen, has a very particular meaning. I did not want to use *artefact* from the beginning because of its connotations of estrangement and the dialectic issues discussed in relation to the subject, for which the term *object* is far more suitable.

References

Adams, P. (1991) 'The art of analysis: Mary Kelly's "Interim" and the Discourse of the Analyst'. *October*, **58**: 81–96.
Alessi, A. (1994) *Alessi: The Design Factory*. London: Academy Editions.
(1998) *The Dream Factory: Alessi since 1921*. Cologne: Könemann.
Alessi (2004) 'Alessi Museum'. Available: www.alessi.com (accessed 17 January 2009).
Association for Computing Machinery (ACM) (2006). Available: www.acm.org (accessed 1 February 2006).
Baudrillard, J. (1988) *The Ecstasy of Communication*. New York: Semiotext(e).
(1991) *Seduction*. New York: Saint Martin's Press.
(1999) *Fatal Strategies*. London: Pluto Press.
Bourdieu, P. (1986) *Distinction: A Social Critique of the Judgement of Taste*. London: Routledge and Kegan Paul.

Bugge, A.B. (2003) 'Cooking as identity work'. *Ageing Societies, New Sociology* (conference), 23–26 September 2003, Murcia, Spain.

Butler, R. (1999) *Jean Baudrillard: The Defence of the Real.* London: Sage.

Clapham, M. (1997) 'Ethical moments in psychotherapy: interpretation, seduction or...?'. *British Journal of Psychotherapy*, 13(4): 506–14.

The Concise Oxford Dictionary of Current English (1964).

Creusen, M.E.H. and Schoormans, J.P.L. (2005) 'The different roles of product appearance in consumer choice'. *Journal of Product Innovation Management*, 22(1): 63–81.

Declercq, F. (2006) 'Lacan on the Capitalist Discourse: its consequences for libidinal enjoyment and social bonds'. *Psychoanalysis, Culture and Society*, 11(1): 74–83.

Evans, D. (1996) *An Introductory Dictionary of Lacanian Psychoanalysis.* London: Routledge.

Fink, B. (1995) *The Lacanian Subject: Between Language and Jouissance.* Princeton University Press.

Gómez Pereira, M. (dir) (1994) *All Men Are the Same* (Todos los hombres sois iguales) DVD. Spain: Ventura Distribution.

Hassenzahl, M. (2004) 'The interplay of beauty, goodness, and usability in interactive products'. *Human-Computer Interaction*, 19(4): 319–49.

Heskett, J. (2003) *Toothpicks and Logos: Design in Everyday Life.* Oxford University Press.

International Conference on Designing Pleasurable Products and Interfaces (ICDPPI) (2003) *Proceedings*. 23–26 June 2003, Pittsburgh, PA. New York: ACM Press.

Julier, G. (2000) *The Culture of Design.* London: Sage.

Khaslavsky, J. and Shedroff, N. (1999) 'Persuasive technologies: understanding the seductive experience'. *Communications of the ACM*, 42 (5), 45–9.

Kivland, S. and du Ry, M. (2000) 'In the place of an object'. *Journal of the Centre for Freudian Analysis and Research*, 12 (Special Issue).

Lacan, J. (1958–9) 'Seminar VI: Le désir et son interprétation'. Unpublished seminar, available: http://nosubject.com/Seminar_VI (accessed 16 January 2009).

(1973–4) 'Seminar XXI: Les non-dupes errent'. Unpublished seminar, available: http://nosubject.com/Seminar_XXI (accessed 16 January 2009).

(1974–5) 'Seminar XXII: RSI'. Unpublished seminar, available: http://nosubject.com/seminar_XXII (accessed 30 August 2009).

Lacan, J., Forrester, J. (transl.) (1975) *The Seminar of Jacques Lacan: Book I: Freud's Papers on Technique 1953–1954.* New York, London: W. W. Norton.

Lacan, J., Sheridan, A. (transl.) (1986) *The Seminar of Jacques Lacan, Book XI: The Four Fundamental Concepts of Psychoanalysis, 1964.* New York, London: W.W. Norton.

Lacan, J. (1991) *Le Séminaire de Jacques Lacan, Livre XVII: L'Envers de la Psychanalyse, 1969–1970.* Paris: Seuil.

Lacan, J., Porter, D. (transl.) (1992) *The Seminar of Jacques Lacan, Book VII: The Ethics of Psychoanalysis 1959 –1960.* London: Routledge.

Lacan, J., Fink, B. (transl.) (1998) *The Seminar of Jacques Lacan, Book XX: Encore, On Feminine Sexuality, The Limits of Love and Knowledge 1972–1973.* New York, London: W.W. Norton.

Lees-Maffei, G. (2002) 'Italianità and internationalism: production, design and mediation at Alessi, 1976–96'. *Modern Italy*, 7(1): 37–57.

Lloyd, P. and Snelders, D. (2003) 'What was Philippe Starck thinking of?' *Design Studies*, 24(3): 237–53.

Marx, K. (1995) *Capital, An Abridged Edition.* Oxford University Press.

McGuirk, J. (2006) 'Philippe Starck'. Available: www.iconeye.com (accessed 19 January 2009).

The Metropolitan Museum (2006) ' "Juicy Salif" lemon squeezer (2001. 523)'. *Heilbrunn Timeline of Art History*. Available: www.metmuseum.org (accessed 19 January 2009).

Morgan, C.L. (1999) *Starck.* New York: Universe Publishing.

Norman, D.A. (2004) *Why We Love (or Hate) Everyday Things.* New York: Basic Books.

Preston, B. (2000) 'The function of things: a philosophical perspective on material culture', in P. Graves-Brown (ed.) *Matter, Materiality and Modern Culture.* London: Routledge.

Osborne, P. (2005) *How to Read Marx.* London: Granta.

Russo, B. and de Moraes, A. (2003) 'The lack of usability in design icons: an affective case study about Juicy Salif', in *Proceedings of the 2003 International Conference on Designing Pleasurable Products and Interfaces*, Pittsburgh, PA, 23–26 June, 2003: 146–7. New York: ACM Press.

Samuels, R. (1995) 'Art and the position of the analyst', in R. Feldstein, B. Fink and M. Jaanus, *Reading Seminar XI: Lacan's Four Fundamental Concepts of Psychoanalysis.* Albany, NY: State University of New York Press.

Scarcella, P. (1987) *Steel and Style: The Story of Alessi Household Ware.* Milano: Arcadia.

Sex and the City, Seasons 1–6 shoebox. DVD (2005). Created by Darren Star. UK: Paramount Home Entertainment.

Stanford University (2005) *Persuasive Technology Lab.* Available: http://captology.stanford.edu (accessed 19 January 2009).

Starck, P. (1997) 'Starck speaks: politics, pleasure and play'. Design Award Lecture, October 1997, Harvard University Graduate School of Design.

(2000) 'Juicy Salif, Alessi, 1990'. Available: www.philippe-starck.com (accessed 19 January 2009).

Tortajada, M. (2004) 'Eric Rohmer and the mechanics of seduction'. *Studies in French Cinema*, 4(3): 229–38.

Unhappy Families (2005). Card game, designed by B. Doldi, S. Kennedy; illustrated by S. Pattenden. Hants: Portobello Games.

Veblen, T. (2004) 'Conspicuous consumption', in V. Buchli (ed.) *Material Culture: Critical Concepts in the Social Sciences*, 1(2). London: Routledge: 309–326.

Weatherill, R. (2000) 'The seduction of therapy'. *British Journal of Psychotherapy*, 16(3): 263–73.

Whitely, N. (1994) 'High art and the high street: the "commerce-and-culture" debate', in R. Keat, N. Whitely and N. Abercrombie (eds.) *The Authority of the Consumer*: 119–137. London: Routledge.

Žižek, S. (1991) *For They Know Not What They Do: Enjoyment as a Political Factor*. London: Verso.

(2006) *Jacques Lacan's Four Discourses*. Available: www.lacan.com/zizfour.htm (accessed 19 January 2009).

15 | 'Time past': the value of remembrance in aesthetic experience

AMY PARKER

'When to the sessions of sweet silent thought, I summon up remembrance of things past', writes Shakespeare (1900) in the opening lines of his thirtieth sonnet. Little do we know that these inviting words will reveal to the reader a sense of melancholy so acute that it could only have been occasioned by the deep sense of grief that we imagine accompanies death. And indeed it is death that permeates this text. However, in this instance, it seems that it is not just the loss of close friends that devastates the author, 'for close friends hid in death's dateless night' but also the loss of one's potential, as if, as an unwelcome accompaniment to the pain he feels as he remembers lost loved ones, this process of recollection, of reflection also requires him to admit to his own sense of unfulfilled ambition and desire, 'I sigh the lack of many a thing I sought'. Remembering seems to expose a lack in the completeness or continuity of a life. Remembering causes him to acknowledge the presence of the empty spaces which bear the traces of unrealised ambitions and departed friends, and which have inevitably been caused, quite simply, though no less gallingly, by time. But is it necessarily the case that memory and the act of remembering cause one to endure the fragmentation of experience?

What might it mean to remember? And why might we want to remember? The etymology of the word reminds us that to remember is essentially to be mindful, to bear something in mind. In the remembering of experience, we might bear the burden of the past, but simultaneously, our remembering also bears us a new experience, remembering yields that which expounds the present moment. In remembering we add to the present, we enrich it, we bring together new and old, present and past. Remembering an experience does not close us off from our current state, rather it actually preserves it, adds to it, and one might even say that remembering contributes to the present. But what is the relation between the concepts of remembering and remembrance and aesthetic experience, and how might this relation shed light upon the idea of value?

This paper will explore the concept of remembrance with respect to aesthetic experience and aesthetic objects. I will attempt to show that *remembrance* and the *act of remembering* contribute to our valuing of works of art and aesthetic experience. Most of the work done in this paper re-examines Walter Benjamin's (1999) essay 'On Some Motifs in Baudelaire' in which the author utilises the concept of memory as a means with which to discuss both psychoanalytic and socio-historical models of understanding and interpreting the experiential, as he understands them to be articulated in the writings of Baudelaire and Proust, amongst others. Furthermore, in an appeal to a critical theoretical discourse, I will attempt to draw a parallel between Proust's literary celebration of remembrance and the attempts of the Frankfurt School to harness the politically and socially revolutionary potential of recollection in an effort to explore how the notions of remembering and remembrance can help us understand the concept of *value* in the context of aesthetic experience.

Forgetting, remembering and reification

In a letter to Walter Benjamin written in 1940 Theodor Adorno (1970) writes, 'Every reification is a forgetting: objects become thinglike at the moment when they are seized without all their elements being contemporaneous, when something of them is forgotten' (Adorno 1970: 321). For critical social theory at least, the concept of reification appears to speak rather directly to the notions of remembering and forgetting, for the reified person is the one whose 'humanness' seems to have been forgotten. Reification depersonalises and deprives the subject of certain essential characteristics. Commodified labour (according to Marx) exemplifies the reification of the individual and transforms them into someone whose human qualities become measurable in the abstract. Reification is structured by and through the forgetting of certain features or essences of the object or person being reified. And in this forgetting, some aspect of the individual is lost. In fact, for the Frankfurt School, the notion of reification is precisely so troubling because it implies a limited potential for self-consciousness within the confines of capitalist structures. When thought of as an abstract thing, when human action and labour become exchangeable and commodifiable, the self becomes fragmented and consciousness becomes masked by ideology. It is in this sense that reification, for the Frankfurt School, implies the loss of the unmediated individual. Reification, therefore, becomes associated with an impoverished experience and existence, and leads to a distorted consciousness in which social relations are transformed into objects.

It becomes clear then that a critical theoretical consideration of reification is dependent upon a corresponding relationship between the ideas of forgetting and loss; reification occurs because some aspect of human existence or experience is lost or forgotten. However, Adorno's quote, as well as introducing the reader, albeit somewhat indirectly, to a discussion of the concepts of memory and value in aesthetic experience, also serves to highlight the inherently paradoxical nature of a contemplation of the notion of forgetting. For, suggesting that 'every reification is a forgetting' and adopting the kind of rhetoric which implies that, consequently, an aspect of the human essence or experience is *lost* in the process of forgetting, would be to forget that one can think of the concepts of forgetting and remembering as coterminous or coextensive. To forget, is at the same time, of course, also to remember. However, what the concept of reification does bring to the fore in this discussion of memory is the notion that forgetting/remembering has a decisive impact upon experience. How would our experience differ if we never forgot anything, indeed, how would the course of the history of experience differ if *we* had never been forgotten? The concept of reification is decisive here because it places the notions of remembering and forgetting in close proximity to the concept of alienation and thus argues that remembering and forgetting contribute to the impoverishment of experience. But there is a way we might put a different spin on the idea of reification in the context of memory. In the process of reification, social relations are made thing-like, they are made abstract, to the detriment of experience. And the way social relations are made thing-like is by and through the forgetting of the human dimension. However, in Benjamin's essay, we are introduced to the idea that memories themselves become thing-like, for the purpose of aesthetic output. And in this sense, it is useful to think of the process of making a memory thing-like *productive* rather than destructive. In other words, by isolating the process of making thing-like such as it is identifiable in the concept of reification, and by appropriating this process to the making thing-like of our memories, it is possible to make a case for the remembering or forgetting of certain experiences as being able to actually contribute to a new experience, as opposed to causing the impoverishment of experience. Of course, in critical-theoretical discourse, reification is a threat because in this making thing-like of social relations, something is forgotten, something is left behind. But what, if anything, is left behind when we remember an aesthetic experience?

To be clear, the aesthetic experience under interrogation here is the one that we wish to articulate, the experience that will be written or spoken about. It is the experience that has been, but that has yet to be formally articulated. In many ways, then, it is the experience to come, but it is also the experience that requires us to remember, to look back and to recollect. But why might we value the recollection of an aesthetic experience in a way that is different to, say, experiencing each moment in its all its 'presentness' or 'nowness'? Might there be something inherently overwhelming and inassimilable, shocking even, about an aesthetic encounter? And might our ability to make sense of aesthetic experience actually be rather limited?

In his essay Benjamin (1999) suggests that the greater the number of data we have to process, the more our consciousness acts as a screen against stimuli. In other words, the greater the number of perceptions we must come to terms with, the better our minds become at filtering and screening out these impressions. This leads one to wonder how we are ever to comprehend aesthetic experiences, if we are biologically and psychologically programmed to start shutting out impressions when they begin to overwhelm us. Perhaps, then, all we can ever do is remember them? Perhaps, once time has passed and we are no longer 'in' the immediacy of experience, we can begin to piece together the fragments of the experience that have remained lodged in our unconscious. A return to the initial question then – what might it mean to remember?

Forgetting, remembering and aesthetic experience

If we admire the painting on the wall of the gallery, we are of course, experiencing the painting as we stand before it; we perceive the colours, the form and the effect the painting may have on us, but how much does our experience of the painting become our memory of it?

Perhaps we might go so far as to ask which the real aesthetic experience is. Is it the few minutes we spend standing in front of the picture, or is it the contemplation of and the delight we take in the after-image of the painting that we are able to experience again and again and again, simply by the act of remembering? Many of these ideas have a long-established history in the domains of critical, philosophical and literary theory, and I will proceed in this paper to draw on ideas that live in the discourses of Walter Benjamin and Marcel Proust. Benjamin's essay 'On Some Motifs in Baudelaire' presents us with the notion of Proustian memory. The introduction of Marcel Proust, at this point, is essential to a discussion of aesthetic experience and memory, yet it is problematic because it is the aesthetic object that remembers. *Remembrance of Things Past* (1983) is itself a testimony to remembrance. However, I want to use some of the theoretical considerations that Proust's work generates, to see if they might illuminate our own reflections on aesthetic experience.

It is of note that in his essay, Benjamin suggests that it is possible to trace out, in the work of Proust, an eminent critique of the philosopher Henri Bergson's theory of experience. In *History of Western Philosophy*, Bertrand Russell (1961) explains that one idea that is crucial to Bergson's philosophy of memory is that of *duration (duree)*, which 'forms the past and present into one organic whole ... in the duration in which we see ourselves acting, there are dissociated elements; but in the duration in which we act, our states melt into each other' (Russell 1961: 759). For Bergson, duration is our 'ultimate' reality in which consciousness gathers information from a past that is receding whilst retaining that information on the basis that it has some contributory worth to the present. In other words, Bergson sees duration as a mode in which the past is somehow preserved in our conception of a present. Furthermore, on the basis of this construction of reality, Bergson argues that it would be at this very moment, this coming together of past and present life in an undivided whole, that one has most possession of oneself. Crucially, Bergson sees the ultimate manifestation of duration in our faculty of memory which contains elements of the past in a present moment, and has two distinct features, as Russell explains:

A man is said to remember a poem if he can repeat it by heart, that is to say if he has acquired a certain habit or mechanism enabling him to repeat a former action. But he might, at least theoretically, be able to repeat the poem without any recollection of the previous occasions on which he has read it; thus there is no consciousness of past events involved in this sort of memory. The second sort, which alone really deserves to be called memory, is exhibited in recollections of separate occasions when he has read the poem, each unique and with a date. (Russell 1961: 760)

In the first instance of Bergson's memory, remembering is said to be brought about by the act of recalling that which, as an activity, as a series of words, or as an object, has its origins in the past. That is to say, we have encountered the thing we are actively recalling before, but importantly, in this specific act of recalling there is no trace of such a past encounter and there is no sense in which our recollection is dependent on a consciousness of the past. In contrast, however, is what Russell refers to as Bergson's second instance of memory in which remembering the past is done in the present moment and the content of which is made up from instances in the past. Thus, this second type of memory is defined by the presence of the past as the mind actively contemplates it, as opposed to the first kind of remembering which involves holding in one's consciousness the means with which to remember something in the past, without necessarily having to be fully conscious of this past. This is what Bergson refers to as *memoire pure*. The sticking point for Benjamin is the antagonism between Bergson's *vita contemplativa* and the *vita activa*. Bergson stipulates that the contemplation of life's experiences comes about through choice. He argues that recollection and memory can be accessed via the means of the free will of the subject. For Proust, the very opposite is the case and he denies the supremacy of the power of the intellect in recalling events of the past. In his discussion of Proust's *Remembrance of Things Past*, Benjamin refers to the introductory passage in which Proust describes the great difficulty with which he recollects his childhood in the town of Combray. This experience (the experience of remembering) is placed in opposition to another, now famous, encounter Proust has with his past as he eats a madeleine and is 'transported' back in time. The difference between these experiences is said to depend upon the distinction that 'before then he had been limited to the promptings of a memory which obeyed the call of attentiveness' (Benjamin 1999: 155). In other words, when Proust attempts with any effort to reflect upon an experience in his past, it is achieved only with great difficulty, precisely because he is attending so directly to the experience he wishes to recall. His childhood in Combray eludes him because he is using the will of his intellect to provoke the recollections. However, when he happens to be engaging in something as relatively banal as eating the madeleine, his access to the past is greatly enhanced, in fact, according to Benjamin, the reflections are so strong that it is as if Proust has actually been 'transported', that is, literally moved back in time. Proustian memory then or *memoire involontaire* is a state of remembering that is occasioned by an encounter or an engagement with something, in the present moment, that triggers or provokes one to recall a moment in one's own past. What happened when Proust ate the madeleine then, according to John Hogan in his 1939 essay on Proust's aesthetic theory, is that 'the past in him rose to the surface, grappled with the present and left him in doubt as to whether he was living in the past or the present, or neither'. Moreover, 'this sensation of simultaneously experiencing both a past and a present had swept him, momentarily, into an undreamed of paradise.' (Hogan 1939: 189)

It becomes apparent then, that Proustian memory is based on a subjective conception of reality. It assumes that the truth of reality lies within us, and not within the object. Though the object may have the power to bring forth from within us a reality, ultimately it is an encounter with ourselves and our own past, just as Proust encounters *his* own past that reveals to us the full significance of our experiences. There is nothing inherently significant about Proust's madeleine, but, by virtue of his memory, his encounter with it becomes almost poetic. The object is made to mean, it becomes sublime and it is given a status above and beyond its ordinary value, because by virtue of it, Proust is able to trace out the experiences of his past, and momentarily, is transported into an unfamiliar paradise.

Let us pause for a moment on this idea of *tracing out experience*. If we consider that a life consists of series of experiences, might it be that some of these experiences leave their mark within us? Might it be that of all the things that happen to us over the course of a lifetime, some of those encounters will have left traces in us, indeed, do some of our experiences still reside in the depths of our memory? Furthermore, and more importantly, might it be that the task of art is to trace out the impressions left in us by experience? If art is bound to the concepts of reality and truth, is it not also bound to the concept of the past? The task of the artist then, becomes the revealing and the translation of the impressions left in us by experience. Following on from this, art cannot therefore, be created, in the divine sense of producing or forming out of nothing, for its subject is always already there; rather art and the artist seek out, search for, recognise and recapture that which has left its mark within us. As Martin Jay (1982) points out in his essay on Marcuse's Theory of Remembrance, Marcuse seized hold of the revolutionary potential of art and remembrance. 'The implication is that forgetting the suffering of men is akin to forgetting the pain caused nature by its human domination ... In short, for Marcuse the promise of future happiness embodied in art was dialectically related to its retention of past instances of joy and fulfilment' (Jay 1982: 6).

An example of such joy can be found in Proust, as Hogan describes a moment from *Remembrance of Things Past* when, positioned on two uneven paving stones, the protagonist is almost run down by a passing carriage and is left, literally, reeling from the experience. 'While under its sway the joyous sensation that swept through him seemed to him to have been the truest, clearest and surest affirmation of life that he had ever known. Taking him outside of time it had yielded him a sense of certainty – sufficient without other proofs to make him indifferent to death' (Hogan 1939: 188). Proust's experience here seems almost transcendent; as he stands swaying on the uneven paving stones, dizzy from his encounter with the wayward carriage, he is apparently lifted out of himself and his immediate surroundings; any worries about the future disappear, and he is momentarily liberated from intellectual anxiety. The place he finds himself in now, moreover, appears to exist outside of time – it has no history, no consequences and, crucially, it doesn't even seem to have a present. But what, one wonders, is the cause of this existential shudder? It seems, according to Hogan (1939: 188), that Proust's 'present experience balancing on the stones in the courtyard was sufficiently like that one in the past to call up from within him that day in Venice, which he had for so long a time kept buried deep inside him'.

In other words, then, as Proust escapes a collision with the carriage, what causes him, at that very moment, to experience an almost sublime sense of liberation is the fact that he simultaneously remembers a similar event that had occurred, before, in Venice. As the two separate events are brought into focus, that is, brought into consciousness, Proust is able to reconcile himself with his previous experience. In this sense, the past is not a distant, long-forgotten, never-to-be-retrieved other dimension, but is a vital, ever-present treasure chest of previous moments that wait to be rediscovered or remembered throughout our lives. What is fundamental here though, is that Proust intimates, realises, or discovers that this place 'outside time' actually furnishes him with a sense of life-affirming certainty. At the heart of Proust's experience, then, is the relationship between the experience in the present and a corresponding experience in his past. In other words, by locating, by discovering or by recognising an equivalent experience in the past, by virtue of an experience in the present, Proust has access to the most complete, most enduring and most spiritually rewarding kind of experience.

Remembering and value

According to Benjamin, Proust imitates the hermetic aspect of art through his writing. That which is concealed from us in art, is precisely what Proust duplicates in his writing. It is not the case that he tries to reveal, or uncover that which we perceive to be hidden from us in artworks, or what could be considered hermetic in art, and simultaneously, he does not expose to us what is beautiful in art, nor does his writing point us in the direction of beauty. Instead, by imitating, copying and essentially reinforcing the concealed aspect of works of art, Proust's writing reveals anew the concept of the beautiful. That which is hidden from us in art, is similar to the kind of memory that Benjamin thinks that Proust gives us, and himself. For, not only could art be considered hermetic, but our experiences too are hermetic, hidden from us somehow, only recollectable through memory, and thus, as long as our experiences remain hidden to us, we remain a mystery to ourselves.

We value remembering and remembrance in aesthetic experience because of all the things that Proust intimates happen to him when he has what we must acknowledge as rather unaesthetic experiences. There is nothing aesthetic about his eating of the madeleine or his standing on the uneven paving stones. Or is there? What Proust does, in fact, is aestheticise his memories. The act of remembering and memory enters into the free play of the imagination, and as he remembers, his memories become aestheticised. We value remembering then, not only because it speaks to an existential notion of subjective unity and spirituality, but because these memories in turn can become the material for a subsequent aesthetic object. We value remembering because it allows us to do two things. First, the act of remembering unites or reconciles us with our own past, and with our own experiences, as well as allowing us to recapture, to project, to fantasise, to embellish and to distort our original experience – thus remembering allows us to aestheticise our memories. Second, remembrance and remembering and memory are tied to aesthetic experience because what we experience in the present moment is never the whole story. When you stand before the painting you value it not just in the present moment, but you value it for all the times you have seen it before, and for all the times you will see it in the future. Seeing the work of art in the present moment is only a fraction of what it promises, because our valuing of art is projected over time, it lives and endures simultaneously in the past, present and in the future. The present moment is in communion with the past. Moreover, while experiencing the work of art in the present moment may provoke memories within us, the work of art also sets itself up to be remembered. We value remembrance in aesthetic experience then, because our remembering of the art work not only guarantees the place of the art work in the future, but also because our remembering allows us to uncover our experiences of the past in such a way that the possibility of art continually penetrates the present moment. And it is in this sense that remembrance of the past in aesthetic experience secures the future of a demystified critical consciousness.

References

Adorno, T. (1970) *Über Walter Benjamin*. Frankfurt: Suhrkamp.

Benjamin, W., Arendt, H. (ed.), Zohn, H. (transl.) (1999) 'On some motifs in Baudelaire', in *Illuminations*, 152–96. London: Pimlico.

Hogan, J. (1939) 'The past recaptured: Marcel Proust's aesthetic theory'. *Ethics*, 49(2): 187–203. University of Chicago Press.

Jay, M. (1982) 'Anamnestic totalisation: reflections on Marcuse's Theory of Remembrance'. *Theory and Society*, 11(1): 1–15.

Proust, M., Scott Moncrieff, C.K. and Kilmartin, T. (transls.) (1983) *Remembrance of Things Past: I, new edition.* London: Penguin Books.

Russell, B. (1961) *History of Western Philosophy.* London: Allen and Unwin.

Shakespeare, W., Fox, L. (ed.) (1900) *The Sonnets of William Shakespeare.* Norwich: Jarrold and Sons.

16 | *What is a creative field?*

ELIZABETH GULLEDGE
AND BARBARA TOWNLEY

An array of processes, individuals and organizations are involved in the production and distribution of cultural objects. Hirsch (1972) observes the trajectory of such objects from creation to consumption, suggesting that cultural objects 'flow', starting with authors, musicians and designers; through publishers, record companies and fashion houses; to booksellers, concert halls and retailers. The final output – the book, the musical recording, the haute couture – represents the collective work of a range of actors who work in and through varied domains. Hirsch's work alerts us to the network of organizational and personal relations that shapes cultural objects, including forces such as changes in technology, developments in copyright law and increased corporate conglomeration. Further to this are the practices and their attendant logics that become institutionalized within creative sectors and the issues of power and control that influence their operation. But the question arises, how do we make sense of, and try to conceptualize this complex picture? What should be the focus of our study of creative sectors? Where do we draw the boundaries when seeking to broaden our analysis? How useful is the concept of 'creative industry' with its connotations? This chapter seeks to address these questions by considering at greater length the concept of a 'field' as developed in the work of Pierre Bourdieu. Using the example of book publishing we illustrate how the concept of the 'field' offers a rich seam of opportunity to better examine how creative products are created, reproduced and distributed by groups of interdependent actors and constituted by an institutional environment.

Above and beyond the organization: sets and systems

Restricting an analysis to a creative organization alone omits much of the dynamics of creative production and we suggest expanding our focus beyond the single organization. Several conceptual frameworks offer different foci from which to choose: 'industry', 'organization sets', 'industry sets' (Perrow 1972). While the term 'industry' usually refers to a group of competing organizations producing similar goods or services, the concept of 'organization set' examines the variety of organizations within an industry (Blau and Scott 1962; Evan 1966). Its focus is on the exchanges between the primary organization and the various organizations in its environment, drawing attention to the flow of information, products/services and personnel that mediate the relationship between the organization and the organization set (Evan 1966). The sole organization and how 'it' strategically manages relations with other members of the organizational set still remains the focal point of analysis, however, with little attention given to the broader structure of the 'organization set' itself.

Hirsch (1972) offers a complementary macro-level concept, the 'industry system', i.e. inter-related organizations that draw on environmental resources, transform them and then send the output to the market or another organization. In his study of books and musical recordings, he highlights the role of gatekeepers who serve as filters or arbiters, influencing which cultural objects will reach the market. His concept of industry system allows analysis to extend beyond issues of competition between similar organizations and a focus on the combination of structures, resources and processes that influence cultural production. Although broadening our analysis, it fails to capture the complexity of processes whereby cultural products are created, reproduced and distributed by groups of interdependent actors, the meanings that attach to these and how these are constituted by an institutional environment (Hirsch 2000; Scott 2006).

These approaches and concepts remain problematic for our intent. The concepts of 'organizational set' and 'industry system' dichotomize the culture–economy relationship, imposing an analytic separation between the production of creative work and its consumption. They do not capture the meanings that cultural and creative products have, and are pre-selective as to who should belong to the object of study. What is required is an approach that takes into consideration issues of ownership and control and, in addition, the analysis and interpretation of creative content and its meaning. This furthers the argument for a perspective that takes into account the inextricably tied processes of production and consumption.

A number of studies included under the banner of the 'production of culture' perspective offer much to this discussion. This body of work places an emphasis on how the organization of cultural production influences cultural content (Peterson 1976; Becker 1982). As artists become conscious of the way the industry system operates, this influences the creation of the cultural object (Becker 1982). As Peterson (1976: 153) notes, 'the milieu in which culture is produced influences its form and content'. The value of this perspective is that it directs our attention to the conditions under which creative ideas and works may be mobilized. As a body of work, however, the focus tends to be on the 'production' of cultural works only.

There is thus a need for an analytical tool that takes into account not only the inextricably tied processes of production and consumption but also considers the range of individual agents involved in these processes beyond those linked by simple relations of interaction (Bourdieu 1993b). In *The Rules of Art*, Bourdieu (1996) stresses the importance of the role played by individuals involved in the process in which cultural goods are constructed as valuable. His emphasis is not just on the material production of the creative objects but also on the construction of the value of the work. Equally, his *Field of Cultural Production* (Bourdieu 1993b) also indicates how an analysis of cultural products must take into consideration their significance both within a field of artistic development and a sociological field of power relations. In this, Bourdieu's development and elaborations of the concept 'field' would appear to offer the prospect of a more nuanced understanding of the nature and operation of creative production.

Fields, capital and Bourdieu

The introduction of the term 'field' into organization studies originally came from Lewin (1951), who drew on the metaphor of magnetic attraction to illustrate how human groupings consolidate into recognized coherent systems. For Lewin, behaviour was shaped by the totality of an individual's situation. In his theory, a 'field' is defined as 'the totality of coexisting facts which are conceived of as mutually interdependent' (Lewin 1951: 240). The more recent invocation of 'field' is found in the neo-institutional literature where it is used to refer to a diverse set of organizations that compete for the same resources and legitimacy in a recognized area of institutional life

(DiMaggio and Powell 1991; Meyer and Rowan 1977; Scott 2001). The focus of analysis is thus on the broader social forces that shape organizational form and practice (Hoffman 1999), and the broader enquiry into the dynamics of organizations and society (Friedland and Alford 1991; Scott 2001; Stinchcombe 1997).

DiMaggio and Powell (1983: 183) define organizational fields as 'those organizations that, in the aggregate, constitute a recognized area of institutional life; key suppliers, resource and product consumers, regulatory agencies, and other organizations that produce similar services or products'. The concept of field includes not just one type of organization (e.g. all book publishing houses, 'the industry'), but all the organizations and actors involved (e.g. writers, literary agents, distributors, printers, freelance editors, reviews and book prizegiving). This focus takes into account the wide variety of agents and organizations that influences production and consumption, broadening analysis to the ideas and interactions that establish practices among actors in addition to factors such as regulation, economic conditions and the changing market (e.g. Jones 2001; Thornton and Ocasio 1999). DiMaggio (1991) demonstrates the utility of this approach in his analysis of art museums, illustrating how ideas about art museums were constructed by the funding bodies. His historical analysis charts how two opposing understandings of their role, as either 'high art' or art that is to be made accessible 'for the masses', influenced their identity and functioning. DiMaggio's analysis draws attention to the political factors involved in the struggle over the role of art museums. Philanthropic agencies and professional organizations influenced the emergence of the 'educational museum' (DiMaggio 1991). The Carnegie Corporation, for example, was able to influence the form and functioning of museums through the types of projects it funded. Similarly, the American Association of Museums spread national norms later adopted by members within local museums.

While research in the neo-institutional literature makes significant headway in developing useful approaches to studying creative sectors, the way in which the concept of 'field' is employed has been the object of criticism. When determining who or what constitutes a field, neo-institutional scholars include organizations in a field if they 'take each other into account' or display 'similar characteristics and relationships' (Scott 1994: 206). Pierre Bourdieu's conceptualization of a 'field' expands the scope of analysis by focusing attention on ways in which actors are embedded in power relations, i.e. are embedded in a struggle for legitimacy or power. This is manifest in a struggle over 'what is at stake' in the field, the meaning of what is shared in common, the understanding of what constitutes 'good art' in the field of arts (Bourdieu 1993b; Oakes *et al.* 1998; Wedlin 2006). This perspective enriches the neo-institutional line of inquiry by taking into account dimensions that structure social interaction and conflict within a field and by seeing these relations as being 'structured' positions. Bourdieu (1993a) regards a field as a socially structured space of positions in which agents struggle over resources and stakes. Because positions reflect relations of power within a field they are described as 'positions of possibility' (Bourdieu 1993a; Oakes *et al.* 1998). Agents hold differing 'points of view' about the field depending on their position and their access to resources in the field (Bourdieu 1985). Positions in the field offer agents possible stances which predispose them toward patterns of thought and action.

While DiMaggio's analysis and other neo-institutional research draw upon the work of Bourdieu, there has been resistance to the use of his concepts of 'field' and 'capital' which are central to the effort to understand the nature of field dynamics. For Bourdieu, a field is defined and structured by forms of 'capital'. In his use of this term, Bourdieu (1993b) extends the traditional understanding of capital from its being economic. Capital is any resource in a field that enables agents to appropriate particular 'profits' arising out of participation in the field (Bourdieu 1993b). In this way, the concepts of field and capital are interrelated: 'capital does not exist and function except in relation to a field' (Bourdieu and Wacquant 1992:97). Positions are characterized by the amount of capital needed to maintain or achieve positions and the degree and type of capital held by an agent influences the relative power the agent wields in a given field. Agents' perceptions of available opportunities and constraints are shaped by their understanding of the locus of capitals in the field. A field's dominant capital may not directly affect an actor's intrinsic abilities but it does affect their relational properties and their sense of positional identity (Oakes *et al.* 1998). The language and concepts Bourdieu offers thus allow us to see how an agent's actions are constrained (and enabled) by external forces but also how agents resist these forces through the accumulation and negotiation of capital.

Along with economic forms of capital, Bourdieu also identifies cultural, social and symbolic forms of capital. He defines social capital as the aggregate of the actual or potential resources linked to the possession of a durable network (Bourdieu 1986: 248). This includes connections or memberships that provide recognized influence in a field. Cultural capital includes both the possession of tangible cultural goods and the formal recognition of particular knowledge and skills. Symbolic capital is a form of legitimacy or respect that is proffered according to terms intrinsic to, or valued within, the field. According to Bourdieu, economic, social, symbolic and cultural forms of capital are equally influential in defining positions and structuring fields. His characterization of the dynamics of action in relation to these capitals acknowledges that they are 'taken for granted' or unconsciously engaged in by individuals and reproduced by practices that are structured in the field.

Agents use economic, cultural, social and symbolic forms of capital to define and negotiate power in a field. They accrue capital as a means of climbing to positions of privilege or power. This struggle has to do with gaining the capacity to produce legitimacy, i.e. help define and influence what is at stake in the field. Especially significant in the struggle for capital is the position of recognition, esteem or honour held by relevant actors within the field; their symbolic influence. Bourdieu suggests that individuals use whatever stores of capital they have to maximize the symbolic capital as defined within an institutional field. Actors who succeed in amassing symbolic capital gain dominant positions. Structural tension thus exists between the dominant and dominated positions within a field. Fields are places of struggle over symbolic capital as agents occupy positions that are endowed with different resources, and are dynamic, because change in one position shifts the possibilities of position-takings of other actors within the field.

Each field has its own logic that determines which forms of capital are required (Bourdieu 1984). For Bourdieu, the approach to analysing the field means that, 'one must identify the forms of specific capital that operate within it, and to construct the forms of specific capital one must know the specific logics of the field' (Bourdieu and Wacquant 1992: 108). A field is defined by a logic through which it operates (Bourdieu 1985). Bourdieu's (1985) definition of field struggles also refers to competing hierarchies of classification, in which power structures are defined by struggles over criteria of legitimacy:

... knowledge of the social world and, more precisely, the categories that make it possible are the stakes, par excellence of political struggle, the inextricably theoretical and practical struggle for the power to conserve or transform the social world by conserving or transforming the categories through which it is perceived ... the work of categorization, i.e. of making explicit and of classification, is performed at every moment of ordinary existence, in the struggles in which agents clash over the meaning of the social world and their positions within it. (Bourdieu 1985: 729)

The object of competing in a field is to control the categories of evaluation that determine the legitimacy of work within that field. This struggle creates flexible and constantly changing boundaries (Wedlin 2006), with actors continually engaged in 'boundary work' in the endeavour to 'determine insiders and outsiders, the criteria that define actors in the field, and who has the authority to judge and set field boundaries' (Wedlin 2006: 14; Gieryn 1999). In continuous interaction with a social context, actors examine their existing activities and identities, naming and categorizing themselves in relation to one another (Bourdieu 1984). Through these processes actors recognize whether they 'fit' or do not fit in a field. This struggle is a contest for authority over the field itself. Without this struggle there is no field. What is at stake are the principles that define the identity of the field and that establish its boundaries (Wedlin 2006). It is precisely the issue of drawing boundaries as to what is included and who is excluded in the field that makes the discussion so complex. It also implies that the boundaries of the field broaden as far as power relations extend and that this can only be demarcated through empirical investigation (Bourdieu and Wacquant 1992).

The field of book publishing

The field of book publishing provides an interesting empirical site to view how Bourdieu's understanding of field dynamics are played out. We can conceptualize the 'publishing field' as a space of positions occupied by a range of different agents, including writers, literary agents, book retailers, libraries, distributors, freelance workers, professional associations, publishers, book prizegiving, book groups and book clubs (Thompson 2005). The publisher is thus one of many agents involved in the chain of tasks and functions related to the publication, sale and distribution of books (Thompson 2005). The disparate players of the field become linked through their various contributions to the process that begins with an idea and ends as a publication. All agents of the field impact in various ways the final production of the publishing industry.

The highly discretionary and evaluative nature of publishing books requires that actors define and set literary standards. The skills and critical discernment of editors and agents play an important role in constructing the values and motives operating in the field. Decisions related to whether to publish or reject manuscripts and the establishment of front and backlists are shaped through logics operating in the field and by the capital of agents who participate in it. For example, an editor's duties involve developing authors and manuscripts. They co-ordinate projects and work with authors, literary agents, advisors, reviewers and other publishers. In these interactions, editors are constructing an understanding of their work in accordance with the dominant capital and operating logic of the field. They play a role as gatekeepers and are empowered to make decisions about which 'products' will be sponsored and distributed (Epstein 2001). Definitions and perceptions about what is valued in manuscripts and why it is valued are thus contested and negotiated through the interaction between the range of agents in the publishing field. The work of these agents plays a part in establishing the boundaries of acceptable activities and how different books will be valued: what types of literature can be acquired or commissioned, what subject matter can be shared, what can be sold and where (Thompson 2005). Power struggles around this classification system take place everywhere in the field, from competition among literary agents who aspire to be associated with certain imprints or authors, to publishers vying for literary reviews in particular newspapers or magazines. All of these inter-relations reflect strategies by agents to acquire capital and position themselves in the field.

A field is defined by a logic through which it operates (Bourdieu 1985). In the case of books, two logics are at work. Under a 'market logic', the book's capital is defined as a commodity to be sold to the public (Thornton 2004). For agents governed by this logic, the primary objective is to make the trade in books like any other type of trade. Success is determined by such measures as the length of print run, marketing methods or overall sales. Judgment and evaluation of a book's value is based on how well it is produced, marketed and sold. The second is an 'editorial logic'. Under this logic, book publishing is associated with the production of 'symbolic' as opposed to consumer goods. As such, books are understood as having intellectual and literary value and are thus seen as distinct from other commodities. Historically, under this logic, the publishing industry was considered a profession with legitimacy based on intellectual reputation. In this way book publishing was not understood as being a conventional business. Rather, it more closely resembled a vocation (Epstein 2001).

These contrasting logics have the effect of establishing beliefs, motives and 'organizing principles' that shape the identities, interests and actions of agents in the field (Friedland and Alford 1991: 248). Agents operating through the business or market logic are oriented toward bottom-line interests as the decision-making process is shaped by the objective of economic success. The focus is on a quick turnover to maximize sales and an emphasis on marketing strategies. Issues such as effective distribution channels and the best ways to accelerate the return on profit are the ultimate imperatives. Publishers may minimize risk by only publishing manuscripts that will have mass appeal (Thompson 2005) or writing on topics of short-term, topical interest. By contrast, an editorial logic entails less emphasis on economic success. Rather, it is based on the building of long-term cultural value and the maximization of cultural and symbolic capital. Under the editorial logic a book is not evaluated solely on the public's willingness to pay for it but also on its literary merit and other types of criteria constructed within publishing networks. The focus is on developing strong relationships with authors, building personal networks and working with editors and literary agents with the best reputations for high-quality work (Thornton 2004).

The mid 1970s marked a period in which new actors emerged and the book publishing industry shifted from a dominant 'editorial logic' to a more 'market logic' (Thornton 2004). During this time, over-riding forces in the broader economic context shifted the culture of book publishing towards a more business or market agenda. Consequently, there was a substantial repositioning of the 'cultural field' of publishing in relation to the 'economic field'. As Epstein (2001: 52) laments, 'book publishing deviated from its true nature by assuming, under duress from unfavourable market conditions and the misconceptions of remote managers, the posture of a conventional business'. As trans-national media conglomerates and globalization reconfigured the operations of the book publishing industry, the 'position taking' of agents and the struggle over capital have become more complex and more intense.

During this period the most striking feature of the publishing industry was industry concentration, in which a select number of global publishing firms dictated the market. In pursuit of international markets and economies of scale, many publishing houses were bought by larger conglomerates. The shift to a market logic which accompanied this marked the reorientation of publishing toward 'bottom line' interests and increased profits. The practice of publishing shifted toward a focus on shaping manuscripts deemed 'market-worthy' and 'bankable' (Greco 2004). Thus, the shift in logics signified a reconfiguration of positions in relation to economic capital. This repositioning led to a new configuration of activity within publishing houses and their staff, and among authors, literary agents, book retailers, distributors and other agents across the field (Wright 2005). A shift took place in which the power of editors declined and the influence of literary agents, professional managers and large retail chains increased. Publishers, which at one time gained credibility through their connections with writers, were increasingly influenced by the corporate world in which they were being assessed. Their criterion of evaluation was based on ability to turn out profitable books (Coser *et al.* 1982). Equally, whereas a close association had existed between publishers, their authors, other writers and literary critics, the shift in orientation and the change in ownership led to a decline in contact between publishing businesses and writers and critics. These relationships were increasingly mediated by agents and lawyers, serving to distance publishers from the creative development of writers and their manuscripts. Publishers became more segregated from intellectual and cultural circles, thus again influencing the nature and operation of book publishing. The dominance of business agenda further intensified as a result of the demise of the Net Book Agreement in 1997 (which had given publishers the legal right to set minimum prices for their books) and the rise of the large retail chains. The historical shifts in the industry and the end of price protection on books had the effect of further diminishing the difference between books and other forms of commodities. This is revealed in the movements within the field and a consequent reorientation of understandings of agents' roles. Increasingly, the dominant position in trade publishing is not occupied by editors but by the buyers and sellers of subsidiary rights.

This brief historical overview serves to emphasize the conflict-ing commercial and cultural processes that exist within the field. Publishing represents a site of both symbolic and cultural conflict. The extent to which the publishing field is shaped by business agendas or, in contrast, operates more as a cultural institution, is governed by power struggles. According to Bourdieu (1985), agents seek to either maintain or overturn the distribution of capital in the field as a way of improving or holding on to their position. Thus the field of book publishing is a site of ongoing battle between those agents occupying dominant positions who seek to preserve the existing (economic) cap-ital and the market logic through which it operates, and those subor-dinated agents who attempt to introduce new standards and practices to improve their position in the field. Mutually opposed interests and conflicting strategies of action are an inherent aspect of fields and are shaped by agents' positioning within it (Fligstein 1997). The field's boundaries are defined by the ideas and assumptions about what con-stitutes 'good practice' by those in the field, serving the purpose of both differentiating and integrating actors within it (Suddaby *et al.* 2007).

Agents' interests are informed by their location within the overall distribution of capital and power relations in the field. In the case of the contemporary book publishing field, publishing houses with substantial amounts of economic, or symbolic capital, and multi-store booksellers are in influential positions to set literary standards. Through processes of naming, categorizing and regularizing, they are able to define a set of meanings in reference to the external market (Oakes *et al.* 1998): what type of manuscripts can be commissioned or acquired, what subjects will be favoured, what can be sold and where. In this sense, publishers and other agents act as cultural medi-ators and arbitrators of what will be accepted in the field. Around this classification system, power struggles take place between authors who aspire to be associated with particular imprints, find recognition and have titles published. Struggles also take place among the literary agents who seek to represent certain authors, develop reputations and specialize in particular genres. These efforts reflect actors' strategies to acquire capital and position themselves vis-à-vis others.

What is at stake in these struggles, in Bourdieu's terms, is the auton-omy of the field of literary production. This may be observed in terms of agents' ability to define their work as being distinctive. The latter may take place at varying points, for example, the sites where books are produced or sites in which 'meanings about books' are produced (Wright 2005: 113). For example, those working in the retail book trade, especially the independents, may construct their work as being different from other types of retail. While the end of price protection and rise of big retailers might be expected to change this, the occupational self-identity of those working in bookshops may be constructed as distinctive and books as something different from other commodities. An analysis using Bourdieu's framework would take into account the cultural capital that allows this construction of identity and the construction of the work as being different. The construction of work as distinctive, or not like any other trade, may be understood as a form of boundary work. It is the attempt to influence the types of capital recognized as legitimate. As Bourdieu (1996) suggests, the field of book publishing constructs itself as autonomous from the economic field. However, at the various points at which books are produced or infused with meaning, this autonomy may be proscribed by the pressure of economic capital (Wright 2005).

Conclusion

This chapter has examined how book publishing may be understood as a field, a space of contestation in which the stakes of the field (a 'cultural logic' or an 'economic logic') and forms of capital define its operation and nature. We would argue that the concept of institutional field, coupled with the elaborations of Pierre Bourdieu, provides the framework for a rich understanding and appreciation of the creative industries. The concept of field reminds us that there are a number of positions that we need to be aware of when understanding the dynamics of what is happening. In doing so, this allows for an appreciation of a range of different actors than would normally be included by the more usual terms of 'industry' and 'set' and the mapping of relations of interaction and exchange. It requires the ability to see the whole board in play, in which a range of potential actors are situated in and constituted by, the capital and logics of the field. Furthermore, Bourdieu's framework also allows for an appreciation of the meaning of cultural goods, and the contests that surround this, to be considered alongside the usual consideration of competitive changes, production processes, markets, etc. The significance of the meanings of the capital and logics over which agents contest, and the way in which they position themselves in relation to dominating positions in the field, shapes how they understand and control organizational purposes and functioning. The contestation and conflict between agents, their struggles over positions and the negotiation of capital, focus attention on how agents located in different structures of power compete for influence to claim what constitutes legitimate creative production. The ability to claim what constitutes legitimate creative production is, after all, what is at stake in the 'creative industries'.

References

Becker, H. (1982) *Art Worlds*. Berkeley: University of California Press.

Blau, P. and Scott, R. (1962) *Formal Organizations: A Comparative Approach*. San Francisco: Chandler.

Bourdieu, P., Nice, R. (transl.) (1984) *Distinction*. Cambridge, MA: Harvard University Press.

(1985) 'The social space and the genesis of groups'. *Theory and Society*, **14**: 723–44.

(1986) 'The forms of capital', in J. Richardson (ed.), *Handbook of Theory and Research for Sociology of Education*: 241–58. Santa Barbara, CA: Greenwood Press.

Nice, R. (transl.) (1993a) 'Some properties of fields'. *Sociology in Question*, 72–7. London: Sage.

(1993b) *The Field of Cultural Production: Essays on Art and Literature*. New York: Columbia University Press.

(1996) *The Rules of Art: Genesis and Structure of the Literary Field*. Cambridge: Polity Press.

Bourdieu, P. and Wacquant, L. (1992) *Invitation to Reflexive Sociology*. Chicago: University of Chicago Press.

Coser, L., Kadushin, C. and Powell, W. (1982). *Books: The Culture and Commerce of Publishing*. Chicago: Basic Books.

DiMaggio, P. (1991) 'Constructing an organizational field as a professional project: US art museums, 1920–1940', in W. Powell and P. DiMaggio (eds.), *The New Institutionalism in Organizational Analysis*: 267–92. Chicago: University of Chicago Press.

DiMaggio, P. and Powell, W. (1983) 'The iron cage revisited: institutional isomorphism and collective rationality in organizational fields'. *American Sociological Review*, **48**: 147–60.

(1991) 'Introduction', in W. Powell and P. DiMaggio (eds.), *The New Institutionalism in Organizational Analysis*: 1–38. Chicago: University of Chicago Press.

Epstein, J. (2001) *Book Business: Publishing Past Present and Future.* New York: W. W. Norton and Company.

Evan, W. (1966) 'The organization set: toward a theory of interorganizational relations', in Thompson (ed.) *Approaches to Organization Design*: 173–88. University of Pittsburgh Press.

Fligstein, N. (1997) 'Social skill and institutional theory'. *American Behavioral Scientist*, 40: 397–405.

Friedland, R. and Alford, R. (1991). 'Bringing society back in: symbols, practices and institutional contradictions', in W. Powell and P. DiMaggio (eds.), *The New Institutionalism in Organizational Analysis.* Chicago: University of Chicago Press.

Gieryn, T. (1999) *Cultural Boundaries of Science: Credibility on the Line.* Chicago: University of Chicago Press.

Greco, A. (2004) *The Book Publishing Industry.* New York: Lawrence Erlbaum.

Hirsch, P. (1972) 'Processing fads and fashions: an organization set analysis of cultural industry systems'. *American Journal of Sociology*, 77: 639–59.

  (2000) 'Cultural industries revisited'. *Organization Science,* 11: 356–61.

Hoffman, A.J. (1999) 'Institutional evolution and change: environmentalism and the US chemical industry'. *Academy of Management Journal*, 42(4): 351–71.

Jones, C. (2001). 'Coevolution of entrepreneurial careers, institutional rules and competitive dynamics in American film, 1895–1920'. *Organization Studies*, 6: 911–44.

Lewin, K. (1951) *Field Theory in Social Science: Selected Theoretical Papers.* New York: Harper & Row.

Meyer, J. and Rowan, B. (1977) 'Institutionalized organizations: formal structure as myth and ceremony'. *American Journal of Sociology*, 103(2): 340–63.

Oakes, L., Townley, B. and Cooper, D. (1998) 'Business planning as pedagogy: language and control in changing institutional field'. *Administrative Science Quarterly*, 43: 257–92.

Perrow, C. (1972). *Complex Organizations: A Critical Essay*, third edn. New York: McGraw-Hill Publishers.

Peterson, R. (1976) 'The production of culture'. *American Behavioral Scientist*, 19: 669–84.

Scott, R. (1994) 'Institutions and organizations: toward a theoretical synthesis', in Scott and Meyer (eds.) *Institutional Environments and Organizations: Structural Complexity and Individualism.* Thousand Oaks, CA: Sage.

(2001) *Institutions and Organization, second edn.* Thousand Oaks, CA: Sage.

(2006) 'Understanding research in the culture industries', in J. Lampel, J. Shamsie and T. Lant (eds.) *The Business of Culture: Emerging Perspectives in Media and Entertainment.* New York: Lawrence Erlbaum.

Stinchcombe, A. (1997) 'On the virtues of old institutionalism'. *Annual Review of Sociology*, **23**: 1–18.

Suddaby, R., Cooper, D.J. and Greenwood, R. (2007) 'Transnational regulation of professional services: governance dynamics of field level organizational change'. *Accounting, Organizations and Society*, **32**(4–5): 333–62.

Thompson, J. (2005) *Books in the Digital Age: The Transformation of Academic and Higher Education Publishing in Britain and the United States.* Cambridge: Polity Press.

Thornton, P. (2004) *Markets from Culture: Institutional Logics and Organizational Decisions in Higher Education Publishing.* Palo Alto, CA: Stanford University Press.

Thornton, P. and Ocasio, H. (1999) 'Institutional logics and the historical contingency of power in organizations: executive succession in the higher education publishing industry, 1958–1990'. *American Journal of Sociology*, **105**: 801–43.

Wedlin, L. (2006) *Ranking Business Schools: Forming Fields, Identities and Boundaries in International Management Education.* Cheltenham: Edward Elgar.

Wright, D. (2005) 'Mediating production and consumption: cultural capital and cultural workers'. *The British Journal of Sociology*, **56**: 105–21.

Managing Creativity: *concluding thoughts*

In this book we set out to give some space to an important and emerging debate. Creative products form a significant and symbolic part of most people's lives. People are defined, and define themselves, through choices they make in the consumption of fashion, literature, art and music. Presaged on these signals, social groups form around creative products, for example by regularly attending events (e.g. cinema, concerts, theatre), clubs or associations devoted to particular genres or artists, or engaging in web interactions with other people with a shared interest. 'Virtual communities' form using web-based interactive digital games and such activities can become significant in people's lives. Increasingly, the creative 'industries' are being seen as crucial elements of Western (and emerging) economies through their provision of employment, big and small business, products, revenues, tourism and taxes. We might question the term 'industry', but certainly creative fields incorporate a plethora of actors, and with the broad definitions of creativity that have been adopted, incorporating design, architecture and advertising, few areas of economic and cultural activity are exempt from the touch of creative processes and products.

The book has been structured around a series of categories derived from Caves (2002), who identified five distinguishing characteristics or properties of creative industries that make its organization and management complex and unpredictable: (a) the inherent unknowability of the outcome and success of creative endeavour prior to its practice (the *nobody knows* property); (b) the intrinsic motivation beyond economic concerns (*art for art's sake* property); (c) the range of factors that sustain appreciation of creative work (*infinite variety* property); (d) the reliance on the skills of a number of talented individuals for creative production (*motley crew* property); and (e) attempts at securing the durability of creative products (*time flies* and *ars longa* properties). In engaging with each of these categories, the purpose has not been to close down thinking or reduce complexity to unrepresentative simple definitions or 'findings'. Rather, we regard them as starting points to stimulate thinking and practice. Hence, the chapters presented here have sought to give some insight into an aspect of creative practice and management, such as the making of a piece of art, decision processes experienced when composing music, the engagement of audience in theatre, the organizing and selling of artistic products and the symbolism of consumption of things, as mundane as kitchen utensils which turn out to be anything but mundane, and value-imbued things such as books, which also rely on the 'mundane' concerns of business for their existence and proliferation. In all of these areas questions open up and stimulate new ways of seeing (or reframing) action and experience. It is not the case simply that managing and creating are oppositional. They are not necessarily in a competitive struggle for legitimacy. Rather, markets, routes to them and returns (revenues) from them are part of normal creative endeavours.

This is not to say that there are not plenty of struggles and conflicts within these fields of practice. There are different 'logics' at play, although rarely are these populated by a single category of person (e.g. 'creatives' or 'managers'). The logics of expression, production, creative consumption and commercial return can be used by divergent actors regardless of whether their (job) titles imply that they should be more interested in one rather than another. Hence, consumers can indulge in the language of production values; commercial agents can be driven by a belief in the importance of art, and artists can see commercial success as a form of feedback on the value of some parts of their output in comparison to others. Equally, none of these agents is passive, and none of the logics fail to be concerned with the adding and operation of value of one sort or another. So, for example, the symbolic importance of The Clash in 2009 rests on their artistic output thirty years before, but equally it relates to the way that consumers of their music construct and perpetuate their image, write and read about them, keeping the symbol and the art alive and growing even though no new music has been produced for a considerable period of time. Hence, that which lasts does so not only because of value recognized in one logic and set of practices (e.g. punk/post-punk music production), but because of translatability between logics and practices (the consumption and re-production of image). Other punk and post-punk bands who were contemporaries of The Clash have not taken a similar position in cross-fertilizing logics and practices, and hence have become the preserve of a small number of consumers/producers for whom the genre is personally significant. One of the real contributions of these diverse logics and practices is that they pose useful questions for each other. When dialogue is effective it typically takes place between positions of difference, and this is only likely to occur where the position of the other is valued rather than being dismissed. In other words, it is important to reject stereotypes of 'creatives' as being concerned only with the intrinsic and immediate quality of producing art, and 'managers' as being concerned only with costs, control and exploitation of products. These stereotypes are dangerous because they militate against debate by setting up an oppositional relationship in which a genuine valuing of the other is unlikely. The real questions are what can we learn from and about each other (and ourselves), and what are the impacts of this learning on what we do?

We hope that the contributions to this book enable each of us to consider these questions. There are theoretical differences between positions taken in the various chapters, and there are divergent views that do not necessarily fit into one way of seeing the world. We regard this as a significant strength of an edited collection and are pleased that the authors presented here have not been constrained to toe a party line or conform to a particular perspective. We have used Caves (2002) to provide a useful framework, not to agree with everything he says, but to use such categories as a means of opening up possibilities for action and dialogue. We would regard this as the first step of management: asking questions, inquiring and exploring. The second step is moving to action and, of course, these steps recur iteratively and become entwined. Often the steps that one takes are taken in conditions of uncertainty. We cannot *know* what lies ahead in a market, production process or interaction between agents in a field any more than we can know in advance what lies ahead when making art. Therefore, our action steps are necessarily experimental, trying something out to see if it works and then deciding which way to go next. Deciding how to evaluate what works (or does not) relates to the dialogue we are suggesting. It may be that one logic dominates all others, for example, it might be that a group of consumers believe one product to be superior to another despite the contrary views of critics and producers. But often logics come into contact with each other and this is likely to be most productive where dialogue occurs through which each position can potentially change and learn.

The title of this book is *Managing Creativity*. There is, however, a question over what constitutes 'managing'. A stereotypical view, one that would be recognized by few who spend their time managing, is that it is all about control and constraint. Actually, management is also about stimulating and supporting, inspiring, communicating and putting values into action. Similarly, a stereotypical view of creativity is that it is something done by lone geniuses who, when they have sparks of inspiration, produce something entirely new. Actually, creativity is also about an assessment of, and a reaction to, the environment, rational decision making and value-adding practices being distributed and enacted by audience members and consumers. Hence, we should question what is meant by 'managing' and 'creativity' and we should question the implications of how we answer these questions. Here, we have argued that the key action is inquiry – therefore questioning – what is valued in other logics? What is valued by the various actors in the field? Where are the areas of translation or shared value? What are the implications for action? How will we know when it is working? None of these questions can or should be answered simply or once and for all. Managing creativity is an ongoing inquiry in which a key strength is the ability to resist pressures that delegitimize uncertainty, questioning, dialogue and experimental action.

References

Caves, R. (2002) *Creative Industries: Contracts Between Art and Commerce*. Cambridge, MA: Harvard University Press.

Index

A&R (Artist and Repertoire)
  departments, 230
accident, in the creative process,
  56–58
action, 47, 50, 52–53
activity theory, 197–99
Adorno, T. W., 8, 130, 132, 141, 150,
  311
AdSense, 204
aesthetic economy, 61–64
aesthetic experience, 310–11,
  313–19
Aesthetic Movement, 89–91
aesthetics
  art for art's sake, 88–91
  artistic form, 91–92, 94–97, 99
  divinity of art, 101–02
  medieval society, 99–101
aleatoric processes, 57–58
Alessi, 287–88, 292, 293, 294,
  304–05
All Men Are the Same (film), 287, 294
ancient societies, 98–99, 100–01
Anderson, C., 201–02
Anthony, S. D., 242
Aquinas, St. Thomas, 101
architecture, 245
Arctic Monkeys, 131
Arendt, Hannah, 48, 50, 58
ars longa, 281–85, 336
art
  and action, 52–59
  ancient societies, 98–99, 100–01
  beauty in, 94–95, 101
  and business, 106–07, 120–22
  collectors, 282–83
  dialogue, 172–75
  durability of, 17, 50
  education, 241–42, 244
  interpretation, 36–37

  and labour, 50
  museums, 324
  performance as, 282
  role of, 8–9
  as social practice, 106–07, 336
  value of, 281
  and work, 51–52
art for art's sake
  vs. commercialization, 81–85,
    106–07
  concept of, 87, 336
  divinity of art, 101–02
  German theatre, 109–11, 118–20
  medieval society, 99–101
  modern usage, 97–98
  in the nineteenth century, 88–91
  opposition to, 92–95
  and position-taking, 118–20
  in the twentieth century, 91–98
artistic form, 91–92, 94–97, 99
artists
  ancient societies, 100–01
  communication with audiences,
    152, 157–58
  conjunction of, 39–44
  context, 165–67
  feedback, 167
  and form, 96–97
  medieval view of, 100–01
  prestige, 114–18
  thought process in drawing art
    works, 31–44
  unknowability in the creative
    process, 44–45
audiences
  The Clash, 129, 136, 139
  communication with artists,
    157–58
  context, 159–60, 165–67
  feedback, 167

340

Printed in the United States
By Bookmasters